ANNUAL EDITIONS

Marketing 09/10

Thirty-Second Edition

EDITOR

John E. Richardson
Pepperdine University

Dr. John E. Richardson is Professor of Marketing in The George L. Graziadio School of Business and Management at Pepperdine University. He is president of his own consulting firm and has consulted with organizations such as Bell and Howell, Dayton-Hudson, Epson, and the U.S. Navy, as well as with various service, nonprofit, and franchise organizations. Dr. Richardson is a member of the American Marketing Association, the American Management Association, the Society for Business Ethics, and Beta Gamma Sigma honorary business fraternity.

McGraw Hill Higher Education

Boston   Burr Ridge, IL   Dubuque, IA   New York   San Francisco   St. Louis
Bangkok   Bogotá   Caracas   Kuala Lumpur   Lisbon   London   Madrid   Mexico City
Milan   Montreal   New Delhi   Santiago   Seoul   Singapore   Sydney   Taipei   Toronto

The McGraw·Hill Companies

Mc Graw Hill **Higher Education**

ANNUAL EDITIONS: MARKETING, THIRTY-SECOND EDITION

1 2 3 4 5 6 7 8 9 0 QPD/QPD 0 9

ISBN 978–0–07–352852–6
MHID 0–07–352852–8
ISSN 0730–2606

Managing Editor: *Larry Loeppke*
Senior Managing Editor: *Faye Schilling*
Developmental Editor: *Dave Welsh*
Editorial Coordinator: *Mary Foust*
Editorial Assistant: *Nancy Meissner*
Production Service Assistant: *Rita Hingtgen*
Permissions Coordinator: *DeAnna Dausener*
Senior Marketing Manager: *Julie Keck*
Marketing Communications Specialist: *Mary Klein*
Marketing Coordinator: *Alice Link*
Project Manager: *Sandy Wille*
Design Specialist: *Tara McDermott*
Senior Production Supervisor: *Laura Fuller*
Cover Graphics: *Kristine Jubeck*

Compositor: Laserwords Private Limited
Cover Image: Courtesy of Travis Kirby (inset); © Getty Images/RF (backround)

Library in Congress Cataloging-in-Publication Data
Main entry under title: Annual Editions: Marketing. 2009/2010.
    1. Marketing—Periodicals. I. Richardson, John E., *comp.* II. Title: Marketing.
658'.05

www.mhhe.com

Editors/Advisory Board

Members of the Advisory Board are instrumental in the final selection of articles for each edition of ANNUAL EDITIONS. Their review of articles for content, level, currentness, and appropriateness provides critical direction to the editor and staff. We think that you will find their careful consideration well reflected in this volume.

Preface

In publishing ANNUAL EDITIONS we recognize the enormous role played by the magazines, newspapers, and journals of the public press in providing current, first-rate educational information in a broad spectrum of interest areas. Many of these articles are appropriate for students, researchers, and professionals seeking accurate, current material to help bridge the gap between principles and theories and the real world. These articles, however, become more useful for study when those of lasting value are carefully collected, organized, indexed, and reproduced in a low-cost format, which provides easy and permanent access when the material is needed. That is the role played by ANNUAL EDITIONS.

The new millennium should prove to be an exciting and challenging time for the American business community. Recent dramatic social, economic, and technological changes have become an important part of the present marketplace. These changes—accompanied by increasing domestic and foreign competition—are leading a wide array of companies and industries toward the realization that better marketing must become a top priority now to assure their future success.

How does the marketing manager respond to this growing challenge? How does the marketing student apply marketing theory to real-world practice? Many reach for the *Wall Street Journal, BusinessWeek, Fortune,* and other well-known sources of business information. There, specific industry and company strategies are discussed and analyzed, marketing principles are often reaffirmed by real occurrences, and textbook theories are supported or challenged by current events.

The articles reprinted in this *Annual Editions: Marketing 09/10* edition have been carefully chosen from numerous public press sources to provide current information on marketing in the world today. Within these pages you will find articles that address marketing theory and application in a wide range of industries. In addition, the selections reveal how several firms interpret and utilize marketing principles in their daily operations and corporate planning.

This volume contains a number of features designed to make it useful for marketing students, researchers, and professionals. These include the *topic guide* to locate articles on specific marketing subjects; *Internet References* pages; the *table of contents* abstracts, which summarize each article and highlight key concepts; and a *glossary* of key marketing terms.

The articles are organized into four units. Selections that focus on similar issues are concentrated into subsections within the broader units. Each unit is preceded by a list of unit selections, as well as a list of key points to consider that focus on major themes running throughout the selections, Web links that provide extra support for the unit's data, and an overview that provides background for informed reading of the articles and emphasizes critical issues.

This is the thirty-second edition of *Annual Editions: Marketing.* Since its first edition in the mid-1970s, the efforts of many individuals have contributed toward its success. We think this is by far the most useful collection of material available for the marketing student. We are anxious to know what you think. What are your opinions? What are your recommendations? Please take a moment to complete and return the *article rating form* on the last page of this volume. Any book can be improved and this one will continue to be, annually.

John E. Richardson
Editor

Contents

UNIT 1
Marketing in the 2000s and Beyond

The concepts in bold italics are developed in the article. For further expansion, please refer to the Topic Guide.

UNIT 2
Research, Markets, and Consumer Behavior

The concepts in bold italics are developed in the article. For further expansion, please refer to the Topic Guide.

UNIT 3
Developing and Implementing Marketing Strategies

The concepts in bold italics are developed in the article. For further expansion, please refer to the Topic Guide.

The concepts in bold italics are developed in the article. For further expansion, please refer to the Topic Guide.

UNIT 4
Global Marketing

The concepts in bold italics are developed in the article. For further expansion, please refer to the Topic Guide.

Correlation Guide

The *Annual Editions* series provides students with convenient, inexpensive access to current, carefully selected articles from the public press. **Annual Editions: Marketing 09/10** is an easy-to-use reader that presents articles on important topics such as the *future of marketing* and *developing marketing strategies*. For more information on *Annual Editions* and other *McGraw-Hill Contemporary Learning Series* titles visit www.mhcls.com.

This convenient guide matches the units in **Annual Editions: Marketing 09/10** with corresponding chapters in two of our best-selling McGraw-Hill Marketing textbooks by Kerin et al. and Perreault et al.

Annual Editions: Marketing 09/10	Marketing: The Core, 3/e by Kerin et al.	Basic Marketing, 17/e by Perreault et al.
Unit 1: Marketing in the 2000s and Beyond	**Chapter 1:** Creating Customer Relationships and Value Through Marketing **Chapter 4:** Ethical and Social Responsibility in Marketing	**Chapter 1:** Marketing's Value to Consumers, Firms, and Society **Chapter 4:** Evaluating Opportunities in the Changing Marketing Environment **Chapter 22:** Ethical Marketing in a Consumer-Oriented World: Appraisal and Challenges
Unit 2: Research, Markets, and Consumer Behavior	**Chapter 5:** Understanding Consumer Behavior **Chapter 6:** Understanding Organizations as Customers **Chapter 8:** Marketing Research: From Customer Insights to Actions	**Chapter 4:** Evaluating Opportunities in the Changing Marketing Environment **Chapter 6:** Final Consumers and Their Buying Behavior **Chapter 7:** Business and Organizational Customers and Their Buying Behavior **Chapter 8:** Improving Decisions with Marketing Information
Unit 3: Developing and Implementing Marketing Strategies	**Chapter 10:** Developing New Products and Services **Chapter 11:** Managing Products, Services and Brands **Chapter 12:** Pricing, Products, Services and Brands **Chapter 16:** Advertising, Sales Promotion, and Public Relations	**Chapter 2:** Marketing Strategy Planning **Chapter 9:** Elements of Product Planning for Goods and Services **Chapter 10:** Product Management and New-Product Development **Chapter 12:** Distribution Customer Services and Logistics **Chapter 14:** Promotion—Introduction to Integrated Marketing Communications **Chapter 17:** Pricing Objectives and Policies
Unit 4: Global Marketing	**Chapter 7:** Understanding and Reaching Global Consumers and Markets	**Chapter 5:** Demographic Dimensions of Global Consumer Markets

Topic Guide

This topic guide suggests how the selections in this book relate to the subjects covered in your course. You may want to use the topics listed on these pages to search the Web more easily.

On the following pages a number of Web sites have been gathered specifically for this book. They are arranged to reflect the units of this Annual Editions reader. You can link to these sites by going to *http://www.mhcls.com*.

All the articles that relate to each topic are listed below the bold-faced term.

Internet References

The following Internet sites have been selected to support the articles found in this reader. These sites were available at the time of publication. However, because Web sites often change their structure and content, the information listed may no longer be available. We invite you to visit *http://www.mhcls.com* for easy access to these sites.

Annual Editions: Marketing 09/10

General Sources

Baruch College BusinessWeek—Harris Poll Demographics
(http://www.businessweek.com/1997/18/b352511.htm)

The Baruch College–Harris poll commissioned by *BusinessWeek* is used at this site to show interested businesses that are on the Net in the United States.

General Social Survey
(http://webapp.icpsr.umich.edu/cocoon/ICPSR-SERIES/00028.xml)

The GSS (see DPLS Archive: http://DPLS.DACC.WISC.EDU/SAF/) is an almost annual personal interview survey of U.S. households that began in 1972. More than 35,000 respondents have answered 2,500 questions. It covers a broad range of variables, many of which relate to microeconomic issues.

BestOfAdvertising.net
(http://www.bestofadvertising.net/)

This is a complete list of sites that include information on marketing research, marketing on the Internet, demographic sources, and organizations and associations. The site also features current books on the subject of marketing.

STAT-USA/Internet Site Economic, Trade, Business Information
(http://www.stat-usa.gov)

This site, from the U.S. Department of Commerce, contains Daily Economic News, Frequently Requested Statistical Releases, Information on Export and International Trade, Domestic Economic News and Statistical Series, and Databases.

U.S. Census Bureau Home Page
(http://www.census.gov)

This is a major source of social, demographic, and economic information, such as income/employment data and the latest indicators, income distribution, and poverty data.

UNIT 1: Marketing in the 2000s and Beyond

American Marketing Association Code of Ethics
(http://www.marketingpower.com/)

At this American Marketing Association site, use the search mechanism to access the organization's Code of Ethics for marketers.

Futures Research Quarterly
(http://www.wfs.org/frq.htm)

Published by the World Future Society, this publication describes future research that encompasses both an evolving philosophy and a range of techniques, with the aim of assisting decision-makers in all fields to understand better the potential consequences of decisions by developing images of alternative futures. From this page explore the current and back issues and What's Coming Up!

Center for Innovation in Product Development (CIPD)
(http://web.mit.edu/cipd/research/prdctdevelop.htm)

CIPD is one of the National Science Foundation's engineering research centers. It shares the goal of future product development with academia, industry, and government.

UNIT 2: Research, Markets, and Consumer Behavior

Canadian Innovation Centre
(http://www.innovationcentre.ca/)

The Canadian Innovation Centre has developed a unique mix of innovation services that can help a company from idea to market launch. Their services are based on the review of 12,000 new product ideas through their technology and market assessment programs over the past 20 years.

BizMiner—Industry Analysis and Trends
(http://www.bizminer.com/market_research.asp)

The importance of using market research databases and pinpointing local and national trends, including details of industry and small business startups, is emphasized by this site of the Brandow Company that offers samples of market research profiles.

Small Business Center—Articles & Insights
(http://www.bcentral.com/articles/krotz/123.asp)

This article discusses five market intelligence blunders made by the giant retailer K-Mart. "There were warning signs that K-Mart management mishandled, downplayed or just plain ignored," Joanna L. Krotz says.

Maritz Marketing Research
(http://www.maritzresearch.com)

Maritz Marketing Research Inc. (MMRI) specializes in custom designed research studies that link the consumer to the marketer through information. Go to Maritz Loyalty Marketing in the Maritz Companies menu to find resources to identify, retain, and grow your most valuable customers. Also visit Maritz Research for polls, stats, and archived research reports.

USADATA
(http://www.usadata.com)

This leading provider of marketing, company, advertising, and consumer behavior data offers national and local data covering the top 60 U.S. markets.

WWW Virtual Library: Demography & Population Studies
(http://demography.anu.edu.au/VirtualLibrary/)

More than 150 links can be found at this major resource to keep track of information of value to researchers in the fields of demography and population studies.

Internet References

UNIT 3: Developing and Implementing Marketing Strategies

American Marketing Association Homepage
(http://www.marketingpower.com)

This site of the American Marketing Association is geared to managers, educators, researchers, students, and global electronic members. It contains a search mechanism, definitions of marketing and market research, and links.

Consumer Buying Behavior
(http://www.courses.psu.edu/mktg/mktg220_rso3/sls_cons.htm)

The Center for Academic Computing at Penn State posts this course data that includes a review of consumer buying behaviors; group, environment, and internal influences; problem-solving; and post-purchasing behavior.

UNIT 4: Global Marketing

International Trade Administration
(http://www.ita.doc.gov)

The U.S. Department of Commerce is dedicated to helping U.S. businesses compete in the global marketplace, and at this site it offers assistance through many Web links under such headings as Trade Statistics, Cross-Cutting Programs, Regions and Countries, and Import Administration.

World Chambers Network
(http://www.worldchambers.net)

International trade at work is viewable at this site. For example, click on Global Business eXchange (GBX) for a list of active business opportunities worldwide or to submit your new business opportunity for validation.

World Trade Center Association OnLine
(http://iserve.wtca.org)

Data on world trade is available at this site that features information, services, a virtual trade fair, an exporter's encyclopedia, trade opportunities, and a resource center.

UNIT 1

Marketing in the 2000s and Beyond

Unit Selections

Key Points to Consider

- Dramatic changes are occurring in the marketing of products and services. What social and economic trends do you believe are most significant today, and how do you think these will affect marketing in the future?

- Theodore Levitt suggests that as times change the marketing concept must be reinterpreted. Given the varied perspectives of the other articles in this unit, what do you think this reinterpretation will entail?

- In the present competitive business arena, is it possible for marketers to behave ethically in the environment and both survive and prosper? What suggestions can you give that could be incorporated into the marketing strategy for firms that want to be both ethical and successful?

Student Web Site

www.mhcls.com

Internet References

American Marketing Association Code of Ethics
   (http://www.marketingpower.com/)
Futures Research Quarterly
   (http://www.wfs.org/frq.htm)
Center for Innovation in Product Development (CIPD)
   (http://web.mit.edu/cipd/research/prdctdevelop.htm)

"If we want to know what a business is we must start with its purpose. . . . There is only one valid definition of business purpose: to create a customer. What business thinks it produces is not of first importance—especially not to the future of the business or to its success. What the customer thinks he is buying, what he considers 'value' is decisive—it determines what a business is, what it produces, and whether it will prosper."

—Peter Drucker, *The Practice of Management*

When Peter Drucker penned these words in 1954, American industry was just awakening to the realization that marketing would play an important role in the future success of businesses. The ensuing years have seen an increasing number of firms in highly competitive areas—particularly in the consumer goods industry—adopt a more sophisticated customer orientation and an integrated marketing focus.

The dramatic economic and social changes of the last decade have stirred companies in an even broader range of industries—from banking and air travel to communications—to the realization that marketing will provide them with their cutting edge. Demographic and lifestyle changes have splintered mass, homogeneous markets into many markets, each with different needs and interests. Deregulation has made once-protected industries vulnerable to the vagaries of competition. Vast and rapid technological changes are making an increasing number of products and services obsolete. Intense international competition, rapid expansion of the Internet-based economy, and the growth of truly global markets have many firms looking well beyond their national boundaries.

Indeed, it appears that during the new millennium marketing will take on a unique significance—and not just within the industrial sector. Social institutions of all kinds, which had thought themselves exempt from the pressures of the marketplace, are also beginning to recognize the need for marketing in the management of their affairs. Colleges and universities, charities, museums, symphony orchestras, and even hospitals are beginning to give attention the marketing concept—to provide what the consumer wants to buy.

The selections in this unit are grouped into four areas. Their purposes are to provide current perspectives on marketing, discuss differing views of the marketing concept, analyze the use of marketing by social institutions and nonprofit organizations, and examine the ethical and social responsibilities of marketing.

The articles in the first subsection provide significant clues about salient approaches and issues that marketers need to address in the future in order to create, promote, and sell their products and services in ways that meet the expectations of consumers.

The selections that address the marketing concept include Levitt's now classic "Marketing Myopia," which first appeared in the *Harvard Business Review* in 1960. This version includes the author's retrospective commentary, written in 1975, in which he discusses how shortsightedness can make management unable to recognize that there is no such thing as a growth industry. "Putting Customers First" suggests nine ways to increase customers' brand loyalty. "Customer

© Stockbyte/Getty Images

Connection" provides five strategies for focusing on customers. The last article in this subsection, "Add Service Element Back In to Get Satisfaction," reflects the importance of companies focusing on customer satisfaction and customer service.

The second article "Surviving in the Age of Rage," reveals ways to manage angry customers. "Attracting Loyalty" covers ways to win customer loyalty with five drivers. The final article in this subsection, "Nonprofits Can Take Cues from Biz World," emphasizes the importance of nonprofits having a carefully developed brand.

In the final subsection, *Marketing Ethics & Social Responsibility,* a careful look is taken at the strategic process and practice of incorporating ethics and social responsibility into the marketplace. "Fidelity Factor" underlines the importance of ensuring customer relationships by infusing them with trust. "Trust in the Marketplace" discusses the importance of gaining and maintaining customers' trust. The last article in this subsection, "Wrestling with Ethics," grapples with the question, "Is marketing ethics an oxymoron?"

1

Hot Stuff

Make These Top Trends Part of Your Marketing Mix

GWEN MORAN

Still using the same marketing tactics you were using five years ago? Those won't work with today's shifting demographics and preferences. The U.S. population is older, more multicultural, more time-pressed and more jaded toward overt sales pitches than ever before. And your marketing strategy should be built accordingly.

So what's working? After consulting over a dozen experts in the field, we've uncovered the following hot trends in marketing.

Market on the Move

According to the Mobile Marketing Association, by 2008, 89 percent of brands will use text and multimedia messaging to reach their audiences, with nearly one-third planning to spend more than 10 percent of their marketing budgets on advertising in the medium. As phones with video capability become more prevalent, expect more rich media marketing options. Plus, now that mobile phone service providers are dipping their toes into the credit card pool—soon your phone or PDA may make plastic obsolete—customers will be relying on these devices more than ever.

"There are some low-cost mobile marketing onramps for small businesses," says Kim Bayne, author of *Marketing Without Wires*. "Businesses can implement opt-in text messaging services and coupons with their loyal customers. We've already seen local restaurants send the day's specials to nearby lunch patrons. The cost is fairly low, and it can be done from a PC, without involving a pricey service provider."

Go Online

"Think globally, act locally" is now the mantra for entrepreneurs advertising online. Online ad spending is up as much as 33 percent over last year, says David J. Moore, chairman and CEO of digital marketing firm 24/7 Real Media Inc. in New York City. Earlier this year, Google announced a new local advertising program linked to its map service and AdWords program, allowing businesses to drive some of Google's traffic to their brick-and-mortar locations.

"[Entrepreneurs] should pay attention to any targeting that allows them to increase advertising efficiency by reaching users in their particular geographic area," says Moore. Online ads are also migrating to podcasts and blogs, where advertisers can reach very specific niche audiences. And with increased access to broadband and the falling cost of video production, Moore foresees a rise in online video ads for businesses as well.

Court the Boom

A baby boomer turns 50 every 7 seconds—joining a population segment that will grow by 25 percent in the next decade while other segments remain flat.

Matt Thornhill, founder of consulting firm The Boomer Project, which helps businesses reach adults born between 1946 and 1964, says it's time for marketers to recalibrate their thinking about marketing to older adults. Boomers are a dynamic group that's much more open to new experiences and brands than previous generations of older adults have been.

Stephanie Lakhani found that to be true at her upscale Breathe Wellness Spas (www.breathetoheal.com) in Boise, Idaho. Catering primarily to boomers, the two spas bring in about $1.2 million per year. She says boomers are an excellent target, with disposable income and a tendency to refer business. "They expect perfect service," says Lakhani, 35, who adds, "They tend to travel and buy in groups, so giving them an incentive to refer a friend in the form of an upgrade or a thank you [gesture] works very well. They are also very responsive to direct mail."

Thornhill adds that marketers should target boomers by what they're doing instead of how old they are. "Boomers are living such cyclical lives. In their 40s or 50s, they could be going back to college, be empty nesters or be married a second time and raising a young family," he explains. "You wouldn't sell the same vacation package to all these people. So pick the lifestyle segment you're targeting, and focus on that."

Sindicate Simply

For something that's named Really Simple Syndication, few tools are more misunderstood or misused than RSS. Provided by such companies as Bloglines (www.bloglines.com) and News-Gator (www.newsgator.com), RSS lets you send and receive information without using e-mail. Instead, the information is sent directly to a subscriber, who receives it through an RSS reader. With browsers like Internet Explorer integrating such readers, we'll be seeing more information feeds. That could be a good thing—or not—depending on whether businesses use them properly.

"You don't need to blog to offer an RSS feed," says online marketing consultant Debbie Weil, author of *The Corporate Blogging Book.* "But you should have a blogging mind-set. Show the reader what's in it for them. Write clear and interesting headlines. There's a bit of an art to writing RSS [content]." She adds that you should break up your feeds by audience—customers, investors, media and the like—just as you would any other message distribution.

Jim Edwards, 38, uses a blog and RSS to promote his business, Guaranteed Response Marketing. "Whenever I publish an article, either through my blog [www.igottatellyou.com/blog] or through another site's RSS feeder, I expect to get 100 to 300 references back to me in a week," says Edwards, whose $2 million Lightfoot, Virginia, business provides electronic tutorials and publications. "It's a quick way to get links back to you, as well as to get on sites that people are actively looking at."

Use Social Networks

Customers are making friends online through social networking sites like MySpace.com. The massive site—boasting millions of users, all segmented by age, geography and interests—offers an unbridled opportunity for marketers, according to Libby Pigg, senior account manager at Edelman Interactive in New York City.

"You [can] launch a profile for your business and give it a personality," says Pigg, who has launched MySpace marketing campaigns for major consumer products companies. "It's simi-

lar to a dating site, where you tell people a bit about yourself. Then, you use the search function to find the group you want to target—maybe single people in New York [City] between 24 and 30—and contact them to become your 'friends.'"

A MySpace profile helped Taylor Bond generate interest in Egismoz.com, the electronics division of his $20 million retail company, Children's Orchard, in Ann Arbor, Michigan. Earlier this year, Bond sent invitations to some of the site's young, tech-savvy users. The key to maintaining their interest, he says, is to provide fresh content and special offers.

"We're seeing more people come into the store saying that they saw us on MySpace," says Bond, 44. "We're definitely seeing more traffic and feedback on the profile, and we're getting some incredible feedback about what's hot and what people want, so it's good for market research, too." Opportunities also exist on other networking sites like Friendster.com, LinkedIn .com, and even niche sites like Adholes.com, which focuses on the advertising community.

Advertise in Unusual Places

From valet tickets and hubcaps to T-shirts emblazoned with video displays, advertising is popping up in new places. A March survey of marketing executives by Blackfriars Communications entitled "Marketing 2006: 2006's Timid Start" found that business spending on traditional advertising continued its decline, and spending on nontraditional marketing methods—from online promotions to buzz marketing—rose 12 percent since late 2005.

Scott Montgomery, principal and creative director of Bradley and Montgomery, an advertising and branding firm in Indianapolis, says the shift in ad spending will continue as advertisers look to make their ad dollars more effective.

Make It Stick

Tap these marketing trends to get into customers' hearts and minds.

- **Multicultural Market:** By 2010, the buying power of American blacks and Hispanics is expected to exceed the gross domestic product of Canada, according to the Selig Center for Economic Growth at the University of Georgia in Athens. Make sure you're not overlooking this market. Rochelle Newman-Carrasco, CEO of Enlace Communications, a Los Angeles multicultural marketing firm, advises companies not only to translate materials when appropriate, but also to be conscious of cultural images: "In lifestyle shots, go beyond multicultural casting. Show scenes where the clothing, food and other backgrounds reflect different cultures."
- **Experiential Marketing:** Kathy Sherbrooke, president of Circles, an experiential marketing firm in Boston, says businesses must figure out the key messages of their brand and find ways for their staffs and locations to reflect that image—young and trendy, sophisticated and elegant, and so on. "Create an environment that's consistent with your brand," she says. She points to Apple Computer's retail stores, where clerks use handheld

checkout machines and pull product bags out of their back pockets to reinforce the ease-of-use and streamlined processes for which Apple is known.
- **Customer Evangelism:** From hiring word-of-mouth marketing companies to creating incentives for customer referrals, businesses are placing more importance on customer evangelism, says Andrew Pierce, senior partner at New York City branding firm Prophet. "Companies need to be customer-centric for this to happen," he explains. "If you're not finding ways to increase value and inspire loyalty, it won't work."

At the simplest level, Pierce advises using customer testimonials to add credibility to marketing efforts, including webinars where customers talk about your company. More extreme examples include buzz marketing campaigns where happy customers talk up the product, or inviting customers to trade shows or other events where they can show their enthusiasm in person.

Montgomery and his team were the first to develop advertising programs on electrical outlets in airports. Reasoning that business travelers—one of the holy grail audiences marketers love—power up portable technology while waiting for their planes, it seemed a natural place to reach them.

"Smart marketers are looking [for] places where people are engaged," says Montgomery. "You have to target your message in a way that makes sense for [how] people behave."

Premium-ize Your Brand

Brands like Coach and Grey Goose vodka have mastered the art of taking everyday items and introducing luxe versions at much higher price points. Now, growing businesses are also going upscale with their products or services.

Andrew Rohm, professor of marketing at Northeastern University's College of Business Administration in Boston, says smaller businesses can often "trickle up" more easily than large brands, which may find that customers are resistant to accepting their more expensive offerings. "A small brand can reinvent itself without having to swim upstream against its image," says Rohm.

To posh up your product, he advises the same best practices as with any new offering: Do your research, and make sure there's a market for the product or service before you make your brand go bling.

Blog On

With the blogosphere more than 43.1 million blogs strong, according to blog search engine Technorati, it appears everyone and his grandmother are blogging. Robert Scoble, technical evangelist at Microsoft and author of *Naked Conversations: How Blogs Are Changing the Way That Businesses Talk With Customers,* believes blogs are important for businesses that want direct customer feedback. And development blogs, where businesses get direct input about products and services from readers, will soon become even more important, he says.

Scoble predicts a rise in regional blogs linked to Google's new local advertising program and Mapquest.com for quick access to directions, giving people more insight into the local businesses they want to frequent. He also says we'll see more video blogs, which won't replace text blogs but will more effectively communicate with some audiences. "If I'm trying to explain to you what [video game] Halo 2 is, I can write 10,000 words and I'm not going to get it right, but you can see a 2-minute video and you'll understand," he says.

Take these trends into consideration as you plan for the coming year. Not every idea may apply to your company, but most are market forces you can't afford to ignore.

GWEN MORAN is Entrepreneur's "Retail Register" and "Quick Pick" columnist.

The World's Most Innovative Companies

Their creativity goes beyond products to rewiring themselves. *BusinessWeek* and the Boston Consulting Group rank the best.

Jena McGregor

It was a fitting way to wrap up the first day of IBM's innovation-themed leadership forum, held in Rome in early April. Guests were treated to small group tours of the Vatican Museum, including Michelangelo's frescoes in the Sistine Chapel. They sipped cocktails on a patio in the back of St. Peter's, the vast dome of the basilica outlined by the light of the moon. They dined in a marble-statue-filled hall inside the Vatican. What better place than Italy to hold a global confab on innovation, the topic *di giorno* among corporate leaders? It was, after all, the birthplace of the Renaissance, another period of great innovation and change.

The next day, at the Auditorium Parco della Musica, 500-odd corporate executives, government leaders, and academics listened as a diverse group of innovative leaders took the stage. Sunil B. Mittal, chief executive officer of Indian telecom company Bharti Tele-Ventures Ltd., described his radical business model, which outsources everything but marketing and customer management, charges 2 cents a minute for calls, and is adding a million customers a month. Yang Mingsheng, CEO of Agricultural Bank of China, the country's second-biggest commercial bank, spoke of building a banking powerhouse from a modest business making micro loans to peasant farmers.

Their stories echoed a comment IBM CEO Samuel J. Palmisano had made the day before: "The way you will thrive in this environment is by innovating—innovating in technologies, innovating in strategies, innovating in business models."

Palmisano, to be sure, was making a subtle pitch for IBM and its ability to help the assembled leaders do well in an increasingly challenging business environment. But he also summed up the broad focus of innovation in the 21st century.

Today, innovation is about much more than new products. It is about reinventing business processes and building entirely new markets that meet untapped customer needs. Most important, as the Internet and globalization widen the pool of new ideas, it's about selecting and executing the right ideas and bringing them to market in record time.

In the 1990s, innovation was about technology and control of quality and cost. Today, it's about taking corporate organizations built for efficiency and rewiring them for creativity and growth. "There are a lot of different things that fall under the rubric of innovation," says Vijay Govindarajan, a professor at Dartmouth College's Tuck School of Business and author of *Ten Rules for Strategic Innovators: From Idea to Execution.* "Innovation does not have to have anything to do with technology."

The Quick and the Blocked

To discover which companies innovate best—and why—*BusinessWeek* joined with The Boston Consulting Group to produce our second annual ranking of the 25 most innovative companies. More than 1,000 senior managers responded to the global survey, making it our deepest management survey to date on this critical issue.

The new ranking has companies evoking all types of innovation. There are technology innovators, such as BlackBerry maker and newcomer Research In Motion Ltd., which makes its debut on our list at No. 24. There are business model innovators, such as No. 11 Virgin Group Ltd., which applies its hip lifestyle brand to ho-hum operations such as airlines, financial services, and even health insurance. Process innovators are there, too: Rounding out the ranking is Southwest Airlines Co. at No. 25, a whiz at wielding operational improvements to outfly its competitors.

At the top of the list are the masters of many genres of innovation. Take Apple Computer Inc., once again the creative king. To launch the iPod, says innovation consultant Larry Keeley of Doblin Inc., Apple used no fewer than seven types of innovation. They included networking (a novel agreement among music companies to sell their songs online), business model (songs sold for a buck each online), and branding (how cool are those white ear buds and wires?). Consumers love the ease and feel of the iPod, but it is the simplicity of the iTunes software platform that turned a great MP3 player into a revenue-gushing phenomenon.

Toyota Motor Corp., which leapt 10 spots this year to No. 4, is becoming a master of many as well. The Japanese auto giant is best known for an obsessive focus on innovating its manufacturing processes. But thanks to the hot-selling Prius, Toyota is earning even more respect as a product innovator. It is also collaborating more closely with suppliers to generate innovation. Last year, Toyota launched its Value Innovation strategy. Rather than work with suppliers just to cut costs of individual parts, it is delving further back in the design process to find savings spanning entire vehicle systems.

OPEN YOUR LABS AND EXPAND YOUR OPPORTUNITIES
Corporate R&D labs are opening their doors—collaborating with suppliers and customers, sharing software code with programmers, and tapping networks of scientists and entrepreneurs for the world's best ideas.

The *BusinessWeek*-BCG survey is more than just a Who's Who list of innovators. It also focuses on the major obstacles to innovation that executives face today. While 72% of the senior executives in the survey named innovation as one of their top three priorities, almost half said they were dissatisfied with the returns on their investments in that area.

The No. 1 obstacle, according to our survey takers, is slow development times. Fast-changing consumer demands, global outsourcing, and open-source software make speed to market

paramount today. Yet companies often can't organize themselves to move faster, says George Stalk Jr., a senior vice-president with BCG who has studied time-based competition for 25 years. Fast cycle times require taking bets even when huge payoffs aren't a certainty. "Some organizations are nearly immobilized by the notion that [they] can't do anything unless it moves the needle," says Stalk. In addition, he says, speed requires coordination from the hub: "Fast innovators organize the corporate center to drive growth. They don't wait for [it] to come up through the business units."

Indeed, a lack of coordination is the second-biggest barrier to innovation, according to the survey's findings. But collaboration requires much more than paying lip service to breaking down silos. The best innovators reroute reporting lines and create physical spaces for collaboration. They team up people from across the org chart and link rewards to innovation. Innovative companies build innovation cultures. "You have to be willing to get down into the plumbing of the organization and align the nervous system of the company," says James P. Andrew, who heads the innovation practice at BCG.

Procter & Gamble Co. (No. 7) has done just that in transforming its traditional in-house research and development process into an open-source innovation strategy it calls "connect and develop." The new method? Embrace the collective brains of the world. Make it a goal that 50% of the company's new products come from outside P&G's labs. Tap networks of inventors, scientists, and suppliers for new products that can be developed in-house.

The radically different approach couldn't be shoehorned into managers' existing responsibilities. Rather, P&G had to tear apart and restitch much of its research organization. It created new job classifications, such as 70 worldwide "technology entrepreneurs," or TEs, who act as scouts, looking for the latest breakthroughs from places such as university

Playbook: Best-Practice Ideas

Ideas from the Innovators

Take a page from some of the world's most respected creative companies:

Bring them together	Think traits as well as numbers	Make a seat at the table	Preserve oral traditions	Get involved on the ground
BMW relocates between 200 and 300 engineers, designers, and managers to its central research and innovation center to design cars. **Face-to-face teams reduce late-stage conflicts and speed development times.**	Tracking innovation results is crucial for any growth-focused company. **But when evaluating managers, subjective metrics, such as risk tolerance or GE's measure of "imagination and courage," can be a better way.**	Infosys selects nine employees under 30 each year to participate in its senior management sessions. These young guns present their ideas for new services and ways to improve the company's processes.	Old-timers at 3M are expected to **hand down tales of the company's long innovation tradition** to new engineers. Before long, every new 3Mer can quote the philosophies of former CEO William McKnight.	Research In Motion co-CEO Mike Lazaridis personally heads engineering teams and hosts weekly innovation-themed "vision" sessions to excite the troops. **A culture of innovation starts from the top.**

labs. TEs also develop "technology game boards" that map out where technology opportunities lie and help P&Gers get inside the minds of its competitors.

To spearhead the connect-and-develop efforts, Larry Huston took on the newly created role of vice-president for innovation and knowledge. Each business unit, from household care to family health, added a manager responsible for driving cultural change around the new model. The managers communicate directly with Huston, who also oversees the technology entrepreneurs and managers running the external innovation networks. "You want to have a coherent strategy across the organization," says Huston. "The ideas tend to be bigger when you have someone sitting at the center looking at the company's growth goals."

Asking the Right Questions

Coordinating innovation from the center is taken literally at BMW Group, No. 16 on the list. Each time BMW begins developing a car, the project team's members—some 200 to 300 staffers from engineering, design, production, marketing, purchasing, and finance—are relocated from their scattered locations to the auto maker's Research and Innovation Center, called FIZ, for up to three years. Such proximity helps speed up communications (and therefore car development) and encourages face-to-face meetings that prevent late-stage conflicts between, say, marketing and engineering. In 2004 these teams began meeting in the center's new Project House, a unique structure that lets them work a short walk from the company's 8,000 researchers and developers and alongside life-size clay prototypes of the car in development.

For many companies, cross-functional collaborations last weeks or months, not years. Southwest recently gathered people from its in-flight, ground, maintenance, and dispatch operations. For six months they met for 10 hours a week, brainstorming ideas to address a broad issue: What are the highest-impact changes we can make to our aircraft operations?

BECOME INNOVATORS-IN-CHIEF
More than 50% of survey respondents said the CEO or chairman was responsible for driving innovation. Without heavy fire cover from the top, innovation efforts will get lost in the shuffle of short-term demands.

The group presented 109 ideas to senior management, three of which involve sweeping operational changes. One solution about to be introduced will reduce the number of aircraft "swaps"—disruptive events that occur when one aircraft has to be substituted for another during mechanical problems. Chief Information Officer Tom Nealon says the diversity of the people on the team was crucial, mentioning one director from the airline's schedule planning division in particular. "He had almost a naive perspective," says Nealon. "His questions were so fundamental they challenged the premises the maintenance and dispatch guys had worked on for the last 30 years."

Managers are scrambling to come up with ways to measure and raise the productivity of their innovation efforts. Yet the *BusinessWeek*-BCG survey shows widespread differences over which metrics—such as the ratio of products that succeed, or the ROI of innovation projects—should be used and how best to use them. Some two-thirds of the managers in the survey say metrics have the most impact in the selection of the right ideas to fund and develop. About half say they use metrics best in assessing the health of their company's innovation portfolio. But as many as 47% said measurements on the impact of innovation after products or services have been launched are used only sporadically.

Actually, most managers in the survey aren't monitoring many innovation metrics at all; 63% follow five gauges or fewer. "Two or three metrics just don't give you the visibility to get down to root causes," says BCG's Andrew. Then there are companies that track far too many. Andrew says one of the top innovators on our list—he's mum as to which one—collects 85 different innovation metrics in one of its businesses. "That means they manage none of them," he says. "They default to a couple, but they spend an immense amount of time and effort collecting those 85."

The sweet spot is somewhere between 8 and 12 metrics, says Andrew. That's about the number that Samsung Electronics Co. uses, says Chu Woosik, a senior vice-president at the South Korean company. Chu says the most important metrics are price premiums and how quickly they can bring to market phones that delight customers. Samsung also watches the allocation of investments across projects and its new-product success ratio. That, Chu says, has nearly doubled in the last five years. "You want to see it from every angle," he says. "A lot of companies fall into the trap that they thought things were really improving, but in the end, it didn't work out that way. We don't want to make that mistake."

Awards and Ethnography

One of the biggest mistakes companies may make is tying managers' incentives too directly to specific innovation metrics. Tuck's Govindarajan warns that linking pay too closely to hard innovation measures may tempt managers to game the system. A metric such as the percentage of revenue from new products, for instance, can lead to incremental brand extensions rather than true breakthroughs. In addition, innovation is such a murky process that targets are likely to change. "There's a dialogue that needs to happen," says Govindarajan. "Operating plans may need to be reviewed, or you may need to change plans because a new competitor came into your space."

Susan Schuman, CEO of Stone Yamashita Partners, which works with CEOs on innovation and change, says that besides numbers-driven metrics, some clients are adding subjective assessments related to innovation, such as a manager's risk tolerance, to performance evaluations. "It's not just about results," she says. "It's how did you lead people to get to those results."

That's one reason the bastion of Six Sigma-dom, General Electric Co., has begun evaluating its top 5,000 managers on "growth traits" that include innovation-oriented themes such as "external focus" and "imagination and courage." GE has also added more flexibility into its traditionally rigid performance rankings. GE will now have to square its traditional Six Sigma metrics, which are all about control, with its new emphasis on innovation, which is more about managing risk. That's a major change in culture.

How do you build an innovation culture? Try carrots. Several companies on our list have formal rewards for top innovators. Nokia Corp. inducts engineers with at least 10 patents into its "Club 10," recognizing them each year in a formal awards ceremony hosted by CEO Jorma Ollila.

3M has long awarded "Genesis Grants" to scientists who want to work on outside projects. Each year more than 60 researchers submit formal applications to a panel of 20 senior scientists who review the requests, just as a foundation would review academics' proposals. Twelve to 20 grants, ranging from $50,000 and $100,000 apiece, are awarded each year. The researchers can use the money to hire supplemental staff or acquire necessary equipment.

MEASURE WHAT MATTERS
Tracking innovation results is hard: You can't reduce it to a single number, and balancing risk is always part of the equation. Just 30% of survey takers said they measure ROI on innovation investments.

Of course, rewards won't help if the inventions aren't focused on customer needs. Getting good consumer insight is the fourth most cited obstacle to innovation in our survey. Blogs and online communities now make it easier to know what customers are thinking. Hiring designers and ethnographers who observe customers using products at work or at home helps, too. But finding that Holy Grail of marketing, the "unmet need" of a consumer, remains elusive. "You need time, just thinking time, to step out of the day to day to see what's going on in the world and what's going on with your customers," says Stone Yamashita's Schuman.

The World Is Your Lab

Try learning journeys. That's what Starbucks Corp., up 10 spots from 2005 to No. 9, does. While the coffee company began doing ethnography back in 2002 and relies on its army of baristas to share customer insights, it recently started taking product development and other cross-company teams on "inspiration" field trips to view customers and trends. Two months ago, Michelle Gass, Starbucks' senior vice-president for category management, took her team to Paris, Düsseldorf, and London to visit local Starbucks and other restaurants to get a better sense of local cultures, behaviors, and fashions. "You come back just full of different ideas and different ways to think about things than you would had you read about it in a magazine or e-mail," says Gass.

A close watch of customer insights can also bring innovation to even the most iconic and established products. Back in 2003, 3M began noticing and monitoring two consumer trends. One

was troubling: Customers were using laptops, cell phones, and BlackBerrys to send quick memos or jot down bits of information. Every thumb-tapped message or stylus-penned note on a personal digital assistant meant one less Post-it note.

The other trend, however, was encouraging: The rise of digital photography. While observing consumers, 3M researchers asked to see their photos. What followed was always a clunky process: Consumers would scroll through screen upon screen of photos or have to dig through a drawer for the few shots they printed. Nine months later a team of one marketer and two lab scientists hit upon the idea of Post-it Picture Paper, or photo paper coated with adhesive that lets people stick their photos to a wall for display. "We listened carefully to what consumers didn't say and observed what they did," says Jack Truong, vice-president of 3M's office supply division.

To get a sense of the value of customer research, imagine you're a Finnish engineer trying to design a phone for an illiterate customer on the Indian subcontinent. That's the problem Nokia faced when it began making low-cost phones for emerging markets. A combination of basic ethnographic and long-term user research in China, India, and Nepal helped Nokia understand how illiterate people live in a world full of numbers and letters. The result? A new "iconic" menu that lets illiterate customers navigate contact lists made up of images.

COORDINATE AND COLLABORATE
There's no simple innovation "on" switch. Building creative companies takes synchronization from the center, cross-boundary collaboration, and structural changes to the org chart.

Other innovative ideas followed. By listening to customers in poorer countries, Nokia learned that phones had to be more durable, since they're often the most expensive item these customers will buy. To function in a tropical climate, it made the phones more moisture-resistant. It even used special screens that are more legible in bright sunlight.

Consumers increasingly are doing the innovation themselves. Consider Google Inc., our No. 2 innovator, and its mapping technology, which it opened to the public. This produced a myriad of "mash-ups" in which programmers combine Google's maps with anything from real estate listings to local poker game sites.

Google's mash-ups are just one example of the escalating phenomenon of open innovation. These days the world is your R&D lab. Customers are co-opting technology and morphing products into their own inventions. Many companies are scouting for outside ideas they can develop in-house, embracing the open-source movement, and joining up with suppliers or even competitors on big projects that will make them more efficient and more powerful. "When you work with outside parties, they bear some of the costs and some of the risks, and can accelerate the time to market," says Henry W. Chesbrough, the University of California at Berkeley Haas School of Business professor who helped establish the concept with his 2003 book, *Open Innovation.*

India and China are growing sources of innovation for companies, too. The *BusinessWeek*-BCG survey shows that they are nearly as popular as Europe among innovation-focused executives. When asked where their company planned to increase R&D spending, 44% answered India, 44% said China, and 48% said Western Europe. Managers tended to look to the U.S. and Canada for idea generation, while a lower percentage looked to Europe for the same tasks. India and China, though, are still seen as centers for product development.

Few companies have embraced the open innovation model as widely as IBM, No. 10 on our list. While the company's proprietary technology is still a force to behold—Big Blue remains the world's largest patent holder, with more than 40,000—the company is opening up its technology to developers, partners, and clients. Last year it made 500 of its patents, mainly for software code, freely available to outside programmers. And in November it helped fund the Open Invention Network, a company formed to acquire patents and offer them royalty-free to help promote the open-source software movement.

Why the generosity? IBM believes that by helping to create technology ecosystems, it will benefit in the long run. "We want to do things that encourage markets to grow," says Dr. John E. Kelly III, senior vice-president for technology and intellectual property at IBM. By helping nurture those markets, says Kelly, "we know we'll get at least our fair share."

Going Outside for Ideas

P&G has helped establish several outside networks of innovators it turns to for ideas the company can develop in-house. These networks include NineSigma, which links up companies with scientists at university, government, and private labs; YourEncore Inc., which connects retired scientists and engineers with businesses; and yet2.com Inc., an online marketplace for intellectual property.

Only a CEO can change a business culture at top speed, and in Alan G. Lafley, P&G has its own innovator-in-chief. Lafley sits in on all "upstream" R&D review meetings, 15 a year, that showcase new products. He also spends three full days a year with the company's Design Board, a group of outside designers who offer their perspective on upcoming P&G products. "He's sort of the chief innovation officer," says P&G's Huston. "He's very, very involved."

That sort of support from the CEO is essential, says Jon R. Katzenbach, co-founder of New York-based management consultancy Katzenbach Partners LLC. "The CEO determines the culture," he says. "If the CEO is determined to [improve] the surfacing of ideas and determined to make critical choices, then the chances of an [organization's] figuring that out are much, much greater."

Infosys Technologies Ltd., the Bangalore-based information technology services company that popped up at No. 10 on our

Asia-Pacific list, takes a direct approach to making sure management stays involved in the innovation process. Chairman and "chief mentor" N.R. Narayana Murthy introduced the company's "voice of youth" program seven years ago. Each year the company selects nine top-performing young guns—each under 30—to participate in its eight yearly senior management council meetings, presenting and discussing their ideas with the top leadership team. "We believe these young ideas need the senior-most attention for them to be identified and fostered," says Sanjay Purohit, associate vice-president and head of corporate planning. Infosys CEO Nandan M. Nilekani concurs: "If an organization becomes too hierarchical, ideas that bubble up from younger people [aren't going to be heard]."

MINE CUSTOMER INSIGHTS
Getting inside the minds of customers is essential for "aha!" moments that lead to innovation. While ethnographers and designers are increasingly helping companies, true insight remains elusive: One quarter of our respondents still call customer awareness an innovation obstacle.

Mike Lazaridis, president and co-CEO of Research In Motion, hosts an innovation-themed, invitation-only "Vision Series" session in the Waterloo (Ont.)-based company's 100-seat auditorium each Thursday. The standing-room-only meetings focus on new research and future goals for the company that gave us the BlackBerry.

Lazaridis is likely the only chief executive of a publicly traded company who has an Academy Award for technical achievement. (He won it in 1999 for an innovative bar-code reader that he helped invent that expedites film editing and production.) He has donated $100 million of his own money to fund a theoretical physics institute and an additional $50 million to a university quantum computing and nanotechnology engineering center in Waterloo. He has even appeared in an American Express commercial, scratching complex equations across a blackboard while proclaiming his commitment to the creative process. "I think we have a culture of innovation here, and [engineers] have absolute access to me," says Lazaridis. "I live a life that tries to promote innovation." As the *BusinessWeek*-BCG survey demonstrates, it is a life every manager around the world must embrace.

JENA MCGREGOR, with Michael Arndt and Robert Berner in Chicago, Ian Rowley and Kenji Hall in Tokyo, Gail Edmondson in Frankfurt, Steve Hamm in Rome, Moon Ihlwan in Seoul, and Andy Reinhardt in Paris.

How the Creative Stay Creative

Innovative companies require innovative people. For lessons on developing a creative work force, we asked some of the nation's top innovation consultants how they do it in their own shop.

Leigh Buchanan

Get Multicultural

Cultural melting pots produce inventive meals, believes Sohrab Vossoughi, CEO of Ziba, an innovation consulting firm in Portland, Oregon. Ziba counts some 26 nationalities and 19 languages among its 120 employees. "People with different genetic backgrounds tend to have healthier children," says Vossoughi, an immigrant from Iran. "It's the same with ideas as it is with biology." Ziba, he says, also benefits from employees' knowledge of global markets.

Encourage Risky Behavior

Every year, BrightHouse holds an event known as March Fo(u)rth. On that date, each employee is encouraged to do something—jump from a plane, scuba-dive, start writing a novel—he or she has never attempted. "If we're known for anything, it's possibilitarianism," says CEO Reiman. Maddock Douglas, meanwhile, gives an annual Fail Forward award, which is designed to celebrate endeavors both ambitious and disastrous. Last year, a designer at the firm won for an unorthodox publication design that wound up laying waste to the production schedule and resulted in a costly error. "It was a total embarrassment" says president Viton. "But she was trying to do something new and different and better. She went for it, and she won an award for it."

Provide Lots of Free Time to Think

"The five last bastions of thinking are the car, the john, the shower, the church or synagogue, and the gym," says Joey Reiman, CEO of BrightHouse, an Atlanta-based innovation consulting firm whose clients include Coca-Cola and Delta Airlines. Note the absence of *office* from that roster. In addition to nearly five weeks' vacation, BrightHouse's 18 staff members get five Your Days, in which they are encouraged to visit a spot conducive to reflection and let their neurons rip. No mandate to solve a particular problem. Just blue-sky thinking—often under actual blue skies. Reiman believes this unstructured cogitation is just as important to a project's success as time spent hunkered down in client meetings. Or as he puts it: "I think; therefore, I am valuable."

Similarly, at Maddock Douglas, an Elmhurst, Illinois, firm that helps companies develop and market new products, employees can bank from 100 to 200 hours a year to pursue whatever intrigues them. (Google popularized a similar model, allotting engineers 20 percent of work hours for personal projects.) "Everybody has a place on their time sheets where they can say, This is not for a billable client," says president Raphael Louis Viton.

Hire Smart

At Innosight, a Watertown, Massachusetts-based firm founded by Clay Christensen, interviewers use case studies to assess problem-solving skills. Partner Julie Sequeira recently asked a job applicant how he would reverse the newspaper industry's declining fortunes. "I couldn't get him to stop thinking about the printed newspaper," she says. "That indicates risk-averse thinking." Chris Conley, co-founder of Gravitytank, a 30-employee firm in Chicago, is interested in how applicants deal with criticism: whether they tear into a creative exchange or defend their first idea to the bitter end. "To innovate, you have to be very open to critique, to why things won't work," says Conley.

Write It Down

Frog Design, a San Francisco-based consulting firm, publishes *Frog Design Mind,* a print and online magazine that serves as a quarterly compendium of staff articles on subjects that excite employees. Each issue is themed, but that's it for boundaries. In the most recent issue, on health, one designer used illustrations and captions to capture the discombobulating experience of being deaf in one ear. Another proposed monitoring people's health using a technologically enabled version of a Tibetan singing bowl. "We do it to keep our employees fresh, but thousands of people read it," says president Doreen Lorenzo. "We recently got a very large health care client because they read that issue."

Bring in Outsiders

Many top innovation firms tap the perspectives of outside experts—be they physicists, poets, actors, archaeologists, theologians, or astronauts. At BrightHouse, such distinguished professionals, otherwise known as "luminaries," are constantly cycling through the office. When the firm was working on a project for Red Lobster, it invited Robert Ballard, the oceanographer who discovered the wreck of the *Titanic;* he helped the team explore the association between its corporate identity and mankind's eternal fascination with the ocean. When working on a major reorganization of Emory University, BrightHouse enlisted Edgar Mitchell, the sixth man to walk on the moon; he talked about how constant training can leach fear from the unknown. CEO Reiman assesses the potential of each project for cross-disciplinary ferment and then consults the company's Rolodex. For employees, the experience is akin to a never-ending liberal arts education with the world's most prestigious faculty.

Be Flexible. Very Flexible

At InnovationLabs, in Walnut Creek, California, almost everyone is an outsider. That's because the company operates on the Hollywood model: It has just four principals and pulls together a new team for each project. Those teams, drawn from a worldwide network developed through referrals, may include business professors, webmasters, scientists, even the occasional dancer. Also, unlike many consulting firms, InnovationLabs has no prescribed process; team members can work any way they like. Given that many may not have met before an assignment, each project becomes a learning experience as contractors share brainstorming and visualization techniques. "Some people are amused when they work with us, because we're so averse to telling people what to do," says managing partner Langdon Morris. "But we want our people to be creative about how they help clients be creative."

Do It for Free

Creative folks enjoy applying their talents to noble causes—and, increasingly, their employers keep them happy by providing opportunities to do so. At BrightHouse, employees with great ideas for improving public life receive a $1,000 bonus on the spot. "It's a way to reward people not for the hours they put in but for the size of their hearts," says CEO Reiman.

Mix Up Your People

Some companies shake things up by letting employees loose in others' playpens. Ziba promotes such cross-fertilization with its Ambassador Program, in which employees spend about three months working in disciplines (known as tribes) different from their own. During that period, employees do their own work but also experience their colleagues' specialties. They sit in on brainstorming sessions and staff meetings and offer their own insights and critiques. Says CEO Vossoughi: "It creates an understanding of another world."

Avoiding Green Marketing Myopia

Ways to Improve Consumer Appeal for Environmentally Preferable Products

Jacquelyn A. Ottman, Edwin R. Stafford, and Cathy L. Hartman

In 1994, Philips launched the "EarthLight," a super energy-efficient compact fluorescent light (CFL) bulb designed to be an environmentally preferable substitute for the traditional energy-intensive incandescent bulb. The CFL's clumsy shape, however, was incompatible with most conventional lamps, and sales languished. After studying consumer response, Philips reintroduced the product in 2000 under the name "Marathon," to emphasize the bulb's five-year life. New designs offered the look and versatility of conventional incandescent light bulbs and the promise of more than $20 in energy savings over the product's life span compared to incandescent bulbs. The new bulbs were also certified by the U.S. Environmental Protection Agency's (EPA) Energy Star label. Repositioning CFL bulbs' features into advantages that resonated with consumer values—convenience, ease-of-use, and credible cost savings—ultimately sparked an annual sales growth of 12 percent in a mature product market.[1]

Philips' experience provides a valuable lesson on how to avoid the common pitfall of "green marketing myopia." Philips called its original entry "EarthLight" to communicate the CFL bulbs' environmental advantage. While noble, the benefit appealed to only the deepest green niche of consumers. The vast majority of consumers, however, will ask, "If I use 'green' products, what's in it for me?" In practice, green appeals are not likely to attract mainstream consumers unless they also offer a desirable benefit, such as cost-savings or improved product performance.[2] To avoid green marketing myopia, marketers must fulfill consumer needs and interests beyond what is good for the environment.

Although no consumer product has a zero impact on the environment, in business, the terms "green product" and "environmental product" are used commonly to describe those that strive to protect or enhance the natural environment by conserving energy and/or resources and reducing or eliminating use of toxic agents, pollution, and waste.[3] Paul Hawken, Amory Lovins, and L. Hunter Lovins write in their book *Natural Capitalism: Creating the Next Industrial Revolution* that greener, more sustainable products need to dramatically increase the productivity of natural resources, follow biological/cyclical production models, encourage dematerialization, and reinvest in and contribute to the planet's "natural" capital.[4] Escalating energy prices, concerns over foreign oil dependency, and calls for energy conservation are creating business opportunities for energy-efficient products, clean energy, and other environmentally-sensitive innovations and products—collectively known as "cleantech"[5] (see the box on page 95). For example, Pulitzer Prize–winning author and *New York Times* columnist Thomas L. Friedman argues that government policy and industry should engage in a "geo-green" strategy to promote energy efficiency, renewable energy, and other cleantech innovations to help alleviate the nation's dependency on oil from politically conflicted regions of the world.[6] Friedman asserts that such innovations can spark economic opportunity and address the converging global challenges of rising energy prices, terrorism, climate change, and the environmental consequences of the rapid economic development of China and India.

To exploit these economic opportunities to steer global commerce onto a more sustainable path, however, green products must appeal to consumers outside the traditional green niche.[7] Looking at sustainability from a green engineering perspective, Arnulf Grubler recently wrote in *Environment,* "To minimize environmental impacts by significant orders of magnitude requires the blending of good engineering with good economics as well as changing consumer preferences."[8] The marketing discipline has long argued that innovation must consider an intimate understanding of the customer,[9] and a close look at green marketing practices over time reveals that green products must be positioned on a consumer value sought by targeted consumers.

Drawing from past research and an analysis of the marketing appeals and strategies of green products that have either succeeded or failed in the marketplace over the past decade, some important lessons emerge for crafting effective green marketing and product strategies.[10] Based on the evidence, successful green products are able to appeal to mainstream consumers or lucrative market niches and frequently command price premiums by offering "non-green" consumer value (such as convenience and performance).

Green Marketing Myopia Defined

Green marketing must satisfy two objectives: improved environmental quality and customer satisfaction. Misjudging either or overemphasizing the former at the expense of the latter can be termed "green marketing myopia." In 1960, Harvard business professor Theodore Levitt introduced the concept of "marketing myopia" in a now-famous and influential article in the *Harvard Business Review.*[11] In it, he characterized the common pitfall of companies' tunnel vision, which focused on "managing products" (that is, product features, functions, and efficient production) instead of "meeting customers' needs" (that is, adapting to consumer expectations and anticipation of future desires). Levitt warned that a corporate preoccupation on products rather than consumer needs was doomed to failure because consumers select products and new innovations that offer benefits they desire. Research indicates that many green products have failed because of green marketing myopia—marketers' myopic focus on their products' "greenness" over the broader expectations of consumers or other market players (such as regulators or activists).

Green marketing must satisfy two objectives: improved environmental quality and customer satisfaction.

For example, partially in response to the 1987 Montreal Protocol, in which signatory countries (including the United States) agreed to phase out ozone-depleting chlorofluorocarbons (CFCs) by 2000, Whirlpool (in 1994) launched the "Energy Wise" refrigerator, the first CFC-free cooler and one that was 30 percent more efficient than the U.S. Department of Energy's highest standard.[12] For its innovation, Whirlpool won the "Golden Carrot," a $30 million award package of consumer rebates from the Super-Efficient Refrigerator Program, sponsored by the Natural Resources Defense Council and funded by 24 electric utilities. Unfortunately, Energy Wise's sales languished because the CFC-free benefit and energy-savings did not offset its $100 to $150 price premium, particularly in markets outside the rebate program, and the refrigerators did not offer additional features or new styles that consumers desired.[13] General Motors (GM) and Ford encountered similar problems when they launched their highly publicized EV-1 and Think Mobility electric vehicles, respectively, in the late 1990s to early 2000s in response to the 1990 zero-emission vehicle (ZEV) regulations adopted in California.[14] Both automakers believed their novel two-seater cars would be market successes (GM offered the EV-1 in a lease program, and Ford offered Think Mobility vehicles as rentals via the Hertz car-rental chain). Consumers, however, found electric vehicles' need for constant recharging with few recharging locations too inconvenient. Critics charged that the automakers made only token efforts to make electric cars a success, but a GM spokesperson recently explained, "We spent more than $1 billion to produce and market the vehicle, [but] fewer than 800 were leased."[15] Most drivers were not willing to drastically change their driving habits and expectations to accommodate electric cars, and the products ultimately were taken off the market.[16]

Aside from offering environmental benefits that do not meet consumer preferences, green marketing myopia can also occur when green products fail to provide credible, substantive environmental benefits. Mobil's Hefty photodegradable plastic trash bag is a case in point. Introduced in 1989, Hefty packages prominently displayed the term "degradable" with the explanation that a special ingredient promoted its decomposition into harmless particles in landfills "activated by exposure to the elements" such as sun, wind, and rain. Because most garbage is buried in landfills that allow limited exposure to the elements, making degradation virtually impossible, the claim enraged environmentalists. Ultimately, seven state attorneys general sued Mobil on charges of deceptive advertising and consumer fraud. Mobil removed the claim from its packaging and vowed to use extreme caution in making environmental claims in the future.[17]

Other fiascos have convinced many companies and consumers to reject green products. Roper ASW's 2002 "Green Gauge Report" finds that the top reasons consumers do not buy green products included beliefs that they require sacrifices—inconvenience, higher costs, lower performance—without significant environmental benefits.[18] Ironically, despite what consumers think, a plethora of green products available in the marketplace are in fact desirable because they deliver convenience, lower operating costs, and/or better performance. Often these are not marketed along with their green benefits, so consumers do not immediately recognize them as green and form misperceptions about their benefits. For instance, the appeal of premium-priced Marathon and other brands of CFL bulbs can be attributed to their energy savings and long life, qualities that make them convenient and economical over time. When consumers are convinced of the desirable "non-green" benefits of environmental products, they are more inclined to adopt them.

Other environmental products have also scored market successes by either serving profitable niche markets or offering mainstream appeal. Consider the Toyota Prius, the gas-electric hybrid vehicle that achieves about 44 miles per gallon of gasoline.[19] In recent years, Toyota's production has hardly kept pace with the growing demand, with buyers enduring long waits and paying thousands above the car's sticker price.[20] Consequently, other carmakers have scrambled to launch their own hybrids.[21] However, despite higher gas prices, analysts assert that it can take 5 to 20 years for lower gas expenses to offset many hybrid cars' higher prices. Thus, economics alone cannot explain their growing popularity.

Analysts offer several reasons for the Prius' market demand. Initially, the buzz over the Prius got a boost at the 2003 Academy Awards when celebrities such as Cameron Diaz, Harrison Ford, Susan Sarandon, and Robin Williams abandoned stretch limousines and oversized sport utility vehicles, arriving in Priuses to symbolize support for reducing America's dependence on foreign oil.[22] Since then, the quirky-looking Prius' badge of "conspicuous conservation" has satisfied many drivers' desires to turn heads and make a statement about their social responsibility, among them Google founders Larry Page and Sergey Brin, columnist Arianna Huffington, comic Bill Maher, and Charles, Prince of Wales.[23] The Prius ultimately was named *Motor Trend's* Car of the Year in 2004. The trendy appeal of the Prius illustrates that some green products can leverage consumer desires for being distinctive. Others say the Prius is just fun to drive—the dazzling digital dashboard that offers continuous feedback on fuel efficiency and other car operations provides an entertaining driving experience. More recently, however, the Prius has garnered fans for more practical reasons. A 2006 Maritz Poll finds that owners purchased hybrids because of the convenience of fewer fill-ups, better performance, and the enjoyment of driving the latest technology.[24] In some states, the Prius and other high-mileage hybrid vehicles, such as Honda's Insight, are granted free parking and solo-occupancy access to high occupancy vehicle (HOV) lanes.[25] In sum, hybrid vehicles offer consumers several desirable benefits that are not necessarily "green" benefits.

Many environmental products have become so common and widely distributed that many consumers may no longer recognize them as green because they buy them for non-green reasons. Green household products, for instance, are widely available at supermarkets and discount retailers, ranging from energy-saving Tide Coldwater laundry detergent to non-toxic Method and Simple Green cleaning products. Use of recycled or biodegradable paper products (such as plates, towels, napkins, coffee filters, computer paper, and other goods) is also widespread. Organic and rainforest-protective "shade grown" coffees are available at Starbucks and other specialty stores and supermarkets. Organic baby food is expected to command 12 percent market share in 2006 as parents strive to protect their children's mental and physical development.[26] Indeed, the organic food market segment has increased 20 percent annually since 1990, five times faster than the conventional food market, spurring the growth of specialty retailers such as Whole Foods Market and Wild Oats. Wal-Mart, too, has joined this extensive distribution of organic products.[27] Indeed, Wal-Mart has recently declared that in North American stores, its non-farm-raised fresh fish will be certified by the Marine Stewardship Council as sustainably harvested.[28]

Super energy-efficient appliances and fixtures are also becoming popular. Chic, front-loading washing machines, for example, accounted for 25 percent of the market in 2004, up from 9 percent in 2001.[29] EPA's Energy Star label, which certifies that products consume up to 30 percent less energy than comparable alternatives, is found on products ranging from major appliances to light fixtures to entire buildings (minimum efficiency standards vary from product to product). The construction industry is becoming increasingly green as government and industry demand office buildings that are "high

Emerging Age of Cleantech

In a 1960 Harvard Business Review article, Harvard professor Theodore Levitt introduced the classic concept of "marketing myopia" to characterize businesses' narrow vision on product features rather than consumer benefits.[1] The consequence is that businesses focus on making better mousetraps rather than seeking better alternatives for controlling pests. To avoid marketing myopia, businesses must engage in "creative destruction," described by economist Joseph Schumpeter as destroying existing products, production methods, market structures and consumption patterns, and replacing them with ways that better meet ever-changing consumer desires.[2] The dynamic pattern in which innovative upstart companies unseat established corporations and industries by capitalizing on new and improved innovations is illustrated by history. That is, the destruction of Coal Age technologies by Oil Age innovations, which are being destroyed by Information Age advances and the emerging Age of Cleantech—clean, energy- and resource-efficient energy technologies, such as those involving low/zero-emissions, wind, solar, biomass, hydrogen, recycling, and closed-loop processes.[3]

Business management researchers Stuart Hart and Mark Milstein argue that the emerging challenge of global sustainability is catalyzing a new round of creative destruction that offers "unprecedented opportunities" for new environmentally sensitive innovations, markets, and products.[4] Throughout the twentieth century, many technologies and business practices have contributed to the destruction of the very ecological systems on which the economy and life itself depends, including toxic contamination, depletion of fisheries and forests, soil erosion, and biodiversity loss. Recent news reports indicate, however, that many companies and consumers are beginning to respond to programs to help conserve the Earth's natural resources, and green marketing is making a comeback.[5] The need for sustainability has become more acute economically as soaring demand, dwindling supplies, and rising prices for oil, gas, coal, water, and other natural resources are being driven by the industrialization of populous countries, such as China and India. Politically, America's significant reliance on foreign oil has become increasingly recognized as a security threat. Global concerns over climate change have led 141 countries to ratify the Kyoto Protocol, the international treaty requiring the reduction of global warming gases created through the burning of fossil fuels. Although the United States has not signed the treaty, most multinational corporations conducting business in signatory nations are compelled to reduce their greenhouse gas emissions, and many states (such as California) and cities (such as Chicago and Seattle) have or are initiating their own global warming gas emission reduction programs.[6] State and city-level policy incentives and mandates, such as "renewable portfolio standards," requiring utilities to provide increasing amounts of electricity from clean, renewable sources such as wind and solar power, are also driving cleaner technology markets.

While some firms have responded grudgingly to such pressures for more efficient and cleaner business practices, others are seizing the cleantech innovation opportunities for new twenty-first-century green products and technologies for competitive advantage. Toyota, for instance, plans to offer an all-hybrid fleet in the near future to challenge competitors on both performance and fuel economy.[7] Further, Toyota is licensing its technology to its competitors to gain profit from their hybrid sales as well. General Electric's highly publicized "Ecomagination" initiative promises a greener world with a plan to double its investments (to $1.5 billion annually) and revenues (to $20 billion) from fuel-efficient diesel locomotives, wind power, "clean" coal, and other cleaner innovations by 2010.[8] Cleantech is attracting investors looking for the "Next Big Thing," including Goldman Sachs and Kleiner Perkins Caufield & Byers.[9] Wal-Mart, too, is testing a sustainable 206,000-square foot store design in Texas that deploys 26 energy-saving and renewable-materials experiments that could set new standards in future retail store construction.[10] In sum, economic, political, and environmental pressures are coalescing to drive cleaner and greener technological innovation in the twenty-first century, and companies that fail to adapt their products and processes accordingly are destined to suffer from the consequences of marketing myopia and creative destruction.

1. T. Levitt, "Marketing Myopia," *Harvard Business Review* 28, July–August (1960): 24–47.
2. See J. Schumpeter, *The Theory of Economic Development* (Cambridge: Harvard University Press, 1934); and J. Schumpeter, *Capitalism, Socialism and Democracy* (New York: Harper Torchbooks, 1942).
3. "Alternate Power: A Change Is in the Wind," *BusinessWeek,* 4 July 2005, 36–37.
4. S. L. Hart and M. B. Milstein, "Global Sustainability and the Creative Destruction of Industries," *MIT Sloan Management Review* 41, Fall (1999): 23–33.
5. See for example T. Howard, "Being Eco-Friendly Can Pay Economically; 'Green Marketing' Sees Growth in Sales, Ads," *USA Today,* 15 August 2005; and E. R. Stafford, "Energy Efficiency and the New Green Marketing," *Environment,* March 2003, 8–10.
6. J. Ball, "California Sets Emission Goals That Are Stiffer than U.S. Plan," *Wall Street Journal,* 2 June 2005; and J. Marglis, "Paving the Way for U.S. Emissions Trading," *Grist Magazine,* 14 June 2005, www.climatebiz.com/sections/news_print.dfm?NewsID=28255.
7. Bloomberg News, "Toyota Says It Plans Eventually to Offer an All-Hybrid Fleet," 14 September 2005, http://www.nytimes.com/2005/09/14/automobiles/14toyota.html.
8. J. Erickson, "U.S. Business and Climate Change: Siding with the Marketing?" *Sustainability Radar,* June, www.climatebiz.com/sections/new_ print .cfm?NewsID=28204.
9. *BusinessWeek,* note 3 above.
10. Howard, note 5 above.

performance" (for example, super energy- and resource-efficient and cost-effective) and "healthy" for occupants (for example, well-ventilated; constructed with materials with low or no volatile organic compounds [VOC]). The U.S. Green Building Council's "Leadership in Energy and Environmental Design" (LEED) provides a rigorous rating system and green building checklist that are rapidly becoming the standard for environmentally sensitive construction.[30]

Home buyers are recognizing the practical long-term cost savings and comfort of natural lighting, passive solar heating, and heat-reflective windows, and a 2006 study sponsored by home improvement retailer Lowe's found nine out of ten builders surveyed are incorporating energy-saving features into new homes.[31] Additionally, a proliferation of "green" building materials to serve the growing demand has emerged.[32] Lowe's competitor The Home Depot is testing an 'EcoOptions' product line featuring natural fertilizers and mold-resistant drywall in its Canadian stores that may filter into the U.S. market.[33] In short, energy efficiency and green construction have become mainstream.

The diversity and availability of green products indicate that consumers are not indifferent to the value offered by environmental benefits. Consumers are buying green—but not necessarily for environmental reasons. The market growth of organic foods and energy-efficient appliances is because consumers desire their perceived safety and money savings, respectively.[34] Thus, the apparent paradox between what consumers say and their purchases may be explained, in part, by green marketing myopia—a narrow focus on the greenness of products that blinds companies from considering the broader consumer and societal desires. A fixation on products' environmental merits has resulted frequently in inferior green products (for example, the original EarthLight and GM's EV-1 electric car) and unsatisfying consumer experiences. By contrast, the analysis of past research and marketing strategies finds that successful green products have avoided green marketing myopia by following three important principles: "The Three Cs" of consumer value positioning, calibration of consumer knowledge, and credibility of product claims.

Consumer Value Positioning

The marketing of successfully established green products showcases non-green consumer value, and there are at least five desirable benefits commonly associated with green products: efficiency and cost effectiveness; health and safety; performance; symbolism and status; and convenience. Additionally, when these five consumer value propositions are not inherent in the green product, successful green marketing programs bundle (that is, add to the product design or market offering) desirable consumer value to broaden the green product's appeal. In practice, the implication is that product designers and marketers need to align environmental products' consumer value (such as money savings) to relevant consumer market segments (for example, cost-conscious consumers).

Efficiency and Cost Effectiveness

As exemplified by the Marathon CFL bulbs, the common inherent benefit of many green products is their potential energy and resource efficiency. Given sky-rocketing energy prices and tax incentives for fuel-efficient cars and energy-saving home improvements and appliances, long-term savings have convinced cost-conscious consumers to buy green.

Recently, the home appliance industry made great strides in developing energy-efficient products to achieve EPA's Energy Star rating. For example, Energy Star refrigerators use at least 15 percent less energy and dishwashers use at least 25 percent less energy than do traditional models.[35] Consequently, an Energy Star product often commands a price premium. Whirlpool's popular Duet front-loading washer and dryer, for example, cost more than $2,000, about double the price of conventional units; however, the washers can save up to 12,000 gallons of water and $110 on electricity annually compared to standard models (Energy Star does not rate dryers).[36]

Laundry detergents are also touting energy savings. Procter & Gamble's (P&G) newest market entry, Tide Cold-water, is designed to clean clothes effectively in cold water. About 80 to 85 percent of the energy used to wash clothes comes from heating water. Working with utility companies, P&G found that consumers could save an average of $63 per year by using cold rather than warm water.[37] Adopting Tide Coldwater gives added confidence to consumers already washing in cold water. As energy and resource prices continue to soar, opportunities for products offering efficiency and savings are destined for market growth.

Health and Safety

Concerns over exposure to toxic chemicals, hormones, or drugs in everyday products have made health and safety important choice considerations, especially among vulnerable consumers, such as pregnant women, children, and the elderly.[38] Because most environmental products are grown or designed to minimize or eliminate the use of toxic agents and adulterating processes, market positioning on consumer safety and health can achieve broad appeal among health-conscious consumers. Sales of organic foods, for example, have grown considerably in the wake of public fear over "mad cow" disease, antibiotic-laced meats, mercury in fish, and genetically modified foods.[39] Mainstream appeal of organics is not derived from marketers promoting the advantages of free-range animal ranching and pesticide-free soil. Rather, market positioning of organics as flavorful, healthy alternatives to factory-farm foods has convinced consumers to pay a premium for them.

A study conducted by the Alliance for Environmental Innovation and household products-maker S.C. Johnson found that consumers are most likely to act on green messages that strongly connect to their personal environments.[40] Specifically, findings suggest that the majority of consumers prefer such environmental household product benefits as "safe to use around children," "no toxic ingredients," "no chemical residues," and "no strong fumes" over such benefits as "packaging can be recycled" or "not tested on animals." Seventh Generation, a brand of non-toxic and environmentally-safe household products, derived its name from the Iroquois belief that, "In our every deliberation, we must consider the impact of our decisions on the next seven generations." Accordingly, its products promote the family-oriented value of making the world a safer place for the next seven generations.

Indoor air quality is also a growing concern. Fumes from paints, carpets, furniture, and other décor in poorly ventilated "sick buildings" have been linked to headaches, eye, nose, and throat irritation, dizziness, and fatigue among occupants. Consequently, many manufacturers have launched green products to reduce indoor air pollution. Sherwin Williams, for example, offers "Harmony," a line of interior paints that is low-odor, zero-VOC, and silica-free. And Mohawk sells EverSet Fibers, a carpet that virtually eliminates the need for harsh chemical cleaners because its design allows most stains to be removed with water. Aside from energy efficiency, health and safety have been key motivators driving the green building movement.

Performance

The conventional wisdom is that green products don't work as well as "non-green" ones. This is a legacy from the first generation of environmentally sensitive products that clearly were inferior. Consumer perception of green cleaning agents introduced in health food stores in the 1960s and 1970s, for example, was that "they cost twice as much to remove half the grime."[41] Today, however, many green products are designed to perform better than conventional ones and can command a price premium. For example, in addition to energy efficiency, front-loading washers clean better and are gentler on clothes compared to conventional top-loading machines because they spin clothes in a motion similar to clothes driers and use centrifugal force to pull dirt and water away from clothes. By contrast, most top-loading washers use agitators to pull clothes through tanks of water, reducing cleaning and increasing wear on clothes. Consequently, the efficiency and high performance benefits of top-loading washers justify their premium prices.

Market positioning on consumer safety and health can achieve broad appeal among health-conscious consumers.

Homeowners commonly build decks with cedar, redwood, or pressure-treated pine (which historically was treated with toxic agents such as arsenic). Wood requires stain or paint and periodic applications of chemical preservatives for maintenance. Increasingly, however, composite deck material made from recycled milk jugs and wood fiber, such as Weyerhaeuser's ChoiceDek, is marketed as the smarter alternative. Composites are attractive, durable, and low maintenance. They do not contain toxic chemicals and never need staining or chemical preservatives. Accordingly, they command a price premium— as much as two to three times the cost of pressure-treated pine and 15 percent more than cedar or redwood.[42]

Likewise, Milgard Windows' low emissivity SunCoat Low-E windows filter the sun in the summer and reduce heat loss in the winter. While the windows can reduce a building's overall energy use, their more significant benefit comes from helping to create a comfortable indoor radiant temperature climate and protecting carpets and furniture from harmful ultraviolet rays. Consequently, Milgard promotes the improved comfort and performance of its SunCoat Low-E windows over conventional windows. In sum, "high performance" positioning can broaden green product appeal.

Symbolism and Status

As mentioned earlier, the Prius, Toyota's gas-electric hybrid, has come to epitomize "green chic." According to many automobile analysts, the cool-kid cachet that comes with being an early adopter of the quirky-looking hybrid vehicle trend continues to partly motivate sales.[43] Establishing a green chic appeal, however, isn't easy. According to popular culture experts, green marketing must appear grass-roots driven and humorous without sounding preachy. To appeal to young people, conservation and green consumption need the unsolicited endorsement of high-profile celebrities and connection to cool technology.[44] Prius has capitalized on its evangelical following and high-tech image with some satirical ads, including a television commercial comparing the hybrid with Neil Armstrong's moon landing ("That's one small step on the accelerator, one giant leap for mankind") and product placements in popular Hollywood films and sitcoms (such as *Curb Your Enthusiasm*). More recently, Toyota has striven to position its "hybrid synergy drive" system as a cut above other car makers' hybrid technologies with witty slogans such as, "Commute with Nature," "mpg:)," and "There's Nothing Like That New Planet Smell."[45] During the 2006

Super Bowl XL game, Ford launched a similarly humorous commercial featuring Kermit the Frog encountering a hybrid Escape sports utility vehicle in the forest, and in a twist, changing his tune with "I guess it *is* easy being green!"[46]

In business, where office furniture symbolizes the cachet of corporate image and status, the ergonomically designed "Think" chair is marketed as the chair "with a brain and a conscience." Produced by Steelcase, the world's largest office furniture manufacturer, the Think chair embodies the latest in "cradle to cradle" (C2C) design and manufacturing. C2C, which describes products that can be ultimately returned to technical or biological nutrients, encourages industrial designers to create products free of harmful agents and processes that can be recycled easily into new products (such as metals and plastics) or safely returned to the earth (such as plant-based materials).[47] Made without any known carcinogens, the Think chair is 99 percent recyclable; it disassembles with basic hand tools in about five minutes, and parts are stamped with icons showing recycling options.[48] Leveraging its award-winning design and sleek comfort, the Think chair is positioned as symbolizing the smart, socially responsible office. In sum, green products can be positioned as status symbols.

Convenience

Many energy-efficient products offer inherent convenience benefits that can be showcased for competitive advantage. CFL bulbs, for example, need infrequent replacement and gas-electric hybrid cars require fewer refueling stops—benefits that are highlighted in their marketing communications. Another efficient alternative to incandescent bulbs are light-emitting diodes (LEDs): They are even more efficient and longer-lasting than CFL bulbs; emit a clearer, brighter light; and are virtually unbreakable even in cold and hot weather. LEDs are used in traffic lights due to their high-performance convenience. Recently, a city in Idaho became a pioneer by adopting LEDs for its annual holiday Festival of Lights. "We spent so much time replacing strings of lights and bulbs," noted one city official, "[using LEDs] is going to reduce two-thirds of the work for us."[49]

To encourage hybrid vehicle adoption, some states and cities are granting their drivers the convenience of free parking and solo-occupant access to HOV lanes. A Toyota spokesperson recently told the *Los Angeles Times,* "Many customers are telling us the carpool lane is the main reason for buying now."[50] Toyota highlights the carpool benefit on its Prius Web site, and convenience has become an incentive to drive efficient hybrid cars in traffic-congested states like California and Virginia. Critics have charged, however, that such incentives clog carpool lanes and reinforce a "one car, one person" lifestyle over alternative transportation. In response, the Virginia legislature has more recently enacted curbs on hybrid drivers use of HOV lanes during peak hours, requiring three or more people per vehicle, except for those that have been grandfathered in.[51]

Solar power was once used only for supplying electricity in remote areas (for example, while camping in the wilderness or boating or in homes situated off the power grid). That convenience, however, is being exploited for other applications. In landscaping, for example, self-contained solar-powered outdoor evening lights that recharge automatically during the day eliminate the need for electrical hookups and offer flexibility for reconfiguration. With society's increasing mobility and reliance on electronics, solar power's convenience is also manifest in solar-powered calculators, wrist watches, and other gadgets, eliminating worries over dying batteries. Reware's solar-powered "Juice Bag" backpack is a popular portable re-charger for students, professionals, and outdoor enthusiasts on the go. The Juice Bag's flexible, waterproof solar panel has a 16.6-volt capacity to generate 6.3 watts to recharge PDAs, cell phones, iPods, and other gadgets in about 2 to 4 hours.[52]

Bundling

Some green products do not offer any of the inherent five consumer-desired benefits noted above. This was the case when energy-efficient and CFC-free refrigerators were introduced in China in the 1990s. While Chinese consumers preferred and were willing to pay about 15 percent more for refrigerators that were "energy-efficient," they did not connect the environmental advantage of "CFC-free" with either energy efficiency or savings. Consequently, the "CFC-free" feature had little impact on purchase decisions.[53] To encourage demand, the CFC-free feature was bundled with attributes desired by Chinese consumers, which included energy efficiency, savings, brand/quality, and outstanding after-sales service.

According to popular culture experts, green marketing must appear grass-roots driven and humorous without sounding preachy.

Given consumer demand for convenience, incorporating time-saving or ease-of-use features into green products can further expand their mainstream acceptance. Ford's hybrid Escape SUV comes with an optional 110-volt AC power outlet suitable for work, tailgating, or camping. Convenience has also enhanced the appeal of Interface's recyclable FLOR carpeting, which is marketed as "practical, goof-proof, and versatile." FLOR comes in modular square tiles with four peel-and-stick dots on the back for easy installation (and pull up for altering, recycling, or washing with water in the sink). Modularity offers versatility to assemble tiles for a custom look. Interface promotes the idea that its carpet tiles can be changed and reconfigured in minutes to dress up a room for any occasion. The tiles come in pizza-style boxes for storage, and ease of use is FLOR's primary consumer appeal.

Finally, Austin (Texas) Energy's "Green Choice" program has led the nation in renewable energy sales for the past three years.[54] In 2006, demand for wind energy outpaced supply so that the utility resorted to selecting new "Green Choice" subscribers by lottery.[55] While most utilities find it challenging to sell green electricity at a premium price on its environmental merit, Austin Energy's success comes from bundling three benefits that appeal to commercial power users: First, Green Choice customers are recognized in broadcast media for their corporate responsibility; second, the green power is marketed as "home grown," appealing to Texan loyalties; and third, the program offers a fixed price that is locked in for 10 years. Because wind power's cost is derived primarily from the construction of wind farms and is not subject to volatile fossil fuel costs, Austin Energy passes its inherent price stability onto its Green Choice customers. Thus, companies participating in Green Choice enjoy the predictability of their future energy costs in an otherwise volatile energy market.

In summary, the analysis suggests that successful green marketing programs have broadened the consumer appeal of green products by convincing consumers of their "non-green" consumer value. The lesson for crafting effective green marketing strategies is that planners need to identify the inherent consumer value of green product attributes (for example, energy efficiency's inherent long-term money savings) or bundle desired consumer value into green products (such as fixed pricing of wind power) and to draw marketing attention to this consumer value.

Calibration of Consumer Knowledge

Many of the successful green products in the analysis described here employ compelling, educational marketing messages and slogans that connect green product attributes with desired consumer value. That is, the marketing programs successfully calibrated consumer knowledge to recognize the green product's consumer benefits. In many instances, the environmental benefit was positioned as secondary, if mentioned at all. Changes made in EPA's Energy Star logo provide an example, illustrating the program's improved message calibration over the years. One of Energy Star's early marketing messages, "EPA Pollution Preventer," was not only ambiguous but myopically focused on pollution rather than a more mainstream consumer benefit. A later promotional message, "Saving The Earth. Saving Your Money." better associated energy efficiency with consumer value, and one of its more recent slogans, "Money Isn't All You're Saving," touts economic savings as the chief benefit. This newest slogan also encourages consumers to think implicitly about what else they are "saving"—the logo's illustration of the Earth suggests the answer, educating consumers that "saving the Earth" can also meet consumer self-interest.

The connection between environmental benefit and consumer value is evident in Earthbound Farm Organic's slogan, "Delicious produce is our business, but health is our bottom line," which communicates that pesticide-free produce is flavorful and healthy. Likewise, Tide Coldwater's "Deep Clean. Save Green." slogan not only assures consumers of the detergent's cleaning performance, but the term "green" offers a double meaning, connecting Tide's cost saving with its environmental benefit. Citizen's solar-powered Eco-Drive watch's slogan, "Unstoppable Caliber," communicates the product's convenience and performance (that is, the battery will not die) as well as prestige. Table 1 on page 89 shows other successful marketing messages that educate consumers of the inherent consumer value of green.

Some compelling marketing communications educate consumers to recognize green products as "solutions" for their personal needs *and* the environment.[56] When introducing its Renewal brand, Rayovac positioned the reusable alkaline batteries as a solution for heavy battery users and the environment with concurrent ads touting "How to save $150 on a CD player that costs $100" and "How to save 147 batteries from going to landfills." Complementing the money savings and landfill angles, another ad in the campaign featured sports star Michael Jordan proclaiming, "More Power. More Music. And More Game Time." to connect Renewal batteries' performance to convenience.[57] In practice, the analysis conducted here suggests that advertising, which draws attention to how the environmental products benefit and also deliver personal value, can broaden consumer acceptance of green products.

Credibility of Product Claims

Credibility is the foundation of effective green marketing. Green products must meet or exceed consumer expectations by delivering their promised consumer value and providing substantive environmental benefits. Often, consumers don't have the expertise or ability to verify green products' environmental and consumer values, creating misperceptions and skepticism. As exemplified in the case of Mobil's Hefty photodegradable plastic trash bag described earlier, green marketing that touts a product's or a company's environmental credentials can spark the scrutiny of advocacy groups or regulators. For example, although it was approved by the U.S. Food and Drug Administration, sugar substitute

Splenda's "Made from sugar, so it tastes like sugar" slogan and claim of being "natural" have been challenged by the Sugar Association and Generation Green, a health advocacy group, as misleading given that its processing results in a product that is "unrecognizable as sugar."[58]

To be persuasive, past research suggests that green claims should be specific and meaningful.[59] Toyota recognizes the ambiguity of the term "green" and discourages its use in its marketing of its gas-electric hybrid cars. One proposed slogan, "Drive green, breathe blue" was dismissed in favor of specific claims about fuel efficiency, such as "Less gas in. Less gasses out."[60] Further, environmental claims must be humble and not over-promise. When Ford Motor Company publicized in *National Geographic* and other magazines its new eco-designed Rouge River Plant that incorporated the world's largest living roof of plants, critics questioned the authenticity of Ford's environmental commitment given the poor fuel economy of the automaker's best-selling SUVs.[61] Even the Prius has garnered some criticism for achieving considerably less mileage (approximately 26 percent less according to *Consumer Reports*) than its government sticker rating claims, although the actual reduced mileage does not appear to be hampering sales.[62] Nonetheless, green product attributes need to be communicated honestly and qualified for believability (in other words, consumer benefits and environmental effectiveness claims need to be compared with comparable alternatives or likely usage scenarios). For example, Toyota includes an "actual mileage may vary" disclaimer in Prius advertising. When Ford's hybrid Escape SUV owners complained that they were not achieving expected mileage ratings, Ford launched the "Fuel-Economy School" campaign to educate drivers about ways to maximize fuel efficiency.[63] Further, EPA is reconsidering how it estimates hybrid mileage ratings to better reflect realistic driving conditions (such as heavy acceleration and air conditioner usage).[64]

Table 1 Marketing Messages Connecting Green Products with Desired Consumer Value

Value	Message and Business/Product
Efficiency and cost effectiveness	"The only thing our washer will shrink is your water bill." —ASKO
	"Did you know that between 80 and 85 percent of the energy used to wash clothes comes from heating the water? Tide Coldwater—The Coolest Way to Clean." —Tide Coldwater Laundry Detergent "mpg:)" —Toyota Prius
Health and safety	"20 years of refusing to farm with toxic pesticides. Stubborn, perhaps. Healthy, most definitely." —Earthbound Farm Organic
	"Safer for You and the Environment." —Seventh Generation Household Cleaners
Performance	"Environmentally friendly stain removal. It's as simple as H_2O." —Mohawk EverSet Fibers Carpet
	"Fueled by light so it runs forever. It's unstoppable. Just like the people who wear it." —Citizen Eco-Drive Sport Watch
Symbolism	"Think is the chair with a brain and a conscience." —Steelcase's Think Chair
	"Make up your mind, not just your face." —The Body Shop
Convenience	"Long life for hard-to-reach places." —General Electric's CFL Flood Lights
Bundling	"Performance and luxury fueled by innovative technology." —Lexus RX400h Hybrid Sports Utility Vehicle

Source: Compiled by J.A. Ottman, E.R. Stafford, and C.L. Hartman, 2006.

Third Party Endorsements and Eco-Certifications

Expert third parties with respected standards for environmental testing (such as independent laboratories, government agencies, private consultants, or nonprofit advocacy organizations) can provide green product endorsements and/or "seals of approval" to help clarify and bolster the believability of product claims.[65] The "Energy Star" label, discussed earlier, is a common certification that distinguishes certain electronic products as consuming up to 30 percent less energy than comparable alternatives. The U.S. Department of Agriculture's "USDA Organic" certifies the production and handling of organic produce and dairy products.

Green Seal and Scientific Certification Systems emblems certify a broad spectrum of green products. Green Seal sets specific criteria for various categories of products, ranging from paints to cleaning agents to hotel properties, and for a fee, companies can have their products evaluated and monitored annually for certification. Green Seal-certified products include Zero-VOC Olympic Premium interior paint and Johnson Wax professional cleaners. Green Seal has also certified the Hyatt Regency in Washington, DC, for the hotel's comprehensive energy and water conservation, recycling programs, and environmental practices. By contrast, Scientific Certification Systems (SCS) certifies specific product claims or provides a detailed "eco-profile" for a product's environmental impact for display on product labels for a broad array of products, from agricultural products to fisheries to construction. For example, Armstrong hard surface flooring holds SCS certification, and SCS works with retailers like The Home Depot to monitor its vendors' environmental claims.[66]

Although eco-certifications differentiate products and aid in consumer decisionmaking, they are not without controversy. The science behind eco-seals can appear subjective and/or complex, and critics may take issue with certification criteria.[67] For example, GreenOrder, a New York-based environmental consulting firm, has devised a scorecard to evaluate cleantech products marketed in General Electric's "Ecomagination" initiative, which range from fuel-efficient aircraft engines to wind turbines to water treatment technologies. Only those passing GreenOrder's criteria are marketed as Ecomagination products, but critics have questioned GE's inclusion of "cleaner coal" (that is, coal gasification for cleaner burning and sequestration of carbon dioxide emissions) as an "Ecomagination" product.[68]

Although eco-certifications differentiate products and aid in consumer decisionmaking, they are not without controversy.

Consequently, when seeking endorsements and eco-certifications, marketers should consider the environmental tradeoffs and complexity of their products and the third parties behind endorsements and/or certifications: Is the third party respected? Are its certification methodologies accepted by leading environmentalists, industry experts, government regulators, and other key stakeholders? Marketers should educate their customers about the meaning behind an endorsement or an eco-seal's criteria. GE recognizes that its cleaner coal technology is controversial but hopes that robust marketing and educational outreach will convince society about cleaner coal's environmental benefits.[69] On its Web site, GE references U.S. Energy Information Administration's statistics that coal accounts for about 24 percent of the world's total energy consumption, arguing that coal will continue to be a dominant source of energy due to its abundance and the increasing electrification of populous nations such as China and India.[70] In response to GE's commitment to clean coal, Jonathan Lash, president of the World Resources Institute, said, "Five years ago, I had to struggle to suppress my gag response to terms like 'clean coal,' but I've since faced the sobering reality that every two weeks China opens a new coal-fired plant. India is moving at almost the same pace. There is huge environmental value in developing ways to mitigate these plants' emissions."[71]

Word-of-Mouth Evangelism and the Internet

Increasingly, consumers have grown skeptical of commercial messages, and they're turning to the collective wisdom and experience of their friends and peers about products.[72] Word-of-mouth or "buzz" is perceived to be very credible, especially as consumers consider and try to comprehend complex product innovations. The Internet, through e-mail and its vast, accessible repository of information, Web sites, search engines, blogs, product ratings sites, podcasts, and other digital platforms, has opened significant opportunities for tapping consumers' social and communication networks to diffuse credible "word-of-mouse" (buzz facilitated by the Internet) about green products. This is exemplified by one of the most spectacular product introductions on the Web: Tide Coldwater.

In 2005, Proctor & Gamble partnered with the non-profit organization, the Alliance to Save Energy (ASE), in a "viral marketing" campaign to spread news about the money-saving benefits of laundering clothes in cold water with specially formulated Tide Coldwater.[73] ASE provided credibility for the detergent by auditing and backing P&G's claims that consumers could save an average of $63 a year if they switched from warm to cold water washes. ASE sent e-mail promotions encouraging consumers to visit Tide.com's interactive Web site and take the "Coldwater Challenge" by registering to receive a free sample. Visitors could calculate how much money they would save by using the detergent, learn other energy-saving laundry tips, and refer e-mail addresses of their friends to take the challenge as well. Tide.com offered an engaging map of the United States where, over time, visitors could track and watch their personal networks grow across the country when their friends logged onto the site to request a free sample.

Given the immediacy of e-mail and the Internet, word-of-mouse is fast becoming an important vehicle for spreading credible news about new products. According to the Pew Internet & American Life

Project, 44 percent of online U.S. adults (about 50 million Americans) are "content creators," meaning that they contribute to the Internet via blogs, product recommendations, and reviews.[74] To facilitate buzz, however, marketers need to create credible messages, stories, and Web sites about their products that are so compelling, interesting, and/or entertaining that consumers will seek the information out and forward it to their friends and family.[75] The fact that P&G was able to achieve this for a low-involvement product is quite remarkable.

International online marketing consultant Hitwise reported that ASE's e-mail campaign increased traffic at the Tide Coldwater Web site by 900 percent in the first week, and then tripled that level in week two.[76] Within a few months, more than one million Americans accepted the "Coldwater Challenge," and word-of-mouse cascaded through ten degrees of separation across all 50 states and more than 33,000 zip codes.[77] In October 2005, Hitwise reported that Tide.com ranked as the twelfth most popular site by market share of visits in the "Lifestyle—House and Garden" category.[78] No other laundry detergent brand's Web site has gained a significant Web presence in terms of the number of visits.

P&G's savvy implementation of "The Three Cs"—consumer value positioning on money savings, calibration of consumer knowledge about cold wash effectiveness via an engaging Web site, and credible product messages dispatched by a respected non-profit group and consumers' Internet networks—set the stage for Tide Coldwater's successful launch.

The Future of Green Marketing

Clearly, there are many lessons to be learned to avoid green marketing myopia (see the box)—the short version of all this is that effective green marketing requires applying good marketing principles to make green products desirable for consumers. The question that remains, however, is, what is green marketing's future? Historically, green marketing has been a misunderstood concept. Business scholars have viewed it as a "fringe" topic, given that environmentalism's acceptance of limits and conservation does not mesh well with marketing's traditional axioms of "give customers what they want" and "sell as much as you can." In practice, green marketing myopia has led to ineffective products and consumer reluctance. Sustainability, however, is destined to dominate twenty-first century commerce. Rising energy prices, growing pollution and resource consumption in Asia, and political pressures to address climate change are driving innovation toward healthier, more-efficient, high-performance products. In short, all marketing will incorporate elements of green marketing.

As the authors of *Natural Capitalism* argue, a more sustainable business model requires "product dematerialization"—that is, commerce will shift from the "sale of goods" to the "sale of services" (for example, providing illumination rather than selling light bulbs).[79] This model is illustrated, if unintentionally, by arguably the twenty-first century's hottest product—Apple's iPod. The iPod gives consumers the convenience to download, store, and play tens of thousands of songs without the environmental impact of manufacturing and distributing CDs, plastic jewel cases, and packaging.

Innovations that transform material goods into efficient streams of services could proliferate if consumers see them as desirable. To encourage energy and water efficiency, Electrolux piloted a "pay-per-wash" service in Sweden in 1999 where consumers were given new efficient washing machines for a small home installation fee and then were charged 10 Swedish kronor (about $1) per use. The machines were connected via the Internet to a central database to monitor use, and Electrolux maintained ownership and servicing of the washers. When the machines had served their duty, Electrolux took them

Summary of Guideposts for the "Three C's"

Evidence indicates that successful green products have avoided green marketing myopia by following three important principles: consumer value positioning, calibration of consumer knowledge, and the credibility of product claims.

Consumer Value Positioning

- Design environmental products to perform as well as (or better than) alternatives.
- Promote and deliver the consumer-desired value of environmental products and target relevant consumer market segments (such as market health benefits among health-conscious consumers).
- Broaden mainstream appeal by bundling (or adding) consumer-desired value into environmental products (such as fixed pricing for subscribers of renewable energy).

Calibration of Consumer Knowledge

- Educate consumers with marketing messages that connect environmental product attributes with desired consumer value (for example, "pesticide-free produce is healthier"; "energy-efficiency saves money"; or "solar power is convenient").

- Frame environmental product attributes as "solutions" for consumer needs (for example, "rechargeable batteries offer longer performance").
- Create engaging and educational Internet sites about environmental products' desired consumer value (for example, Tide Coldwater's interactive Web site allows visitors to calculate their likely annual money savings based on their laundry habits, utility source (gas or electricity), and zip code location).

Credibility of Product Claims

- Employ environmental product and consumer benefit claims that are specific, meaningful, unpretentious, and qualified (that is, compared with comparable alternatives or likely usage scenarios).
- Procure product endorsements or eco-certifications from trustworthy third parties, and educate consumers about the meaning behind those endorsements and eco-certifications.
- Encourage consumer evangelism via consumers' social and Internet communication networks with compelling, interesting, and/or entertaining information about environmental products (for example, Tide's "Coldwater Challenge" Web site included a map of the United States so visitors could track and watch their personal influence spread when their friends requested a free sample).

back for remanufacturing. Pay-per-wash failed, however, because consumers were not convinced of its benefits over traditional ownership of washing machines.[80] Had Electrolux better marketed pay-per-wash's convenience (for example, virtually no upfront costs for obtaining a top-of-the-line washer, free servicing, and easy trade-ins for upgrades) or bundled pay-per-wash with more desirable features, consumers might have accepted the green service. To avoid green marketing myopia, the future success of product dematerialization and more sustainable services will depend on credibly communicating and delivering consumer-desired value in the marketplace. Only then will product dematerialization steer business onto a more sustainable path.

Notes

1. G. Fowler, "'Green Sales Pitch Isn't Moving Many Products," *Wall Street Journal,* 6 March 2002.

2. See, for example, K. Alston and J. P. Roberts, "Partners in New Product Development: SC Johnson and the Alliance for Environmental Innovation," *Corporate Environmental Strategy* 6, no. 2: 111–28.

3. See, for example, J. Ottman, *Green Marketing: Opportunity for Innovation* (Lincolnwood [Chicago]: NTC Business Books, 1997).

4. P. Hawken, A. Lovins, and L. H. Lovins, *Natural Capitalism: Creating the Next Industrial Revolution* (Boston: Little, Brown, and Company, 1999).

5. See, for example, *BusinessWeek,* "Alternate Power: A Change in the Wind," 4 July 2005, 36–37.

6. See T. L. Friedman, "Geo-Greening by Example," *New York Times,* 27 March 2005; and T. L. Friedman, "The New 'Sputnik' Challenges: They All Run on Oil," *New York Times,* 20 January 2006.

7. There is some debate as to how to define a "green consumer." Roper ASW's most recent research segments American consumers by their propensity to purchase environmentally sensitive products into five categories, ranging from "True Blue Greens," who are most inclined to seek out and buy green on a regular basis (representing 9 percent of the population), to "Basic Browns," who are the least involved group and believe environmental indifference is mainstream (representing 33 percent of the population); see Roper ASW "Green Gauge Report 2002:Americans Perspective on Environmental Issues—Yes . . . But," November 2002, http://www.windustry.com/conferences/november2002/nov2002_proceedings/plenary/greenguage2002.pdf(accessed 7 February 2006). Alternatively, however, some marketers view green consumers as falling into three broad segments concerned with preserving the planet, health consequences of environmental problems, and animal welfare; see Ottman, note 3 above, pages 19–44. Because environmental concerns are varied, ranging from resource/energy conservation to wildlife protection to air quality, marketing research suggests that responses to green advertising appeals vary by consumer segments. For example, in one study, young college-educated students were found to be drawn to health-oriented green appeals, whereas working adults were more responsive toward health, waste, and energy

appeals; see M. R. Stafford, T. F. Stafford, and J. Chowdhury, "Predispositions Toward Green Issues: The Potential Efficacy of Advertising Appeals," *Journal of Current Issues and Research in Advertising* 18, no. 2 (1996): 67–79. One of the lessons from the study presented here is that green products must be positioned on the consumer value sought by targeted consumers.

8. A. Grubler, "Doing More with Less: Improving the Environment through Green Engineering," *Environment 48,* no. 2 (March 2006): 22–37.

9. See, for example, L.A. Crosby and S. L. Johnson, "Customer-Centric Innovation," *Marketing Management* 15, no. 2 (2006): 12–13.

10. The methodology for this article involved reviewing case descriptions of green products discussed in the academic and business literature to identify factors contributing to consumer acceptance or resistance. Product failure was defined as situations in which the green product experienced very limited sales and ultimately was either removed from the marketplace (such as General Motor's EV1 electric car and Electrolux's "pay-per-wash" service) or re-positioned in the marketplace (such as Philips' "EarthLight"). Product success was defined as situations in which the green product attained consumer acceptance and was widely available at the time of the analysis. Particular attention centered on the market strategies and external market forces of green products experiencing significant growth (such as gas-electric hybrid cars and organic foods), and the study examined their market context, pricing, targeted consumers, product design, and marketing appeals and messages.

11. See T. Levitt, "Marketing Myopia," *Harvard Business Review* 28, July–August (1960): 24–47.

12. A. D. Lee and R. Conger, "Market Transformation: Does it Work? The Super Energy Efficient Refrigerator Program," *ACEEE Proceedings,* 1996, 3.69–3.80.

13. Ibid.

14. The California Air Resources Board (CARB) adopted the Low-Emission Vehicle (LEV) regulations in 1990. The original LEV regulations required the introduction of zero-emission vehicles (ZEVs) in 1998 as 2 percent of all vehicles produced for sale in California, and increased the percentage of ZEVs from 2 percent to 10 percent in 2003. By 1998, significant flexibility was introduced through partial ZEV credits for very-low-emission vehicles. For a review, see S. Shaheen, "California's Zero-Emission Vehicle Mandate," *Institute of Transportation Studies,* Paper UCD-ITS-RP-04-14, 2 September 2004.

15. C. Palmeri, "Unplugged," *BusinessWeek,* 20 March 2006, 12.

16. "Think Tanks," *Automotive News,* 6 March 2006, 42; J. Ottman, "Lessons from the Green Graveyard," *Green@Work,* April 2003, 62–63.

17. J. Lawrence, "The Green Revolution: Case Study," *Advertising Age,* 29 January 1991, 12.

18. See Roper ASW, note 7 above.

19. "Fuel Economy: Why You're Not Getting the MPG You Expect," *Consumer Reports,* October 2005, 20–23.

20. J. O'Dell, "Prices Soar for Hybrids with Rights to Fast Lane," *Los Angeles Times,* 27 August 2005.

21. M. Landler and K. Bradsher, "VW to Build Hybrid Minivan with Chinese," *New York Times,* 9 September 2005.

22. K. Carter, "'Hybrid' Cars Were Oscars' Politically Correct Ride," *USA Today,* 31 March 2003.

23. See, for example, H. W. Jenkins, "Dear Valued Hybrid Customer . . . ," *Wall Street Journal,* 30 November 2005; E. R. Stafford, "Conspicuous Conservation," *Green@Work,* Winter 2004, 30–32. A recent Civil Society Institute poll found that 66 percent of survey participants agreed that driving fuel efficient vehicles was "patriotic"; see Reuters, "Americans See Fuel Efficient Cars as 'Patriotic,'" 18 March 2005, http://www.planetark.com/avantgo/dailynewsstory.cfm?newsid=29988.

24. "Rising Consumer Interest in Hybrid Technology Confirmed by Maritz Research," PRNewswire, 5 January 2006.

25. O'Dell, note 20 above.

26. J. Fetto, "The Baby Business," *American Demographics,* May 2003, 40.

27. See D. McGinn, "The Green Machine," *Newsweek,* 21 March 2005, E8–E12; and J. Weber, "A Super-Natural Investing Opportunity," *Business 2.0,* March 2005, 34.

28. A. Murray, "Can Wal-Mart Sustain a Softer Edge?" *Wall Street Journal,* 8 February 2006.

29. C. Tan, "New Incentives for Being Green," *Wall Street Journal,* 4 August 2005.

30. For an overview of the Leadership in Energy and Environmental Design Green Building Rating System, see http://www.usgbc.org. The 69-point LEED rating system addresses energy and water use, indoor air quality, materials, siting, and innovation and design. Buildings can earn basic certification or a silver, gold, or platinum designation depending on the number of credits awarded by external reviewers. Critics charge, however, that the costly and confusing administration of the LEED system is inhibiting adoption of the program and impeding the program's environmental objectives; see A. Schendler and R. Udall, "LEED is Broken; Let's Fix It," *Grist Magazine,* 16 October 2005, http://www.grist.com/comments/soapbox/2005/10/26/leed/index1.html.

31. GreenBiz.com, "Survey: Home Builders Name Energy Efficiency as Biggest Industry Trend," 26 January 2006, http://www.greenerbuildings.com/news_details.cfm?NewsID=30221.

32. D. Smith, "Conservation: Building Grows Greener in Bay Area," *San Francisco Chronicle,* 1 June 2005.

33. E. Beck, "Earth-Friendly Materials Go Mainstream," *New York Times,* 5 January 2006, 8.

34. J. M. Ginsberg and P. N. Bloom, "Choosing the Right Green Marketing Strategy," *MIT Sloan Management Journal,* Fall 2004: 79–84.

35. Tan, note 29 above.

36. Tan, note 29, above.

37. C. C. Berk, "P&G Will Promote 'Green' Detergent," *Wall Street Journal,* 19 January 2005.

38. K. McLaughlin, "Has Your Chicken Been Drugged?" *Wall Street Journal,* 2 August 2005; and E. Weise, "Are Our Products Our Enemy?" *USA Today,* 13 August 2005.

39. McLaughlin, ibid.

40. Alston and Roberts, note 2 above.

41. R. Leiber, "The Dirt on Green Housecleaners," *Wall Street Journal,* 29 December 2005.

42. M. Alexander, "Home Improved," *Readers Digest,* April 2004, 77–80.

43. For example, see D. Leonhardt, "Buy a Hybrid, and Save a Guzzler," *New York Times,* 8 February 2006.

44. See, for example, D. Cave, "It's Not Sexy Being Green (Yet)," *New York Times,* 2 October 2005.

45. G. Chon, "Toyota Goes After Copycat Hybrids; Buyers are Asked to Believe Branded HSD Technology is Worth the Extra Cost," *Wall Street Journal,* 22 September 2005.

46. B. G. Hoffman, "Ford: Now It's Easy Being Green," *Detroit News,* 31 January 2006.

47. See W. McDonough and M. Braungart, *Cradle to Cradle: Remaking the Way We Make Things* (New York: North Point Press, 2002).

48. R. Smith, "Beyond Recycling: Manufacturers Embrace 'C2C' Design," *Wall Street Journal*, 3 March 2005.

49. K. Hafen, "Preston Festival Goes LED," *Logan Herald Journal,* 21 September 2005.

50. O'Dell, note 20 above.

51. A. Covarrubias, "In Carpool Lanes, Hybrids Find Cold Shoulders," *Los Angeles Times,* 10 April 2006.

52. M. Clayton, "Hot Stuff for a Cool Earth," *Christian Science Monitor,* 21 April 2005.

53. See Ogilvy & Mather Topline Report, *China Energy-Efficient CFC-Free Refrigerator Study* (Beijing: Ogilvy & Mather, August 1997); E. R. Stafford, C. L. Hartman, and Y. Liang, "Forces Driving Environmental Innovation Diffusion in China: The Case of Green-freeze," *Business Horizons* 9, no. 2 (2003): 122–35.

54. J. Baker, Jr., K. Denby, and J. E. Jerrett, "Market-based Government Activities in Texas," *Texas Business Review,* August 2005, 1–5.

55. T. Harris, "Austinites Apply to Save With Wind Power," *KVUE News,* 13 February 2006.

56. J. Ottman, note 3 above.

57. J. Ottman, note 3 above.

58. Generation Green, "Splenda Letter to Federal Trade Commission," 13 January 2005, http://www.generationgreen .org/2005_01-FTC-letter.htm (accessed 7 February 2006).

59. J. Davis, "Strategies for Environmental Advertising," *Journal of Consumer Marketing* 10, no. 2 (1993): 23–25.

60. S. Farah, "The Thin Green Line," CMO Magazine, 1 December 2005, http://www.cmomagazine.com/read/120105/green_line. html (accessed 9 February 2006).

61. Ibid.

62. See Jenkins, note 23 above.

63. See Farah, note 60 above.

64. M. Maynard, "E.P.A. Revision is Likely to Cut Mileage Ratings," *New York Times,* 11 January 2006.

65. For a more comprehensive overview of eco-certifications and labeling, see L. H. Gulbrandsen, "Mark of Sustainability? Challenges for Fishery and Forestry Eco-labeling," *Environment* 47, no. 5 (2005): 8–23.

66. For a comprehensive overview of other eco-certifications, see Consumers Union's Web site at http://www.eco-labels. org/home.cfm.

67. Gulbrandsen, note 65 above, pages 17–19.

68. Farah, note 60 above.

69. Farah, note 60 above.

70. See GE Global Research, *Clean Coal,* http://ge.com/research/ grc_2_1_3.html (accessed 16 April 2006).

71. A. Griscom Little, "It Was Just My Ecomagination," *Grist Magazine,* 10 May 2005, http://grist.org/news/ muck/2005/05/10/little-ge/index.html.

72. E. Rosen, *The Anatomy of Buzz: How to Create Word-of-Mouth Marketing* (New York: Doubleday, 2000).

73. Viral marketing is a form of "word-of-mouse" buzz marketing defined as "the process of encouraging honest communication among consumer networks, and it focuses on email as the channel." See J. E. Phelps, R. Lewis, L. Mobilio, D. Perry, and N. Raman, "Viral Marketing or Electronic Word-of-Mouth Advertising: Examining Consumer Responses and Motivation to Pass Along Email," *Journal of Advertising Research* 44, no. 4 (2004): 333–48.

74. G. Ramsey, "Ten Reasons Why Word-of-Mouth Marketing Works," Online Media Daily, 23 September 2005, http:// publications.mediapost.com/index.cfm?fuseaction=Articles .san&s=34339&Nid=15643&p=114739 (accessed 16 February 2006).

75. See Rosen, note 72 above.

76. Ramsey, note 74 above.

77. Tide press release, "ColdWater Challenge Reaches One Million," http://www.tide.com/tidecoldwater/challenge.html (accessed 13 September 2005).

78. L. Prescott, "Case Study: Tide Boosts Traffic 9-fold," iMedia Connection, 30 November 2005, http://www.imdiaconnection .com/content/7406.asp.

79. Hawken, Lovins, and Lovins, note 4 above; see also A. B. Lovins, L. H. Lovins, and P. Hawken, "A Road Map for Natural Capitalism," *Harvard Business Review,* May–June 1999, 145–58.

80. J. Makower, "Green Marketing: Lessons from the Leaders," Two Steps Forward, September 2005, http://makower.typepad. com/joel_makower/2005/09/green_marketing.html.

JACQUELYN A. OTTMAN is president of J. Ottman Consulting, Inc. in New York and author of *Green Marketing: Opportunity for Innovation,* 2nd edition (NTC Business Books, 1997). She can be reached at jaottman@greenmarketing.com. **EDWIN R. STAFFORD** is an associate professor of marketing at Utah State University, Logan. He researches the strategic marketing and policy implications of clean technology (also known as "cleantech") and is the co-principal investigator for a $1 million research grant from the U.S. Department of Energy on the diffusion of wind power in Utah. He may be reached at ed.stafford@ usu.edu. **CATHY L. HARTMAN** is a professor of marketing at Utah State University, Logan. Her research centers on how interpersonal influence and social systems affect the diffusion of ideas and clean products and technology. She is principal investigator on a $1 million U.S. Department of Energy grant for developing wind power in the state of Utah. She can be contacted at cathy.hartman@usu.edu.

From *Environment,* June 2006, pp. 23–36. Reprinted by permission of the Helen Dwight Reid Educational Foundation. Published by Heldref Publications, 1319 Eighteenth St., NW, Washington, DC 20036-1802. Copyright © 2006. www.heldref.org

Doing Whatever Gets Them in the Door

Merchants are going back to basics—cutting prices, broadening product lines, and even teaming up.

JANE PORTER AND BURT HELM

Whenever the economy slackens, America's shop-keepers slash prices and pray for consumers to pull out the plastic. Once again, retailers are doing their part, although perhaps with more zeal than usual. Discounts are deeper than they were a year ago. Nordstrom has slashed prices, starting at 40%, vs. 33% last year. Sales have begun earlier. Saks Fifth Avenue opened its first big sale in April, rather than May. And loyalty programs are getting sweeter. Neiman Marcus just handed out $200 gift cards to those who spent $500 or more.

Of course, this is no ordinary downturn. Yes, tax rebates from the federal government pushed retail sales higher in May than many economists had expected. But consumers will be paying lofty prices at the gas pump and supermarket long after the stimulus checks stop arriving. That leaves less for discretionary buying. "Moms who used to buy every member of the family their own brand of shampoo are buying one big cheap one," says Sheila McKusker, who notes that, in 20 years of tracking the retail industry for market researcher Information Resources, she's never seen such a profound or sudden shift in shopping behavior. In May, consumer confidence hit its lowest level since 1992.

New York shoppers in a Sephora boutique at Penney's (top); FAO Schwarz in a Macy's in Chicago.

Cutting prices may not be enough to get people into stores. So while Lowe's is offering low-cost versions of Shop-Vacs and air purifiers, the home-improvement chain has also launched an advertising campaign to reposition itself as something that looks a lot like the local hardware store (the very mom-and-pop shop that Lowe's and Home Depot helped drive out of business). In one TV commercial, a father and his sons marvel as a Lowe's employee cuts duplicate house keys.

In many cases, retailers are going after a different customer altogether. Earlier this year, Gap's troubled Old Navy chain began pitching trendier clothing at twentysomethings. Sales continued to tank, and the retailer is refocusing its message on price. Now the ideal customer is the budget-conscious mom shopping for herself and the family. Unlike this spring's safari- and surfer-themed clothes, the fall line will include more basics, and TV ads now emphasize price over style.

Saks Fifth Avenue, too, is focusing more on value. This fall, the upscale department store will reintroduce a private-label line for women in their 40s and 50s. Called Real Clothes, the skirts, blouses, and dresses will be priced 20% below the store's average brand-name items. "For a high-end customer, it's not about a trade-off between food [and] gasoline," says Saks CEO Stephen I. Sadove, "[but] how they feel about their net worth." He also notes that, during tough economic times, consumers expect better service, too. That's why Saks is putting more of its sales staff on commission—the better to compete for shoppers' affections.

As they seek to hang on to existing customers and attract new ones, retailers are teaming up. In May, Macy's announced it would partner with FAO Schwarz to bring toys back to its stores. Over the next two years, Macy's will put an FAO Schwarz inside 685 of its locations. "If gas prices continue to rise, being in Macy's is a really smart move," says FAO Schwarz CEO Edward M. Schmults. "Customers aren't going to want to drive to five different places looking for products." The partnership also allows Macy's to lease excess space and gives the toy retailer access to millions of new shoppers.

Pricey Bargains

On May 23, *Women's Wear Daily* reported that such designer boutiques as Escada, Calvin Klein, and St. John are feeling pressure from the weak economy, deep department-store discounts, and record-high gas prices, and are marking down items more rigorously this season.

J.C. Penney is using an existing partnership with Sephora USA, the cosmetics and fragrance merchant, to go after freer-spending consumers. Sephora has opened boutiques inside 72 (of 300 planned) Penney stores, catering to 18- to 35-year-old women who typically spend more per item than Penney's traditional base of middle-aged moms. Penney CEO Myron E. Ullman III says he's discounting to keep his regulars buying while Sephora lures those willing to pay full price for new products.

Even as stores scramble to broaden their appeal, they are minding their core customers. Rite Aid is offering a $30 gift card and a chance to win a year's worth of free gasoline to customers who transfer their prescriptions to the chain (page 18). Target is pushing its cheaper private-label food and beverages. And Saks in April rolled out no-interest loans on top-drawer jewelry. As Saks CEO Sadove says: "The high-end consumer likes a deal like everybody else."

Marketing Myopia
(with Retrospective Commentary)

Shortsighted managements often fail to recognize that in fact there is no such thing as a growth industry.

THEODORE LEVITT

How can a company ensure its continued growth? In 1960 "Marketing Myopia" answered that question in a new and challenging way by urging organizations to define their industries broadly to take advantage of growth opportunities. Using the archetype of the railroads, Mr. Levitt showed how they declined inevitably as technology advanced because they defined themselves too narrowly. To continue growing, companies must ascertain and act on their customers' needs and desires, not bank on the presumptive longevity of their products. The success of the article testifies to the validity of its message. It has been widely quoted and anthologized, and HBR has sold more than 265,000 reprints of it. The author of 14 subsequent articles in HBR, Mr. Levitt is one of the magazine's most prolific contributors. In a retrospective commentary, he considers the use and misuse that have been made of "Marketing Myopia," describing its many interpretations and hypothesizing about its success.

Every major industry was once a growth industry. But some that are now riding a wave of growth enthusiasm are very much in the shadow of decline. Others which are thought of as seasoned growth industries have actually stopped growing. In every case the reason growth is threatened, slowed, or stopped is *not* because the market is saturated. It is because there has been a failure of management.

Fateful purposes: The failure is at the top. The executives responsible for it, in the last analysis, are those who deal with broad aims and policies. Thus:

- The railroads did not stop growing because the need for passenger and freight transportation declined. That grew. The railroads are in trouble today not because the need was filled by others (cars, trucks, airplanes, even telephones), but because it was *not* filled by the railroads themselves. They let others take customers away from them because they assumed themselves to be in the railroad business rather than in the transportation business. The reason they defined their industry wrong was because they were railroad-oriented instead of transportation-oriented; they were product-oriented instead of customer-oriented.

- Hollywood barely escaped being totally ravished by television. Actually, all the established film companies went through drastic reorganizations. Some simply disappeared. All of them got into trouble not because of TV's inroads but because of their own myopia. As with the railroads, Hollywood defined its business incorrectly. It thought it was in the movie business when it was actually in the entertainment business. "Movies" implied a specific, limited product. This produced a fatuous contentment which from the beginning led producers to view TV as a threat. Hollywood scorned and rejected TV when it should have welcomed it as an opportunity—an opportunity to expand the entertainment business.

Today TV is a bigger business than the old narrowly defined movie business ever was. Had Hollywood been customer-oriented (providing entertainment), rather then product-oriented (making movies), would it have gone through the fiscal purgatory that it did? I doubt it. What ultimately saved Hollywood and accounted for its recent resurgence was the wave of new young writers, producers, and directors whose previous successes in television had decimated the old movie companies and toppled the big movie moguls.

There are other less obvious examples of industries that have been and are now endangering their futures by improperly defining their purposes. I shall discuss some in detail later and analyze the kind of policies that lead to trouble. Right now it may help to show what a thoroughly customer-oriented management can do to keep a growth industry growing, even after the obvious opportunities have been exhausted; and here there are two examples that have been around for a long time. They are nylon and glass—specifically, E. I. duPont de Nemours & Company and Corning Glass Works.

Both companies have great technical competence. Their product orientation is unquestioned. But this alone does not explain their success. After all, who was more pridefully product-oriented and product-conscious than the erstwhile New England textile companies that have been so thoroughly massacred? The DuPonts and the Cornings have succeeded not primarily because of their product or research orientation but because they have been thoroughly customer-oriented also. It is constant watchfulness for opportunities to apply their technical knowhow to the creation of customer-satisfying uses which accounts for their prodigious output of successful new products. Without a very sophisticated eye on the customer, most of their new products might have been wrong, their sales methods useless.

Aluminum has also continued to be a growth industry, thanks to the efforts of two wartime-created companies which deliberately set about creating new customer-satisfying uses. Without Kaiser Aluminum & Chemical Corporation and Reynolds Metals Company, the total demand for aluminum today would be vastly less.

Error of analysis: Some may argue that it is foolish to set the railroads off against aluminum or the movies off against glass. Are not aluminum and glass naturally so versatile that the industries are bound to have more growth opportunities than the railroads and movies? This view commits precisely the error I have been talking about. It defines an industry, or a product, or a cluster of know-how so narrowly as to guarantee its premature senescence. When we mention "railroads," we should make sure we mean "transportation." As transporters, the railroads still have a good chance for very considerable growth. They are not limited to the railroad business as such (though in my opinion rail transportation is potentially a much stronger transportation medium than is generally believed).

What the railroads lack is not opportunity, but some of the same managerial imaginativeness and audacity that made them great. Even an amateur like Jacques Barzun can see what is lacking when he says:

"I grieve to see the most advanced physical and social organization of the last century go down in shabby disgrace for lack of the same comprehensive imagination that built it up. [What is lacking is] the will of the companies to survive and to satisfy the public by inventiveness and skill."[1]

Shadow of Obsolescence

It is impossible to mention a single major industry that did not at one time qualify for the magic appellation of "growth industry." In each case its assumed strength lay in the apparently unchallenged superiority of its product. There appeared to be no effective substitute for it. It was itself a runaway substitute for the product it so triumphantly replaced. Yet one after another of these celebrated industries has come under a shadow. Let us look briefly at a few more of them, this time taking examples that have so far received a little less attention:

- *Dry cleaning*—This was once a growth industry with lavish prospects. In an age of wool garments, imagine being finally able to get them safely and easily clean. The boom was on.

  Yet here we are 30 years after the boom started and the industry is in trouble. Where has the competition come from? From a better way of cleaning? No. It has come from synthetic fibers and chemical additives that have cut the need for dry cleaning. But this is only the beginning. Lurking in the wings and ready to make chemical dry cleaning totally obsolete is that powerful magician, ultrasonics.

- *Electric utilities*—This is another one of those supposedly "no-substitute" products that has been enthroned on a pedestal of invincible growth. When the incandescent lamp came along, kerosene lights were finished. Later the water wheel and the steam engine were cut to ribbons by the flexibility, reliability, simplicity, and just plain easy availability of electric motors. The prosperity of electric utilities continues to wax extravagant as the home is converted into a museum of electric gadgetry. How can anybody miss by investing in utilities, with no competition, nothing but growth ahead?

  But a second look is not quite so comforting. A score of nonutility companies are well advanced toward developing a powerful chemical fuel cell which could sit in some hidden closet of every home silently ticking off electric power. The electric lines that vulgarize so many neighborhoods will be eliminated. So will the endless demolition of streets and service interruptions during storms. Also on the horizon is solar energy, again pioneered by nonutility companies.

  Who says that the utilities have no competition? They may be natural monopolies now, but tomorrow they may be natural deaths. To avoid this prospect, they too will have to develop fuel cells, solar energy, and other power sources. To survive, they themselves will have to plot the obsolescence of what now produces their livelihood.

- *Grocery stores*—Many people find it hard to realize that there ever was a thriving establishment known as the "corner grocery store." The supermarket has taken over with a powerful effectiveness. Yet the big food chains of the 1930s narrowly escaped being completely wiped out by the aggressive expansion of independent supermarkets. The first genuine supermarket was opened in 1930, in Jamaica, Long Island. By 1933 supermarkets were thriving in California, Ohio, Pennsylvania, and elsewhere. Yet the established chains pompously ignored them. When they chose to notice them, it was with such derisive descriptions as "cheapy," "horse-and-buggy," "cracker-barrel storekeeping," and "unethical opportunists."

The executive of one big chain announced at the time that he found it "hard to believe that people will drive for miles to shop for foods and sacrifice the personal service chains have perfected and to which Mrs. Consumer is accustomed."[2] As late as 1936, the National Wholesale Grocers convention and the New Jersey Retail Grocers Association said there was nothing to fear. They said that the supers' narrow appeal to the price buyer limited the size of their market. They had to draw from miles around. When imitators came, there would be wholesale liquidations as volume fell. The current high sales of the supers was said to be partly due to their novelty. Basically people wanted convenient neighborhood grocers. If the neighborhood stores "cooperate with their suppliers, pay attention to their costs, and improve their service," they would be able to weather the competition until it blew over.[3]

It never blew over. The chains discovered that survival required going into the supermarket business. This meant the wholesale destruction of their huge investments in corner store sites and in established distribution and merchandising methods. The companies with "the courage of their convictions" resolutely stuck to the corner store philosophy. They kept their pride but lost their shirts.

Self-deceiving cycle: But memories are short. For example, it is hard for people who today confidently hail the twin messiahs of electronics and chemicals to see how things could possibly go wrong with these galloping industries. They probably also cannot see how a reasonably sensible businessman could have been as myopic as the famous Boston millionaire who 50 years ago unintentionally sentenced his heirs to poverty by stipulating that his entire estate be forever invested exclusively in electric streetcar securities. His posthumous declaration, "There will always be a big demand for efficient urban transportation," is no consolation to his heirs who sustain life by pumping gasoline at automobile filling stations.

Yet, in a casual survey I recently took among a group of intelligent business executives, nearly half agreed that it would be hard to hurt their heirs by tying their estates forever to the electronics industry. When I then confronted them with the Boston streetcar example, they chorused unanimously, "That's different!" But is it? Is not the basic situation identical?

In truth, *there is no such thing* as a growth industry, I believe. There are only companies organized and operated to create and capitalize on growth opportunities. Industries that assume themselves to be riding some automatic growth escalator invariably descend into stagnation. The history of every dead and dying "growth" industry shows a self-deceiving cycle of bountiful expansion and undetected decay. There are four conditions which usually guarantee this cycle:

1. The belief that growth is assured by an expanding and more affluent population.
2. The belief that there is no competitive substitute for the industry's major product.
3. Too much faith in mass production and in the advantages of rapidly declining unit costs as output rises.
4. Preoccupation with a product that lends itself to carefully controlled scientific experimentation, improvement, and manufacturing cost reduction.

I should like now to begin examining each of these conditions in some detail. To build my case as boldly as possible, I shall illustrate the points with reference to three industries—petroleum, automobiles, and electronics—particularly petroleum, because it spans more years and more vicissitudes. Not only do these three have excellent reputations with the general public and also enjoy the confidence of sophisticated investors, but their managements have become known for progressive thinking in areas like financial control, product research, and management training. If obsolescence can cripple even these industries, it can happen anywhere.

Population Myth

The belief that profits are assured by an expanding and more affluent population is dear to the heart of every industry. It takes the edge off the apprehensions everybody understandably feels about the future. If consumers are multiplying and also buying more of your product or service, you can face the future with considerably more comfort than if the market is shrinking. An expanding market keeps the manufacturer from having to think very hard or imaginatively. If thinking is an intellectual response to a problem, then the absence of a problem leads to the absence of thinking. If your product has an automatically expanding market, then you will not give much thought to how to expand it.

One of the most interesting examples of this is provided by the petroleum industry. Probably our oldest growth industry, it has an enviable record. While there are some current apprehensions about its growth rate, the industry itself tends to be optimistic.

But I believe it can be demonstrated that it is undergoing a fundamental yet typical change. It is not only ceasing to be a growth industry, but may actually be a declining one, relative to other business. Although there is widespread unawareness of it, I believe that within 25 years the oil industry may find itself in much the same position of retrospective glory that the railroads are now in. Despite its pioneering work in developing and applying the present-value method of investment evaluation, in employee relations, and in working with backward countries, the petroleum business is a distressing example of how complacency and wrongheadedness can stubbornly convert opportunity into near disaster.

One of the characteristics of this and other industries that have believed very strongly in the beneficial consequences of an expanding population, while at the same time being industries with a generic product for which there has appeared to be no competitive substitute, is that the individual companies have sought to outdo their competitors by improving on what they are already doing. This makes sense, of course, if one assumes that sales are tied to the country's population strings, because the customer can compare products only on a feature-by-feature basis. I believe it is significant, for example, that not since John D. Rockefeller sent free kerosene lamps to China has the oil industry done anything really outstanding to create a demand for its product. Not even in product improvement has it showered itself with eminence. The greatest single improvement—namely, the development of tetraethyl lead—came from outside the industry, specifically from General Motors and DuPont. The big contributions made by the industry itself are confined to the technology of oil exploration, production, and refining.

Asking for trouble: In other words, the industry's efforts have focused on improving the *efficiency* of getting and making its product, not really on improving the generic product or its marketing. Moreover, its chief product has continuously been defined in the narrowest possible terms, namely, gasoline, not energy, fuel, or transportation. This attitude has helped assure that:

- Major improvements in gasoline quality tend not to originate in the oil industry. Also, the development of superior alternative fuels comes from outside the oil industry, as will be shown later.

- Major innovations in automobile fuel marketing are originated by small new oil companies that are not primarily preoccupied with production or refining. These are the companies that have been responsible for the rapidly expanding multipump gasoline stations, with their successful emphasis on large and clean layouts, rapid and efficient driveway service, and quality gasoline at low prices.

Thus, the oil industry is asking for trouble from outsiders. Sooner or later, in this land of hungry inventors and entrepreneurs, a threat is sure to come. The possibilities of this will become more apparent when we turn to the next dangerous belief of many managements. For the sake of continuity, because this second belief is tied closely to the first, I shall continue with the same example.

Idea of indispensability: The petroleum industry is pretty much persuaded that there is no competitive substitute for its major product, gasoline—or if there is, that it will continue to be a derivative of crude oil, such as diesel fuel or kerosene jet fuel.

There is a lot of automatic wishful thinking in this assumption. The trouble is that most refining companies own huge amounts of crude oil reserves. These have value only if there is a market for products into which oil can be converted—hence the tenacious belief in the continuing competitive superiority of automobile fuels made from crude oil.

This idea persists despite all historic evidence against it. The evidence not only shows that oil has never been a superior product for any purpose for very long, but it also shows that the oil industry has never really been a growth industry. It has been a succession of different businesses that have gone through the usual historic cycles of growth, maturity, and decay. Its overall survival is owed to a series of miraculous escapes from total obsolescence, of last-minute and unexpected reprieves from total disaster reminiscent of the Perils of Pauline.

Perils of petroleum: I shall sketch in only the main episodes.

First, crude oil was largely a patent medicine. But even before that fad ran out, demand was greatly expanded by the use of oil in kerosene lamps. The prospect of lighting the world's lamps gave rise to an extravagant promise of growth. The prospects were similar to those the industry now holds for gasoline in other parts of the world. It can hardly wait for the underdeveloped nations to get a car in every garage.

In the days of the kerosene lamp, the oil companies competed with each other and against gaslight by trying to improve the illuminating characteristics of kerosene. Then suddenly the impossible happened. Edison invented a light which was totally nondependent on crude oil. Had it not been for the growing use of kerosene in space heaters, the incandescent lamp would have completely finished oil as a growth industry at that time. Oil would have been good for little else than axle grease.

Then disaster and reprieve struck again. Two great innovations occurred, neither originating in the oil industry. The successful development of coal-burning domestic central-heating systems made the space heater obsolescent. While the industry reeled, along came its most magnificent boost yet—the internal combustion engine, also invented by outsiders. Then when the prodigious expansion for gasoline finally began to level off in the 1920s, along came the miraculous escape of a central oil heater. Once again, the escape was provided by an outsider's invention and development. And when that market weakened, wartime demand for aviation fuel came to the rescue. After the war the expansion of civilian aviation, the dieselization of railroads, and the explosive demand for cars and trucks kept the industry's growth in high gear.

Meanwhile, centralized oil heating—whose boom potential had only recently been proclaimed—ran into severe competition from natural gas. While the oil companies themselves owned the gas that now competed with their oil, the industry did not originate the natural gas revolution, nor has it to this day greatly profited from its gas ownership. The gas revolution was made by newly formed transmission companies that marketed the product with an aggressive ardor. They started a magnificent new industry, first against the advice and then against the resistance of the oil companies.

By all the logic of the situation, the oil companies themselves should have made the gas revolution. They not only owned the gas; they also were the only people experienced in handling, scrubbing, and using it, the only people experienced in pipeline technology and transmission, and they understood heating problems. But, partly because they knew that natural gas would compete with their own sale of heating oil, the oil companies pooh-poohed the potentials of gas.

The revolution was finally started by oil pipeline executives who, unable to persuade their own companies to go into gas, quit and organized the spectacularly successful gas transmission companies. Even after their success became painfully evident to the oil companies, the latter did not go into gas transmission. The multibillion dollar business which should have been theirs went to others. As in the past, the industry was blinded by its narrow preoccupation with a specific product and the value of its reserves. It paid little or no attention to its customers' basic needs and preferences.

The postwar years have not witnessed any change. Immediately after World War II the oil industry was greatly encouraged about its future by the rapid expansion of demand for its traditional line of products. In 1950 most companies projected annual rates of domestic expansion of around 6% through at least 1975. Though the ratio of crude oil reserves to demand in the Free World was about 20 to 1, with 10 to 1 being usually considered a reasonable working ratio in the United States, booming demand sent oil men searching for more without sufficient regard to what the future really promised. In 1952 they "hit" in the Middle East; the ratio skyrocketed to 42 to 1. If gross additions to reserves continue at the average rate of the past five years (37 billion barrels annually), then by 1970 the reserve ratio will be up to 45 to 1. This abundance of oil has weakened crude and product prices all over the world.

Uncertain future: Management cannot find much consolation today in the rapidly expanding petrochemical industry, another oil-using idea that did not originate in the leading firms. The total United States production of petrochemicals is equivalent to about 2% (by volume) of the demand for all petroleum products. Although the petrochemical industry is now expected to grow by about 10% per year, this will not offset other drains

28

on the growth of crude oil consumption. Furthermore, while petrochemical products are many and growing, it is well to remember that there are nonpetroleum sources of the basic raw material, such as coal. Besides, a lot of plastics can be produced with relatively little oil. A 5,000-barrel-per-day oil refinery is now considered the absolute minimum size for efficiency. But a 5,000-barrel-per-day chemical plant is a giant operation.

Oil has never been a continuously strong growth industry. It has grown by fits and starts, always miraculously saved by innovations and developments not of its own making. The reason it has not grown in a smooth progression is that each time it thought it had a superior product safe from the possibility of competitive substitutes, the product turned out to be inferior and notoriously subject to obsolescence. Until now, gasoline (for motor fuel, anyhow) has escaped this fate. But, as we shall see later, it too may be on its last legs.

The point of all this is that there is no guarantee against product obsolescence. If a company's own research does not make it obsolete, another's will. Unless an industry is especially lucky, as oil has been until now, it can easily go down in a sea of red figures—just as the railroads have, as the buggy whip manufacturers have, as the corner grocery chains have, as most of the big movie companies have, and indeed as many other industries have.

The best way for a firm to be lucky is to make its own luck. That requires knowing what makes a business successful. One of the greatest enemies of this knowledge is mass production.

Production Pressures

Mass-production industries are impelled by a great drive to produce all they can. The prospect of steeply declining unit costs as output rises is more than most companies can usually resist. The profit possibilities look spectacular. All effort focuses on production. The result is that marketing gets neglected.

John Kenneth Galbraith contends that just the opposite occurs.[4] Output is so prodigious that all effort concentrates on trying to get rid of it. He says this accounts for singing commercials, desecration of the countryside with advertising signs, and other wasteful and vulgar practices. Galbraith has a finger on something real, but he misses the strategic point. Mass production does indeed generate great pressure to "move" the product. But what usually gets emphasized is selling, not marketing. Marketing, being a more sophisticated and complex process, gets ignored.

The difference between marketing and selling is more than semantic. Selling focuses on the needs of the seller, marketing on the needs of the buyer. Selling is preoccupied with the seller's need to convert his product into cash, marketing with the idea of satisfying the needs of the customer by means of the product and the whole cluster of things associated with creating, delivering, and finally consuming it.

In some industries the enticements of full mass production have been so powerful that for many years top management in effect has told the sales departments, "You get rid of it; we'll worry about profits." By contrast, a truly marketing-minded firm tries to create value-satisfying goods and services that consumers will want to buy. What it offers for sale includes not only the generic product or service, but also how it is made available to the customer, in what form, when, under what conditions, and at what terms of trade. Most important, what it offers for sale is determined not by the seller but by the buyer. The seller takes his cues from the buyer in such a way that the product becomes a consequence of the marketing effort, not vice versa.

Lag in Detroit: This may sound like an elementary rule of business, but that does not keep it from being violated wholesale. It is certainly more violated than honored. Take the automobile industry.

Here mass production is most famous, most honored, and has the greatest impact on the entire society. The industry has hitched its fortune to the relentless requirements of the annual model change, a policy that makes customer orientation an especially urgent necessity. Consequently the auto companies annually spend millions of dollars on consumer research. But the fact that the new compact cars are selling so well in their first year indicates that Detroit's vast researches have for a long time failed to reveal what the customer really wanted. Detroit was not persuaded that he wanted anything different from what he had been getting until it lost millions of customers to other small car manufacturers.

How could this unbelievable lag behind consumer wants have been perpetuated so long? Why did not research reveal consumer preferences before consumers' buying decisions themselves revealed the facts? Is that not what consumer research is for—to find out before the fact what is going to happen? The answer is that Detroit never really researched the customer's wants. It only researched his preferences between the kinds of things which it had already decided to offer him. For Detroit is mainly product-oriented, not customer-oriented. To the extent that the customer is recognized as having needs that the manufacturer should try to satisfy, Detroit usually acts as if the job can be done entirely by product changes. Occasionally attention gets paid to financing, too, but that is done more in order to sell than to enable the customer to buy.

As for taking care of other customer needs, there is not enough being done to write about. The areas of the greatest unsatisfied needs are ignored, or at best get stepchild attention. These are at the point of sale and on the matter of automotive repair and maintenance. Detroit views these problem areas as being of secondary importance. That is underscored by the fact that the retailing and servicing ends of this industry are neither owned and operated nor controlled by the manufacturers. Once the car is produced, things are pretty much in the dealer's inadequate hands. Illustrative of Detroit's arm's-length attitude is the fact that, while servicing holds enormous sales-stimulating, profit-building opportunities, only 57 of Chevrolet's 7,000 dealers provide night maintenance service.

Motorists repeatedly express their dissatisfaction with servicing and their apprehensions about buying cars under the present selling setup. The anxieties and problems they encounter during the auto buying and maintenance processes are probably more intense and widespread today than 30 years ago. Yet the automobile companies do not *seem* to listen to or take their cues from the anguished consumer. If they do listen, it must be through the filter of their own preoccupation with production.

The marketing effort is still viewed as a necessary consequence of the product, not vice versa, as it should be. That is the legacy of mass production, with its parochial view that profit resides essentially in low-cost full production.

What Ford put first: The profit lure of mass production obviously has a place in the plans and strategy of business management, but it must always *follow* hard thinking about the customer. This is one of the most important lessons that we can learn from the contradictory behavior of Henry Ford. In a sense, Ford was both the most brilliant and the most senseless marketer in American history. He was senseless because he refused to give the customer anything but a black car. He was brilliant because he fashioned a production system designed to fit market needs. We habitually celebrate him for the wrong reason, his production genius. His real genius was marketing. We think he was able to cut his selling price and therefore sell millions of $500 cars because his invention of the assembly line had reduced the costs. Actually he invented the assembly line because he had concluded that at $500 he could sell millions of cars. Mass production was the *result* not the cause of his low prices.

Ford repeatedly emphasized this point, but a nation of production-oriented business managers refuses to hear the great lesson he taught. Here is his operating philosophy as he expressed it succinctly:

"Our policy is to reduce the price, extend the operations, and improve the article. You will notice that the reduction of price comes first. We have never considered any costs as fixed. Therefore we first reduce the price to the point where we believe more sales will result. Then we go ahead and try to make the prices. We do not bother about the costs. The new price forces the costs down. The more usual way is to take the costs and then determine the price; and although that method may be scientific in the narrow sense, it is not scientific in the broad sense, because what earthly use is it to know the cost if it tells you that you cannot manufacture at a price at which the article can be sold? But more to the point is the fact that, although one may calculate what a cost is, and of course all of our costs are carefully calculated, no one knows what a cost ought to be. One of the ways of discovering . . . is to name a price so low as to force everybody in the place to the highest point of efficiency. The low price makes everybody dig for profits. We make more discoveries concerning manufacturing and selling under this forced method than by any method of leisurely investigation."[5]

Product provincialism: The tantalizing profit possibilities of low unit production costs may be the most seriously self-deceiving attitude that can afflict a company, particularly a "growth" company where an apparently assured expansion of demand already tends to undermine a proper concern for the importance of marketing and the customer.

The usual result of this narrow preoccupation with so-called concrete matters is that instead of growing, the industry declines. It usually means that the product fails to adapt to the constantly changing patterns of consumer needs and tastes, to new and modified marketing institutions and practices, or to product developments in competing or complementary industries. The industry has its eyes so firmly on its own specific product that it does not see how it is being made obsolete.

The classical example of this is the buggy whip industry. No amount of product improvement could stave off its death sentence. But had the industry defined itself as being in the transportation business rather than the buggy whip business, it might have survived. It would have done what survival always entails, that is, changing. Even if it had only defined its business as providing a stimulant or catalyst to an energy source, it might have survived by becoming a manufacturer of, say, fanbelts or air cleaners.

What may some day be a still more classical example is, again, the oil industry. Having let others steal marvelous opportunities from it (e.g., natural gas, as already mentioned, missile fuels, and jet engine lubricants), one would expect it to have taken steps never to let that happen again. But this is not the case. We are now getting extraordinary new developments in fuel systems specifically designed to power automobiles. Not only are these developments concentrated in firms outside the petroleum industry, but petroleum is almost systematically ignoring them, securely content in its wedded bliss to oil. It is the story of the kerosene lamp versus the incandescent lamp all over again. Oil is trying to improve hydrocarbon fuels rather than develop *any* fuels best suited to the needs of their users, whether or not made in different ways and with different raw materials from oil.

Here are some things which nonpetroleum companies are working on:

- Over a dozen such firms now have advanced working models of energy systems which, when perfected, will replace the internal combustion engine and eliminate the demand for gasoline. The superior merit of each of these systems is their elimination of frequent, time-consuming, and irritating refueling stops. Most of these systems are fuel cells designed to create electrical energy directly from chemicals without combustion. Most of them use chemicals that are not derived from oil, generally hydrogen and oxygen.

- Several other companies have advanced models of electric storage batteries designed to power automobiles. One of these is an aircraft producer that is working jointly with several electric utility companies. The latter hope to use off-peak generating capacity to supply overnight plug-in battery regeneration. Another company, also using the battery approach, is a medium-size electronics firm with extensive small-battery experience that it developed in connection with its work on hearing aids. It is collaborating with an automobile manufacturer. Recent improvements arising from the need for high-powered miniature power storage plants in rockets have put us within reach of a relatively small battery capable of withstanding great overloads or surges of power. Germanium diode applications and batteries using sintered-plate and nickel-cadmium techniques promise to make a revolution in our energy sources.

- Solar energy conversion systems are also getting increasing attention. One usually cautious Detroit auto executive recently ventured that solar-powered cars might be common by 1980.

As for the oil companies, they are more or less "watching developments," as one research director put it to me. A few are doing a bit of research on fuel cells, but almost always confined to developing cells powered by hydrocarbon chemicals. None of them are enthusiastically researching fuel cells, batteries, or solar power plants. None of them are spending a fraction as much on research in these profoundly important areas as they are on the usual run-of-the-mill things like reducing combustion chamber deposit in gasoline engines. One major integrated petroleum company recently took a tentative look at the fuel cell and concluded that although "the companies actively working on it indicate a belief in ultimate success . . . the timing and magnitude of its impact are too remote to warrant recognition in our forecasts."

One might, of course, ask: Why should the oil companies do anything different? Would not chemical fuel cells, batteries, or solar energy kill the present product lines? The answer is that they would indeed, and that is precisely the reason for the oil firms having to develop these power units before their competitors, so they will not be companies without an industry.

Management might be more likely to do what is needed for its own preservation if it thought of itself as being in the energy business. But even that would not be enough if it persists in imprisoning itself in the narrow grip of its tight product orientation. It has to think of itself as taking care of customer needs, not finding, refining, or even selling oil. Once it genuinely thinks of its business as taking care of people's transportation needs, nothing can stop it from creating its own extravagantly profitable growth.

'Creative destruction': Since words are cheap and deeds are dear, it may be appropriate to indicate what this kind of thinking involves and leads to. Let us start at the beginning—the customer. It can be shown that motorists strongly dislike the bother, delay, and experience of buying gasoline. People actually do not buy gasoline. They cannot see it, taste it, feel it, appreciate it, or really test it. What they buy is the right to continue driving their cars. The gas station is like a tax collector to whom people are compelled to pay a periodic toll as the price of using their cars. This makes the gas station a basically unpopular institution. It can never be made popular or pleasant, only less unpopular, less unpleasant.

To reduce its unpopularity completely means eliminating it. Nobody likes a tax collector, not even a pleasantly cheerful one. Nobody likes to interrupt a trip to buy a phantom product, not even from a handsome Adonis or a seductive Venus. Hence, companies that are working on exotic fuel substitutes which will eliminate the need for frequent refueling are heading directly into the outstretched arms of the irritated motorist. They are riding a wave of inevitability, not because they are creating something which is technologically superior or more sophisticated, but because they are satisfying a powerful customer need. They are also eliminating noxious odors and air pollution.

Once the petroleum companies recognize the customer-satisfying logic of what another power system can do they will see that they have no more choice about working on an efficient, long-lasting fuel (or some way of delivering present fuels without bothering the motorist) than the big food chains had a choice about going into the supermarket business, or the vacuum tube companies had a choice about making semiconductors. For their own good the oil firms will have to destroy their own highly profitable assets. No amount of wishful thinking can save them from the necessity of engaging in this form of "creative destruction."

I phrase the need as strongly as this because I think management must make quite an effort to break itself loose from conventional ways. It is all too easy in this day and age for a company or industry to let its sense of purpose become dominated by the economies of full production and to develop a dangerously lopsided product orientation. In short, if management lets itself drift, it invariably drifts in the direction of thinking of itself as producing goods and services, not customer satisfactions. While it probably will not descend to the depths of telling its salesmen, "You get rid of it; we'll worry about profits," it can, without knowing it, be practicing precisely that formula for withering decay. The historic fate of one growth industry after another has been its suicidal product provincialism.

Dangers of R&D

Another big danger to a firm's continued growth arises when top management is wholly transfixed by the profit possibilities of technical research and development. To illustrate I shall turn first to a new industry—electronics—and then return once more to the oil companies. By comparing a fresh example with a familiar one, I hope to emphasize the prevalence and insidiousness of a hazardous way of thinking.

Marketing shortchanged: In the case of electronics, the greatest danger which faces the glamorous new companies in this field is not that they do not pay enough attention to research and development, but that they pay *too much* attention to it. And the fact that the fastest growing electronics firms owe their eminence to their heavy emphasis on technical research is completely beside the point. They have vaulted to affluence on a sudden crest of unusually strong general receptiveness to new technical ideas. Also, their success has been shaped in the virtually guaranteed market of military subsidies and by military orders that in many cases actually preceded the existence of facilities to make the products. Their expansion has, in other words, been almost totally devoid of marketing effort.

Thus, they are growing up under conditions that come dangerously close to creating the illusion that a superior product will sell itself. Having created a successful company by making a superior product, it is not surprising that management continues to be oriented toward the product rather than the people who consume it. It develops the philosophy that continued growth is a matter of continued product innovation and improvement.

A number of other factors tend to strengthen and sustain this belief:

1. Because electronic products are highly complex and sophisticated, managements become top-heavy with engineers and scientists. This creates a selective bias in favor of research and production at the expense of

marketing. The organization tends to view itself as making things rather than satisfying customer needs. Marketing gets treated as a residual activity, "something else" that must be done once the vital job of product creation and production is completed.

2. To this bias in favor of product research, development, and production is added the bias in favor of dealing with controllable variables. Engineers and scientists are at home in the world of concrete things like machines, test tubes, production lines, and even balance sheets. The abstractions to which they feel kindly are those which are testable or manipulatable in the laboratory, or, if not testable, then functional, such as Euclid's axioms. In short, the managements of the new glamour-growth companies tend to favor those business activities which lend themselves to careful study, experimentation, and control—the hard, practical realities of the lab, the shop, the books.

What gets shortchanged are the realities of the *market.* Consumers are unpredictable, varied, fickle, stupid, shortsighted, stubborn, and generally bothersome. This is not what the engineer-managers say, but deep down in their consciousness it is what they believe. And this accounts for their concentrating on what they know and what they can control, namely, product research, engineering, and production. The emphasis on production becomes particularly attractive when the product can be made at declining unit costs. There is no more inviting way of making money than by running the plant full blast.

Today the top-heavy science-engineering-production orientation of so many electronics companies works reasonably well because they are pushing into new frontiers in which the armed services have pioneered virtually assured markets. The companies are in the felicitous position of having to fill, not find markets; of not having to discover what the customer needs and wants, but of having the customer voluntarily come forward with specific new product demands. If a team of consultants had been assigned specifically to design a business situation calculated to prevent the emergence and development of a customer-oriented marketing viewpoint, it could not have produced anything better than the conditions just described.

Stepchild treatment: The oil industry is a stunning example of how science, technology, and mass production can divert an entire group of companies from their main task. To the extent the consumer is studied at all (which is not much), the focus is forever on getting information which is designed to help the oil companies improve what they are now doing. They try to discover more convincing advertising themes, more effective sales promotional drives, what the market shares of the various companies are, what people like or dislike about service station dealers and oil companies, and so forth. Nobody seems as interested in probing deeply into the basic human needs that the industry might be trying to satisfy as in probing into the basic properties of the raw material that the companies work with in trying to deliver customer satisfactions.

Basic questions about customers and markets seldom get asked. The latter occupy a stepchild status. They are recog-

nized as existing, as having to be taken care of, but not worth very much real thought or dedicated attention. Nobody gets as excited about the customers in his own backyard as about the oil in the Sahara Desert. Nothing illustrates better the neglect of marketing than its treatment in the industry press.

The centennial issue of the *American Petroleum Institute Quarterly,* published in 1959 to celebrate the discovery of oil in Titusville, Pennsylvania, contained 21 feature articles proclaiming the industry's greatness. Only one of these talked about its achievements in marketing, and that was only a pictorial record of how service station architecture has changed. The issue also contained a special section on "New Horizons," which was devoted to showing the magnificent role oil would play in America's future. Every reference was ebulliently optimistic, never implying once that oil might have some hard competition. Even the reference to atomic energy was a cheerful catalogue of how oil would help make atomic energy a success. There was not a single apprehension that the oil industry's affluence might be threatened or a suggestion that one "new horizon" might include new and better ways of serving oil's present customers.

But the most revealing example of the stepchild treatment that marketing gets was still another special series of short articles on "The Revolutionary Potential of Electronics." Under that heading this list of articles appeared in the table of contents:

- "In the Search for Oil"
- "In Production Operations"
- "In Refinery Processes"
- "In Pipeline Operations"

Significantly, every one of the industry's major functional areas is listed, *except* marketing. Why? Either it is believed that electronics holds no revolutionary potential for petroleum marketing (which is palpably wrong), or the editors forgot to discuss marketing (which is more likely, and illustrates its stepchild status).

The order in which the four functional areas are listed also betrays the alienation of the oil industry from the consumer. The industry is implicitly defined as beginning with the search for oil and ending with its distribution from the refinery. But the truth is, it seems to me, that the industry begins with the needs of the customer for its products. From that primal position its definition moves steadily back-stream to areas of progressively lesser importance, until it finally comes to rest at the "search for oil."

Beginning & end: The view that an industry is a customer-satisfying process, not a goods-producing process, is vital for all businessmen to understand. An industry begins with the customer and his needs, not with a patent, a raw material, or a selling skill. Given the customer's needs, the industry develops backwards, first concerning itself with the physical *delivery* of customer satisfactions. Then it moves back further to *creating* the things by which these satisfactions are in part achieved. How these materials are created is a matter of indifference to the customer, hence the particular form of manufacturing, processing, or what-have-you cannot be considered as a vital aspect of the industry. Finally, the industry moves back still further to *finding* the raw materials necessary for making its products.

The irony of some industries oriented toward technical research and development is that the scientists who occupy the high executive positions are totally unscientific when it comes to defining their companies' overall needs and purposes. They violate the first two rules of the scientific method—being aware of and defining their companies' problems, and then developing testable hypotheses about solving them. They are scientific only about the convenient things, such as laboratory and product experiments.

The reason that the customer (and the satisfaction of his deepest needs) is not considered as being "the problem" is not because there is any certain belief that no such problem exists, but because an organizational lifetime has conditioned management to look in the opposite direction. Marketing is a stepchild.

I do not mean that selling is ignored. Far from it. But selling, again, is not marketing. As already pointed out, selling concerns itself with the tricks and techniques of getting people to exchange their cash for your product. It is not concerned with the values that the exchange is all about. And it does not, as marketing invariably does, view the entire business process as consisting of a tightly integrated effort to discover, create, arouse, and satisfy customer needs. The customer is somebody "out there" who, with proper cunning, can be separated from his loose change.

Actually, not even selling gets much attention in some technologically minded firms. Because there is a virtually guaranteed market for the abundant flow of their new products, they do not actually know what a real market is. It is as if they lived in a planned economy, moving their products routinely from factory to retail outlet. Their successful concentration on products tends to convince them of the soundness of what they have been doing, and they fail to see the gathering clouds over the market.

Conclusion

Less than 75 years ago American railroads enjoyed a fierce loyalty among astute Wall Streeters. European monarchs invested in them heavily. Eternal wealth was thought to be the benediction for anybody who could scrape a few thousand dollars together to put into rail stocks. No other form of transportation could compete with the railroads in speed, flexibility, durability, economy, and growth potentials.

As Jacques Barzun put it, "By the turn of the century it was an institution, an image of man, a tradition, a code of honor, a source of poetry, a nursery of boyhood desires, a sublimest of toys, and the most solemn machine—next to the funeral hearse—that marks the epochs in man's life."[6]

Even after the advent of automobiles, trucks, and airplanes, the railroad tycoons remained imperturbably self-confident. If you had told them 30 years ago that in 30 years they would be flat on their backs, broke, and pleading for government subsidies, they would have thought you totally demented. Such a future was simply not considered possible. It was not even a

discussable subject, or an askable question, or a matter which any sane person would consider worth speculating about. The very thought was insane. Yet a lot of insane notions now have matter-of-fact acceptance—for example, the idea of 100-ton tubes of metal moving smoothly through the air 20,000 feet above the earth, loaded with 100 sane and solid citizens casually drinking martinis—and they have dealt cruel blows to the railroads.

What specifically must other companies do to avoid this fate? What does customer orientation involve? These questions have in part been answered by the preceding examples and analysis. It would take another article to show in detail what is required for specific industries. In any case, it should be obvious that building an effective customer-oriented company involves far more than good intentions or promotional tricks; it involves profound matters of human organization and leadership. For the present, let me merely suggest what appear to be some general requirements.

Visceral feel of greatness: Obviously the company has to do what survival demands. It has to adapt to the requirements of the market, and it has to do it sooner rather than later. But mere survival is a so-so aspiration. Anybody can survive in some way or other, even the skid-row bum. The trick is to survive gallantly, to feel the surging impulse of commercial mastery; not just to experience the sweet smell of success, but to have the visceral feel of entrepreneurial greatness.

No organization can achieve greatness without a vigorous leader who is driven onward by his own pulsating *will to succeed.* He has to have a vision of grandeur, a vision that can produce eager followers in vast numbers. In business, the followers are the customers.

In order to produce these customers, the entire corporation must be viewed as a customer-creating and customer-satisfying organism. Management must think of itself not as producing products but as providing customer-creating value satisfactions. It must push this idea (and everything it means and requires) into every nook and cranny of the organization. It has to do this continuously and with the kind of flair that excites and stimulates the people in it. Otherwise, the company will be merely a series of pigeonholed parts, with no consolidating sense of purpose or direction.

In short, the organization must learn to think of itself not as producing goods or services but as *buying customers,* as doing the things that will make people *want* to do business with it. And the chief executive himself has the inescapable responsibility for creating this environment, this viewpoint, this attitude, this aspiration. He himself must set the company's style, its direction, and its goals. This means he has to know precisely where he himself wants to go, and to make sure the whole organization is enthusiastically aware of where that is. This is a first requisite of leadership, for *unless he knows where he is going, any road will take him there.*

If any road is okay, the chief executive might as well pack his attaché case and go fishing. If an organization does not know or care where it is going, it does not need to advertise that fact with a ceremonial figurehead. Everybody will notice it soon enough.

Retrospective Commentary

Amazed, finally, by his literary success, Isaac Bashevis Singer reconciled an attendant problem: "I think the moment you have published a book, it's not any more your private property. . . . If it has value, everybody can find in it what he finds, and I cannot tell the man I did not intend it to be so." Over the past 15 years, "Marketing Myopia" has become a case in point. Remarkably, the article spawned a legion of loyal partisans—not to mention a host of unlikely bedfellows.

Its most common and, I believe, most influential consequence is the way certain companies for the first time gave serious thought to the question of what businesses they are really in.

The strategic consequences of this have in many cases been dramatic. The best-known case, of course, is the shift in thinking of oneself as being in the "oil business" to being in the "energy business." In some instances the payoff has been spectacular (getting into coal, for example) and in others dreadful (in terms of the time and money spent so far on fuel cell research). Another successful example is a company with a large chain of retail shoe stores that redefined itself as a retailer of moderately priced, frequently purchased, widely assorted consumer specialty products. The result was a dramatic growth in volume, earnings, and return on assets.

Some companies, again for the first time, asked themselves whether they wished to be masters of certain technologies for which they would seek markets, or be masters of markets for which they would seek customer-satisfying products and services.

Choosing the former, one company has declared, in effect, "We are experts in glass technology. We intend to improve and expand that expertise with the object of creating products that will attract customers." This decision has forced the company into a much more systematic and customer-sensitive look at possible markets and users, even though its stated strategic object has been to capitalize on glass technology.

Deciding to concentrate on markets, another company has determined that "we want to help people (primarily women) enhance their beauty and sense of youthfulness." This company has expanded its line of cosmetic products, but has also entered the fields of proprietary drugs and vitamin supplements.

All these examples illustrate the "policy" results of "Marketing Myopia." On the operating level, there has been, I think, an extraordinary heightening of sensitivity to customers and consumers. R&D departments have cultivated a greater "external" orientation toward uses, users, and markets—balancing thereby the previously one-sided "internal" focus on materials and methods; upper management has realized that marketing and sales departments should be somewhat more willingly accommodated than before, finance departments have become more receptive to the legitimacy of budgets for market research and experimentation in marketing, and salesmen have been better trained to listen to and understand customer needs and problems, rather than merely to "push" the product.

A Mirror, Not a Window

My impression is that the article has had more impact in industrial-products companies than in consumer-products companies—perhaps because the former had lagged most in customer orientation. There are at least two reasons for this lag: (1) industrial-products companies tend to be more capital intensive, and (2) in the past, at least, they have had to rely heavily on communicating face-to-face the technical character of what they made and sold. These points are worth explaining.

Capital-intensive businesses are understandably preoccupied with magnitudes, especially where the capital, once invested, cannot be easily moved, manipulated, or modified for the production of a variety of products—e.g., chemical plants, steel mills, airlines, and railroads. Understandably, they seek big volumes and operating efficiencies to pay off the equipment and meet the carrying costs.

At least one problem results: corporate power becomes disproportionately lodged with operating or financial executives. If you read the charter of one of the nation's largest companies, you will see that the chairman of the finance committee, not the chief executive officer, is the "chief." Executives with such backgrounds have an almost trained incapacity to see that getting "volume" may require understanding and serving many discrete and sometimes small market segments, rather than going after a perhaps mythical batch of big or homogeneous customers.

These executives also often fail to appreciate the competitive changes going on around them. They observe the changes, all right, but devalue their significance or underestimate their ability to nibble away at the company's markets.

Once dramatically alerted to the concept of segments, sectors, and customers, though, managers of capital-intensive businesses have become more responsive to the necessity of balancing their inescapable preoccupation with "paying the bills" or breaking even with the fact that the best way to accomplish this may be to pay more attention to segments, sectors, and customers.

The second reason industrial products companies have probably been more influenced by the article is that, in the case of the more technical industrial products or services, the necessity of clearly communicating product and service characteristics to prospects results in a lot of face-to-face "selling" effort. But precisely because the product is so complex, the situation produces salesmen who know the product more than they know the customer, who are more adept at explaining what they have and what it can do than learning what the customer's needs and problems are. The result has been a narrow product orientation rather than a liberating customer orientation, and "service" often suffered. To be sure, sellers said, "We have to provide service," but they tended to define service by looking into the mirror rather than out the window. They *thought* they were looking out the window at the customer, but it was actually a mirror—a reflection of their own product-oriented biases rather than a reflection of their customers' situations.

A Manifesto, Not a Prescription

Not everything has been rosy. A lot of bizarre things have happened as a result of the article:

- Some companies have developed what I call "marketing mania"—they've become obsessively responsive to every fleeting whim of the customer. Mass production operations have been converted to approximations of job shops, with cost and price consequences far exceeding the willingness of customers to buy the product.

- Management has expanded product lines and added new lines of business without first establishing adequate control systems to run more complex operations.

- Marketing staffs have suddenly and rapidly expanded themselves and their research budgets without either getting sufficient prior organizational support or, thereafter, producing sufficient results.

- Companies that are functionally organized have converted to product, brand, or market-based organizations with the expectation of instant and miraculous results. The outcome has been ambiguity, frustration, confusion, corporate infighting, losses, and finally a reversion to functional arrangements that only worsened the situation.

- Companies have attempted to "serve" customers by creating complex and beautifully efficient products or services that buyers are either too risk-averse to adopt or incapable of learning how to employ—in effect, there are now steam shovels for people who haven't yet learned to use spades. This problem has happened repeatedly in the so-called service industries (financial services, insurance, computer-based services) and with American companies selling in less-developed economies.

"Marketing Myopia" was not intended as analysis or even prescription; it was intended as manifesto. It did not pretend to take a balanced position. Nor was it a new idea—Peter F. Drucker, J. B. McKitterick, Wroe Alderson, John Howard, and Neil Borden had each done more original and balanced work on "the marketing concept." My scheme, however, tied marketing more closely to the inner orbit of business policy. Drucker—especially in *The Concept of the Corporation* and *The Practice of Management*—originally provided me with a great deal of insight.

My contribution, therefore, appears merely to have been a simple, brief, and useful way of communicating an existing way of thinking. I tried to do it in a very direct, but responsible fashion, knowing that few readers (customers), especially managers and leaders, could stand much equivocation or hesitation.

I also knew that the colorful and lightly documented affirmation works better than the tortuously reasoned explanation.

But why the enormous popularity of what was actually such a simple preexisting idea? Why its appeal throughout the world to resolutely restrained scholars, implacably temperate managers, and high government officials, all accustomed to balanced and thoughtful calculation? Is it that concrete examples, joined to illustrate a simple idea and presented with some attention to literacy, communicate better than massive analytical reasoning that reads as though it were translated from the German? Is it that provocative assertions are more memorable and persuasive than restrained and balanced explanations, no matter who the audience? Is it that the character of the message is as much the message as its content? Or was mine not simply a different tune, but a new symphony? I don't know.

Of course, I'd do it again and in the same way, given my purposes, even with what more I now know—the good and the bad, the power of facts and the limits of rhetoric. If your mission is the moon, you don't use a car. Don Marquis's cockroach, Archy, provides some final consolation: "an idea is not responsible for who believes in it."

Notes

1. Jacques Barzun, "Trains and the Mind of Man," *Holiday,* February 1960, p. 21.

2. For more details see M. M. Zimmerman, *The Super Market: A Revolution in Distribution* (New York, McGraw-Hill Book Company, Inc., 1955), p. 48.

3. Ibid., pp. 45–47.

4. *The Affluent Society* (Boston, Houghton Mifflin Company, 1958), pp. 152–160.

5. Henry Ford, *My Life and* Work (New York, Doubleday, Page & Company, 1923), pp. 146–147.

6. Jacques Barzun, "Trains and the Mind of Man," *Holiday,* February 1960, p. 20.

At the time of the article's publication, **THEODORE LEVITT** was lecturer in business administration at the Harvard Business School. He is the author of several books, including *The Third Sector: New Tactics for a Responsive Society* (1973) and *Marketing for Business Growth* (1974).

Putting Customers First
Nine Surefire Ways to Increase Brand Loyalty

Kyle LaMalfa

"Customers first." It's the mantra of businesses everywhere. Yet the average company still loses 10% to 15% of customers each year. Most of them leave due to poor service or a disappointing product experience, yet only 4% of them will tell you about it. And once they've left, it's difficult (not to mention expensive) to get them back.

Fostering true loyalty and engagement with customers starts at a basic level, but here are nine techniques you can employ to make customer loyalty a powerful competitive advantage for your company. They can be broken down into three categories: loyalty basics (one through four), loyalty technologies (five through seven) and loyalty measurement (eight and nine).

1. Give Customers What They Expect

Knowing your customer's expectations and making sure your product or service meets them is Business 101, yet often ignored. At the basic level, business needs to be a balanced transaction where someone pays for something and expects a fair trade in return.

Expectations of product quality come from many sources, including previous quality levels set by your organization, what competitors are saying about you, and the media. Marketing and sales should work together to monitor customer expectations through feedback and surveys.

2. Go Beyond Simple Reward Programs

Points and rewards encourage repeat purchases, but don't actually build loyalty. This is demonstrated by a drop in sales when the rewards are no longer offered. True loyalty comes when customers purchase products without being bribed.

3. Turn Complaints into Opportunities

Managing questions, comments and concerns benefits your business in two important ways. First, research indicates that an upset customer whose problem is addressed with swiftness and certainty can be turned into a highly loyal customer. Second, unstructured feedback, gathered and managed appropriately, can be a rich source of ideas. To that end:

- Establish channels (electronic, phone and written) to build engagement, one customer at a time.
- Encourage customers to voice their thoughts.
- Create metrics to improve response to concerns (i.e., "time to first response," "time to resolution," etc.).
- Create metrics to measure loyalty before and after the problem.
- Use technology to help you centralize the information, create reports and structure drill-downs.

4. Build Opportunities for Repeat Business

Give your customers a chance to be loyal by offering products for repeat business. Monitor what customers request most and offer products or services that compliment other purchases. In addition, exceed expectations by driving product development to offer more value for less cost. Use technology to track, classify and categorize open-ended feedback.

5. Engage Customers in a Two-Way Dialogue

An engaged customer is more than satisfied and more than loyal. They support you during both good and bad times because they believe what you have to offer is superior to others.

Engagement takes your customer beyond passive loyalty to become an active participant and promoter of your product. Engaged customers will give you more feedback so you should be ready to handle it! All this translates into a customer who will spend more money with you over time. Accordingly:

- Listen to customer feedback from comment cards, letters, phone calls and surveys.
- Respond quickly and personally to concerns of high interest to your customers.
- Organize unstructured feedback for tracking and trending over time.

- Trust your customers to tell you what the problem is.
- Use statistical techniques to discover which action items will have the most impact on your business.

6. Survey Customers and Solicit Feedback

Actively soliciting information from a population of customers is a time-tested technique pioneered by Arthur Nielsen (creator of the Nielsen ratings) in the 1920s. Survey research can be used for problem identification or solving. Questions with simple scales such as "agree/disagree" deliver quantitative insight for problem identification. Open-ended follow-up questions can provide rich insight for solving problems. Some tips:

- Make sure your surveys are short, bias-free and well structured.
- Use random sampling to gather feedback continuously without over-surveying.
- Create summary survey indices that can be displayed graphically and tracked over time.

7. Create a Centralized System for Managing Feedback throughout the Enterprise

Technology such as enterprise feedback management (EFM) helps to centralize surveys and customer feedback and track both qualitative and quantitative information. EFM involves more than just collecting data, though; it adopts a strategic approach to building dialogs with your customers. Follow these steps:

- Empower customers to give feedback through common advertised channels.
- Centralize reporting for proactive surveys and complaint management solutions.
- Structure quantitative feedback into a drill-down or rollup report.
- Make open-ended feedback intuitively searchable.

8. Tie Customer Loyalty and Engagement to Business Outcomes

Orienting your organization to focus on satisfaction, loyalty and engagement is no panacea. But researchers have clearly documented evidence of short-term benefits to customer/ employee retention and long-term benefits to profitability. Hence:

- Determine whether to measure your engagement outcome by satisfaction, likelihood to purchase again, likelihood to recommend, or another voice of the customer (VOC) metric.
- If necessary, create hybrid VOC measurements using more than one metric.
- Link your VOC metrics with business outcomes like shareholder returns, annual sales growth, gross margin, market share, cash flows, Tobin's Q or customer churn.
- Be aware that changes in loyalty/engagement scores generally precede changes in business outcomes.

9. Use Analysis to Predict Future Loyalty

Businesses use a variety of statistical techniques to make predictions about the potential for future events. Furthermore, predictive analytics may be used to ascertain the degree to which answers from a survey relate to particular goals (such as loyalty and engagement). Tactical knowledge of how action items impact an outcome discourages the wasting of resources on ineffective programs, and competent statistical modeling reveals which tactical options work. Consequently:

- Analyze data using a statistical technique to reveal the most important areas of focus.
- Ask your analyst about common statistical methods, including correlation and logit models.
- Recognize that the major areas of focus may change in response to changes in your economic, competitive and demographic environments.

Following these steps may not be the easiest process, but stay focused. Increasing your engagement and loyalty equals increasing profits and a competitive edge.

Kyle LaMalfa is the best practices manager and loyalty expert for Allegiance, Inc. He can be reached at kyle.lamalfa@allegiance.com. For more information about how to increase your loyalty and engagement, visit www.allegiance.com.

Customer Connection

We started winning when we listened to customers.

ANNE M. MULCAHY

I came by my passion for the customer naturally. I began my Xerox career in sales, and I have never stopped selling Xerox. Staying connected with customers is part of my DNA, and I'm trying to keep it a part of the Xerox DNA. As our founder, Joe Wilson, said: "Customers determine whether we have a job or not. Their attitude determines our success." This legacy is what saved Xerox from our worst crisis. We got into trouble by losing sight of the customer, and we got out of trouble by redoubling our focus on the customer.

Just five years ago, the prospect of bankruptcy loomed over us. Revenue and profits were declining. Cash was shrinking. Debt was mounting. Customers were irate. Employees were defecting. The day the value of Xerox stock had been cut in half (May 11, 2000), I was named president and COO.

One of the first things I did was call Warren Buffet to get his advice. He told me, "You've been drafted into a war you didn't start. Focus on your customers and lead your people as though their lives depended on your success."

Fortunately, I had not one but two aces in the hole: 1) a loyal customer base that wanted Xerox to survive, and 2) a talented and committed workforce—people who love Xerox and would do anything to help save the company and return it to greatness.

And so we went to work. We spent lots of time with customers, industry experts, and employees—listening. Customers told us we had great technology, but our response to them had slipped. Industry experts told us our technology was leading-edge, but we had to focus on doing a few things very well. And employees told us they would do whatever it took to save the company, but they needed clear direction.

We laid out a bold plan to turn Xerox around. The results have been stunning in magnitude and swiftness. We cut our debt by more than half; most of what remains is in the form of receivables. We more than doubled our equity. We took more than $2 billion out of our cost base through tough choices. And we increased earnings—building value for our shareholders, customers, and employees. Four years ago we lost $273 million. Last year we made $978 million. Our margins are healthy. We have money in the bank, and we're buying back stock.

Leading Xerox has been the opportunity of a lifetime, and I've learned that you can't do enough communications; that you need to change the bad and leverage the good in your culture; that you need to articulate a vision of where you are taking the company; that bad leadership can ruin a company overnight, and good leadership can move mountains over time; and that good people, aligned around a common set of objectives, can do almost anything. Mostly I learned that the customer is the center of our universe. Forget that and nothing much else matters: employees lose jobs, shareholders lose value, suppliers lose business, the brand deteriorates, and the firm spirals downward.

Consider the value of customer service: 1) If you can retain 5 percent more of your customers than you currently do, your bottom-line profit will grow from 25 to 50 percent; and 2) it takes five times more money and effort to attract a new customer as it does to retain an old one. We all know that customers are the reason we exist, yet we don't always behave that way. That's what got Xerox in trouble. We made decisions that didn't have the customer in mind. We weren't listening to our customers, and we started to take them for granted. We learned a powerful lesson the hard way.

Five Strategies

We've since made the customer our priority by focusing on five strategies:

Strategy 1: Listen and leant what your customers are facing—what their problems and opportunities are. It's not something you can delegate. It starts at the top. Every week I sit down with some of our key customers. In 2005 and 2006, I spent 25 percent of my time in direct contact with customers. Our entire leadership team at Xerox shares the same passion. Our 500 major accounts are assigned to our top executives. All our executives are involved. Each executive is responsible for communicating with at least one of our customers—understanding their concerns and requirements, and making sure that Xerox resources are marshaled to fix problems, address issues, and capture opportunities.

All of our officers do something to keep in touch with customers. There are about 20 of us, and we rotate responsibility to be "Customer Officer of the Day." It works out to about a day a month. When you're in the box, you assume responsibility for dealing with complaints from customers who have had a bad experience. They're angry, frustrated, and calling headquarters as their court of last resort. The "Officer of the Day" is required to listen, resolve the problem, and fix the underlying cause. It keeps us in touch with the real world, permeates our decision-making, impacts the way we allocate resources, and keeps us passionate about serving our customers.

Strategy 2: Even in the worst of times, invest in the best of times. As proud as I am of out financial turnaround, what gives me even greater satisfaction is the progress we've made on strengthening our core business to ensure future growth. Even as we dramatically reduced our costs, we maintained R&D spending in our core business. This was not a universally applauded decision: our financial advisors thought that slashing R&D was necessary; the bankers thought I didn't understand the problem; but our customers knew it would be a hollow victory if we avoided financial bankruptcy today only to face a technology drought tomorrow.

So we continued to invest in innovation. We're glad we did. In recent years, we have brought to market scores of new products and services. These investments are paying off. In fact, three-quarters of our revenues are coming from offerings that were introduced in the past two years.

Strategy 3: Align: Focus all your employees on creating customer value. A CEO I met with during our turnaround advised me to ask the question: "Would the customer pay for this? Would the customer think this was helpful?" I've tried to use that as a guideline. It has a double-payoff—streamlined costs and customer focus.

Top to bottom, Xerox people are tightly connected to our customers and their businesses. For us, it's personal. Our customers are real people with aspirations that we want to help them realize. We treat each customer as an individual—using our own technology to communicate with them one-to-one.

Strategy 4: Deliver value: Don't sell the customer your products, offer them solutions to their problems. In the recent decades, organizations have poured billions of dollars into technology. And the ROI hasn't always lived up to the promise because the focus was always on the technology. Our focus is on what really matters—information and what our customers do with it. We focus not on hardware and technology for the sake of technology, but on reducing cost and complexity while improving the customer experience. And the customer experience is more about striving problems.

Strategy 5: Serve: Provide service beyond the customer's expectations. About 75 percent of customers who defect say they were satisfied. When our customers tell us they are *very* satisfied, they are six times more likely to continue doing business with us than those who are merely "satisfied." If you're providing your customers with good service, they're probably satisfied. But only about 40 percent of satisfied people repurchase! This should set off alarm bells. In a world of increasing competition and expectations, standards like *good* and *satisfied* don't cut it.

We realize that our customers have choices about whom they do business with, that their expectations continue to escalate, and that our competitors continue to improve.

We embrace those challenges. We know that our success depends on customer loyalty. Customers put a lot of trust in us, and we're on a crusade to give them a good return on trust.

The idea of putting the customer first is powerful, and we stray from it at our own peril. Our recent successes all stem from putting the customer at the center of decision-making.

ANNE M. MULCAHY is chairman and CEO of Xerox Corporation. This article is adapted from her speech at the World Business Forum, October 25, 2006. Frankfurt, Germany. Visit www.xerox.com or call 203-968-3000.

Add Service Element Back in to Get Satisfaction

TODD POLIFKA

We live in a customer-focused society. That is, as business owners and managers we focus all of our attention on customers. For several hours a day, corporate energy is focused on how to find new customers, repeat customers, loyal customers and more customers than our competition. Once acquired, customers are then *segmented*, upsold and processed. In the rush to be focused on all aspects of the customer, it appears that many companies seem to have forgotten about the two most important—customer satisfaction and customer service.

Many companies talk about customer service, but sadly for most it has become just that—talk. While companies are busy knocking down the barriers for customers to buy from us, they are putting up more barriers than ever for maintaining that relationship with the customer, especially if something goes wrong.

Business executives apply a great deal of energy and effort to the immediate sale, but we are in danger of missing the forest for the trees. Rather than try to build a relationship that translates into not only a sale today but future sales and relationships and incremental sales due to referrals, companies are stuck in a mode where they are focusing only on getting that immediate sale.

How about your business? Is everyone at your company on the same page regarding customer service? Do you think it's possible? The Walt Disney Co.'s 50,000-plus employees consistently deliver legendary customer service, which has kept them ranked as an elite customer service company for well over a decade. There are several other companies doing this as well, such as Nordstrom, Southwest Airlines, Build-A-Bear Workshop Inc. and Marriot International Inc. to name a few. How do they do it?

The answer is actually very simple. They have made customer service part of their everyday business activity, or what is more commonly being referred to as their customer culture. Customer service has become infused throughout everything they do, from answering the phones, to solving problems, to ensuring that the customer is completely satisfied. It will require companies to assess every aspect of their operations, but the reward of life-long customers who become advocates for your brand and refer you to others is worth it.

Here are six areas to begin focusing on that in the long run will help you change your company's culture to one of customer service and customer satisfaction.

Accessibility—Remove Barriers to Customer Lines of Communication

The No. 1 complaint of customers, according to the U.S. Department of Commerce's Office of Consumer Affairs, is that they are not able to speak to someone about their issue. If they are able to get a hold of a live person, their second biggest complaint is that it is not someone with the authority to solve their issues. In a customer service culture, it is not only important to have someone answering phones and e-mails in a timely manner, it is important that every employee, from the president on down, is empowered to solve the customers' problems, or to immediately involve someone who can.

Transparent Pricing—No Hidden Costs or Secondary Costs

Customers feel immediately cheated when they have to pay more than the agreed upon price. No matter how legitimate the reason, it is the perception of customers who have to pay an amount different than the agreed upon price that they have become a victim of fraud.

In a customer service culture, upfront and transparent pricing has to happen; if there are any further charges that may be applicable, such as service contracts or warranties, present those options and prices to the customer before closing the sale.

What You See Is What You Get—Avoid the Feeling of Bait-and-Switch

With the increasing amount of Internet purchases, customers are no longer so concerned about being able to stop by the showroom and "kick a few tires." They are, however, more and more concerned about receiving the goods they have seen represented. In your advertising, photos and descriptions that provide visual demonstration of services, you must be exacting in how truly you represent your offerings.

Constant Communications— Quick Response

The communication can be live or virtual, but it has to happen freely and timely. We are increasingly becoming a society that expects instant gratification. With technology today, there is no reason that your people do not have access to communications, whether it is via phone or Internet. Quick and frequent communication goes a long way toward giving the perception that you are taking action on their problem, and attempting to resolve it.

Quality Products, Services and Craftsmanship

It would seem that quality on all levels should be an obvious part of any company's way of doing business, but if it really is in place, it means that there are fewer opportunities for a customer to have an issue with the goods or services they are purchasing. The longer a product lasts, the longer a customer is satisfied.

Unmatched Passion for the Customer

As a company you probably got into a business because you had a passion for the product or services you were selling. You should have that same level of passion for the people who buy those products or services. And if you want them to be satisfied and to keep purchasing from you, you need to be more passionate about the customers than your competition. This is extremely important in a crowded industry where your product may be rather similar to those of a competitor.

Putting the service back into customer service may take a commitment from you and your team and will require that a lot of time and effort be invested in your customer service and care, but the dividends are well worth it. Your company can join the select group of those companies that walk the talk and don't just pay lip service to customer service and actually achieve customer satisfaction.

Now, how may I help you?

TODD POLIFKA is co-owner and sales director for Vision Remodeling, a full-service home remodeling company based in the Twin Cities, Minn.

School Your Customers

Marketing executives from PepsiCo to General Mills to The Home Depot are learning that educating consumers about a product category can help build brand loyalty.

TAMARA E. HOLMES

Two years ago, in a bit of a marketing gamble, PepsiCo launched a massive campaign that would place it in the role of educator. Recognizing that Americans were becoming increasingly interested in health and wellness, the Purchase, N.Y.–based company began masking its product pitches with more instructive information on the benefits of nutritious foods. The program, called Smart Spot, was designed to help consumers choose healthier products while it subtly promoted PepsiCo-produced foods and beverages that met certain nutritional guidelines.

Today, more than 250 PepsiCo products sport a green Smart Spot stamp, which shows they contain at least 10 percent of the recommended daily value of a targeted nutrient, have specific health and wellness benefits, contain limited amounts of fat, sodium, and/or sugar, or also include healthier ingredients, such as whole grains. "The Smart Spot products grew at more than two and a half times the rate of the rest of our portfolio in 2005," says Lynn Markley, vice president of public relations for health and wellness at PepsiCo. "Consumers are looking for healthier products. Clearly we're meeting the demand."

PepsiCo, which actively promotes Smart Spot through television and print advertisements, recently announced a partnership with the nonprofit organization KaBOOM! to create Smart Spot playgrounds across the country, providing children with a safe place to get more exercise. The company is also partnering with the YMCA of the USA and America on the Move to raise health awareness and promote active, healthy lifestyles.

PepsiCo isn't the only company that has embraced the educational marketing concept. Several major brands in a variety of industries are using promotions to educate consumers about not only specific products but also entire product categories. As a result, consumers not only make well-informed buying decisions, experts say, they also become more receptive to product pitches because they are more trusting of the companies they do business with. "Marketers can change people's behavior by educating them," contends Fred Senn, founding partner of the Minneapolis, Minn.–based advertising agency Fallon Worldwide and coauthor of *Juicing the Orange: How to Turn Creativity into a Powerful Competitive Advantage.*

Enhancing Lives

General Mills recognizes the value in helping to educate health-conscious consumers on eating well and living better. In 2004, it launched the interactive Web site BrandNewYou.com, where visitors get tips on calorie counting, portion control, and exercise. Consumers can learn about General Mills' portion-controlled offerings, such as 100-calorie popcorns and soups, and can download Betty Crocker low-fat recipes.

Another online campaign of General Mills' revolves around Green Giant, the leading vegetable brand in the country. To help consumers better understand the importance of vegetables to a healthy diet, the company launched Greengiant.com in 2005. The site offers quizzes, recipes, and even a vegetable tracker to help consumers ensure that they're fulfilling the dietary guidelines established by the Department of Health and Human Services and the Department of Agriculture.

In fact, after the guidelines were announced in April 2005, General Mills launched a nutrition education initiative, the highlight of which was displaying the food pyramid on the boxes of its Big G cereal brands—including Total Raisin Bran, Cheerios, and Wheaties. "The guidelines are the collective efforts of the American nutrition community, and we want to help communicate these important messages by using some of the best real estate there is," said John Haugen, vice president of Big G marketing, when the initiative was launched. "The cereal box is one of the most read items in the home. With cereal consumed in 93 percent of American households and with the information on more than 100 million General Mills cereal boxes, this is a powerful step forward in nutrition education."

"The cereal box is one of the most read items in the home . . . With information on more than 100 million General Mills cereal boxes, this is a powerful step forward in nutrition education."

—John Haugen, vice president of Big G marketing

Kraft Foods took a different approach to educational marketing by focusing on a niche market: South Beach dieters. In January, as this target audience looked for ways to start the year off right, the Northfield, Ill.–based company launched the Beach in a Box Tour. Kraft officials traveled to nine cities to inform consumers about how to prepare nutritious meals and maintain good eating habits while, at the same time, they were softly selling healthy Kraft products. Although it's too early to determine how product sales will be affected by the tour, the company has deemed it a success thanks to the high consumer turnout, says Sydney S. Lindner, associate director of corporate affairs for Kraft Foods.

The health and wellness industry is not the only one for which educational marketing has worked. The Home Depot has succeeded in building customer loyalty through its popular how-to clinics. "Our how-to clinics started in the aisles years ago," says John Clay-brooks, director of brand marketing. "An associate would be helping a customer and explaining how to do different projects, and before you knew it, a crowd of people would gather around to listen and learn."

The Home Depot stores started conducting how-to clinics based on customer requests in select locations around 2001, and then other stores across the country began to follow suit. In 2003, the company launched Do-It-Herself, women-only clinics that have attracted more than 280,000 participants. The company also offers Kids Workshops, in which children are taught about tool safety and allowed to take part in some do-it-yourself projects.

---

4 Ways to Stand Out

1. **Keep It Light.** While customers want to learn, they don't want to feel like they're in school. Avoid information overload.
2. **Make It Entertaining.** People like to be amused when they learn. Promotions such as games, quizzes, and contests can inform while they engage.
3. **Incorporate Interactive Elements.** The best campaigns allow customers to interact with others, whether it's through an in-store presentation or an interactive Web site. An emotional connection can make consumers more loyal to your brand.
4. **Point Out the Reward.** Tell customers why the information you're presenting will benefit them; then point out the value of your respective products.

"The how-to clinics provide an opportunity for customers to receive personal attention to assist with their do-it-yourself projects. In doing so, customers develop a level of comfort with the store."

—John Claybrooks, director of brand marketing for The Home Depot

---

"The how-to clinics provide an opportunity for customers to receive personal attention to assist with their do-it-yourself projects," Claybrooks says. "In doing so, customers develop a level of comfort with the store and with the products needed to help finish the job. This confidence and comfort with The Home Depot and its associates bring customers back again and again."

Tying It Together

The key to a successful educational marketing campaign is recognizing the needs of the consumer. The more entertaining and creative the information, the more engaged customers will be, and the more likely they will be to trust that company's products. However, there are instances when educational marketing could easily take the wrong approach. "Most advertising that we see treats people like they're stupid," says Bart Cleveland, partner and creative director at McKee Wallwork Cleveland, a full service advertising agency based in Albuquerque, N.M. "It's either too obvious or it's condescending, and education-based campaigns can be especially guilty of that."

Cleveland was particularly cognizant of that fact when he headed a recent anti-smoking campaign for the New

Mexico Health Department. "These people are addicted to something and they feel vulnerable," he says. "You have to be very careful not to be condescending." Rather than go out with an educational message about the dangers of smoking, the company created documentary-style commercials that ran late last year and during the 2006 Super Bowl, contrasting smoking with other bad habits, such as nose-picking.

The company used humor to show people that smoking is not a bad habit, it's an addiction. According to Cleveland, the New Mexico Health Department has seen spikes in its Help Line when the ads have run.

If a company does decide to embark on an education-based marketing campaign, Fallon Worldwide's Senn says, it must first figure out what its audience wants to know and then craft a message accordingly. If there is something crucial about the product category that consumers don't know, "you can have not only a creative campaign but a campaign that is bankable," he says. "When it comes down to the bottom line, that's all an advertiser can ask for."

Surviving in the Age of Rage

Learning to manage angry customers is a crucial part of today's service landscape.

STEPHEN J. GROVE, RAYMOND P. FISK, AND JOBY JOHN

We seem to live in an age of rage. What once were isolated incidents of volatile customer behavior have become commonplace. News reports from around the world chronicle a growing number of customer rage incidents. These incidents create serious problems for managers of service organizations. Consider the following episodes:

Checkout counter rage. A woman had half her nose bitten off by a fellow shopper when she insisted on remaining in an express lane with more than the 12 permitted items.

Parking rage. Youths screamed, swore at, and verbally abused a man in a dispute over a parking space in front of a Costco store and later severely scratched his automobile.

Air rage. A disruptive passenger who attempted to break into the cockpit on a Southwest Airlines flight to Salt Lake City was beaten, choked, and eventually killed by other passengers. (This happened before Sept. 11, 2001.)

Snowplow rage. Frustrated by the never-ending snowfall and the snowplow generated mountain of white blocking his driveway, a Framingham, Mass., man beat the town's plow driver with his snow shovel.

Pub rage. Incensed for being refused service at a pub at closing time, a man with a tractor repeatedly smashed into the establishment, causing the pub's walls to crumble.

ATM rage. When a bank machine at a convenience store swallowed his card, an enraged patron stuck the ATM machine with a utility knife, cursed a nearby clerk, hurled the knife at a cashier, and smashed an adjacent fax machine to the ground. These incidents only hint at the breadth and severity of customer rage. Damage caused by rage episodes varies from verbal indignation, to vandalism, to physical injury, and even death. Fellow patrons and workers alike have been unsuspecting targets of rage. Clearly, disruptive customer behaviors pose severe problems for businesses afflicted by rage episodes. These problems might include negative publicity, costs of legal actions, and the untold ramifications of traumatized customers and employees.

Service organizations should have policies and procedures to prevent or reduce the occurrence of customer rage.

Many customer rage incidents go unreported, so the precise number of rage episodes is difficult to determine. Indications are, however, that customer rage is on the upswing. Consider the airline industry prior to Sept. 11. A *New York Times* article reported that Swissair witnessed nearly a 100% increase over a three-year period in the occurrence of passenger interference with crew members' in-flight duties. CNN reported that an estimated 4,000 air rage episodes occurred in the United States (where airlines are not required to register such instances) in the year 2000 alone. While the number of air rage incidents has declined since 2001 according to the Federal Aviation Administration, a new phenomenon called "ground rage" is growing. Aggressive behavior toward airline personnel on the ground is now so prevalent that British Airways issues soccer-style yellow cards as a final warning to disruptive travelers that any further disturbance will result in refusal of service.

On another front, a recent survey of call center personnel found that nearly 60% of the respondents reported an increased incidence of phone rage over the past five years. Regardless of the range or severity of customer rage, it's the service sector that is most frequently afflicted with rage incidents. Service organizations, such as hotels, banks, restaurants, airlines, and theme parks, require interaction between customers and employees, often in the presence of multiple consumers sharing a common service setting. In addition, service quality provided by such organizations is notoriously variable due to the "real time" character of service delivery and the many uncontrollable elements that combine to create customers' service experience. Further, service organizations are often capacity constrained. It's not surprising then that service encounters are a veritable petri dish for customer rage. According to a 2002 study by the Public Agenda research group, shopping malls, airports, airplanes, and government offices are particularly vulnerable to rude or disrespectful behavior.

Customer behaviors in service settings can range from those that are too friendly to those that constitute rage. Obviously, pleasant interactions between customers and employees are

Executive Briefing

With civility on a seemingly downward path, customer rage has become a common problem for many service organizations. This article discusses "the four Ts of customer rage," which include the targets of customer rage behavior, the influence of temperament on customers expressing rage, the triggers that spark customers' rage, and the treatments for preventing or managing customer rage. In this environment, smart service managers are doing all they can to improve the service environment for their customers.

desirable. However, if customers are excessively friendly, they can be a major distraction to employees and may delay service to subsequent customers. Under such circumstances, the service process bogs down and workers search for ways to chill customers' friendly advances. Hence, we label the boundary line between too friendly and the range of acceptable behaviors as the freezing point. Toward the other extreme of acceptable behaviors, unfriendly situations occur when customers are irritating or rude to employees. Unfriendly interactions can escalate to rage if the customer or the employee hits the other's hot button with an inappropriate comment, misguided gesture, or other affront. We label the boundary line between rage and the range of acceptable behaviors as the boiling point.

The Four Ts of Customer Rage

Targets. Since customer rage is a common service phenomenon, it's not surprising that the targets of customer rage are other customers, employees, or elements of the service environment. In reality, no aspect of a service organization is immune from rage. In most cases, the rage exhibited far exceeds the transgression that triggered the anger. An unsolicited comment or an accidental bump by a fellow patron may unleash astonishing fury. Harried employees who snub or overlook demanding customers may experience their uncontrolled wrath. Not even innocent bystanders are sheltered from customer rage. Bottled up angst may find an outlet in the nearest unsuspecting soul. Sometimes it's the adjacent passenger, fellow shopper, or exuberant fan that draws the rage of nearby customers. Sharing the service setting with one who is predisposed to rage is not unfathomable.

When fellow customers or employees are not targets of rage, fury may be directed at inanimate objects or others' possessions. Angry ATM users relentlessly pound the machine that swallowed their debit card. Frustrated golfers hurl the clubs that humiliate them into the nearest water hazard. Enraged diners slam tables and toss food on the floor when offended by a waiter. Clearly, when anger boils over, neither people nor property is safe.

Temperament. Service organizations that cater to large numbers of customers simultaneously must be aware that some

people are prone to customer rage. Most people know somebody who can "go off" at the slightest provocation. Perhaps it can be traced to personality or maybe other personal factors are at play. Regardless, not all service customers are equally likely to exhibit rage.

Modern technology has created a world where the boundaries between work and leisure are blurred. Where can one escape the responsibilities of the workplace? Cell phones, pagers, laptop computers, and Internet access keep us tethered to obligations that follow us everywhere. We seem to live in a world where we're on stage 24 hours a day, seven days a week, and 365 days a year. These stressful circumstances provide ample kindling to ignite rage in some customers.

> **Unfriendly interactions can escalate to rage if the customer or the employee hits the other's hot button with an inappropriate comment, misguided gesture, or other affront.**

Is it possible that some people fly into rage more quickly? Perhaps. There is some evidence that anger is inherited, yet it seems more likely that rage behaviors are learned via socialization as appropriate responses to certain situations. Some people may have internalized rage as a typical response for some occasions, possibly through a previous experience or by observing others. Further contributing to the likelihood of rage may be the absence of one's spouse or close friends, whose presence might normally keep one's aggressive behavior in check. At the very least, the enraged customer may lack strong social or personal norms that prevent them from boiling over when faced with challenging circumstances.

Many other temperament factors can make some people susceptible to rage. Aggressive personality types are prone to heated verbal exchanges and attempt retribution for even the smallest perceived transgressions. Customers who exhibit type A behavior patterns (i.e., intense achievement strivings, strong sense of competition) often find themselves in situations where their impatience or obsessive nature sparks confrontation. Those who feel controlled by circumstances may be prone to display aggression as well. Even physiological conditions, such as reduced amounts of serotonin and low levels of cholesterol in one's blood system, have been linked with aggressive tendencies. These are just a handful of individual characteristics associated with rage. In short, some customers enter a service encounter with their rage sensors loaded and ready.

The task of identifying likely candidates for rage is fraught with issues. There is an important but subtle difference between engaging in customer segmentation and discrimination. Customer segmentation involves offering different customers different service based on their distinctive characteristics. (Service businesses that provide a more protective environment for parents with small children engage in customer segmentation.) Discrimination occurs when customers are given poor service because of their race, age, sex, religion, or other distinctive characteristic. Discrimination can take the form of "profiling." For instance, a business may decide that males with beards are prone to rage and subject such customers to obtrusive scrutiny. Since Sept. 11, profiling has become a controversial issue. The U.S. Transportation Security Administration's computer-assisted passenger profiling system (or CAPPS II) classifies prospective passengers with a three-level rating—green, yellow, or red. A green rating yields minimal security screening, a yellow rating leads to extensive searches and interrogation, and a red rating prevents boarding the plane.

Triggers. The interactive nature of services offers many potential triggers for customer rage. Some of the strongest triggers occur when customers believe they have been treated unfairly, neglected, or negated in a service encounter. Perceived unjust treatment, such as a later-arriving patron being seated first at a restaurant, may fuel rage. Customers sometimes become angry when their needs are neglected. One who endures a long wait at an unattended customer service counter may commence yelling when the service representative finally arrives. If customers believe they are being treated with disrespect, hostility may ensue. A patronizing attitude from an employee tells customers that they are unimportant and can send the customer into a fury. Ironically, it seems that some organizations knowingly trigger "righteous indignation" from customers and may deserve the rage responses they prompt.

We seem to live in a world where we're on stage 24 hours a day, seven days a week, and 365 days a year. These stressful circumstances provide ample kindling to ignite rage in some customers.

Situational influences on customer behavior, such as those described by Russell Belk, may play a role in triggering rage in any service encounter. Consider the rage-generating effect of these in the following:

- *Physical surrounding:* Aspects of the service environment may rub customers the wrong way. Room temperatures can be oppressively warm or chillingly cold, noise levels can be painfully loud, filthy service settings can anger customers, and/or cramped facilities can make the service setting seem too crowded.
- *Social surroundings:* Other customers often negatively affect each other by violating normative expectations (e.g., standing too close in line or smoking in nonsmoking areas). Crowded service settings can push customers to their limits and may initiate jostling among customers.
- *Temporal perspective:* Long delays or being rushed for time can ignite rage. Time is one of the most sensitive of situational triggers. For example, most customers detest

waiting in line, and time delays can cause tempers to rushed often become aggravated and lash out.
- *Task definition:* Extraordinary obligations Heightened expectations and desires can increase customer sensitivity. For example, a married couple celebrating a special occasion may become quite agitated when things don't go as planned at a fancy restaurant.
- *Antecedent states:* Temporary conditions that customers experience, such as hunger or thirst, may cause people to become easily enraged. But the most troubling of such antecedent states is drunkenness, a circumstance that escalates when businesses such as bars, nightclubs, or sporting events serve large numbers of drinking customers.

Treatment. People's emotions can soar during a rage-precipitating incident to the point where management must get involved during or after the episode. Less astute organizations occasionally find themselves tackling uncomfortable negative publicity and possibly liability issues. Clearly, it's in any organization's best interest to have a well-designed set of procedures and policies to manage customer rage.

The first management step is to prevent customer rage by preempting such situations. To do this, firms should focus on the triggers that activate rage. Organizations that understand the triggers that prompt rage can institute procedures to manage outbursts. For example, an unfulfilled promise of a "freebie" supplemental service, an unbearably long wait for service due to unforeseen circumstances, an aggressive customer in a bad mood, or a poorly trained employee serving an "important customer" may each require different treatment. Consider how Disney Corp. successfully manages waiting time for rides at its theme parks. For years, Disney has communicated average waiting times, kept lines moving, and made the wait entertaining. But the most significant improvement is Disney's Fastpass virtual queue system that allows guests to reserve a place in line without having to queue up.

When rage incidents occur, frontline service staff must scramble to defuse the situation and protect the personal safety of those present. At the very least, customer rage may have harmful effects on frontline employees, on customers who share the service setting, and on the perception of service quality. If an employee is the target of rage, this can affect subsequent encounters with future customers. If other patrons are present, they may witness the rage incident and their own experience may be affected negatively. The 2002 Public Agenda study found that nearly three of every four customers report seeing fellow customers behaving badly toward service personnel, and more than 60% said such incidents bothered them a lot. All in all, the costs of mishandling customer rage are too great to be ignored.

Once a rage episode has occurred, organizations are faced with the difficult task of determining the appropriate remedial action for that specific incident and learning from the event to prevent future occurrences. Service organizations should be attuned to how the nature of services can affect customer rage.

BEFORE

Ensure that people and processes are in place to recognize customers who are prone to rage and potential customer rage situations

DURING

Empower employees with the skills and reward mechanisms to manage customer rage as it occurs

AFTER

Investigate, analyze, and learn from customer rage incidents

Figure 1 Living with Customer Rage

Since services occur in real time, the risk of failure is always high. Therefore, it is imperative that organizations take a systematic approach to managing rage incidents. For example, the C.H.A.R.M. School provides lessons in Customer Hostility and Rage Management. Employees learn various identification techniques to spot potential incidents before they happen and plausible tactics to defuse potentially dangerous customers. Forward thinking organizations that prepare employees for rage through such programs are making a commitment to a better service experience.

In Figure 1, we suggest how firms might establish customer rage management protocols.

There are several managerial actions that organizations can take before, during, or after a customer rage incident occurs.

"Before" Actions

Before customer rage occurs, managers can take preemptive actions to lock the trigger. First, organizations should identify and institute early warning mechanisms and procedures for handling rage episodes. The specific devices involved may vary across service types. Nevertheless, frontline employees need to be trained, motivated, and rewarded for handling difficult customer rage incidents. These actions demonstrate to employees and customers that management takes rage situations seriously. It also facilitates any legal defense if an unfortunate event should occur. As a manager, you might do the following:

- Train employees to anticipate and manage service failures and customer rage.
- Empower employees to act on the incidents without waiting for supervisory assistance.
- Establish reward systems that motivate all employees to attend to customer rage incidents.
- Design early warning mechanisms to anticipate circumstances and situations leading to customer rage.

As an example, Caterpillar Inc. depends a great deal on service enhancements to its products. The company monitors customer equipment remotely, sending electronic warning signals to its service technicians when necessary. These employees are given information indicating the parts and tools needed to make the repair.

"During" Actions

During a rage incident, other procedures may be engaged. Such procedures might include employee actions that seek to respond to the situation. The status of the customer could dictate the type of procedure to invoke. For example, an important client might be handled by senior management with a just amount of apologies and offers for redemption. During a rage incident, you should do the following:

- Take immediate action
- Maintain decorum and remain calm
- Listen to the customer, show empathy, assume responsibility, apologize, and make amends
- Separate or isolate the enraged customer, especially in a shared customer experience
- Document everything about the incident including witness reports
- Involve superiors, if necessary

Marriott, for example, specifies the situations that call for empowered actions based on the nature of the customer problem and the value of the customer to the company. Employees are given "safe zones" for spending up to $2,500 to compensate a customer grievance or inconvenience.

"After" Actions

After a rage incident, management must analyze each episode and follow up with the individuals involved. For long-term actions, incidents must be recorded, categorized by level of severity and frequency of occurrence, stored as information, and then analyzed so that systemic improvements might be designed into the service delivery processes. Managers should take the following steps after an episode of customer rage:

- Investigate causes of the incident
- Follow-up with customers by apologizing, explaining, and reinstating the organization's commitment to preventing similar occurrences in the future

- Depending on the severity and pervasiveness of an incident, involve upper management. If service failure was the reason, determine what can be done to prevent it in the future
- If a customer is at fault, determine if an individual or a customer segment should be avoided
- If a service employee is at fault, determine if screening, hiring, training, or supervision is to be changed or improved

Westpac Bank of Melbourne, Australia, has adopted an innovative way to respond to customer rage. It recruits "middle-aged mums" to cool customer rage since mothers tend to have the proper skills from managing their families. They have a general willingness to listen, an increased level of patience, and are naturally empathetic.

Figure 2 outlines the series of steps that firms might formally establish to manage customer rage. Step 1 is to analyze rage incidents to understand what triggered the rage. Process design is Step 2, which requires designing and implementing methods for preempting customer rage. Step 3 stresses action during rage incidents by employing prevention methods to manage raging customers. Taking action after a rage incident is Step 4, following up with individuals who became enraged. This is essentially a damage control step. If the customer was enraged about legitimate complaints, then corrective actions must be taken. If, however, the customer was primarily to blame for the rage incident, then it might be necessary to ask the customer to take their patronage elsewhere. Step 5 is process improvement. The organization should follow up on any lessons learned regarding managing customer rage.

The Prognosis

In some ways, it's surprising that the customer rage problem isn't worse. Civility seems to be scarce in modern times. The 2002 Public Agenda study documented a perception of growing rudeness in America with 80% of Americans surveyed viewing rudeness as a very serious problem. Among the reasons that customers become rude or even enraged is that their public and private lives leave them pressed for time. In addition, rising education levels have led to rising customer expectations. Information age technology will continue to present opportunities

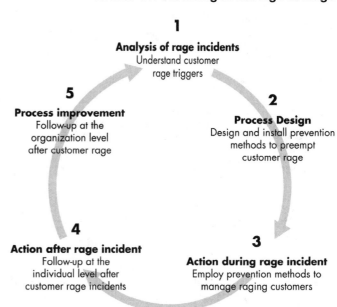

Figure 2 Phases in the Treatment of Customer Rage

for customer rage as it provides new methods for interaction between firm and customer, and for interaction among customers. Against this backdrop, it's clear that more needs to be done to manage and prevent customer rage.

Will service encounters in the future contain even more hostility than today? We believe that customer rage is more likely unless service managers reduce common targets of customer rage, manage customer temperaments, prevent triggers, and pursue treatments for customer rage. Smart services managers will do everything possible to make sure that their customer interactions are characterized by civility rather than marred by rage. They know that customers prefer businesses that provide predictably pleasant service environments.

STEPHEN J. GROVE is professor, department of marketing, college of business, Clemson University, Clemson, S.C. He may be reached at groves@clemson.edu. **RAYMOND P. FISK** is professor and chair of marketing, department of marketing, college of business administration, University of New Orleans. He may be reached at rfisk@uno.edu. **JOBY JOHN** is professor and chair, marketing department, Bentley College, Waltham, Mass. He may be reached at jjohn@bentley.edu.

From *Marketing Management,* March/April 2004, pp. 41–46. Copyright © 2004 by American Marketing Association. Reprinted by permission.

Attracting Loyalty
From All the New Customers

CHIP R. BELL AND JOHN R. PATTERSON

Today's customers get terrific service in pockets of their life, and use those experiences to judge everyone else. When the UPS or FedEx delivery person walks with a sense of urgency, we expect the mail carrier to do likewise. Customers also have choices. Shop for a loaf of bread, and you're confronted with 16 brands and 23 varieties packaged 12 different ways.

Today's customers are smarter buyers. Considering Sleepwell Hotel for your next vacation trip? You can get web-based information complete with evaluations from 40 previous guests. Everyone is everyone's *Consumers Report*. Watchdog websites can give you the lowdown on why one company is better than another. It means companies must monitor all the details (now transparent to customers) and get early warning on emerging glitches.

Figuring out how to attract and retain loyal customers today is not easy.

Five Loyalty Drivers

Five loyalty drivers fit most customers most of the time about most services.

1. Include me. Customers' loyalty soars when they discover they can be active participants in the service experience. Harley-Davidson created the Harley Owners Group (HOG) as a forum to bring Harley loyalists together for education and recreation. Membership comes with the purchase of a Harley. Managers often join in the fun and fellowship as HOG members reunite around a barbeque or motorcade on a Sunday afternoon.

Dealers for BMW's Mini-brand automobile mail to buyers a "birth certificate" once the customer pays a deposit. The customer then receives a link to go on line and follow their car's production. Build-A-Bear Workshop with their interactive build-a-stuff-toy experience has grown to 200 stores worldwide in 10 years. If customers know they have a chance to be included, the impact is almost as powerful as if they actually put "skin in the game."

2. Protect me. A value proposition is the complete package of offerings a seller proposes to a customer in exchange for the customer's funds. It includes the product (or outcome), the price, and the process (or experience) involved in getting the product or outcome. There are certain qualities or features all buyers assume will typify that value proposition—the products they buy will be as promised, the price fair, and the process comfortable. These are "givens"—taken for granted unless removed—but they do not make us happy campers. If the commercial plane we board lands in the right city, we do not cheer; but, if it lands in the wrong city, we're upset. We assume banks will be safe, hotels comfortable, and hospitals clean. Customers are loyal to organizations that make sure the basics are always done perfectly.

3. Understand me. Service goes deeper than just meeting a customer's need. All needs are derived from a problem to be solved. Great service providers are great listeners. They know that unearthing the essence of the problem will point to a solution that goes beyond the superficial transaction. It takes building rapport with customers to engender trust. It entails standing in the customers shoes to get sense their hopes and aspirations.

Understanding customers takes more than surveys and focus groups. It means viewing every person who comes in contact with the customer as a vital listening post—a scout who gathers intelligence about the customer's changing requirements and provides early warning about issues and concerns. It involves gathering customer intelligence and mining the intelligence from front-line contacts.

4. Surprise me. Today's customers want sparkle and glitter; a cherry on top of everything. They want all their senses stimulated, not just those linked to the buyer-seller exchange. Features have become far more titillating than function; extras more valued than the core offering. Attracting customer loyalty today requires thinking of service as an attraction. Examine how Cabelas and Bass Pro Shops decorate the service experience. If your enterprise was "choreographed" by Walt Disney World, a Lexus dealership, MTV or Starbucks, how would it change?

Think of the service experience like a box of Cracker Jacks. What can be your "free prize inside?" The power of surprise lies in its capacity to enchant, not just entertain; to be value-unique, not just value-added. Service innovation works best when it is simple and unexpected. Hotel Monaco puts a live goldfish in your room; Sewell Infiniti dealership programs in your radio stations from your trade-in; servers at Macaroni Grill introduce themselves by writing their name with a crayon upside down (right side up to the customer) on the butcher paper table cloth.

5. Inspire me. Customers are tired of plain-vanilla service. It attracts their loyalty if it reflects a deeper purpose or destiny, befitting of the organization's values—not just its strategy. Service with character means a sense of innocence, naturalness, purity—a solid grounding. We like being charmed by what we don't understand; we do not enjoy being hoodwinked by what we should have understood. Such service need not be obvious to customers in its design, but it must never feel devious in its execution.

What makes service inspirational? It moves us when it comes from people who are passionate about their work. We are stirred by professionalism and pride when it reflects a zeal to "do the right thing." It leaves customers wanting to return when they've had an encounter with goodness and purity.

Loyal customers act as a volunteer sales force, championing you to others at home, work, social circles, blogs, bulletin boards, and web sites. Because they feel committed to you and see both emotional and business value in the relationship, they'll often pay more for what they get from you.

The formula for creating and sustaining loyalty comes through inclusion, trust, understanding, joy, and character. Put these in your customers' experience, and watch their admiration soar along with your bottom line!

CHIP R. BELL is senior partner of The Chip Bell Group. JOHN R. PATTERSON is president of Progressive Insights, a CBG alliance company. Their new book is *Customer Loyalty Guaranteed!* Visit www.loyaltycreators.com.

Nonprofits Can Take Cues from Biz World

Branding Roadmap Shapes Success

LARRY CHIAGOURIS

Individual nonprofit organizations face unique challenges. Consider the following examples:

- A leading provider of social services is confronting a major challenge: It has substantial resources, but its major contributors, who are more than 60 years old on average, are dying off. This charity is not signing up meaningful numbers of baby boomers as members, donors or volunteers. Consequently, its leaders are concerned about future levels of financial support.
- A state-of-the-art science museum is about to open when it receives inquiries from the media, concerning its mission. Will the museum celebrate current global environmental issues or will it speak to the ecological beauty of its location? Will it engage adults about the world or will it raise children's awareness of science and the environment? Its leaders cannot agree on the answers and thus cannot move forward on communications activities.
- An international institution organized to fight hunger recognizes that it needs more than government donations to perform. It conducts a fund-raising project among corporations and the general public. The project is not successful because most people had never heard of the institution.

    Each of these organizations lacked a coherent brand strategy and program. Whether recruiting new members, responding to the media or generating donations, nonprofits are more likely to succeed if their target audiences know who they are and what they stand for. In other words, nonprofits must have a carefully developed brand.

    The pressures on nonprofit brands have increased dramatically over the last decade, for several reasons.
- Many of them are managed with small staffs and tight budgets.
- More than 1.5 million nonprofits now are competing for scarce resources and attention from public and private

donors in the United States. This estimate primarily encompasses charitable causes, universities, foundations, and professional societies and associations. But there are more nonprofits: hospitals, governmental organizations, political candidates and committees, and even branches of the military.
- The Internet offers new and exciting ways to attract volunteers and donations. With new concerns about scams and spam, however, an Internet presence demands a brand be credible and meaningful to prospective supporters.

Establish mission statement, brand promise.

Given this challenging environment, what brand components will target audiences view as compelling? What should nonprofits borrow from the commercial sector, to aid them in brand building? To answer these questions, my organization studied the best branding practices of leading nonprofits. We also interviewed several nonprofit managers breaking ground in the branding arena. Brand mission, unique selling proposition and reason to believe, personality, graphic identity and measurement emerged as highly relevant components.

Make a Statement

Nonprofit brands do not have to answer to the vagaries of Wall Street or the short-term demands publicly held companies face daily. In many ways, however, they have to meet more exacting requirements. They are under constant scrutiny to efficiently deliver on missions that answer to a higher calling—delivery that can mean the difference between life and death for some, and improved quality of life for many.

Most consumers don't know or even care what the mission is for Nike, Charmin, McDonald's or other leading brands. But for nonprofits, the lead brand element is its mission. If people are going to donate time or money or become members, they want to know what the brand is all about; they want to know the mission statement.

Specific

Most nonprofit mission statements fail to provide sufficient specificity. For example, many museums state broadly that they will educate the public on their subject matter. They do not differentiate their purpose from that of other museums. In contrast, the Chicago Children's Museum's mission statement is rather specific: "to create a community where play and learning connect." It does not fall in step with so many other routine promises.

Realistic

Another problem is that many nonprofits compose unrealistic mission statements that exceed their abilities. It is wonderful to reach and stretch, but not if it negatively affects credibility. A mission statement to rid the world of a crippling disease may be admirable, but isn't believable if it's coming from a small or unknown entity without a strong track record. A mission statement with a reasonable chance of being accomplished is a major step toward brand credibility.

Show Promise

Nonprofits should then look at what they would like target audiences to take from encounters with the brand, as well as build a case to support such reasoning.

Unique Selling Proposition (USP)

The USP is central to the brand message. Some call it the brand promise, others refer to it as the net impression. Whatever the label, it is the primary thought the target audience should take from encounters with the brand—a composite of brand attributes and benefits. The most effective commercial sector USPs convey what the brand will do for or give to the consumer. USPs such as "melts in your mouth—not in your hand" (M&M's) or "We try harder" (Avis) live on long after tag lines change.

The USPs of nonprofit brands are quite different. Nonprofit USPs frequently reflect what the brand will do for others—not just the target audience. The benefits are often to be experienced by all. Instead of promising that your skin will look younger or your house will be cleaner, nonprofit brands pledge to make the world better with their work.

Consider the USP of St. Jude Children's Research Hospital: "Finding cures. Saving children." It is clear and specific. It does not promise it will cure the world, but focuses on searching for cures—for children. Not complicated, yet very compelling.

Reason to Believe (RTB)

An RTB should always accompany a USP. Some label it the "support." It builds the case for the target audience accepting a USP as true and highly credible. A car buried for months in the Alaskan snow, only to start immediately when the driver turns

the ignition key, is an effective image because it prompts the prospective consumer to think, "If this battery can start a car in the middle of an Alaskan winter, it surely can start my car." The RTB can similarly serve nonprofit branding objectives.

So, why should we believe St. Jude's USP? In a recently televised appeal to prospective donors, the spokesperson noted that because of St. Jude's research, the survival rates for childhood cancers have increased substantially in recent years. This proves St. Jude's support is producing results. Other St. Jude's communications, such as press releases, also reveal many research breakthroughs in combating childhood diseases.

The most important consideration for the RTB is that in a highly segmented market, different support points will be called on to convince the different target audiences of the USP's believability. It is acceptable to have several, as long as you don't throw them into the same communication in an "everything but the kitchen sink" style. That will only lead to confusion about the brand.

Multiple Personality

Brand personality is a valuable way to enhance the relationship between organization and target audience. Key personality attributes will vary according to the nonprofit's mission: Hospitals and social service organizations benefit if consumers see them as caring and maternal; museums benefit if consumers see them as highly competent and knowledgeable.

Just as one attribute is not enough to capture a person's essence, so it is with brand personality. For example, it's important for people to view museum staff as competent, but it's even more important for them to view the staff as accessible. Visitors do not want tour guides or personnel to treat them in a condescending manner. They want them to courteously answer their questions and encourage their curiosity. A museum supportive in this multidimensional way is likely to receive more visitors and donor contributions.

Values

A nonprofit's values can also make a difference in brand perception. Although not the same as personality, they can convince people of a brand relationship's appeal. The U.S. military understands this. The Army conveys and operates by seven key values—loyalty, duty, respect, selfless service, honor, integrity and personal courage—and integrates them into many of its soldier training programs.

Track progress with measurement system.

Graphic Content

If you have held a Fortune 500 company's corporate identity and style manual, you can appreciate the degree to which it documents what one can and can't do to portray brand identity. These manuals are often up to 100 pages long and cover every visual element of materials, including shapes, colors and sizes. For nonprofits, graphic identity can also be complex. The University of Virginia Web site, for example, notes: "A significant factor in the success of the University's unified identity is adherence to a standard color palette."

Name

The name of a brand is central to its success. The principles that guide name development in the commercial sector also apply to nonprofits: The name should be memorable, distinctive, ownable, easy to pronounce, and relevant to the organization's mission and benefits. The Museum of Modern Art's name and logo is the perfect combination of these elements. The Manhattan museum's abbreviation had been MOMA for many years. One day the director had an epiphany: Why not use a lowercase "o"—portray it as MoMA? Today, everyone recognizes MoMA as the museum's graphic identity (and the sound of its name). It is the gold standard of what nonprofits can achieve.

Logo

Nonprofits need to exercise serious thought and reflection in developing a logo. The Carnegie Museum of Art's logo is a good representation. The golden-yellow "C" is for Carnegie, and its form of a brush stroke symbolizes the wonderful art at this Pittsburgh museum.

Tag Line

The tag line completes the picture. Each telegraphs different impressions. More importantly, the tag line needs to communicate the USP. "Explore & Learn" (the Smithsonian), "Advance Humanity" (UNICEF), "Where the End of Poverty Begins" (CARE) and "Bringing the Real World to Kids" (Junior Achievement) are tag lines that provide additional relevance to brand objectives.

For Good Measure

The brand program is not complete until nonprofits create a system for measuring how well the brand is connecting with its target audience. Too often, they limit their evaluations to levels of donations or sales; focus exclusively on the number of members, volunteers or visitors; or simply note the quality and quantity of mentions in the media, or letters from the public. Although these measurements are important, they do not go far enough. To determine the nature of brand development progress, it is important to track the images, attitudes and perceptions of each target audience.

Common commercial sector tools can work quite well for nonprofits in conducting assessments. Strategic planning sessions among internal and external constituencies can unearth substantial guidance, market research can identify the brand-building elements a nonprofit should execute, and brand equity studies are now using measures that assess a nonprofit brand's financial worth. This can provide considerable insight into what nonprofits are accomplishing.

The best tools go a step further: They identify the drivers contributing most to a brand's success, and pinpoint the barriers nonprofits must remove to achieve higher and faster levels of progress in the brand's health. This allows brand managers to make the necessary adjustments—to attributes such as brand trust, credibility, responsiveness, competence and knowledge—to keep the brand strong and relevant.

Brand-Building Profits

A compelling brand image is more important to nonprofits than commercial sector companies for one fundamental reason: Nonprofits do not have the resources to send their messages to large numbers of people through the media.

They cannot solve awareness challenges with more advertising weight, but must define and execute their branding objectives right out of the gate. However, they also can't afford to do so by just delegating brand management responsibilities to a junior staffer, a well-intentioned but untrained volunteer or the person who recently mastered a graphic art software package.

There is so much depending on professional brand development and execution that it must be one of the nonprofit's key priorities. The potential impact on fundraising is substantial. Michael Hoffman, CEO of Changing Our World (a New York City philanthropic services company), puts it in perspective. "The brand tells the story. A strong brand is vital to long-term development and fundraising because it connects the mission with the organization and potential donors."

Professional brand development and execution must be one of the nonprofit's key priorities.

In fact, a strong brand may lead to profit-generating activities that can underwrite social programs. Many nonprofits are beginning to experiment with these initiatives and are experiencing success. Steve Case, co-founder of America Online, established a foundation to encourage entrepreneurial behavior among nonprofit managers—including development of professional skills integral to brand building. His view, stated in a May 2005 *Wall Street Journal* article, is that brand programs can contribute to "significant social change." I can't agree more, but would add this: These programs will drive social change that will endure.

LARRY CHIAGOURIS is associate professor of marketing at Pace University's Lubin School of Business in New York City and a senior partner at Brand Marketing Services Ltd. He may be reached at lchiagouris@pace.edu. This article originally appeared in the September/October 2005 issue of Marketing Management magazine and was edited for style and length before being reprinted. For more information on subscribing to Marketing Management, please call AMA at 800/262-1150.

From *Marketing News*, July 15, 2006, pp. 20–22. Copyright © 2006 by American Marketing Association. Reprinted by permission.

Fidelity Factor

Ensure Loyal Customer Relationships by Infusing Them with Trust

JEFF HESS AND JOHN W. STORY

Until recently, marketers and academics were convinced that the ultimate goal of marketing was to satisfy customers. An entire generation of business students was sent forth with the conviction that all good things come from meeting or exceeding customers' expectations—that once they are satisfied, loyalty is inevitable.

On the contrary, more than 25 years of exhaustive investigation and simple observation have left us with an undeniable conclusion: Lasting profitability results more from enduring customer relationships than from a collection of satisfying transactions.

As a result, companies now are committed to customer relationships—building them, managing them, and asking marketing researchers to tell them how well they're doing. The belief that strong relationships are a significant market advantage has firms racing with competitors to bond with their customers.

But false starts, with promising new technologies such as those supporting customer relationship management (CRM), suggest we may have gotten ahead of ourselves.

To realize the promise of relationships, we first must understand them. What do they look like, where do they come from, what do we get out of them, and how are they different from the ongoing transactions we currently measure with loyalty programs? Once we learn the language of relationships, and formalize models and methods to build and track them, tools such as CRM can transform how marketing gets done.

The relationship framework has quickly emerged from a clever promotional differentiator to a competitive imperative, and is the dominant paradigm of marketing. In *Total Relationship Marketing* (Butterworth-Heinemann, 2002), Evert Gummesson writes that there's a built-in profitability to relationships, as they provide companies several bottom-line benefits not offered by customers participating in random transactions. From sales promotion to pricing, most marketing activities become more effective and less expensive when customers are on your side.

Professor Susan Fournier and Jeff Hess (one of the authors of this article) report the real secret behind the relationship

Executive Briefing

Although it is important to know the strength of customer bonds, it is absolutely essential to understand their nature. Just as personal relationships have many dimensions (friends, acquaintances, and romantic attachments), so do customer-brand relationships. To ignore these dimensions would be perilous. The trust-based commitment relationship model formalizes the processes by which multidimensional relationships develop—as well as the benefits that ensue.

revolution: Many customers form brand relationships similar to the bonds they form with other people, complete with personal and functional characteristics. And it is in this multidimensional relationship space that new classes of loyal behavior emerge, all of which can have a profound impact on the bottom line.

Figure 1 displays two views of how customers respond to their interactions with your brand. The traditional view represents the familiar process in which they evaluate your products and services on a set of performance attributes they deem important. The primary arbiter of return on investment (ROI) is whether customers are satisfied with performance, and whether overall satisfaction with your products and services leads to functional loyalty: "I stay with the brand because it does what it says it'll do, and because I get a good value for the money."

In the relationship view, trust resides in the center of the model, as a fundamental condition. Once the role of trust is recognized, a new world of diagnostics and benefits emerges, and the ultimate relationship disposition transforms from primarily functional to including personal dimensions. This model does not propose new types of relationships where none existed, but instead promotes a deeper understanding of previously studied behaviors and hidden motivations. Trust is the primary condition for personal connections, which (with functional connections)

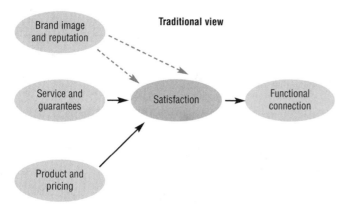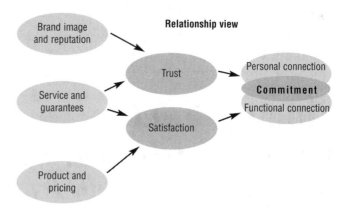

Figure 1   How Customers Interact with the Brand.

translate into truly committed relationships. And committed relationships are profitable relationships. The trust-based commitment model described in Figure 2 formalizes the interaction among these relationship constructs.

Problematic Approaches

There are basic deficiencies with current configurations of loyalty, and little agreement on what loyalty is. Some companies portray it as behavioral (proportional or sequential behavior), some measure it as an attitude intended to predict behavior, and some build indices based on several behavioral and attitudinal measures. The problem with these approaches is that they take a narrow, purely revenue-based view of loyalty.

Certainly share and revenue are important business goals, but they often overlook customer behaviors that drive profitability. A typical functional loyalty model focuses on the revenue outcomes of functional connections. However, unless you take a multidimensional view of your customer interactions, a broad range of loyal behaviors remains behind a veil of conventional measures. A multidimensional commitment framework describes the personal connections leading to profitable behavior:

- Paying premium prices for the brand's products.
- Seeking a company's Web site to purchase products.
- Overcoming purchase barriers such as inconvenience or competitive offers.
- Forgiving the brand's minor failures.
- Trying the brand's new products.

Most companies agree that it makes good business sense to form bonds with customers, but the real epiphany is that customers enjoy being in relationships with their favorite companies. They are often willing and active partners in such connections. If you're looking at relationships from a purely functional perspective, there's a good chance you're missing significant opportunities to build partnerships of a personal nature—attachments yielding much more than repeat purchases and improved satisfaction scores.

Consider the customer ready to pay a higher price or endure inconvenient schedules to fly his or her favorite airline. Or think about the relatively unreliable, moderately performing,

premium-priced auto brand known for its devoted long-term customer relationships. In various retail contexts where convenience and price competition dominate, many profitable brands rely on their customers driving past more convenient competitors to pay a premium at their locations. These events signify relational bonds not described by standard satisfaction and loyalty measures.

Beyond Satisfaction

Trust is at the center of customer relationship phenomena, and is the key to understanding relationships of a personal character. In fact, misunderstanding and misplacement of trust has led to an anemic knowledge of customer-brand relationships, misapplication of investment, and the inability to accurately assess returns.

Although satisfaction is the indicator of perceived brand performance, trust is an acknowledgment of brand motivation. It's the powerful idea that a brand has its customers' best interests in mind, and that it'll do whatever it takes to make them happy. Trust lives in the dissatisfied customer happily marching into a favorite store, fully expecting a swift and peaceful resolution; it is absent in the dissatisfied customer anticipating conflict and aggravation.

When customers believe in your brand, they no longer worry you'll take advantage when their guards are down. Consequently, as in human relationships, they may engage in deeper commitment. Although customers may be skeptical that altruistic brand motivations exist, the idea becomes plausible when you implement actions and policies demonstrating your dedication to pleasing them.

Just like relationships with other people, customer relationships are built on trust—becoming more profound and expansive as trust endures. Introducing trust as the gateway to profitable relationships not only improves the precision with which you deploy precious resources, but also allows for a much more sophisticated assessment of customer-focused activities. But despite its essential role in building trust and personal relationships, many a customer-centered initiative has been erroneously marginalized because of the minimal impact on customer satisfaction. Until trust is defined and measured, important activities will continue to die on the vine with the relationships they support.

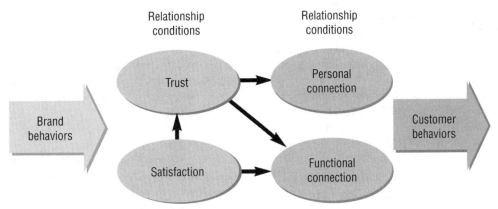

Figure 2 Trust-based Commitment Model.

For instance, allowing customers to interact with people—rather than routing them through frustrating automated response systems—might seem a frivolous and inefficient use of resources. But person-to-person interaction is fundamental to forming trust. The surest way of undermining trust is to tell customers you're not interested in talking to them.

Trust as the key to enduring relationships is not a novel concept. Ad agencies have been using the language of trust and commitment for several years. But unlike satisfaction, which captured the imagination of marketing scholars and practitioners more than 25 years ago, trust has remained a chiefly intuitive application.

The Trust-Based Commitment Model

Many brands understand the importance of communicating their motivations through actions and promotions, but rarely do they formalize processes and measures for reliably planning and assessing relationship success. Marketers and academics have been slow to create a usable customer relationship model revolving around a rigorous understanding of trust. In this vacuum, they continue to rely on transactional satisfaction and traditional loyalty concepts.

Once the antecedents and implications of trust are elaborated, marketers can confidently invest in the next frontier: customer-brand relationships. The promise of technologies such as CRM, data management, and the Internet will be realized only when their places in true relationship building and management are understood.

In the past, as relationship tools outpaced understanding of customer relationship development's social and psychological processes, marketers were quick to throw money at the problem of disconnected, random transactions. When first conceived, data management promised a rich, quantifiable understanding of individual customers and the ability to customize marketing activity to targeted customer segments. Although often increasing the efficiency with which brands promote to accessible customers, CRM activities and protocols rarely result in real customer relationships. These practices revealed hidden behaviors and patterns influencing the definition of customer-brand relationships, yet they could not reveal relational components of these behaviors. According to Atul Parvatiyar and Jag Sheth's article "Customer Relationship Management: Emerging Practice, Process, and Discipline" in the *Journal of Economic and Social Research,* it's possible that CRM systems may impede real relationship building; they've nearly become a mere surrogate for the technology applied to data management methods.

The trust-based commitment model in Figure 2 seeks to put "relationship" back into CRM by devising a formal structure of customer relationship concepts, upon which marketing can be built and assessed. This structure transcends behaviors and purchase patterns, to encompass relational components of attitudes and customer-brand interactions.

A relationship view doesn't aim to undermine the importance of classic marketing ideas (e.g., satisfaction, value, loyalty) or merely freshen up traditional models with new nomenclature. Rather, it reorganizes the basic customer process model so that satisfaction and related concepts take their places in a constellation of ideas, resulting in real relationships and relationship-specific benefits for customers and brands. This has significant financial implications.

Loyalty Redefined

In the relationship world, when we speak of loyalty we are ultimately speaking of commitment. Although it is tempting to define loyalty as simply repurchase, marketers often have little power over the variables and constraints directly controlling how customers pass through the purchase environment. In addition, repurchase is only one of several outcomes that can be described as loyal behaviors; some refer to sales volume and share, and some to profitability.

As Dave Aaker states in his recent *Planning Review* article "Managing the Most Important Asset: Brand Equity," strong brands certainly have loyal customers. But are such brands fully taking advantage of the benefits these customers offer? From customers' perspectives, loyalty is an intuitively adopted strategy, to maximize the value of their consuming skills and win the cost/utility game (reduce risk, increase information processing effectiveness, and gain tangible frequent-user benefits). However, it's also a way to take advantage of their customer status' hidden pleasures. Even more revolutionary than economic efficiency is that relationships allow customers to enjoy relational benefits alien to utility maximization (e.g., affiliation, association, value matching).

And the essence of how customer-brand relationship outcomes differ from those of more traditional loyalty models is that relationship connections significantly contribute to customer behaviors and result in increased profits.

STANDARD research methods are often ill-suited to describe a customer's disposition and resilience in the marketplace.

The assumption underpinning all loyalty and satisfaction models is that the measured customer processes reflect attitudes that determine behavior. The most expedient and common measures of attitudes and behavior assess repurchase intent or overall satisfaction, which extend to financial performance. This calculus often undermines the credibility of the research: Such models rarely yield accurate financial predictions, leaving decision makers to ponder the value of research data.

The heart of the dilemma is in the assumptions, and in the fact that standard research methods are often well removed from ultimate market behavior—or ill-suited to describe a customer's disposition and resilience in the marketplace. The best case: These assessments are an unreliable reflection of behavioral trends. The worst case: They mislead strategic planning regarding market share or volume superiority, by masking underlying relational weaknesses. It's important to remember that, by traditional criteria, customers repeatedly buying out of convenience appear loyal.

While competitors are content striving to meet expectations, the savvy brand moves beyond a transactional view—prizing relationships over unqualified repeat purchases. For instance, the fast-food market is often dominated by convenience and price considerations; relationship building in this environment might seem an exercise in futility with fleeting benefits. Competitive advantage can be gained in the face of transactional constraints, via customer relationship building. For example, restaurant brand A has nearly twice as many locations as restaurant brand B, with associated superiority in revenue. On a transactional basis, B's customers are slightly more satisfied; however, its customers have greater commitment. Consequently, they're more willing to pay premium prices and try the restaurant's new products. In this case, an assessment of relationship vs. transactional constructs will be much more revealing regarding B's potential emergence in the marketplace. B can use this information to capitalize on a potential competitive opportunity, whereas A is alerted to an emerging competitive threat.

As marketers, we are primarily managing the attitudes that customers take into the purchase environment. It is those attitudes that determine how they'll respond to competitive actions, inconvenience, pricing, and situational factors. Commitment is

a customer's ultimate relationship disposition—a fundamental and powerful concept carrying beliefs and attitudes that result in actions toward the brand, understood only when decomposed into its primary dimensions. It is the distinct personal and functional connections that separate commitment from standard loyalty and intention. And trust is the key to understanding how these connections develop.

At least as important as assessing customer bond strength is understanding its nature. Just as human relationships have many dimensions (friends, acquaintances, and romantic attachments), so do customer-brand relationships. And to ignore these dimensions is perilous; just ask The Coca-Cola Company. It may have underestimated the profound, personal nature of customers' bonds with Coke, and the betrayal felt from any change to the beloved brand. A negative response to a demonstrably superior product innovation can best be understood in a relationship light.

Connection Dimensions

The key to understanding and managing customer-brand relationships is the process by which trust and satisfaction evolve into commitment. Whether relationship partners are human or brands, trust is necessary for breaking down intellectual and emotional barriers to personal connection.

Satisfying transactions might continue indefinitely without transcending this interaction because customer-brand ties remain vulnerable to incident failure or competitive action and brand investment requirements proceed unabated. Trust can transform such repeated interactions into enduring relationships. Elena Delgado-Ballester and José Luis Munuera-Alemán—in their recent *European Journal of Marketing* article, "Brand Trust in the Context of Consumer Loyalty"—claim that all relationships, whether with people or brands, are built on trust. The point is that if you satisfy customers you are still vulnerable to competitive actions, but when trust develops, the relationship is more resilient. Trust allows customers to relax perpetual brand critiques and enjoy the benefits.

Marketers evaluate ROI more accurately when they understand that trust and satisfaction require different activities and that each communicates different motivations and competencies. The trust-based commitment model describes a process in which marketing activity investments have a specific and individual impact on trust and satisfaction. For example, in the retail category: Store environment, high-quality products, and easy-to-find merchandise lead to satisfaction; generous warranties and return policies, service guarantees, resolving problems with attentive and pleasant employees, and standing behind products lead to trust. Because such investments might not always be justified by short-term financial results, their real return is assessed only when trust is included as a central judge of ROI.

Just as relationship commitment is composed of functional and personal dimensions, satisfaction and trust uniquely contribute to each dimension of commitment. For instance, personal connections are primarily a function of high levels of trust. And customers who are habitually satisfied with the brand's products will form functional connections.

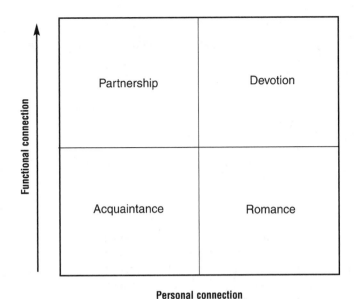

Figure 3 Relationship Types.

Interpersonal allegories illuminate the nature of customer-brand relationships. Figure 3 suggests four types—based on the relative strength of functional and personal connections.

- Customers with strong functionally specific relationships may view them as partnerships, formed to achieve discrete functional outcomes free of personal investment.
- Customers with solid personal and functional connections offer a company many benefits associated with interpersonal devotion, such as immunity against failure and partner generosity.
- Personally connected customers invest in more emotive bonds, seeking to reap relational benefits. These bonds are more elaborately formed and regretfully severed, like romance.

- Disconnected customers are in relationships akin to acquaintances, in which interaction and benefits are incidental and fluid.

These four customers behave differently toward the brand and promotional efforts. Combining the trust-based commitment model with an understanding of the different classes allows a brand to manage customer relationships, and assess the value of investments in relationship development.

Ultimately, this permits firms to design strategies for developing committed relationships, map their brands relative to competitors by relationship type, and anticipate customer response to product introductions and promotional efforts (theirs and their competitors'). Placing trust in the center of customer-brand relationships—and expanding their conceptualization to multiple dimensions—opens the door to a new era of understanding, managing, and profiting from them.

Additional Readings

Armstrong, G. and P. Kotler (2002), *Principles of Marketing,* 9th ed. Englewood Cliffs, N.J.: Prentice Hall.

Fournier, S. (1998), "Consumers and Their Brands: Developing Relationship Theory in Consumer Research," *Journal of Consumer Research,* 24 (March), 343–373.

Garbarino, E. and M. S. Johnson (1999), "The Different Roles of Satisfaction, Trust, and Commitment in Customer Relationships," *Journal of Marketing,* 63 (April), 70–87.

Hess, J. (1995), "Construction and Assessment of a Scale to Measure Consumer Trust," in *Proceedings of the American Marketing Association Educators' Conference,* eds. B.B. Stern et G.M. Zinkhan, 6 (Summer), 20–25.

Jeff Hess is vice president and senior methodologist at Harris Interactive in Rochester, N.Y. He may be reached at jhess@harrisinteractive.com.
John W. Story is assistant professor of marketing at Idaho State University in Pocatello. He may be reached at storjohn@isu.edu.

From *Marketing Management,* Vol. 14, no. 6, November/December 2005, pp. 43–48. Copyright © 2005 by American Marketing Association. Reprinted by permission.

Trust in the Marketplace

JOHN E. RICHARDSON AND LINNEA BERNARD McCORD

Traditionally, ethics is defined as a set of moral values or principles or a code of conduct.

. . . Ethics, as an expression of reality, is predicated upon the assumption that there are right and wrong motives, attitudes, traits of character, and actions that are exhibited in interpersonal relationships. Respectful social interaction is considered a norm by almost everyone.

. . . the overwhelming majority of people perceive others to be ethical when they observe what is considered to be their genuine kindness, consideration, politeness, empathy, and fairness in their interpersonal relationships. When these are absent, and unkindness, inconsideration, rudeness, hardness, and injustice are present, the people exhibiting such conduct are considered unethical. A genuine consideration of others is essential to an ethical life. (Chewning, pp. 175–176).

An essential concomitant of ethics is of trust. Webster's Dictionary defines trust as "assured reliance on the character, ability, strength or truth of someone or something." Businesses are built on a foundation of trust in our free-enterprise system. When there are violations of this trust between competitors, between employer and employees, or between businesses and consumers, our economic system ceases to run smoothly. From a moral viewpoint, ethical behavior should not exist because of economic pragmatism, governmental edict, or contemporary fashionability—it should exist because it is morally appropriate and right. From an economic point of view, ethical behavior should exist because it just makes good business sense to be ethical and operate in a manner that demonstrates trustworthiness.

Robert Bruce Shaw, in *Trust in the Balance,* makes some thoughtful observations about trust within an organization. Paraphrasing his observations and applying his ideas to the marketplace as a whole:

1. Trust requires consumers have confidence in organizational promises or claims made to them. This means that a consumer should be able to believe that a commitment made will be met.
2. Trust requires integrity and consistency in following a known set of values, beliefs, and practices.
3. Trust requires concern for the well-being of others. This does not mean that organizational needs are not given appropriate emphasis—but it suggests the importance of understanding the impact of decisions and actions on others—i.e. consumers. (Shaw, pp. 39–40)

Companies can lose the trust of their customers by portraying their products in a deceptive or inaccurate manner. In one recent example, a Nike advertisement exhorted golfers to buy the same golf balls used by Tiger Woods. However, since Tiger Woods was using custom-made Nike golf balls not yet available to the general golfing public, the ad was, in fact, deceptive. In one of its ads, Volvo represented that Volvo cars could withstand a physical impact that, in fact, was not possible. Once a company is "caught" giving inaccurate information, even if done innocently, trust in that company is eroded.

Companies can also lose the trust of their customers when they fail to act promptly and notify their customers of problems that the company has discovered, especially where deaths may be involved. This occurred when Chrysler dragged its feet in replacing a safety latch on its Minivan (Geyelin, pp. A1, A10). More recently, Firestone and Ford had been publicly brought to task for failing to expeditiously notify American consumers of tire defects in SUVs even though the problem had occurred years earlier in other countries. In cases like these, trust might not just be eroded, it might be destroyed. It could take years of painstaking effort to rebuild trust under these circumstances, and some companies might not have the economic ability to withstand such a rebuilding process with their consumers.

A *20/20* and *New York Times* investigation on a recent *ABC 20/20* program, entitled "The Car Dealer's Secret" revealed a sad example of the violation of trust in the marketplace. The investigation divulged that many unsuspecting consumers have had hidden charges tacked on by some car dealers when purchasing a new car. According to consumer attorney Gary Klein, "It's a dirty little secret that the auto lending industry has not owned up to." (*ABC News 20/20*)

The scheme worked in the following manner. Car dealers would send a prospective buyer's application to a number of lenders, who would report to the car dealer what interest rate the lender would give to the buyer for his or her car loan. This interest rate is referred to as the "buy rate." Legally a car dealer is not required to tell the buyer what the "buy rate" is or how much the dealer is marking up the loan. If dealers did most of the loans at the buy rate, they only get a small fee. However, if they were able to convince the buyer to pay a higher rate, they made considerably more money. Lenders encouraged car dealers to charge the buyer a higher rate than the "buy rate" by agreeing to split the extra income with the dealer.

David Robertson, head of the Association of Finance and Insurance Professionals—a trade group representing finance managers—defended the practice, reflecting that it was akin to a retail markup on loans. "The dealership provides a valuable service on behalf of the customer in negotiating these loans," he said. "Because of that, the dealership should be compensated for that work." (*ABC News 20/20*)

Careful examination of the entire report, however, makes one seriously question this apologetic. Even if this practice is deemed to be legal, the critical issue is what happens to trust when the buyers discover that they have been charged an additional 1–3% of the loan without their knowledge? In some cases, consumers were led to believe that they were getting the dealer's bank rate, and in other cases, they were told that the dealer had shopped around at several banks to secure the best loan rate they could get for the buyer. While this practice may be questionable from a legal standpoint, it is clearly in ethical breach of trust with the consumer. Once discovered, the companies doing this will have the same credibility and trustworthiness problems as the other examples mentioned above.

The untrustworthiness problems of the car companies was compounded by the fact that the investigation appeared to reveal statistics showing that black customers were twice as likely as whites to have their rate marked up—and at a higher level. That evidence—included in thousands of pages of confidential documents which *20/20* and *The New York Times* obtained from a Tennessee court—revealed that some Nissan and GM dealers in Tennessee routinely marked up rates for blacks, forcing them to pay between $300 and $400 more than whites. (*ABC News 20/20*)

This is a tragic example for everyone who was affected by this markup and was the victim of this secret policy. Not only is trust destroyed, there is a huge economic cost to the general public. It is estimated that in the last four years or so, Texas car dealers have received approximately $9 billion of kickbacks from lenders, affecting 5.2 million consumers. (*ABC News 20/20*)

Let's compare these unfortunate examples of untrustworthy corporate behavior with the landmark example of Johnson & Johnson which ultimately increased its trustworthiness with consumers by the way it handled the Tylenol incident. After seven individuals, who had consumed Tylenol capsules contaminated by a third party died, Johnson & Johnson instituted a total product recall within a week costing an estimated $50 million after taxes. The company did this, not because it was responsible for causing the problem, but because it was the right thing to do. In addition, Johnson & Johnson spearheaded the development of more effective tamper-proof containers for their industry. Because of the company's swift response, consumers once again were able to trust in the Johnson & Johnson name. Although Johnson & Johnson suffered a decrease in market share at the time because of the scare, over the long term it

has maintained its profitability in a highly competitive market. Certainly part of this profit success is attributable to consumers believing that Johnson & Johnson is a trustworthy company. (Robin and Reidenbach)

The e-commerce arena presents another example of the importance of marketers building a mutually valuable relationship with customers through a trust-based collaboration process. Recent research with 50 e-businesses reflects that companies which create and nurture trust find customers return to their sites repeatedly. (Dayal. . . . p. 64)

In the e-commerce world, six components of trust were found to be critical in developing trusting, satisfied customers:

- State-of-art reliable security measures on one's site
- Merchant legitimacy (e.g., ally one's product or service with an established brand)
- Order fulfillment (i.e. placing orders and getting merchandise efficiently and with minimal hassles)
- Tone and ambiance—handling consumers' personal information with sensitivity and iron-clad confidentiality
- Customers feeling that they are in control of the buying process
- Consumer collaboration—e.g., having chat groups to let consumers query each other about their purchases and experiences (Dayal. . . , pp. 64–67)

Additionally, one author noted recently that in the e-commerce world we've moved beyond brands and trademarks to "trustmarks." This author defined a trustmark as a

. . . (D)istinctive name or symbol that emotionally binds a company with the desires and aspirations of its customers. It's an emotional connection—and it's much bigger and more powerful than the uses that we traditionally associate with a trademark. . . . (Webber, p. 214)

Certainly if this is the case, trust—being an emotional link—is of supreme importance for a company that wants to succeed in doing business on the Internet.

It's unfortunate that while a plethora of examples of violation of trust easily come to mind, a paucity of examples "pop up" as noteworthy paradigms of organizational courage and trust in their relationship with consumers.

In conclusion, some key areas for companies to scrutinize and practice with regard to decisions that may affect trustworthiness in the marketplace might include:

- Does a company practice the Golden Rule with its customers? As a company insider, knowing what you know about the product, how willing would you be to purchase it for yourself or for a family member?
- How proud would you be if your marketing practices were made public. . . . shared with your friends. . . . or family? (Blanchard and Peale, p. 27)
- Are bottom-line concerns the sole component of your organizational decision-making process? What about human rights, the ecological/environmental impact, and other areas of social responsibility?

- Can a firm which engages in unethical business practices with customers be trusted to deal with its employees any differently? Unfortunately, frequently a willingness to violate standards of ethics is not an isolated phenomenon but permeates the culture. The result is erosion of integrity throughout a company. In such cases, trust is elusive at best. (Shaw, p. 75)
- Is your organization not only market driven, but also value-oriented? (Peters and Levering, Moskowitz, and Katz)
- Is there a strong commitment to a positive corporate culture and a clearly defined mission which is frequently and unambiguously voiced by upper-management?
- Does your organization exemplify trust by practicing a genuine relationship partnership with your customers—*before, during, and after* the initial purchase? (Strout, p. 69)

Companies which exemplify treating customers ethically are founded on a covenant of trust. There is a shared belief, confidence, and faith that the company and its people will be fair, reliable, and ethical in all its dealings. ***Total trust is the belief that a company and its people will never take opportunistic advantage of customer vulnerabilities.*** (Hart and Johnson, pp. 11–13)

References

ABC News 20/20, "The Car Dealer's Secret," October 27, 2000.

Blanchard, Kenneth, and Norman Vincent Peale, *The Power of Ethical Management,* New York: William Morrow and Company, Inc., 1988.

Chewning, Richard C., *Business Ethics in a Changing Culture* (Reston, Virginia: Reston Publishing, 1984).

Dayal, Sandeep, Landesberg, Helen, and Michael Zeissner, "How to Build Trust Online," *Marketing Management,* Fall 1999, pp. 64–69.

Geyelin, Milo, "Why One Jury Dealt a Big Blow to Chrysler in Minivan-Latch Case," *Wall Street Journal,* November 19, 1997, pp. A1, A10.

Hart, Christopher W. and Michael D. Johnson, "Growing the Trust Relationship," *Marketing Management,* Spring 1999, pp. 9–19.

Hosmer, La Rue Tone, *The Ethics of Management,* second edition (Homewood, Illinois: Irwin, 1991).

Kaydo, Chad, "A Position of Power," *Sales & Marketing Management,* June 2000, pp. 104–106, 108ff.

Levering, Robert; Moskowitz, Milton; and Michael Katz, *The 100 Best Companies to Work for in America* (Reading, Mass.: Addison-Wesley, 1984).

Magnet, Myron, "Meet the New Revolutionaries," *Fortune,* February 24, 1992, pp. 94–101.

Muoio, Anna, "The Experienced Customer," *Net Company,* Fall 1999, pp. 025–027.

Peters, Thomas J. and Robert H. Waterman Jr., *In Search of Excellence* (New York: Harper & Row, 1982).

Richardson, John (ed.), *Annual Editions: Business Ethics 00/01* (Guilford, CT: McGraw-Hill/Dushkin, 2000).

———, *Annual Editions: Marketing 00/01* (Guilford, CT: McGraw-Hill/Dushkin, 2000).

Robin, Donald P., and Erich Reidenbach, "Social Responsibility, Ethics, and Marketing Strategy: Closing the Gap Between Concept and Application," *Journal of Marketing,* Vol. 51 (January 1987), pp. 44–58.

Shaw, Robert Bruce, *Trust in the Balance,* (San Francisco: Jossey-Bass Publishers, 1997).

Strout, Erin, "Tough Customers," *Sales Marketing Management,* January 2000, pp. 63–69.

Webber, Alan M., "Trust in the Future," *Fast Company,* September 2000, pp. 209–212ff.

Dr. John E. Richardson is Professor of Marketing in the Graziadio School of Business and Management at Pepperdine University, Malibu, California. **Dr. Linnea Bernard McCord** is Associate Professor of Business Law in the Graziadio School of Business and Management at Pepperdine University, Malibu, California.

Wrestling with Ethics
Is Marketing Ethics an Oxymoron?

Every profession and business has to wrestle with ethical questions. The recent wave of business scandals over inaccurate reporting of sales and profits and excessive pay and privileges for top executives has brought questions of business ethics to the fore. And lawyers have been continuously accused of "ambulance chasing," jury manipulation, and inflated fees, leaving the plaintiffs with much less than called for in the judgment. Physicians have been known to recommend certain drugs as more effective while receiving support from pharmaceutical companies.

PHILIP KOTLER

Marketers are not immune from facing a whole set of ethical issues. For evidence, look to Howard Bowen's classic questions from his 1953 book, *Social Responsibilities of the Businessman:*

"Should he conduct selling in ways that intrude on the privacy of people, for example, by door-to-door selling? Should he use methods involving ballyhoo, chances, prizes, hawking, and other tactics which are at least of doubtful good taste? Should he employ 'high pressure' tactics in persuading people to buy? Should he try to hasten the obsolescence of goods by bringing out an endless succession of new models and new styles? Should he appeal to and attempt to strengthen the motives of materialism, invidious consumption, and keeping up with the Joneses?" (Also see Smith, N. Craig and Elizabeth Cooper-Martin (1997), "Ethics and Target Marketing: The Role of Product Harm and Consumer Vulnerability," *Journal of Marketing,* July, 1–20.)

The issues raised are complicated. Drawing a clear line between normal marketing practice and unethical behavior isn't easy. Yet it's important for marketing scholars and those interested in public policy to raise questions about practices that they may normally endorse but which may not coincide with the public interest.

We will examine the central axiom of marketing: Companies that satisfy their target customers will perform better than those that don't. Companies that satisfy customers can expect repeat business; those that don't will get only one-time sales. Steady profits come from holding onto customers, satisfying them, and selling them more goods and services.

This axiom is the essence of the well-known marketing concept. It reduces to the formula "Give the customer what he wants." This sounds reasonable on the surface. But notice that it carries an implied corollary: "Don't judge what the customer wants."

Marketers have been, or should be, a little uneasy about this corollary. It raises two public interest concerns: (1) What if the customer wants something that isn't good for him or her? (2) What if the product or service, while good for the customer, isn't good for society or other groups?

EXECUTIVE briefing
Marketers should be proud of their field. They have encouraged and promoted the development of many products and services that have benefited people worldwide. But this is all the more reason that they should carefully and thoughtfully consider where they stand on the ethical issues confronting them today and into the future. Marketers are able to take a stand and must make the effort to do so in order to help resolve these issues.

When it comes to the first question, what are some products that some customers desire that might not be good for them? These would be products that can potentially harm their health, safety, or well-being. Tobacco and hard drugs such as cocaine, LSD, or ecstasy immediately come to mind.

As for the second question, examples of products or services that some customers desire that may not be in the public's best interest include using asbestos as a building material or using lead paint indiscriminately. Other products and services where debates continue to rage as to whether they are in the public's interest include the right to own guns and other weapons, the right to have an abortion, the right to distribute hate literature, and the right to buy large gas guzzling and polluting automobiles.

We now turn to three questions of interest to marketers, businesses, and the public:

1. Given that expanding consumption is at the core of most businesses, what are the interests and behaviors of companies that make these products?
2. To what extent do these companies care about reducing the negative side effects of these products?
3. What steps can be taken to reduce the consumption of products that have questionable effects and is limited intervention warranted?

Expanding Consumption

Most companies will strive to enlarge their market as much as possible. A tobacco company, if unchecked, will try to get everyone who comes of age to start smoking cigarettes. Given that cigarettes are addictive, this promises the cigarette company "customers for life." Each new customer will create a 50-year profit stream for the cigarette company if the consumer continues to favor the same brand—and live long enough. Suppose a new smoker starts at the age of 13, smokes for 50 years, and dies at 63 from lung cancer. If he spends $500 a year on cigarettes, he will spend $25,000 over his lifetime. If the company's profit rate is 20%, that new customer is worth $5,000 to the company (undiscounted). It is hard to imagine a company that doesn't want to attract a customer who contributes $5,000 to its profits.

The same story describes the hard drug industry, whose products are addictive and even more expensive. The difference is that cigarette companies can operate legally but hard drug companies must operate illegally.

Other products, such as hamburgers, candy, soft drinks, and beer, are less harmful when consumed in moderation, but are addictive for some people. We hear a person saying she has a "sweet tooth." One person drinks three Coca-Colas a day, and another drinks five beers a day. Still another consumer is found who eats most of his meals at McDonald's. These are the "heavy users." Each company treasures the heavy users who account for a high proportion of the company's profits.

All said, every company has a natural drive to expand consumption of its products, leaving any negative consequences to be the result of the "free choice" of consumers. A high-level official working for Coca-Cola in Sweden said that her aim is to get people to start drinking Coca-Cola for breakfast (instead of orange juice). And McDonald's encourages customers to choose a larger hamburger, a larger order of French fries, and a larger cola drink. And these companies have some of the best marketers in the world working for them.

Reducing Side Effects

It would not be a natural act on the part of these companies to try to reduce or restrain consumption of their products. What company wants to reduce its profits? Usually some form of public pressure must bear on these companies before they will act.

The government has passed laws banning tobacco companies from advertising and glamorizing smoking on TV. But Philip Morris' Marlboro brand still will put out posters showing its mythical cowboy. And Marlboro will make sure that its name is mentioned in sports stadiums, art exhibits, and in labels for other products.

Tobacco companies today are treading carefully not to openly try to create smokers out of young people. They have stopped distributing free cigarettes to young people in the United States as they move their operations increasingly into China.

Beer companies have adopted a socially responsible attitude by telling people not to over-drink or drive during or after drinking. They cooperate with efforts to prevent underage people from buying beer. They are trying to behave in a socially responsible manner. They also know that, at the margin, the sales loss resulting from their "cooperation" is very slight.

McDonald's has struggled to find a way to reduce the ill effects (obesity, heart disease) of too much consumption of their products. It tried to offer a reduced-fat hamburger only to find consumers rejecting it. It has offered salads, but they weren't of good quality when originally introduced and they failed. Now it's making a second and better attempt.

Limited Intervention

Do public interest groups or the government have the right to intervene in the free choices of individuals? This question has been endlessly debated. On one side are people who resent any intervention in their choices of products and services. In the extreme, they go by such names as libertarians, vigilantes, and "freedom lovers." They have a legitimate concern about government power and its potential abuse. Some of their views include:

- The marketer's job is to "sell more stuff." It isn't the marketer's job to save the world or make society a better place.
- The marketer's job is to produce profits for the shareholders in any legally sanctioned way.
- A high-minded socially conscious person should not be in marketing. A company shouldn't hire such a person.

On the other side are people concerned with the personal and societal costs of "unregulated consumption." They are considered do-gooders and will document that Coca-Cola delivers six teaspoons of sugar in every bottle or can. They will cite statistics on the heavy health costs of obesity, heart disease, and liver damage that are caused by failing to reduce the consumption of some of these products. These costs fall on everyone through higher medical costs and taxes. Thus, those who don't consume questionable products are still harmed through the unenlightened behavior of others.

Ultimately, the problem is one of conflict among different ethical systems. Consider the following five:

Ethical Egoism

Your only obligation is to take care of yourself (Protagoras and Ayn Rand).

Government Requirements

The law represents the minimal moral standards of a society (Thomas Hobbes and John Locke).

Personal Virtues

Be honest, good, and caring (Plato and Aristotle).

Utilitarianism

Create the greatest good for the greatest number (Jeremy Bentham and John Stuart Mill).

Universal Rules

"Act only on that maxim through which you can at the same time will that it should become a universal law" (Immanuel Kant's categorical imperative).

Clearly, people embrace different ethical viewpoints, making marketing ethics and other business issues more complex to resolve.

> **Every company has a natural drive to expand consumption of its products, leaving any negative consequences to be the result of the "free choice" of consumers.**

Let's consider the last two ethical systems insofar as they imply that some interventions are warranted. Aside from the weak gestures of companies toward self-regulation and appearing concerned, there are a range of measures that can be taken by those wishing to push their view of the public interest. They include the following six approaches:

1. Encouraging these companies to make products safer. Many companies have responded to public concern or social pressure to make their products safer. Tobacco companies developed filters that would reduce the chance of contracting emphysema or lung cancer. If a leaf without nicotine could give smokers the same satisfaction, they would be happy to replace the tobacco leaf. Some tobacco companies have even offered information or aids to help smokers limit their appetite for tobacco or curb it entirely.

Food and soft drink companies have reformulated many of their products to be "light," "nonfat," or "low in calories." Some beer companies have introduced non-alcoholic beer. These companies still offer their standard products but provide concerned consumers with alternatives that present less risk to their weight or health.

Auto companies have reluctantly incorporated devices designed to reduce pollution output into their automobiles. Some are even producing cars with hybrid fuel systems to further reduce harmful emissions to the air. But the auto companies still insist on putting out larger automobiles (such as Hummers) because the "public demands them."

What can we suggest to Coca-Cola and other soft drink competitors that are already offering "light" versions of their drinks? First, they should focus more on developing the bottled water side of their businesses because bottled water is healthier than sugared soft drinks. Further, they should be encouraged to add nutrients and vitamins in standard drinks so these drinks can at least deliver more health benefits, especially to those in undeveloped countries who are deprived of these nutrients and vitamins. (Coca-Cola has some brands doing this now.)

What can we suggest to McDonald's and its fast food competitors? The basic suggestion is to offer more variety in its menu. McDonald's seems to forget that, while parents bring their children to McDonald's, they themselves usually prefer to eat healthier food, not to mention want their children eating healthier foods. How about a first-class salad bar? How about moving more into the healthy sandwich business? Today more Americans are buying their meals at Subway and other sandwich shops where they feel they are getting healthier and tastier food for their dollar.

There seems to be a correlation between the amount of charity given by companies in some categories and the category's degree of "sin." Thus, McDonald's knows that overconsumption of its products can be harmful, but the company is very charitable. A cynic would say that McDonald's wants to build a bank of public goodwill to diffuse potential public criticism.

2. Banning or restricting the sale or use of the product or service. A community or nation will ban certain products where there is strong public support. Hard drugs are banned, although there is some debate about whether the ban should include marijuana and lighter hard drugs. There are even advocates who oppose banning hard drugs, believing that the cost of policing and criminality far exceed the cost of a moderate increase that might take place in hard drug usage. Many people today believe that the "war on drugs" can never be won and is creating more serious consequences than simply dropping the ban or helping drug addicts, as Holland and Switzerland have done.

Some products carry restrictions on their purchase or use. This is particularly true of drugs that require a doctor's prescription and certain poisons that can't be purchased without authorization. Persons buying guns must be free of a criminal record and register their gun ownership. And certain types of guns, such as machine guns, are banned or restricted.

3. Banning or limiting advertising or promotion of the product. Even when a product isn't banned or its purchase restricted, laws may be passed to prevent producers from advertising or promoting the product. Gun, alcohol, and tobacco manufacturers can't advertise on TV, although they can advertise in print media such as magazines and newspapers. They can also inform and possibly promote their products online.

Manufacturers get around this by mentioning their brand name in every possible venue: sports stadiums, music concerts, and feature articles. They don't want to be forgotten in the face of a ban on promoting their products overtly.

4. Increasing "sin" taxes to discourage consumption. One reasonable alternative to banning a product or its promotion is to place a "sin" tax on its consumption. Thus, smokers pay hefty government taxes for cigarettes. This is supposed to have three effects when done right. First, the higher price should discourage consumption. Second, the tax revenue could be used to finance the social costs to health and safety caused by the consumption of the product. Third, some of the tax revenue could be used to counter-advertise the use of the product or support public education against its use. The last effect was enacted by California when it taxed tobacco companies and used the money to "unsell" tobacco smoking.

5. Public education campaigns. In the 1960s, Sweden developed a social policy to use public education to raise a nation of non-smokers and non-drinkers. Children from the first grade up were educated to understand the ill effects of tobacco and alcohol. Other countries are doing this on a less systematic and intensive basis. U.S. public schools devote parts of occasional courses to educate students against certain temptations with mixed success. Girls, not boys, in the United States seem to be more prone to taking up smoking. The reason often given by girls is that smoking curbs their appetite for food and consequently helps them avoid becoming overweight, a problem they consider more serious than lung cancer taking place 40 years later.

Sex education has become a controversial issue, when it comes to public education campaigns. The ultra-conservative camp wants to encourage total abstinence until marriage. The more liberal camp believes that students should be taught the risks of early sex and have the necessary knowledge to protect themselves. The effectiveness of both types of sex education is under debate.

6. Social marketing campaigns. These campaigns describe a wide variety of efforts to communicate the ill effects of certain behaviors that can harm the person, other persons, or society as a whole. These campaigns use techniques of public education, advertising and promotion, incentives, and channel development to make it as easy and attractive as possible for people to change their behavior for the better. (See Kotler, Philip, Eduardo Roberto, and Nancy Lee (2002), *Social Marketing: Improving the Quality of Life,* 2nd ed. London: Sage Publications.) Social marketing uses the tools of commercial marketing—segmentation, targeting, and positioning, and the four Ps (product, price, place, and promotion)—to achieve voluntary compliance with publicly endorsed goals. Some social marketing campaigns, such as family planning and anti-littering, have achieved moderate to high success. Other campaigns including anti-smoking, anti-drugs ("say no to drugs"), and seat belt promotion have worked well when supplemented with legal action.

Social Responsibility and Profits

Each year *Business Ethics* magazine publishes the 100 best American companies out of 1,000 evaluated. The publication examines the degree to which the companies serve seven stakeholder groups: shareholders, communities, minorities and women, employees, environment, non-U.S. stakeholders, and customers. Information is gathered on lawsuits, regulatory problems, pollution emissions, charitable contributions, staff diversity counts, union relations, employee benefits, and awards. Companies are removed from the list if there are significant scandals or improprieties. The research is done by Kinder, Lydenberg, Domini (KLD), an independent rating service. (For more details see the Spring 2003 issue of *Business Ethics*.)

The 20 best-rated companies in 2003 were (in order): General Mills, Cummins Engine, Intel, Procter & Gamble, IBM,

Hewlett-Packard, Avon Products, Green Mountain Coffee, John Nuveen Co., St. Paul Companies, AT&T, Fannie Mae, Bank of America, Motorola, Herman Miller, Expedia, Autodesk, Cisco Systems, Wild Oats Markets, and Deluxe.

The earmarks of a socially responsible company include:

- Living out a deep set of company values that drive company purpose, goals, strategies, and tactics
- Treating customers with fairness, openness, and quick response to inquiries and complaints
- Treating employees, suppliers, and distributors fairly
- Caring about the environmental impact of its activities and supply chain
- Behaving in a consistently ethical fashion

The intriguing question is whether socially responsible companies are more profitable. Unfortunately, different research studies have come up with different results. The correlations between financial performance (FP) and social performance (SP) are sometimes positive, sometimes negative, and sometimes neutral, depending on the study. Even when FP and SP are positively related, which causes which? The most probable finding is that high FP firms invest slack resources in SP and then discover the SP leads to better FP, in a virtuous circle. (See Waddock, Sandra A. and Samuel B. Graves (1997), "The Corporate Social Performance-Financial Performance Link," *Strategic Management Journal,* 18 (4), 303–319.)

Marketers' Responsibilities

As professional marketers, we are hired by some of the aforementioned companies to use our marketing toolkit to help them sell more of their products and services. Through our research, we can discover which consumer groups are the most susceptible to increasing their consumption. We can use the research to assemble the best 30-second TV commercials, print ads, and sales incentives to persuade them that these products will deliver great satisfaction. And we can create price discounts to tempt them to consume even more of the product than would normally be healthy or safe to consume.

But, as professional marketers, we should have the same ambivalence as nuclear scientists who help build nuclear bombs or pilots who spray DDT over crops from the airplane. Some of us, in fact, are independent enough to tell these clients that we will not work for them to find ways to sell more of what hurts people. We can tell them that we're willing to use our marketing toolkit to help them build new businesses around substitute products that are much healthier and safer.

But, even if these companies moved toward these healthier and safer products, they'll probably continue to push their current "cash cows." At that point, marketers will have to decide whether to work for these companies, help them reshape their offerings, avoid these companies altogether, or even work to oppose these company offerings.

Remember Marketing's Contributions

Nothing said here should detract from the major contributions that marketing has made to raise the material standards of living around the world. One doesn't want to go back to the kitchen where the housewife cooked five hours a day, washed dishes by hand, put fresh ice in the ice box, and washed and dried clothes in the open air. We value refrigerators, electric stoves, dishwashers, washing machines, and dryers. We value the invention and diffusion of the radio, the television set, the computer, the Internet, the cellular phone, the automobile, the movies, and even frozen food. Marketing has played a major role in their instigation and diffusion. Granted, any of these are capable of abuse (bad movies or TV shows), but they promise and deliver much that is good and valued in modern life.

Marketers have a right to be proud of their field. They search for unmet needs, encourage the development of products and services addressing these needs, manage communications to inform people of these products and services, arrange for easy accessibility and availability, and price the goods in a way that represents superior value delivered vis-à-vis competitors' offerings. This is the true work of marketing.

PHILIP KOTLER is S.C. Johnson and Son Distinguished Professor of International Marketing, Kellogg School of Management, Northwestern University. He may be reached at pkotler@nwu.edu.

Author's note—The author wishes to thank Professor Evert Gummesson of the School of Business, Stockholm University, for earlier discussion of these issues.

UNIT 2

Research, Markets, and Consumer Behavior

Unit Selections

Key Points to Consider

• As marketing research techniques become more and more advanced, and as psychographic analysis leads to more and more sophisticated models of consumer behavior, do you believe marketing will become more capable of predicting consumer behavior? Explain.

• Where the target population lives, its age, and its ethnicity are demographic factors of importance to marketers. What other demographic factors must be taken into account in long-range market planning?

• Psychographic segmentation is the process whereby consumer markets are divided up into segments based upon similarities in lifestyles, attitudes, personality type, social class, and buying behavior. In what specific ways do you envision psychographic research and findings helping marketing planning and strategy in the next decade?

Student Web Site
www.mhcls.com

Internet References

Canadian Innovation Centre
(http://www.innovationcentre.ca/)
BizMiner—Industry Analysis and Trends
(http://www.bizminer.com/market_research.asp)
Small Business Center—Articles & Insights
(http://www.bcentral.com/articles/krotz/123.asp)
Maritz Marketing Research
(http://www.maritzresearch.com)
USADATA
(http://www.usadata.com)
WWW Virtual Library: Demography & Population Studies
(http://demography.anu.edu.au/VirtualLibrary/)

If marketing activities were all we knew about an individual, we would know a great deal. By tracing these daily activities over only a short period of time, we could probably guess rather accurately that person's tastes, understand much of his or her system of personal values, and learn quite a bit about how he or she deals with the world.

In a sense, this is a key to successful marketing management: tracing a market's activities and understanding its behavior. However, in spite of the increasing sophistication of market research techniques, this task is not easy. Today a new society is evolving out of the changing lifestyles of Americans, and these divergent lifestyles have put great pressure on the marketer who hopes to identify and profitably reach a target market. At the same time, however, each change in consumer behavior leads to new marketing opportunities.

The writings in this unit were selected to provide information and insight into the effect that lifestyle changes and demographic trends are having on American industry.

The first article in the *Marketing Research* subsection describes how as more companies are refocusing more squarely on the consumer, ethnography and its proponents have become star players. The second article provides eight tips outlining the best practices for conducting surveys via the Internet. The third article furnishes insight on how new technology is ideal for capitalizing on the consistent accuracy of a household-level segmentation system. The last article in this subsection, "A Clean Slate," presents a case reflecting how marketing research helped WD-40 fill in gaps in its product line.

The articles in the *Markets and Demographics* subsection examine the importance of demographic and psychographic data, economic forces, and age considerations in making marketing decisions.

The articles in the final subsection, *Consumer Behavior,* analyze how consumer behavior, social attitudes, cues, and quality considerations all have an impact on the evaluation and purchase of various products and services for different consumers.

The Science of Desire

As more companies refocus squarely on the consumer, ethnography and its proponents have become star players.

SPENCER E. ANTE

The satellite-radio war can't be won by Howard Stern alone. So shortly after signing the shock jock to a $500 million contract in 2004, Sirius Satellite Radio called on a small Portland (Ore.) consulting firm to envision a device that would help it catch up with bigger rival XM Satellite Radio Holdings. Ziba Design dispatched a team of social scientists, designers, and ethnographers on a road trip to Nashville and Boston. For four weeks they shadowed 45 people, studying how they listen to music, watch TV, and even peruse gossip magazines. Their conclusion: A portable satellite-radio player that was easy to use and load with music for later playback could be a killer app in the competition against XM.

Last November, Sirius began selling the Sirius S50, a device the size of a slim cigarette pack that stores up to 50 hours of digital music and commentary. It features a color screen and handy buttons that let you easily pick your favorite song to listen to. Slip it into a docking station and it automatically gathers and refreshes programming from your favorite Sirius channels. Techies praised the device, declaring it better than XM's competing player, the MyFi, launched in October, 2004. The S50 became one of the holiday season's hottest sellers. Sirius says it has helped the company sign up more subscribers than XM has since last fall. "[Ziba's] research capabilities and innovative approach to design concepts were most impressive," says Sirius President James E. Meyer.

A portable satellite radio from Sirius. Hipper, more user-friendly lobbies at hotels owned by Marriott International Inc. A cheap PC from Intel Corp. designed to run in rural Indian villages on a truck battery in 113-degree temperatures. All these brainstorms happened with the guidance of ethnographers, a species of anthropologist who can, among other things, identify what's missing in people's lives—the perfect cell phone, home appliance, or piece of furniture—and work with designers and engineers to help dream up products and services to fill those needs.

Companies have been harnessing the social sciences, including ethnography, since the 1930s. Back then executives were mostly interested in figuring out how to make their employees more productive. But since the 1960s, when management gurus crowned the consumer king, companies have been tapping ethnographers to get a better handle on their customers. Now, as more and more businesses re-orient themselves to serve the consumer, ethnography has entered prime time.

The beauty of ethnography, say its proponents, is that it provides a richer understanding of consumers than does traditional research. Yes, companies are still using focus groups, surveys, and demographic data to glean insights into the consumer's mind. But closely observing people where they live and work, say executives, allows companies to zero in on their customers' unarticulated desires. "It used be that design features were tacked on to the end of a marketing strategy," says Timothy deWaal Malefyt, an anthropologist who runs "cultural discovery" at ad firm BBDO Worldwide. "Now what differentiates products has to be baked in from the beginning. This makes anthropology far more valuable."

Ethnography's rising prominence is creating unlikely stars within companies in retailing, manufacturing, and financial services, as well as at consulting firms such as IDEO, Jump Associates, and Doblin Group. Three years ago, IBM's research group had a handful of anthropologists on staff. Today it has a dozen. Furniture maker Steelcase Inc. relies heavily on in-house ethnographers to devise new products. Intel, in the midst of a wrenching transition from chipmaker to consumer-products company, has moved several of its senior social scientists out of the research lab and into leadership positions. "Technology is increasingly being designed from the outside in, putting the needs of people first and foremost," says Intel CEO Paul S. Otellini. "Intel's researchers are giving our designers a deeper understanding of what real people want to do with computers."

With more companies putting ethnographers front and center, schools around the country are ramping up social science programs or steering anthropology students toward jobs in the corporate world. In recent years, New York's Parsons School for Design and Illinois Institute of Technology's Institute of Design have put anthropologists on the faculty. Ditto for many business

Ethnography: Do It Right . . .

Anthropological research can be a potent tool—or a waste of time and money. Here's how to get the most bang for your buck:

Think Big Thoughts

Ethnography is **most effective when it's used to spot breakthrough innovations.** Don't use it for incremental improvements or to solve small problems. Ethnography works best when the questions are big and broad. "The good time to use it is with futuristic research," says Natalie Hanson, SAP's director for business operations.

Due Diligence

Many companies do not have the resources to hire their own anthropologists or social scientists. So **picking the right consultants can make or break a project.** With many poseurs jumping on the bandwagon, it's important to hire a firm with a track record, client references, and a staff with a mix of skills in social science, design, and business.

Start Early

Using ethnography at the beginning of the product development process is key because **it helps identify consumers' unmet needs.** It's those findings that can inspire a hit product or service. One danger of waiting too long to bring in social scientists is that you might end up with "feature creep," simply adding unnecessary bells and whistles.

Sell, Sell, Sell

Let's face it: Many executives think ethnography is bunk. So **managers must constantly educate others about its value.** Be clear that ethnography is not a cure-all but can spark innovation. "To get people to think about a softer approach is a challenge," says GE's marketing operations manager, Dominic McMahon.

Build a Culture

Organizations that have used ethnography to the greatest effect have usually made such research an integral part of their culture. "I don't believe it is one person's job to figure out user problems," says Alex Lee, president of OXO, a long-time user of ethnography. "What's important is the mindset of the people. Ideas come from every which way."

. . . and Reap the Rewards

Motorola A732

After observing how popular Chinese-character text messaging was in Shanghai, Motorola researchers developed a cell phone that lets you send messages by writing directly on the keypad using your finger.

TownePlace Suites

A team of ethnographers and designers from IDEO found that TownePlace guests often turn their bedrooms into work spaces. So it came up with a flexible modular wall unit where there had been only a dining table. Guests can use the unit either as an office or a place to eat.

OXO Hammer

To develop a line of professional-grade tools for consumers, OXO and Smart Design visited contractors and home renovators. One result: A hammer with a fiberglass core to cut vibration and a rubber bumper on top to avoid leaving marks when removing nails.

Citigroup PayPass

Citigroup teamed up with Doblin Group to brainstorm new payment services for consumers. This summer, Citi will launch a pilot project called PayPass that lets New York City subway riders pay with a special key chain tag that debits their checking accounts.

Sirius S50

Sirius and Ziba Design studied how people listen to music, read magazines, and watch TV. That led them to develop a portable satellite-radio player that is easily loaded with up to 50 hours of digital music for later playback.

---

schools. And going to work for The Man is no longer considered selling out. Says Marietta L. Baba, Michigan State University's dean of social sciences: "Ethnography [has] escaped from academia, where it had been held hostage."

Up Close and Personal

We know what you're thinking: Corporate ethnography can sound a little flaky. And a certain amount of skepticism is in order whenever consultants hype trendy new ways to reach the masses. Ethnographers' findings often don't lead to a product or service, only a generalized sense of what people want. Their research can also take a long time to bear fruit. Intel's India Community PC emerged only after ethnographer Tony Salvador spent two years traipsing around the developing world, including a memorable evening in the Ecuadorean Andes when the town healer conducted a ceremony that included spitting the local hooch on him.

Practitioners caution that all the attention ethnography is getting could lead to a backlash. Many ethnographers already complain about poseurs flooding the field. Others gripe that corporations are hiring anthropologists to rubber-stamp bone-headed business plans. Norman Stolzoff, founder of Ethnographic Insight Inc., a Bellingham (Wash.) consulting firm, says he has worked with several companies that insist on changing the line of questioning when they're not getting the answers

Eric Dishman

Title
General Manager & Global Director, Intel Health Research & Innovation Group

Education
Masters in communications from Southern Illinois University; PhD candidate in anthropology, University of Utah

Research
Dishman and his team are working with medical and engineering schools to help discover new technologies to improve health care for seniors. One innovation: A special PC that flashes the photo of a person calling, along with personal details, to help Alzheimer's sufferers remember whom they're talking to.

Jane Fulton Suri

Title
IDEO's Director for Human Factors Design & Research

Education
Masters in architecture from the University of Strathclyde, Glasgow

Research
Her 40 researchers help the likes of Procter & Gamble and Marriott detect unmet consumer needs and divine products to serve them. Suri's team came up with the idea for P&G's Magic Reach tool after watching people struggle to clean their bathrooms. The device's long handle and swivel head gets into those hard-to-reach places.

they need to justify a decision. "There's a lot of pressure to ratify decisions that are already being made," says Stolzoff, who holds a PhD from the University of California at Davis in cultural anthropology.

TRUE, ethnography can sound a bit flaky and take a while to bear fruit. But one B-school dean says "it could become a core competence" for executives.

Still, in an accelerated global society where consumers are inundated with choices, markets are sliced into ever-thinner pieces, product cycles are measured not in years but in months or weeks, and new ideas zip around the planet at the speed of light, getting up close and personal with Joe and Jane Consumer is increasingly important. Ethnography may be no silver bullet, says Roger Martin, dean of the University of Toronto's Rotman School of Business, but "it could become a core competence" in the executive tool kit. Here are three case studies that demonstrate how businesses are using it to spark innovation:

Refreshing a Product

While many companies embrace ethnography to create something new, others are using it to revitalize an existing product or service. In 2004, Marriott hired IDEO Inc. to rethink the hotel experience for an increasingly important customer: the young, tech-savvy road warrior. "This is all about looking freshly at business travel and how people behave and what they need," explains Michael E. Jannini, Marriott's executive vice-president for brand management.

To better understand Marriott's customers, IDEO dispatched a team of seven consultants, including a designer, anthropologist, writer, and architect, on a six-week trip. Covering 12 cities, the group hung out in hotel lobbies, cafés, and bars, and asked guests to graph what they were doing hour by hour.

What they learned: Hotels are generally good at serving large parties but not small groups of business travelers. Researchers noted that hotel lobbies tend to be dark and better suited to killing time than conducting casual business. Marriott lacked places where guests could comfortably combine work with pleasure outside their rooms. IDEO consultant and Marriott project manager Dana Cho recalls watching a female business traveler drinking wine in the lobby while trying not to spill it on papers spread out on a desk. "There are very few hotel services that address [such] problems," says Cho.

Having studied IDEO's findings, Marriott in January announced plans to reinvent the lobbies of its Marriott and Renaissance Hotels, creating for each a social zone, with small tables, brighter lights, and wireless Web access, that is better suited to meetings. Another area will allow solo travelers to work or unwind in larger, quiet, semiprivate spaces where they won't have to worry about spilling coffee on their laptops or papers. Guests would also like the option of checking themselves in, so Marriott is considering a new kiosk where they can swipe a credit card to do just that. Says Jannini: "We wanted something new but not gimmicky."

Cracking Markets

Breaking into a new market is a classic path to growth. But how do you infiltrate an industry about which you know next to nothing? For General Electric Co., ethnography was the answer. GE was already selling plastic materials to makers of cell phones and car parts. But executives wanted to get into the plastic-fiber business, which provides material for higher-value, higher-margin products such as fire-retardant jackets and bulletproof vests. So two years ago, GE Plastics Marketing Operations Manager Dominic McMahon hired Jump Associates. Says

McMahon: "We couldn't go to someone in the fiber world and say: 'Please tell us how to take your business."

In fact, it took many months to persuade a few manufacturers to participate in the study. They cooperated only because they figured GE would someday provide them with materials that would help their businesses. "The idea that GE could become a supplier to the industry was hugely exciting," says Jump researcher Lauren Osofsky. Customers refused to be videotaped, but they agreed to be tape-recorded. For a few months, GE execs and researchers from Jump interviewed presidents, managers, and engineers at textile makers, touring their offices and photographing their plants. An engineer told Jump he pulled off the highway one day to collect a bunch of milkweed so he could take it home and run it through a fiber-processing machine he keeps in his garage just to see what would happen. "It told us these people like to get their hands dirty," says Osofsky.

The yearlong study produced one profound insight that led GE to pull a strategic U-turn. GE thought the fibers industry was a commodity business focused on quickly obtaining the cheapest materials. What it found instead was an artisanal industry with customers who want to collaborate from the earliest stages to develop high-performance materials. As a result, GE now shares prototypes with customers. And instead of currying favor with executives, it works closely with engineers to solve technical problems. "That was a breakthrough and a huge opportunity," says McMahon. Before, GE was having a hard time even getting meetings. Now, says McMahon, "we were suddenly welcomed wherever we went."

> **GE discovered it was approaching its bid to break into the fibers biz all wrong: Instead of cheap commodities, customers want help developing advanced materials.**

Transforming a Culture

For big corporations that don't market directly to consumers, ethnography has a singular appeal. This is especially true of Intel, which is facing tough competition from rival Advanced Micro Devices Inc. and believes it badly needs to branch out beyond its core chipmaking business. Since taking over a year ago, CEO Otellini has started to turn Intel into a company that is much more focused on consumer products: entertainment systems for the home; handheld computers for doctors; cheap, rugged PCs for emerging markets. Getting those gadgets right, Intel has concluded, requires closer relationships with customers. That means bringing in ethnographers at the highest levels of management.

> **INTEL has an ethnographer heading research for its new emerging-markets unit, with development centers in Bangalore, Cairo, São Paulo, and Shanghai.**

Intel has used them since the early 1990s. But it wasn't until the late '90s that their work began to influence the company's direction. One of the first breakthroughs came in 1997 when two Intel anthropologists, Tony Salvador and John Sherry, launched a project called "Anywhere at Work." The study took them to Alaska's Bristol Bay, where they realized that fishermen could use wireless technology to transmit the tally of their daily catch directly to the Alaska Fish & Game Dept. That observation, and others like it, helped persuade Intel to put its brainpower behind mobile computing and, eventually, into its popular wireless Centrino mobile technology.

Now, Salvador & Co. are studying the elderly to see how Intel can provide medical technology for the coming wave of retiring boomers, including a device to track and help ensure that patients take their meds. And, of course, Intel ethnographers helped devise the $500 Community India PC, which could turn into a big seller as hundreds of millions of rural Indians access the Web.

J. Wilton L. Agatstein Jr., who runs Intel's new emerging-markets unit, knows it's crucial to figure out the unique needs and aspirations of different cultures. That's why he hired Salvador to head research for the whole group. The pair have created a network of "platform-definition centers" in Bangalore, Cairo, São Paulo, and Shanghai. Agatstein describes the facilities— staffed by local engineers, designers, and marketers—as highly tuned antennae to help define and develop products for local markets. Agatstein is such a fervent believer in ethnography that he often tags along with Salvador on field trips: "He has taught me to look in ways I've never looked before."

Timothy deWaal Malefyt

Title
BBDO's Director for Cultural Discovery

Education
PhD in anthropology from Brown University

Research
Drawing on a network of anthropologists, Malefyt discovered that teens use e-mail for serious communication, instant messaging for informal chats, and text messaging to reach people they don't want to talk to. BBDO is talking with Frito-Lay and Campbell Soup about using this research to help them craft new marketing campaigns.

Not everyone at Intel shares their enthusiasm. This, after all, is a company that was founded and long run by data-driven engineers. Recently, Genevieve Bell, an ethnographer at Intel's Digital Home unit, asked engineers to identify experiences to categorize various technologies. Movies, music, and games were placed under the Escape rubric. Health and wellness were put in the Life & Spirituality basket.

The exercise elicited grumbles from a few Intel traditionalists. Says division chief Don McDonald: "We've had people say: 'Life and spirituality? What the !@#& are you talking about?'" But with anthropologists in ascendance, engineers—and everyone else—had better get used to it.

With Cliff Edwards, San Mateo, Calif.

Eight Tips Offer Best Practices for Online MR

RICHARD KOTTLER

"You don't need a weatherman to know which way the wind blows."—Bob Dylan, 1965

Four decades ago, Bob Dylan's lyric was a call for dynamic individual thought. Today, it can be interpreted more literally: You really don't need a weatherman, you just need a Web browser. As we progress through the second decade of the Internet Age, the sheer ubiquity of the Internet as a consumer and business communications medium is absolute, and it is providing a dynamic means to get visibility into your customers' often-changing thoughts.

It has also altered the way we market and are marketed to, primarily by providing that same ubiquitous access to information and communication for marketers. In 2005, companies will spend more than $1.1 billion on online market research, a 16% increase over 2004, according to *Inside Research.*

The advantages of online research are self-evident: There's no need for data entry or interviews, and responses are collected automatically, saving time and money while eliminating coding errors and interviewer bias. Also, respondents may feel more comfortable in answering sensitive questions with their anonymity ensured.

With the increasing prevalence of online research, a handful of tips can begin to outline the best practices for maximizing the efficacy of conducting surveys via the Internet. Some of the tips outlined in this article, such as suggestions on planning, are equally relevant to offline and online research. Others are specific to the online realm.

No. 1: Planning—Real-World Common Sense for the Online Realm

If you are planning an online survey, do you know why you and your organization want to conduct it? If so, use these reasons to develop your survey's mission. Once developed, the mission should drive everything throughout the survey process to make sure that every action taken supports it. If you're uncertain as to why you are conducting your survey, or if your answer is, "We do it every year," dig deeper for the real reason before you

begin plotting steps toward implementation. Once your survey is drafted, test it on a sample audience and include questions that elicit feedback on how the survey can be improved before it is put into play. And make certain your sample size maps to your budget and time constraints and the type of analysis to be conducted.

No. 2: Understand Your Population

Clearly, the population influences the entire research process— methodology, layout, content, incentives; everything is driven by their influence. The inability to properly define your population has serious ramifications.

If you're uncertain as to why you are conducting your survey, dig deeper for the real reason before plotting steps toward implementation.

No. 3: Use the Correct Medium to Contact Participants

Researchers can use a variety of media to invite participants to take part in online surveys, such as e-mail, Web links and pop-ups:

- E-mail notifications work best for a well-defined audience, and a well-written missive provides a cost-effective means of reaching existing customers and prospects.
- Web links provide an easy means to elicit general feedback from Web site visitors. However, it is more difficult to target particular respondent profiles using Web links.
- Pop-ups have fallen out of favor, particularly as federal and state legislation are limiting such windows when they are triggered by adware and spyware. Broad consumer dissatisfaction, coupled with free blockers from

online properties such as Google and Yahoo!, has led to a veritable pop-up rebellion.

No. 4: Keep It Simple

Creating a short survey to answer a few questions is easy . . . and it's easy to create a long survey to answer many questions. The challenge is finding the balance between survey length and depth of questions and answers. The holy grail is the short survey that's long on answers. Here are some tips to make that happen:

- Keep questions and answer lists short and to the point.
- Use pre-existing questions when possible (the tried and true).
- Avoid using double negatives.
- Avoid double-barreled questions.
- Avoid leading questions.
- Avoid using loaded questions.
- Avoid vague quantifiers such as "few," "many" or "usually."
- Don't assume knowledge about specific topics or issues.
- Consider the location of open-ended questions.
- Remember the audience for each particular question, not just the overall survey.
- Always offer a "prefer not to answer" on sensitive questions and topics.
- Pretest whenever possible.
- Get feedback early in the process.

No. 5: Set Expectations—Then Reset Them

The top two respondents' questions are "How long will this take?" and "What will I get for doing this?" We'll answer the first question here and the second in No. 8.

- Briefly state the purpose of the survey and how long it should take to complete.
- Make sure the length of the survey is appropriate for your audience and purpose.
- Let your respondents know their progress throughout the survey using a bar or percentage section.

No. 6: Utilize the Power of Open-Ended Questions

Traditionally, researchers think of closed-ended questions when drafting a survey, meaning you provide response choices for participants. Traditionally, they provide two major benefits: They're easy for respondents to answer, and they're easier for surveyors to tabulate. However, they do limit the breadth of responses to predefined answers.

Now, new text mining technologies are emerging that make it possible to harvest data and knowledge from open-ended questions by exploring a greater breadth of respondent attitudes and preferences.

There are two types of open-ended questions: those with a predetermined set of answers and those with a nearly infinite range of potential answers. For example, "Which soft drinks have you enjoyed in the past month?" allows the respondent to answer the question without supplying a list, yet there are only a certain number of beverages on the market. However, "Are there additional features you'd like to see in our products?" will generate comments that are not as quickly classified as a simple list might be. However, it may uncover views or preferences that were heretofore unimagined.

Place open-ended questions at the end, as it gives you greater flexibility and more room to record verbatim responses. At the same time, be certain not to overuse open-ended questions. They do take more thought and time from the respondent and a slew of early open-ended questions may cause your respondent to quit.

No. 7: Monitor the Field

Be prepared to make changes, if necessary. Monitor for the following:

- If the completion rate is low, why?
- Is there a pattern to respondent dropout?
- Have the respondents been appropriately screened?
- If the survey is media-intensive, have you screened for connection speed?
- Is the survey taking longer than stated?

Offer respondents a chance to rate their survey experience in a closed- and open-ended question.

No. 8: Make It Worth Their While

Offering an incentive helps motivate people to take part in your survey. When choosing incentives, though, think about how these might influence the types of participants they could attract, or ultimately, deter. No one wants a cadre of survey respondents who are the online equivalent of the trade show swindlers who load up on shopping bags full of free vendor T-shirts, pins and hats, with no intention of becoming a customer any time soon. At the same time, it's important to match the relative value of an incentive to the effort required to complete the survey.

With the Internet, time is on your side. Data from a Web survey can be collected in a few days or a few weeks, while a survey via the mail adds at least a month to the process. By using online surveys, you'll save on postage, printing and wages for interviewers, and minimize the costs of data entry and data cleansing.

Ultimately, the Internet, if used properly, can provide the quickest path to valuable insight into your customers' minds.

RICHARD KOTTLER, based in the London office, is vice president of survey applications product management for SPSS Inc., a Chicago-based data analysis software provider.

Consumers on the Move

*Improved Technology Should Help Marketers
Reach Prospects—Wherever They May Be*

Josh Herman

The *good* news is you've got lots of customer data! The *bad* news is you've got lots of customer data! How can the promise of true integrated marketing be possible in that sea of disparate details? And how can you quickly tease meaningful information from it that will make a tangible impact on your company's bottom line?

One of the most effective ways to demonstrate the value of your database investment is to ensure it can answer core marketing questions, such as:

- *Who* buys from me?
- *What* are they going to buy from me?
- *Where* can I find them geographically?
- *How* can I best communicate with them?

Answering these questions is possible only if you have a consistent framework to define and describe each customer or prospect. A segmentation system allows you to identify opportunities and take marketing action. And advances in database technology are allowing us to go beyond "who, what, where and how" and add two new questions: "when" and "on which screen."

Where We Started

The most common approaches to segmenting a customer database are through demographics, buying behaviors or geography. More than a quarter century ago, Jonathan Robbin helped create the first geodemographic segmentation system called Prizm (Potential Ratings in ZIP Markets), a marketing database that combined geographic and demographic characteristics of neighborhoods. By analyzing the aggregated 1970 decennial census data, Robbin was able to differentiate and describe each census neighborhood in the United States. A sociologist, he uncovered the correlation between a neighborhood's demographic characteristics and the likely consumer behaviors of those who lived there.

But where did this intersect with marketing decisions? Each neighborhood could be labeled with a geodemographic segment code and every record on a customer database could be tagged with segment codes. This allowed marketers to calculate the kinds of neighborhoods likely to have a concentration of a company's best prospects.

And that's how we lived for most of a quarter century, with that static snapshot taken from area-level, decennial census data. But in the last few years there have been dramatic changes in marketers' data and targeting choices.

What's Changed

Advances in computing technology, data quality and statistical techniques have allowed us to break the yoke of the once-every-10-years census data and deploy segmentation systems using household-level data. Now, instead of being able to differentiate between whole neighborhoods, marketers can differentiate between next-door neighbors. This is significant if you consider the average number of households in a census block group is 600. Rather than papering the entire neighborhood with your marketing message, now you can select the specific households most likely to respond to your offer.

> **New technology in addressable advertising across 'all three screens'—computer, cable television and wireless—is terrific for capitalizing on the consistent accuracy of a household-level segmentation system.**

The overall effect is to dramatically improve targeting power. Core demographics like age, marital status, income, kids and net worth still play a powerful role, but now it's with household-level accuracy covering some 120 million U.S. households. And the old mythology of poor household data has dissolved with routine household-level match rates consistently in the 90% range, *plus* the ability to code tens of millions of records in just hours.

The framework for a segmentation system also had to change. Instead of simply finding differences between neighborhoods, the "life stage" concept is most meaningful when differentiating consumer behaviors, media preferences and lifestyles among next door neighbors. It's as intuitive as it is practical.

Moving from that old, static snapshot to the reality of a changing, dynamic marketplace is where the advantages of a household system come into play. Most compelling is that the segment codes for each household can be updated every time the household database is updated—approximately once a month, not once a year. This allows marketers to identify when a household migrates from one life-stage cluster to another.

When life-stage changes happen, previous attachments to purchasing behaviors, media preferences and lifestyles destabilize. Consumers are then open to trying new brands and products through new channels. This is a great opportunity for marketers that want to add the "when" to their targeting strategy. For example, when consumers have babies they're suddenly acutely aware of where the diaper aisle is in the supermarket. And they're more likely to stay at home watching "America's Funniest Home Videos" on a Friday evening rather than go out nightclubbing.

Life-stage migrations, from getting your first apartment to retirement, have a dramatic impact on our consumer behaviors and media preferences. If 90,000 households just moved into your most profitable life-stage segment this month, you want to talk to them before the competition does.

Even syndicated survey data like MRI or IRI works better because the surveys are coded at the household level. Maps can be articulated with the latitude/longitude accuracy of dot-density maps to indicate where the target households are—a huge improvement over ordinary thematic maps and their blankets of color. So now marketers have a consistent framework with which to view their customer and prospect universe.

Looking to the Future

As new media channels proliferate and mature, marketers must strike a balance between their choice of targeted households and the media selected to reach those prospects. New technology in addressable advertising across "all three screens"—computer, cable television and wireless—is terrific for capitalizing on the consistent accuracy of a household-level segmentation system. It's the computer screen where the "geo" is really becoming less central to targeting since information can be found anywhere and at any time. Let's take a look at each screen's targeting capabilities.

- *Computer:* For lack of a better term, "PersonicX®" cookies" are the next step for boosting the effectiveness of online ad targeting. Right now most online advertising is done in an untargeted "spray and pray" style. But with a cookie tied to a household segmentation system, both the advertiser and Web site publisher can dramatically improve targeting and site performance.

- For example, when a computer with a PersonicX cookie indicates the user is from a particular household cluster, the Web publisher will know how to improve users' site experience with targeted content for households in that cluster. This will improve the quality of ad delivery and allow a sponsor to buy X number of impressions in that cluster.

- *Cable television.* After years of talk, addressable advertising over cable TV is ready to take its first real steps. But while the plumbing may be in place, the work of deciding which ad goes through which pipe still needs to be done thoughtfully. This is changing television into a real direct marketing vehicle—one requiring the same targeting expertise as traditional DM channels.

- Consider the power of using the same consistent household-level segmentation framework online and off, and with "directcast" TV (as opposed to broadcast). And, in the same way advertisers can pay for and measure reaching 2 million households in a given cluster online, they will he able to make similar targeted media buys via cable TV.

- *Wireless.* The "third screen" offers DMers the same opportunity to know a subscriber's consumer life-stage segment and to deliver targeted content whenever and wherever that person happens to be. The geographic independence of today's mobile consumer renders the traditional "You are where you live" approach of classic geodemographic systems more or less irrelevant. Not only will we marketers need to know the predictive and descriptive characteristics of the mobile subscriber looking for information about our products, we'll have to provide meaningful information that's applicable to where they are at any given moment.

A lot has changed in the science and art of consumer segmentation in recent years. Improvements in the power and cost of computer technology, data quality and statistical techniques have provided DMers some powerful new tools. The opportunity to achieve true integrated marketing across all channels puts more control into marketers' hands than ever before. These are exciting times indeed.

JOSH HERMAN (Joshua.Herman@acxiom.com) is data product innovation leader at Acxiom Corp. in Little Rock, AR.

A Clean Slate

Open-ended qualitative, quantitative research helped WD-40 fill in gaps in product line.

MICHAEL FIELDING

While the company is largely noted for its well-known line of household lubricants, San Diego-based WD-40 Co. has repositioned one of its product lines as essential bathroom cleaners—the result of a research process whose goal was deliberately left open-ended.

While sales of the company's six household product brands (of which X-14 is one) make up a sizable percentage—more than 31%—of the overall portfolio, according to the company's 2006 annual report, the X-14 packaging belied a reputable brand in its lack of cohesiveness in design and positioning. Marketed as individual items, rather than as a family of products, it was overshadowed on the retail store shelves by more popular rival brands. "Something had to happen with the packaging, and we needed to figure out how to tell consumers about the products, (and) improve how we were talking about them," says Heidi Noorany, director of marketing.

While the X-14 line is not new, its repositioning helped the $287 million company find the brand's niche. "We previously had products that focused on the bathroom, but there wasn't a unified line in its positioning. We had a line of cleaning products that were not meeting their potential in the marketplace," Noorany says of the desire to re-examine the brand.

Research studies typically have specific goals, but the company began this project by trying to understand how consumers clean and how they shop. In January 2006, the team set out to analyze the market—and more than 3,400 consumers through quantitative research and about 100 through qualitative research—and see where the research took them.

Several phases of both qualitative and quantitative research helped: Noorany did qualitative research that used in-home ethnographies and focus groups to understand consumer cleaning habits and product usage, and quantitative research into positioning of the brand, bottle structure, label graphics and packaging claims. All research was conducted among the general population, not just X-14 users. Additional qualitative research followed with blind products (not branded) in home-use tests, as well as in-lab scientific studies of product effectiveness.

The team concluded that there was a need for a "bathroom expert" line of products. "We knew we had the positioning and the quality of products within the current line, but we had to communicate it," Noorany adds. That would be translated through the line's packaging.

The quantitative research, which was used to measure product effectiveness vs. competitors' products, found that the X-14 Foaming Bathroom Cleaner scored 4.5 on a scale of 1 to 5 and that its Trigger Bathroom Cleaner scored a 91% approval rating, placing it higher than four other competing brands.

The research also found that consumers engage in two types of cleaning—weekly deep cleanings and quick daily cleanings. "We saw an opportunity for a bathroom expert line of products," says Noorany, who acknowledges that while X-14's applications aren't unique (its main competitors are Oakland, Calif.-based Clorox Co., Racine, Wis.-based S. C. Johnson & Son Inc. and Princeton, N.J.-based Church & Dwight Co. Inc.'s Arm & Hammer products), consumers were looking for products that focus solely on the bathroom.

"People liked the idea about a brand focused clearly on the bathroom. It was clear to us that there was a gap in the category and one that we could already fill with our products," she says.

Research Also Provided Data Useful for Future Products

"But we also clearly saw where future gaps were."

Among those future gaps was the need for more products within the X-14 line. While WD-40 has just recently begun development for those additional products (and, as a result, declines to say much about them), Noorany credits the open-mindedness of her research team with the introduction of those new products to the line.

The open-ended research approach paid off: Not only did WD-40 learn how to best reposition the X-14 line, but it garnered enough insight from the research process that it could use the data in future product development. WD-40 was able to get the most out of its investment (it was the largest investment in research for X-14 since the company acquired the brand) since it can use the data over and over, she explains.

While the company declines to give further details, Noorany says it expects to save "thousands of dollars" in research of future products. "New product opportunities were clearly identified," says Noorany, who admits that she never overtly planned to add new products. Still, several additions to the line are expected to be released in 2008.

The brand's new positioning—X-14 as The Bathroom Expert—is the centerpiece around which its new product line re-enters the market. Completely redesigned, the line provides a family look for the set of products rather than a disjointed set of similar products, with packaging characterized by a variety of pinks, oranges and blues as well as several bottle designs. Yet it also includes two additions: Foaming Bathroom Cleaner and Bathroom Cleaner, which combines oxy and citrus for general bathroom cleaning. Additionally, several future products are expected to be released some time next year.

"It wasn't the objective of the first study, but by the end we felt the opportunity was clear that there was a lot more we could add to the line," she explains. "We weren't looking for a specific answer. Instead, we were simply saying to consumers: 'Tell us how you clean'."

In all, the company had spent eight months by the time it completed the process in August 2006. The company declines to say how much it spent on the research, though. The company began shipping the new line in February.

"What we learned was to start the research process with the consumer; we didn't go to them with any preconceived notions," Noorany says. "We were just listening to them."

Wooing Luxury Customers

To win over today's upscale customers, brands must ensure a flawlessly engaging and emotional experience with every interaction.

Suzanne Hader

While the current economic forecast for most business sectors is dim, a bright light still shines on the luxury marketplace. Estimated by analysts to be a $220 billion (and growing) market, it's one by which many brands wish to be illuminated.

But luxury goods and service provision is a high-margin game in which fewer customers purchase more expensive items, making competition for the luxury customer's share of wallet fierce. Not surprisingly, there is a big push by marketers to position—or reposition—their brands to better capture the attention of this specific demographic.

Their challenge is reaching today's luxury consumer. Connecting with this group is no longer just about proper messaging; it's also (perhaps even more so) about creating a positive, memorable, and emotion-evoking experience. Brands that are upscale—or aspire to those heights—must understand that the experience they create around their brand is now the critical differentiator. The brands that come out ahead will be those that collect and then leverage their knowledge of the needs and desires of this sector, and consistently exceed its expectations.

Consider the tales of two luxury shoppers. Cindy N., a young research professional living and working in New York, is not rich. But she is a luxury goods customer who spends much of her discretionary income on high-end handbags, coats, and shoes. Shopping online recently at high-fashion apparel retailer Net-a-Porter.com, she had a question about sizing on an item and sent a brief e-mail to customer service. In short order, she received a detailed reply that answered her question about the item—and also suggested additional items that could tie an outfit together around it.

Net-a-Porter's highly personalized service has won critical acclaim from the luxury marketplace, along with equal financial rewards: Net-a-Porter's business has almost doubled in size every year since its inception in 2000, and ambitious growth plans are in place to continue the trend.

Then there's Jane D. Enticed by a pair of Jimmy Choo boots she saw in a magazine, she went to the upscale boutique that carried them, credit card in hand. Jane approached the salesperson

Executive Briefing

In this article, the author examines the evolving habits and desires of luxury consumers, who are driving a $220 billion (and growing) market. To be considered truly luxurious, she says brands must wrap exclusive first quality offerings in a consistently flawless and emotionally positive customer experience. Through a variety of examples, the author demonstrates the core motivations of luxury consumers and outlines five things brands must do to build lasting relationships with them.

at the counter who was filing receipts; a second salesperson was talking to a customer—about her dog. When Jane asked for the boots, the counter salesperson pointed to the other one and said: "I'm sorry, I'm busy right now, you'll have to wait for her." Incensed, Jane walked out—without the boots, and with a very bad feeling about the brand.

Many a once-lustrous luxury brand has fallen from its pedestal (think Audi in the early 2000s), not only because of questionable product quality, but also by failing to provide the flawless customer experience this increasingly demanding and fragmented consumer segment expects. More disturbing to brands, however, should be the amount of profit that is assuredly lost at the hands of poorly trained, apathetic, or aloof customer-facing staff. This lack of recognition that times have changed—and with them, the demands of the luxury clientele—is part of the issue.

What Is Luxury?

Although it depends on which dictionary you consult, luxury has been defined as "something inessential but conducive to pleasure and comfort; something expensive or hard to obtain; sumptuous living or surroundings: lives in luxury." But to the luxury customer, luxury is a promise. It's a brand's commitment that you (the customer) will be taken care of in exactly the way expect, whether purchasing a $20 million yacht, a diamond encrusted cell phone, or a $20 chocolate bar.

Truly luxurious brands allow customers to give up control and to trust that they will not be disappointed in the item's quality—or in the service and ownership experience around it. The service aspect cannot be uncoupled from the product where luxury is concerned; the two are completely intertwined and interdependent. Delivering on this customer category's expectations, which are very subjective and sometimes vague, is a daunting task—but it is also the main reason people are willing to pay the premium.

That said, all luxury is not created equal. And the term "luxurious" is becoming so overused it has almost lost all meaning.

For example, the Four Seasons and the Mandarin Oriental both consider themselves luxury hotels. The Four Seasons develops egalitarian workers who can respond intelligently and independently to keep customers satisfied. They're very careful to promise only what they can deliver, so they can deliver on what they promise—every time.

Rather than overselling the customer with hype and superlatives, the Four Seasons focuses on the provision of a great hotel experience, which is achieved by setting expectations appropriately and then trying to exceed those expectations whenever and wherever possible. The Four Seasons is confident in the value of the product being provided and what it is worth to customers—so much so that the hotel group does not participate in the prevalent industry discount game. Finally, its marketing efforts are very narrowly targeted in terms of advertising, direct mail, and one-to-one relationship building. The Four Seasons does not advertise in *Vogue.*

The Mandarin Oriental's approach is more scripted and "by the book," as a consultant who travels frequently recently discovered. Ann T. booked a room through the Mandarin Oriental's Web site, which said the room had a balcony. Once there, she saw the "balcony" was a six-inch beam with a railing attached. Disappointed, Ann took the elevator back to the lobby and asked to switch to a room with a real balcony.

Begrudgingly, the agent switched the room and escorted her to see the new one. On the way, he told her that this new room was his "favorite." Later, when ordering room service, Ann heard that the wine she selected was the order-taker's "favorite." And the next day, she was told that her spa package was the receptionist's "favorite." By the third time, Ann was hip to the script.

It's a small detail, but true luxury is getting all of the small details right. Today's luxury customers are extremely sensitive and intolerant of the slightest whiff of disingenuousness. They know when they're being put on. In this case, the Mandarin Oriental's patronizing treatment put Ann on the defensive for the rest of her stay and dissolved all trust in the staff—and any desire to interact with the brand in the future.

The Four Seasons is a certifiably luxurious experience, precisely because customers know they can trust the brand to provide an experience that's worth every penny and more. They know that once they step over that threshold, they can relax and enjoy the stay because their treatment will be authentic and consistently outstanding.

New Wealth Begets New Customers

Twenty years ago, luxury goods and services were marketed primarily (if not exclusively) to the ultra-wealthy. Brands promoted their premium goods and services as indicators of class and status, outward signs that the purchaser had "arrived." In the intervening years, however, a variety of economic factors have created enormous new wealth—and with it, a new type of luxury consumer with different motivations and needs. While the marketplace still consists of the ultra-wealthy, it now also encompasses a much broader customer base of both aspirational and solidly affluent customers, all desiring upscale products and services—delivered on their terms. Today's luxury market comprises three main segments:

- Ultra-high net worth. This segment includes company owners, entrepreneurs, and entertainment moguls who are so well-funded that they don't need to work (although many still do). Some can't spend all the money they have. Many of their purchases are made by advisers or house managers. Think Bill Gates, Warren Buffett, and Oprah Winfrey.
- Wealthy. These are high-income earners such as doctors, lawyers, the C-suite elite, entrepreneurs, and celebrities. Think sports stars, actors, musicians, and so on. Loss of a job or an economic downturn (without proper financial planning) could land them back where they began. Many also advance to the "ultra" category.
- Aspirational. These are people who are typically affluent, but not always, though many may become affluent and even wealthy. These customers trade up and use discretionary income to purchase luxury items, but shop for more basic items at mass or "masstige" levels. The category includes the affluent stay-at-home mom who books five-star vacations, but shops for paper goods at Target; the high school or college student who spends $200 on a pair of jeans, and the bartender who spends $300 on a pair of sunglasses.

What Shapes Luxury Habits

Whatever category they fall into, most of today's upscale customers share four characteristics that brands need to consider when shaping the customer experience.

First, it's all about indulgence and expression. Selecting a brand is a means to explore and express an identity; these customers won't be forced into a mold. Rather than dressing in one fashion label from head to toe, luxury fashionistas combine pieces from multiple brands to create a unique signature statement. It's not unusual to find this new type of luxury customer in a 3.1 Phillip Lim top, J Brand jeans and Christian Louboutin boots, carrying a Miu Miu bag.

This means that customers are engaging with four or more luxury brands to assemble each and every outfit. And it puts the pressure on marketers to first find out what products resonate with this empowered, creative demographic—and then wrap an experience around their acquisitions that will keep them coming back for more.

Second, experiences trump "things." Especially in a down economy, luxury customers will splurge on experiences, rather than items. When money gets tight (or is perceived so), guilt becomes a factor. Sharing indulgences helps disarm the guilt. It requires providers of luxury services to not only surprise and delight initiators of these luxury experiences (such as exotic trips, special events, or gifts), but also to make them look good in the eyes of the recipients.

Third, it must be "worth it." These consumers will indulge in purchases they believe are "worth it," but buy lower-cost items when no luxury option satisfies their expectations: The woman who spends a small fortune on interior design, but gets her pots and pans at Target; the family that flies coach, but stays at the Ritz-Carlton; or the younger career woman who buys thousand-dollar handbags, but gets everything else from H&M and Zara. The aspirational customer, however, is not the only one with an eye for value. High net worth shoppers also evaluate purchases and judge whether they merit their lofty price tags.

Still, this market enjoys spending money when the value of the product and the experience of purchasing and using it are perceived to be in line with the price. For example, before Apple, purchasing a personal computer was a largely undifferentiated experience because the end product made little difference once it was in use. Apple conceived and delivered a clearly superior luxurious computing experience (both in purchase and in use) that people consider to be well worth its premium price.

Finally, today's luxury customers expect an emotionally rewarding and affirmative experience with each and every premium brand interaction—from introduction to acquisition and beyond. In exchange for their attention—and share of wallet—they expect favored upscale brands to evolve, surprise, and delight them. Kate Spade, for example, created great, inclusive experiences by the continuous development, experimentation, and evolution of her brand. Spade's ads, Web content, diverse array of products, and inspired collaborations kept everyone's curiosity piqued. A prime example of this was her "Behind the Curtain" Web site, a pop-culture collage that catalogued her influences, interests, and whatever she thought was cool. Customers let in on these "secrets" felt like they knew the brand in friendship, further deepening the emotional connection.

Operationalize the Brand

Where luxury brands face the greatest risk of compromising the experiential connection is at the point of sale, making operationalization of the brand their biggest obstacle to success. Many spend millions getting their products in front of potential customers, and spurring them to action. But bland or less-than-pristine store environments, non-empathetic sales-people, and poorly designed Web sites negate the investment by alienating the customers that the brand's marketing programs were able to attract.

The challenge brands face is finding ways to provide a luxurious customer experience at every juncture. Here are some guidelines for doing it right.

Whenever possible, use market re[...] graphic and ethnographic profiling to [...] customers and understand why they b[...] want to feel like the brand is speaking to [...] The first step to achieving this goal is [...] better than your competition.

Note that you should expect to pay a tidy sum for research. Recruiting research subjects for this segment is very challenging, and incentives must be factored in, as most luxury consumers do not want to be found or identified due to privacy concerns. It can cost more than $1,000 to secure a small amount of information from just one person. If purchasing or using existing research to make decisions, make sure that the sample set includes actual luxury customers.

For example, one recently released and highly-publicized "luxury survey" conducted by a well-known research outfit asked a number of non-luxury customers what brand they would buy if money were no object. The results, while interesting from a pop culture standpoint, provided no insight into the behavior or wishes of those who actually can and do buy those products.

Aim for brand engagement and sales will follow. Luxury customers are extremely wary of being sold to, and will reject overtures that are too forceful or blatant. Instead, they look for rich experiences that wrap the purchase in an emotional connection based on shared values like privacy and quality. Marketers should concentrate on inspiring the recipient to engage with the brand at an emotional level, driving interest rather than sales. Marketing initiatives should emphasize quality over quantity every time.

For example, biking and walking trip purveyor Butterfield & Robinson (www.butterfield.com) combines a spectacular and content-rich Web site with emotional and inspirational direct mail—designed to get travelers to start thinking of the company while on a tour with them, but not selling any one particular thing. Full color pieces feature a large photograph of an amazing destination with the words "Slow Down" or "You, Here" with an arrow into the landscape written across the front. Another brand that uses direct mail to further embrace its customer base is luxury retailer Coach, which occasionally sends out a bound booklet of its products as a special sneak peek at its new collections. Because the catalog is so well done and is mailed only when there's a powerful merchandise message behind it, customers tend to look for it and save it.

Hire people who already have a "heart for service," then train and empower them to act on behalf of your brand. Luxury retailer Ralph Lauren's sales staff is empowered to make split-second decisions they think will keep the customer happy—without having to check with a manager. Staff also is expected to become intimately acquainted with—and remember—client needs and desires. Additionally, Lauren's standardized suite of shopper services provides a consistent framework for appropriate customer service.

The brand may be what piques the luxury consumer's attention, but it's the service that forges and solidifies the bond. This bond, and the high degree of trust that comes with it, is the reason why luxury customers are willing to pay so much more for the privilege.

also important to hire the right customer service people to respond quickly to direct mail and Web site-generated inquiries. This human connection provides a vital opportunity to extend the customer relationship and reinforce your brand's personality through warm and friendly interactions. Staff should also have all the resources they need to provide useful information, above and beyond what's been requested.

Develop programs to reengage dormant and ex-customers. The luxury population is so small that many times it is much easier (and less expensive) to woo back a former customer than to find and engage a new one. In communicating with these customers, be sure to place the emphasis on what makes your luxury brand special and different from the rest.

One powerful way to re-pique interest in a brand is to invite customers to an event, especially if it features a person of note connected with the brand. Events need not be extravagant, but they must be special. For example, Lexus put on "Taste of Lexus: Luxury Living Edition" in 2007. It was a suite of events held in major cities, where former and potential customers were invited to come out and test drive different models on a professionally designed performance track. Events are incredibly successful for the luxury market, because the messaging is one-to-one and personal attention is assured.

Embrace online commerce—now. The e-commerce-enabled Web site already has proven to be the most profitable, highest traffic entry point for Chanel, Rolex, and Gucci—proof that luxury consumers are ready and willing to spend large sums of money online. In fact, when it comes to online commerce,

luxury brands already are late to the party—as most waited until customers clamored to shop online.

Luxury brands also need to stop looking at online customers as separate from offline customers. Many run their dot-coms as competing storefronts, instead of as a channel that complements real-life retail. Consider the customer who purchases a blouse in black at the flagship, and is so delighted with it she decides she wants one in every color. It should be made easy for her to go online, find her original in-store purchase and order the additional items (with free overnight delivery).

Though the technology already exists to facilitate this type of integration, it still remains a huge untapped opportunity—meaning luxury brands seem to be arriving (unfashionably) late to this party too. Just as they expect to be recognized and remembered when they shop in person, customers will soon come to expect (and demand) that their luxury brands integrate this knowledge of their preferences and shopping history between brick and mortar stores and online commerce outlets.

Reaching today's luxury customer has never been more challenging—or financially rewarding. Marketers who understand the nuances of what motivates this sector to establish relationships with exclusive brands—and design high-touch and high-trust experiences in response—will be best positioned to reap the rewards.

SUZANNE HADER is principal of 400twin (www.400twin.com), a New York-based consulting firm that provides evaluation of and strategic direction for luxury brands. She may be reached at shader@400twin.com.

The Halo Effect

Christian Consumers Are a Bloc That Matters to All Marketers

MICHAEL FIELDING

Politics. Sex. Religion.

Classic dinner-talk taboos, every one, although marketers for all kinds of products and services have largely capitalized on them—religion being a notable exception. For years it was a risk: "It's like being behind a political party," says Irene Dickey, lecturer in management and marketing at the School of Business Administration at the University of Dayton in Ohio. "Businesses just didn't go there."

Yet the United States has been getting religion. It was the talk of the presidential political campaign, enrollment in religiously based colleges is soaring, and some elements of religious pop culture, such as the ersatz rock group Creed and the "Left Behind" fiction series, have found fans among those who don't necessarily believe.

And some mainstream marketers have discovered an entrée to Christians' life style, in particular, that offers many earthly rewards. Major retailers, consumer products companies and marketing consultants have found that through Scriptures and sponsorship, viral marketing and targeting the right media, they can tap the secular benefits of the born-again Christian community. Those benefits include spending power, education, loyal buying habits—and a vocal culture that can spread good news far and wide, or trash an insincere company's empty efforts.

While it has yet to reach the status of a major targeted segment, the born-again Christian market has turned the heads of a few big-name companies, from Target to Disney.

"(Most) national brands have not targeted the segment because they don't understand it," posits Jeff Lambert, managing partner of 6-year-old public relations firm Lambert, Edwards & Associates Inc., based in Grand Rapids, Mich.

Born-again Christians are generally defined as those who follow literal interpretations of the Bible and acknowledge being born again through religious conversion. Theirs is among the fastest growing religious affiliations in the United States. (The born-again Christian community includes a subset, evangelicals, who generally believe that they have a personal responsibility to share their religious beliefs about Christ with

Christian Characteristics

32%
say they drank an alcoholic beverage in the last month

74%
of evangelicals are white and married

33%
are baby boomers

54%
live in the South

36%
of born-agains have volunteered to help with their church in the past week, compared with 24% of average adults

non-Christians. Although they are not the same—many born-again Christians are not evangelicals—the terms often are used interchangeably.)

According to Ventura, Calif.-based independent market research company Barna Research Group, about 72 million of the 235 million Christians in the United States, or 30.6%, say they are born-again. Some 14 million of that group, or 19.4%, consider themselves evangelical.

"(God and religion are) a part of their daily activities," Dickey says. "Their interests and opinions are often linked with their religion."

If any time is the right time to take a marketing message to the born-again segment, it is now.

"Religious Congregations and Membership," a 2000 study by the Nashville, Tenn.-based Glenmary Research Center, found that among the fastest-growing church denominations in America are many conservative Christian churches (numbering more than 100 evangelical denominations), some of which grew more than 20% over the 10-year period beginning in 1990, when the center conducted a previous survey. That surpassed the 16.2% growth rate of members of the Roman Catholic faith, the nation's largest denomination.

By comparison, more mainline Protestant denominations experienced some of the slowest growth rates, ranging from a high of 10.2% for the North American Baptist Conference for the decade to a drop of −51.4% among independent congregational churches not affiliated with the National Association of Congregational Christian Churches. The Jewish faith overall grew by 2.7%.

A marketer's message may be conveyed to born-again Christians in several ways—some inexpensive, some insightful.

First, a marketer may turn to the Scriptures. "If the company has a Christian founder or philosophy, it can communicate easily through Scriptures on its packaging," says John Nardini, vice president of marketing at Wayland, Mich.-based Denali Flavors. "It's really subtle, but Christians notice things like that."

While Denali is a company that follows Christian values, it does not play that fact up on its packaging, but other national companies do. Consider *Woman's Day* magazine, published by Hachette Filipacchi Media U.S. Inc.: A biblical verse runs along the top of the table of contents page in each issue. Recently, "Psalm 100: 5" greeted readers before leading them to stories about health and decorating.

Remember, though, that for born-again Christians, their religion is their life. They'll notice an empty marketing message. "With religion, it's a level higher than whether you like the Mets or whether you like the Yankees," warns Jonathan Jaffe, owner of Westfield, N.J.-based Jaffe Communications, a 3-year-old public relations consulting firm whose clients include a company catering to Christian consumers.

A separate step would be to consider sponsorship. A company could sponsor an event, as Target Corp. did in 2004, when the Minneapolis-based retailer sponsored a portion of a 2004–05 tour by Christian musical group the Newsboys. The retailer used in store positioning, promotion through local media outlets and the Newsboys' own Internet site. Separately, for more than two decades Walt Disney Co. has sponsored the "Night of Joy" at its Walt Disney World resort in Florida, featuring Christian music.

On a smaller scale, "Look beyond (big-scale ideas) to partner with an organization that reaches that audience," Lambert says, suggesting that prison ministries and youth organizations are ripe for sponsorship.

Indeed, Christian groups tend to be tremendously well organized at the grassroots level, which allows for effective and affordable marketing to small, highly involved groups of consumers.

Sponsorship also has a high ROI potential. "It is a terrific use of a company's marketing dollars," says Julie Fairchild, co-founder of Dallas-based public relations/marketing firm Lovell-Fairchild Communications, who considers herself a born-again Christian. At a 2004 Christian festival in Atlanta, for example, more than 100,000 attendees converged on downtown Atlanta

for several days—an infectious viral marketing opportunity, Fairchild points out.

For PR and advertising purposes, consider using Christian media as a vehicle for the marketing message. The right media don't even have to be particularly Christian: Jaffe alerts religion writers in the general media both locally and nationally of product updates by his clients that cater to Christian consumers.

> **'Grassroots marketing campaigns are the most effective because (Christian consumers) are connected. They really appreciate a company or product that does pay attention to their interests.'**

Elsewhere, Denali owns lines of sub-branded premium ice creams and distributes them regionally. Among its products is Moose Tracks ice cream, which is produced by 85 dairies and distributed across the United States. The company has captured a solid Christian market by brokering on-air promotions for Moose Tracks with Christian radio stations. "Christian radio stations are personal fans of the ice cream, so they give it away," Nardini explains. "It's not 'Christian' ice cream, though. It's a national brand."

Nardini's home-run pitch to Moose Tracks' Christian consumers is that the company returns part of its profits to Christian causes.

As Jaffe says, "One of the biggest struggles of faith-based organizations is raising the money. When a for-profit company comes to them and says, 'We're willing to give you X amount of money,' that puts it at a higher level."

Finally, don't underestimate the impact of word-of mouth marketing. "Marketing to a Christian audience is no different from marketing to any other audience. It's just that they exercise choice based on a value system," Fairchild explains. "Grassroots marketing campaigns are the most effective because (Christian consumers) are connected, and they really appreciate a company or product that does pay attention to their interests. When they find something that lines up with that, they pass it along."

For example, Wal-Mart Stores Inc.'s charitable giving programs are secular and aimed at the local level. The company donates to religious organizations, among other groups, but only for programs that benefit the community in general. Still, in recent years, the stores have carried a broader selection of Christian books while continuing to refuse to carry what many conservative Christians consider offensive magazines. (Try finding laddie mags such as *Stuff, FHM* and *Maxim* on the shelves at the world's largest retailer.) So while Wal-Mart can disassociate itself from religious affiliation, company officials can boast that they're taking a moral stand. The word gets out—and viral marketing takes over.

Nardini touts the efficiencies of marketing to large numbers of consumers during gatherings of born-again Christians. Women of Faith and Promise Keepers confabs may draw up to

30,000 people per event, and the Billy Graham Crusades continue to fill stadiums nightly with three- and four-night stands.

And viral marketing has been a boon for One Christian Voice, one of Jaffe's clients, a Vancouver, Wash.-based long-distance telephone company. It has gained customers in 48 states in its first year of business.

'If they're interested in the values that are behind a company, they tend to stick with that company.'

A bonus for marketers: Born-again Christians are fiercely loyal once they've been effectively courted. "If you believe in something as fundamental (as religion), it pervades every single part of (your life)," Nardini says. "If there is a brand that supports those causes, they're going to support that 100%."

What marketers miss about Christians is that while they do all the things everyone else does, they're more passionate about certain things, Fairchild says. "If they're interested in the values that are behind a company, they tend to stick with that company," she says. "The values they're looking for are what everyone desires. It's peace and warmth and togetherness."

Finding these 72 million desirable consumers isn't difficult, marketers say.

- According to Barna:
  —just 32% of Christians say they drank an alcoholic beverage in the last month;
  —74% of evangelicals are white and married;
  —33% are baby boomers;
  —54% live in the South; and
  —36% of born-agains have volunteered to help with their church in the past week, compared with 24% of average adults.
- Born-again Christians are highly educated and intelligent. According to Barna, 29% of evangelical Christians have a college degree. That's higher than the national average of 26%. Furthermore, author Naomi Schaefer Riley reports in her latest book, *God on the Quad,* that enrollment at the 100 schools of the Council for Christian Colleges & Universities jumped 60% between 1990 and 2002—as attendance at colleges not affiliated with a religion remained flat.

- With the average lifetime cost to raise a child hovering above $200,000, and a marked preference for children among Christian couples, marketers infer there's no lack of spending power.
- Raleigh, N.C.-based construction consultancy FMI Corp. estimates the value of the religious building market at more than $8 billion, and expects it to grow 3.9% in 2005. That's much smaller than the $62.7 billion commercial building market or the $566 billion residential building market—but church construction is driven by individual giving, unlike other industry segments, so the theory is that booming church construction indicates Christian consumers with plenty of resources.

Prominent Christians include preacher Billy Graham, who continues to be listed as one of the 10 most admired men in the world, according to Gallup Polls; Rick Warren, author of *The Purpose Driven Life,* which has topped the *The New York Times* Bestseller list for nonfiction for nearly two years straight; and President Bush, whose wizard strategist Karl Rove stimulated a massive turnout among Christian voters to secure a second term for Bush in the 2004 general election. Speaker of the House Dennis Hastert, a Republican from Illinois, is a graduate of Wheaton College, an evangelical Christian school in Wheaton, Ill.

Yet despite their attractive demographics, marketers say, Christian consumers are often thought to be less discerning than others shoppers.

Wrong, Lambert says: "Don't assume the Christian consumer is less (savvy) than any other consumer. They're more educated than most other consumer audiences." Lambert's clients include the Colorado Spring, Colo.-based Christian Booksellers' Association, the world's largest Bible publisher, and Grand Rapids, Mich.-based Family Christian Stores, the nation's largest Christians retailer.

Part of the demystification of the segment is realizing that, just as other niche markets—Hispanics and African-Americans, for example—shop at all kinds of retail stores, so do born-again Christians. "It's about how they shop but also what they don't buy and where they don't want to shop," Lambert adds.

Dickey suggests that it's not difficult to send the right message to born-again Christians in order to raise their awareness of a product. "The elements there are pretty clear: Respect that this is a lifestyle and communicate with them with words and images . . . that are respectful of that target market."

Youth Marketing, Galvanized

Media & Marketers Diversify to Reach A Mercurial Market

DANIEL B. HONIGMAN

Ten years ago, marketers looking to target the youth segment didn't need to look much further than one channel: MTV. But changing media consumption habits are splintering media buys, shards of which are being claimed by other networks, experiential promotions and social networks. The fight to claim the bleeding edge of youth marketing is fierce and is forcing marketers to innovate beyond the pale.

"People live and breathe advertising and marketing in a different way now; they relate to it individually," says John Koller, senior marketing manager in charge of Sony's PlayStation Portable (PSP) video game console.

In 1998, the multimillion-dollar PlayStation marketing budget allocation was 75% broadcast, 20% print, and 5% events and online. "It's splintered significantly since then," Koller says, reporting that the allocation is now closer to 55% broadcast and 20%–25% online. The last quarter is split across mobile, outdoor and retail channels.

"Broadcast is great for awareness, but it's not a 100% driver to the retail environment. Working with PR and great editorial or being able to have a PSP truck outside a Wal-Mart, those are some of our drivers [now]," Koller says.

This splintering of media budgets is common across all segments, but figuring out how to balance these spinning plates is essential to brand survival, says Andrew Frank, research vice president of New York-based Gartner Research. "Anyone who's trying to reach the youth market can't put their eggs in one basket," he says. "Fragmentation has led to a situation in which there's not one seller of ad services that can reach it all. The most successful brands are using a variety of techniques to reach young consumers, but the challenge is keeping them all integrated and complementary."

One such innovator is Cartoon Network, a cable network created in 1992 by Atlanta-based Turner Broadcasting System Inc. Its heavy-hitting, late-night Adult Swim block of programming is the largest draw for men aged 18–34, according to Nielsen Media Research. Despite being a single cable outlet, it offers a mixed bag of marketing touch points for media buyers to choose among.

John O'Hara, senior vice president and general sales manager for Cartoon Network, attributes Adult Swim's success to the network's overall wackiness quotient. But even more, he says, is its pickiness when selecting and integrating an advertiser—and its campaign—into its lineup. This, he says, helps Adult Swim maintain credibility in the youth segment. "You can become uncool with this segment quickly," he says. "We want to make sure we do things with a partner that makes sense and [with whom] we can work something . . . that maintains that 'cool' element."

To do this, Adult Swim takes alternative paths for its ads. For example, in December 2007 its program *Aqua Teen Hunger Force* featured an in-show ad for XM Satellite Radio. The show's plot featured the main characters hijacking the signal of a fictitious hard-rock satellite radio station. During the program, viewers could tune in to the XM channel for a "live" broadcast, and XM posted a fake complaint letter against the program's characters on its Web site.

For an experiential promotion, Adult Swim teamed up with Virgin Mobile and video game developer Activision Inc. to sponsor a 12-show college tour featuring faux-hard rock band Dethklok from the program *Metalocalpyse*. At the band's stage shows, students—who received free tickets—got a chance to play the video game *GuitarHero III: Legends of Rock* and use Virgin cell phones to text messages that were viewable on the stage's video screen.

When it comes to engaging the youth segment, Adult Swim usually incorporates humor and music, but creativity is what advertisers look for most. "Adult Swim [shows have] some off-the-wall characters, and the sky's the limit for us," O'Hara says. "So creativity, in terms of what we can do with an advertiser across our platforms, will lead to engagement. If you start out with an audience that's so engaged with the network, you'll find a way to engage them with your product."

Utilizing the Web is no different. Simply measuring eyeballs, MTV.com drew 7.5 million unique viewers in October 2007, which pales in comparison with social networks MySpace and Facebook, which drew 123.4 million and 40.1 million unique visitors, respectively, according to Nielsen

Online. MTV.com traffic also trails music giants like Yahoo! Music and Project Playlist. MTV declined to comment for this story.

"You can become uncool with this segment quickly," he says. "We want to make sure we do things with a partner that makes sense and [with whom] we can work something . . . that maintains that 'cool' element."

Anastasia Goodstein, founder and editor of Ypulse.com and author of *Totally Wired: What Teens And Tweens Are Really Doing Online,* says a big reason why MTV is trailing online is because it missed the boat with social networking. "You have the long-tail effect of people going to smaller sites or checking out their friends' blogs, all of which nibble away at MTV's Web properties," Goodstein says. "[And] MTV also [can't compete with] some of the authentic grassroots sites that are created by people within specific subcultures. [For marketers] trying to reach influencers in the snowboarding community, for example, they should find out what site or publication is embraced by the core group within that subculture."

This is not to say that MTV and its Web properties haven't responded to the more segmented markets. "From a youth marketing perspective, is MTV still the place to go? Of course it is," says Josh Weil, partner at Ramsey, N.J.-based youth marketing research firm Youth Trends. "They've made great inroads in the college market with mtvU, they're launching a ton of vertical Web sites against different music genres and, at some point, they're going to launch a social network. They consistently reach, through their TV channels, mobile and online, more people than any other platform." For MTV, it's just a matter of figuring out a combination that works for its audience and its advertisers. "On the digital end, like everyone else, MTV is trying to figure out how to best leverage its digital assets. Right now, its strategy is to throw a bunch of [stuff] up there and see what sticks," Weil says.

Peter Gardiner, partner and chief media officer with New York-based ad agency Deutsch, agrees. "It would be a bit over-blown to say MTV doesn't work anymore," he says. "Ten years ago, youth marketing started and ended with MTV, but while MTV isn't what it used to be in terms of its dominance over the youth market, it's still an incredibly powerful part of the mix."

In the end, however, whether marketers use MTV, Adult Swim, online or targeted verticals, media channels are only a part of what marketers need to do to effectively reach the youth market. "You hear a lot from marketing executives about the fracturing of media," says Sony's Koller. If you can parse the youth demographic into the smallest segment and can market to [each segment accordingly], you'll be ahead of the game."

Sowing the Seeds

A deeper understanding of the customer buying process can drive organic growth.

Mark Pocharski and Sheryl Jacobson

Marketers love to talk about getting closer to customers. But the reality today for most companies is that they aren't very close at all to the people or companies that purchase their products or services. The problem: It's a complicated world out there. What was once a fairly straightforward buying process that consumers followed—comprising one or two channels and an orderly progression of steps from awareness to purchase—has now morphed into a complex and constantly changing ecosystem made up of multiple channels, more competition, and less-attentive and increasingly empowered customers.

As a result, traditional sales and marketing tools that have worked for decades are no longer adequate. Consider how the scope and complexity of the buying process has grown for a product as simple as a doorknob. Not so long ago, a homeowner would go to a local hardware store or a big-box retailer such as Sears, maybe speak with an associate and choose from perhaps a half-dozen different types of doorknobs.

Now the consumer might start with a Google search of "new doorknob," which would turn up literally thousands of information sources on buying and replacing doorknobs (home improvement sites such as HGTV or This Old House) along with myriad purchase options, ranging among the following:

- retail giants such as The Home Depot, Lowe's, Wal-Mart, and Target
- regional hardware stores such as Ace, Aubuchon, and True Value
- for-sale-by-owner sites such as eBay and Craigslist
- numerous e-retailers such as doorknobdiscountcenter.com and knobsandhardware.com

It's safe to say, however, that none of those retailers has deep insight about that potential consumer other than his perceived need for a new doorknob. Is he building a house

Executive Briefing

With the increasing complexity of business today, many marketers have forgotten the fundamental principal that growth occurs only when you're able to change specific behaviors in customers during their buying process. That's harder today because the typical buying process is a complex ecosystem of channels, information sources, and marketing mix options—but it's absolutely essential. This article outlines specific ways companies can develop insights from the customer buying process and then focus their marketing efforts on the things that really matter.

or replacing a door? Does he want more security or is the new knob strictly for looks? How much of a factor is price? Did someone refer him to this brand? Beyond offering basic price information and product descriptions, most retailers are not likely to take any action to lead the consumer through a detailed buying process. And yet if companies don't invest in understanding where they can win or lose that customer in the buying process, then how can they invest in the marketing programs that matter most?

The irony is that marketers are being asked with increasing urgency to help drive organic business growth by acquiring and retaining customers—and by convincing them to buy more products or services. In many cases, however, their methods have yet to catch up with the madness of the current marketplace, in which consumers are less attentive to traditional messaging and just as likely to follow advice on a new product from a Web log (blog) or third-party Web site. Although most companies have a very good understanding of the transactions that a customer has historically engaged in, they have very little understanding of why an individual behaves in the way he does and what they could do to alter that behavior to their advantage.

Marketers need new tools that will help them develop deeper insights into customer behavior and identify key points in which they can influence purchase decisions. Conducting an in-depth analysis of the buying process to uncover these "leverage points" can help marketers define the best tactics to alter (or reinforce)–to increase sales and ultimately drive profitable growth.

New Buying Process

The proliferation of product choices, information sources, distribution channels, and marketing platforms has made the world a complex place for both buyers and sellers of goods and services. For marketers, it's the equivalent of moving from a simple game of checkers to trying to solve a Rubik's Cube and Sudoku puzzle simultaneously. Unfortunately, existing models for understanding the buying process—particularly the specificity of how a customer is motivated and influenced at each step along the way—are constrained by two significant flaws in conventional wisdom.

The buying process is nonlinear. The first flaw is viewing the buying process as a linear progression. Many marketing and sales teams still group the customer life cycle into orderly and discrete stages: awareness, trial, consideration, purchase, and repeat. They have systems in place to monitor what happens at each stage (e.g., customer relationship management, sales-force automation, loyalty analysis), but those systems don't show the numerous paths customers use to navigate throughout the process. That used to matter less when there were one or two ways of creating awareness or purchasing a product; the linkages then were fairly obvious. Now, however, the paths are so varied that companies cannot effectively track them. A customer might enter a store ready to buy a specific make and model of a computer after researching the product online, or he might be a novice looking for information and guidance. Those are two customers with very different purchase contexts that require two separate marketing approaches. Marketing tactics for the computer-savvy shopper might include word-of-mouth strategies, blogs, and third-party endorsements, whereas the computer-novice shopper might require aggressive sales promotions, in-store purchase displays, and endorsements from well-known media outlets such as *Consumer Reports.*

Compounding the problem: Marketing and sales personnel who treat the buying-process stages as a straight line (awareness leads to consideration, which leads to a purchase, which leads to repeat purchases) incorrectly assume that all buying processes begin with awareness and that success in one stage will naturally lead to success in the next. That attitude ignores other influences at various points in the buying process, which can lead a customer down an entirely different path.

Take, for example, a technology distributor that grew successfully over the years by following a simple marketing premise: that high-quality technical support was good for business, especially during the consideration phase. The company developed an unrivaled (online and offline) pre-sales technical support group to help customers configure complex technology solutions to meet their needs. Although this approach allowed the company to win customers and build share for a number of years, it also created a bloated cost structure that ate into margins. More alarmingly, the company was not aware of the increasing number of prospects—including some long-term customers—that were (1) using the distributor's best-in-class support to configure solutions but then (2) purchasing the solution from one of several new and lower-cost competitors that didn't offer technical support.

Acquisition and retention are interrelated. The second flaw involves treating customer acquisition and customer retention as independent processes. In too many companies, an artificial wall exists between the two. Sales and marketing will focus on the former (if sales are down) or the latter (if defection rates are high), but rarely does it examine the interdependencies between them. Viewing acquisition and retention separately ignores the fact that customers today may make frequent and often overlapping trips through the buying process and therefore cannot be categorized as either a prospect or an existing customer—they are often both.

How frequently do you see promotions from cell phone providers or credit card companies offering low rates or giveaways for new customers—deals for which long-term and loyal customers are not eligible? Companies spend billions on advertising and promotion to entice new customers while saddling existing customers with inferior prices, even when those current customers come with zero acquisition costs. Consumers are fighting back, either by canceling their subscriptions and re-engaging as new customers (to get the better prices) or by canceling their service altogether and purchasing a competitive offering.

A more subtle example comes from the pharmaceuticals industry. Many drug companies have developed a marketing approach of investing significant dollars into direct-to-consumer advertising—to convince patients to inquire about certain branded drugs with their physicians. In doing so, however, drug companies often overlook other, higher-potential growth opportunities. For example, recent research we conducted in the pharmaceutical industry showed that in some sectors, lack of patient compliance (e.g., taking less than the prescribed medication or stopping the medication early) was in fact the biggest barrier to long-term, profitable growth. By viewing acquisition and retention as inter-related processes we were able to demonstrate that focusing marketing and sales activities on compliance issues (targeted at doctors and patients to ensure patients took their full regimen of medication) rather than direct-to-consumer advertising would make certain drug classes grow faster and more profitably. The resulting marketing programs helped turn a negative-growth product into a 30% growth rate in just one year.

Understanding Buying Behaviors

As the examples here demonstrate, organic growth is driven by behavioral change in customers. A company can control and accelerate its growth rate only if it knows the specific customer behaviors it wants to change and focuses its marketing and sales teams on influencing the behaviors that have the highest potential for return.

How to begin the process of understanding customer behavior? The first step is developing a comprehensive understanding of where the leverage points exist in the buying process. Leverage points represent the place in the buying process where customers or prospects either enter or drop out of your process. By influencing prospects to move to the next stage instead of leaving, marketers can directly increase the purchase or usage of a product.

In many cases, leverage points are not obvious; they might even conflict with accepted beliefs about the business. Management teams often guess wrong about customer behavior because they neither see changes occurring in the marketplace quickly enough, nor have the data to challenge their operating assumptions. The following examples show how uncovering leverage points led to changes in marketing activities that provided a big payback.

The men's high-end fashion industry. For years, the prevailing wisdom was that men buy high-end clothing and accessories because they want to dress like Tiger Woods, George Clooney, or some other handsome and successful personality. One fashion retailer played this aspirational card to the hilt: investing heavily in celebrity-endorsed print ads in men's magazines and TV spots during sporting events, hoping to influence its target audience. However, after careful examination of the buying process, that retailer found that many of its targeted segments didn't buy fashion and accessories that way at all.

For many segments, purchase decisions were made in the racks of high-end specialty stores. The retailer's primary target group was gathering only 5% of its information from television and 7% from magazines. Its main influence was word of mouth; 68% of all information was gathered from the subject's wife, girlfriend, or mother. And at the point of sale, more than two-thirds based their purchase decision on the fit and feel of the product. If the consumer tried on the product, then he disproportionally bought it over competitors' brands. To address those behaviors, the company shifted a significant amount of its marketing spend from celebrity sponsorship to point-of-purchase promotion designed to experience the product. It has since tripled the annual growth rate of its core business.

A watch manufacturer. Not all companies should move their marketing dollars downstream to the point of sale; sometimes the best move is in the opposite direction. Another example is of a watch manufacturer that historically had invested heavily with retailers to create attractive in-store promotional displays and signage. The marketing team spent a robust 85% of its budget on point-of-sale tactics. However, as younger consumers (a critical segment for this company) started using cell phones instead of watches to tell time, the watchmaker was experiencing significantly lower growth rates. Yet a closer examination of customer behaviors revealed that (1) younger shoppers didn't see the value of using a watch to keep time and (2) the point-of-purchase displays were having little impact on them. After examining the data, the watchmaker realized that the key leverage point—the opportunity to influence the youth segment's buying decisions and change its behavior—came well before they entered the store. The company shifted more than 60% of its marketing resources toward a broad-based campaign to promote the benefits and style of wearing a watch. The shift of marketing tactics had a significant impact in turning the brand around and driving new growth.

As the clothing retailer and watchmaker both discovered, focusing on the leverage points in the buying process can help you understand where you are winning and losing your customers. An in-depth analysis of the buying process provides specificity around the behavior that a company seeks to change among its target audience. Those insights include how and why people make decisions leading to purchase—and ultimately usage—of the product or where and why people drop out of the process. They can illuminate (1) where competition is really happening and (2) its impact on winning or losing customers. Importantly, they identify the role of influencers—any word-of-mouth advocacy manifested in blogs, chat rooms, or other venues—on the customer's behavior.

Most companies are swimming in the wrong kind of data, or they're analyzing the right data the wrong way.

The spirits world. Such outputs convinced one spirits maker to change its in-store promotional tactics. The marketing team knew that most of the company's customers were men, and it knew that the segment bought spirits roughly once a month. It didn't know much more than that, so it performed a deeper analysis to uncover the motivations behind the monthly visits. It uncovered two main scenarios. The first was the "special-occasions run," made when friends were coming over at the last minute. The second was the "stock-up," done monthly to replenish the customer's inventory. The last-minute shoppers cared more about packaging: opting for specialized glass bottles, often in smaller quantities. And in that segment of customers, the spirits maker was losing ground to new competitors. With that insight in hand, the spirits maker changed its in-store packaging to reinforce special-occasions buying behaviors. The change resulted in close to doubling the growth and profit from its primary spirits brand.

Turning Insights into Action

A key point to remember is you need the data to act. It's incredibly tempting to think you already know how consumers behave and to simply assume that you can rely on your intuition, years of experience, and macro-trend analysis to come up with the best approach. That's a tempting and sometimes fatal mistake. Most companies are swimming in the wrong kind of data, or they're analyzing the right data the wrong way. As we've highlighted, typical models for understanding buying and usage behaviors are not rich enough; you must go deeper where it really matters. There are two points to bear in mind.

Be broader in scope when you start analyzing the situation. Look at multiple buying processes in all corners of the market. Think more broadly about competitors/substitutes, consumers, geographies, and occasions. Have an unconstrained view of the opportunity first; then use feasibility and economics to highlight the best leverage points.

Don't get lost in the woods. At the end of the day, data must be actionable to have value (e.g., there are too many customer segmentations out there in which sales can't find the target). It's important to use interactive, hypothesis-driven processes combined with managerial insight to cut through the data clutter. Translate those data into holistic, living and breathing representations of your customers. To find the best opportunities, it's important to keep three questions in mind:

- Would the desired behavioral change drive significant profitable growth for the company? Does it provide a large-enough opportunity? (Unless the desired behavioral change tilts customers to your brand and results in profitable growth, there is limited upside to focusing on it.)
- Are the required skills and capabilities resident in the organization to execute on this opportunity? (If you don't have the marketing capabilities to affect this behavior, then it is not feasible in the short term.)
- Will it be cost-prohibitive to obtain the expected gains? (If you cannot overcome barriers through

appropriate and affordable marketing tactics, then you won't achieve the desired behavioral change.)

With the leverage points identified in the buying process, a marketing team can then define a few critical "behavioral objectives" that will form the foundation of a sustainable growth strategy. These behavioral objectives help reinforce or change a customer's behavior to increase purchase and usage of a product. It's what you want the customer to do differently or more frequently. A behavioral objective is more actionable than a traditional marketing campaign goal.

For a financial services company, "attract new customers to the category" is a broad objective that is difficult to build a campaign around. A more important and valuable behavioral objective, such as "convert automatic teller machine users to debit cards," will allow for greater precision in marketing programs. The same lesson applies for a telecommunications company: Refining the behavioral objective from "initiate new cell phone usage" to "make personal calls with cell phone instead of home phone" provides enough specificity for a more targeted—and ultimately more successful—campaign. The point is that you can't be specific enough in targeting what customer behavior to change or reinforce without knowing where the leverage point is in the first place.

Focusing on What Matters

Leverage points and behavioral objectives are important elements of a detailed buying-process analysis. Done right, that type of analysis will move marketing's collective mind-set away from assumptions, estimates, and "spread-your-bet" marketing plans—toward a focus on the customer behaviors it needs to change (and where). A buying-process analysis is particularly helpful in multichannel industries such as pharmaceuticals, technology, and financial services. In such industries, the multiple constituencies involved in decision making make it even more critical to understand the behaviors and opportunities at each stage.

Buying-process analysis can also help a management team pinpoint the greatest achievable economic opportunities instead of spending too much time on broad-based ideas such as customer loyalty, awareness, and satisfaction. It also enables a company to see the marketplace in a way that's different from competitors, which will open up new opportunities upstream or downstream—and away from a head-to-head battle over market share.

Think about the elements that drive top-line growth: getting customers to buy more frequently, buy more products, buy instead of browse, or purchase from you instead of your competitor. Changing or reinforcing behaviors that affect any of those drivers in a positive way will directly contribute to increased revenue. Although it's easy for a company to state that it is focused on understanding its customers better, executing on that mission is the true challenge. The most successful companies have made a real commitment to developing deep insights into customer behavior—and they are taking steps to influence that behavior. Only by under-standing the different dimensions of the buying process can companies solve the puzzle of sustainable organic growth.

MARK POCHARSKI is a partner of Monitor Group (which helps organizations grow by working with leading corporations, governments, and social sector organizations around the world on the growth issues that are most important to them) and leader of Monitor's marketing strategy unit, Market2Customer (M2C), in Cambridge, Mass. He may be reached at mark_pocharski@monitor.com. **SHERYL JACOBSON** is a global account manager of M2C and may be reached at sheryl_jacobson@monitor.com. To join the discussion about this article, please visit www.marketingpower.com/marketingmanagementblog.

From *Marketing Management*, September/October 2007, pp. 26–31. Copyright © by American Marketing Association. Reprinted by permission.

You Choose, You Lose

Unrestrained customer choices can derail manufacturing productivity and profitability.

GEORGE H. LEON

"Have it your way" began as Burger King's declaration of customer freedom of choice in burger building, but quickly became the mantra of consumer marketing. Now there are a variety of categories that have climbed on the bandwagon. Dell Inc. offers online personal computer (PC) customization, and even humble Carmelite nuns provide online, interactive rosary bead configuration. The theory is that customer choice differentiates the brand, sells more product, and engenders customer loyalty.

But if customer freedom of choice has fully blossomed in consumer marketing, why is it being challenged in certain quarters of the B2B world? Specifically, manufacturers of heavy trucks—which historically have been built to customer specifications—are increasingly narrowing choices. Why do they seem to be moving opposite the rest of the world? Are they risking customer alienation in limiting choices? And how are they getting away with it—even positioning it as a benefit to customers?

Black or Black?

In the pioneering days of the automobile assembly line, the old joke that "a Model T Ford is available in any color, as long as it's black" implied that some degree of choice was sacrificed for the benefits of inexpensive mass production. More subtly and perhaps more importantly, the joke implied that customers should have a choice of color. Today, customers take for granted free choice of color when purchasing an automobile, whereas other options (such as a sunroof) add to the price. In other words, customer choice motivates customers not only to buy a particular brand, but also to spend more.

Of course, it's no coincidence that none of the available options requires the car to be reengineered. Assembly line production has evolved to where it can accommodate a certain level of customer choice—hence, the blanks on the

Executive Briefing

"Have it your way" quickly became the focus of consumer marketing in a variety of categories. The theory has been that customer choice differentiates the brand and engenders customer loyalty. However, in some segments of the B2B world, unconstrained customer choice translates into manufacturing platform complexity, maintenance of multiple supplier relationships, and higher engineering and development costs.

dashboard for controls of unselected options. One could say that automobile customer choice and production technology are in a state of equilibrium: The degree of customer choice offered is that which is economically supported by the production technology, and no more.

Big Macs. Mass production of fast food came much later than automobile assembly lines, in the 1950s. Initially, only a small variety of products was available, with no real choice of how each was configured; a hamburger was a hamburger. In fact, the uniformity of the customer experience initially served to differentiate McDonald's from the unpredictable mom-and-pop burger joints. It minimized customer risk of disappointment when exploring unknown territory. Later, Burger King tapped the latent customer need for choice when it declared: "Have it your way." Neither a quantum leap in production technology nor new-product development was required to withhold ingredients in burger hand-assembly. Competitors had to get on board, and fastfood production technology advanced to offer ever-increasing customer choice.

PCs. In contrast to the fast food industry, the early years of PC production presented customers with a chaotic environment of choices. In the late 1970s, buyers could decide from an array of architectures, associated processors, memory configurations, and disk-drive formats. It was easy to make a mistake, because software that ran on one brand might not run on another (it usually didn't). And no one knew for sure which standard, if any, would prevail. But as developers migrated to the IBM/MS-DOS standard in the early 1980s, owners of alternative architectures became increasingly marginalized, despite the alleged technological superiority of their machines over the somewhat bland IBM PC. IBM didn't attempt to build the "best" machine; it opted for a relatively plain "vanilla" box with open architecture and an operating system that would become the de facto world standard, accelerating technology adoption across the entire market. Although buyers still can choose from a variety of machine configurations, it's a lot more difficult for them to make a costly mistake than it was 25 years ago.

Dell pioneered customer choice by allowing customers to configure their PCs, but today one just as easily can configure an Apple iMac online: select a care plan and software, add an iPod, pay for the whole package, and have it delivered to his or her doorstep. Both Dell and Apple offer a number of desktop and laptop models, plus additional memory, hard-disk drives, wireless networking, and other configuration choices. Of course, this self-service approach assumes that customers know what will best meet their needs, and probably results in customers sometimes buying too much or too little. Because components essentially are "plug-in" or "bolt-on," the online customer interface nicely fits with the "pick-and-pack" production technology, where no reengineering of the basic product is required.

Rosary beads. Most of the world's 1 billion plus Catholics have at least one set of rosary beads, typically from their first Holy Communion. Although in 1961 there were black beads for boys, white beads for girls, and adult choices limited to wood or glass beads of various colors, today one can visit www.sistersofcarmel.com and build a fully customized rosary. More that 17 million combinations are possible online, with further options available by contacting the Carmelite nuns in Colorado Springs, Colo. Like burgers, rosaries are hand-assembled. And like PCs, the components are completely interchangeable, despite significant variations in value. Most importantly, the choices are completely in sync with the production technology, which is relatively primitive compared with the highly sophisticated customer interface.

Mack trucks. Heavy-truck buyers traditionally have been able to specify choice of engine, transmission, axles, tires, and other components. And they can select not only technical specifications (e.g., engine displacement, torque, horsepower, transmission gearing), but also component brands. For example, Freightliner Class 8 diesel trucks are available with a Detroit Diesel, Caterpillar, or Cummins engine, and with an Eaton Fuller, Meritor, or Allison transmission.

In contrast, Volvo Class 8 trucks come with only Volvo engines: the single-hood design of Volvo's top-of-the line

VT 880 melding "the traditional styling you want" with "the fuel-saving aerodynamics you need."

And although "a Mack truck can be spec'ed and customized to meet just about any requirement" (per Mack's Web site), don't ask for a Caterpillar engine. Instead, Mack offers an integrated drive train entirely consisting of Mack components. "Our engines, transmissions, and axles work better because they were designed to work together."

Self-service assumes that customers know what will best meet their needs, and might result in them buying too much or too little.

In fact, the overall trend in the market has been toward narrower choice sets and increasingly vertically integrated products. Even those manufacturers who've traditionally allowed customers to "spec a truck from the ground up" have significantly narrowed brand choices for major components (e.g., engines, transmissions, axles) and altogether eliminated them for minor components, in some cases.

The Nature of Choice

Automobile buyers have never experienced the array of choices traditionally afforded heavy-truck buyers, particularly when it comes to component brand. Don't ask your Toyota dealer for a Camry with a Ford engine or Honda transmission, for example. For wheels and tires, however, customers might have a choice of either standard wheels and tires or upgraded alloy wheels and high-performance tires. These choices increase the car's price and allow the dealer or manufacturer to make more on the sale. Typical "sport package" options that add value to the sale are engineered into the car, but in no way radically alter the design.

The bolt-on principle also applies to most PC configuration choices. For example, the Dell Web site recently offered six sizes of flat-screen and conventional display units (from 15 inches to 20 inches) for its Dimension 3000 PC. It also offered two sizes of hard-disk drive, three memory configurations, and two types of optical drive—but not the brand of these components. Commoditization of components allows manufacturers to get the best prices from suppliers while providing customers choice of technical specifications, but not component brand.

It is the simplicity of the Carmelite sisters' production technology, combined with a sophisticated customer interface, that allows them to present 17 million rosary choices. For a burger, though, pickles and lettuce are default options. No choices are available on how the burger is cooked, and don't even think about altering the 'technical specifications' of the components—asking for Vidalia onions and Jersey tomatoes.

The Value of Choice

In the heavy truck category, the trend toward narrower choices and integrated products is bringing it closer in options to other categories, with choices available in specification, not brand. Indeed, in the medium truck market, integrated products already are much more prevalent.

Truck buyers value choice of component brand primarily for functional reasons, but these reasons are often tinged with emotion. Functionally, customers select particular brands because they meet their technical specification requirements, have particular valued characteristics, and fit into their existing operations. Emotionally, customers might fear that alternative choices won't meet their requirements, doubt that other brands share characteristics of the preferred brand, and feel uncertain that an alternative brand will fit into their operations.

The bottom line is that customers might feel tied to specific brands to meet their technical specification requirements, depending on the demands of their applications. Moreover, even if an equivalent product is available, in terms of technical specifications, a customer might believe that one brand is better-constructed, more durable, easier to service, or simply superior in performance. Obviously, it is in the truck manufacturer's interest to understand how to get customers switching component brand rather than truck brand, and to know when a component switch would constitute a deal breaker (customers would change manufacturers to maintain the choices).

The Cost of Choice

When choices are interchangeable, bolt-on, or even commodity, they have four common elements.

- Customers typically can't pick the brand, and sometimes can't pick the type.
- Customers are offered fairly constrained technical specification choices.
- The options require little or no engineering modifications to the core product.
- In a commodity environment, the manufacturer can apply price pressure to suppliers of largely interchangeable parts and, by implication, maintain relatively simple supplier relationships.

Except for the simplest of components, none of these principles holds in the heavy-truck manufacturing industry. However:

- customers traditionally have been allowed to "spec a truck from the ground up," including choice of component brand.
- technical specifications are far more complex.
- particularly for major components, options might require a substantial amount of engineering effort on the manufacturer's part.

- because of the complexity of the technical specifications and engineering requirements, supplier relationships are far more complicated.

Not surprisingly, customer choice of components is considerably more costly in the truck category. Supply-chain management, inventory control, and contract management are especially complicated by multiple vendor relationships. In a nutshell, customer choice presents an expensive headache for manufacturers: It complicates day-to-day operations, potentially slows product development and launch, and creates uncertainty in forecasting earnings. The answer, of course, is rationalization: consolidation of suppliers, vertical integration of the product, simplified engineering, streamlined supply chain, reduced operations costs, and more certainty in forecasting. Life would be much simpler if manufacturers didn't need to accommodate customer choice. And that's the direction truck manufacturers seem to be taking.

Does this mean that truck manufacturers are increasingly insensitive to customer needs? Not at all. In fact, most would argue that they can better meet customer needs by providing an integrated product, or at least selecting components for customers. In other words, an integrated product—consisting of components that are designed to work together—should be better than a product consisting of different manufacturers' components. But even if the product is not fully integrated (the same brand components), one that's optimally assembled from various components should be better than one assembled from customer-selected components. Unlike the Dell self-service model, the assumption here is that customers might not be the best people to specify a truck.

In addition to improving the product, rationalization can enhance post-sale service and support. With fewer component brands for an organization to manage, technicians can be trained quicker and more thoroughly, service coverage can be more universal, and parts and supplies can be more readily available. The idea is a well-oiled machine of post-sale service and support. From a strictly rational/economic point of view, rationalization should command a price premium, which customers should be able to recover through improved product performance, less downtime, and reduced operating and maintenance costs. But customers must be convinced of the benefits, and possibly compensated for the loss of free choice.

The question, in the minds of customers and manufacturers, is how far can and will rationalization go? How much can customers' choices be narrowed, what will customers require in exchange, and what are the deal breakers?

Mistakes can be made in pricing and positioning rationalization. Insufficient rewards (e.g., price points, warranty terms) for fewer choices can result in share erosion. Conversely, excessive rewards can leave money on the table and substantially offset the financial gains realized through rationalization. So, despite the potential advantages, rationalization is a risky business in which bad decisions can spiral out of control. How can a manufacturer minimize the risks?

Customer Perspective

In an environment of increasingly constrained choices, customers face trade-offs between free choice in specifying a truck, the potential advantages of accepting a rationalized value proposition, and the risks of making changes. Customers might be willing to forgo some choices in exchange for the intrinsic benefits; this willingness probably is contingent on the importance of a particular feature, how well the product will meet their requirements, and the perceived value of the rewards.

The lesson is that when it comes to customer choice, more is not necessarily better.

Ideally, the manufacturer can anticipate and pre-engineer customers' requirements, and appropriately price and position the product. And it's understood that, at least for some customer segments, loss of a particular choice can be a deal breaker. In these instances, the manufacturer must decide between allowing that choice to continue or cutting loose the segment. To do so, the manufacturer must identify the deal breakers and understand customers' requirements, perceptions of benefits value, and willingness to trade choice for those benefits. Without this information, the manufacturer cannot make reasonable decisions about rationalization, and is in grave danger of presenting a suboptimal value proposition.

The manufacturer can get that information through market research. Typically some sort of conjoint design is the best approach toward understanding and quantifying customer trade-offs. When properly conducted, conjoint design not only identifies the deal breakers and informs the optimal configuration of the value proposition, but also estimates the share and revenue impacts of optimal and suboptimal solutions. Some examples of conjoint design guidelines:

- Most traditional discrete-choice conjoint design approaches are not up to the task. All except the smallest owner-operators among truck buyers do not pick a product, but rotate their fleet through a prescribed replacement cycle. Also, despite (or because of) frequent preferences for fleet uniformity, truck buyers tend to try new products a little at a time. To be realistic to customers, the conjoint design must accommodate their intentions to purchase multiple trucks in a given period, and allow them to try assorted value propositions in the exercise.
- Attributes of the conjoint design must not be fixed product features; they must represent realms of choices. Although traditional conjoint designs test

various product features and prices, this conjoint design would need to test various types of choices, prices, and benefits.

- The conjoint design should present customers with a realistic, multi-brand scenario. For example, truck buyers simultaneously consider multiple proposals, so the conjoint design should simultaneously present eight or more branded choices to represent the major suppliers.
- The conjoint design should incorporate and test positioning statements, such as "optimally engineered product," "higher quality and greater reliability," "faster, more responsive servicing," "lower operating costs," and "extended warranty."
- Qualitative research conducted with customers should precede and inform the conjoint design, to ensure identification and proper articulation of the conjoint design attributes.

When More Isn't Better

Examining the current relationships between production technology and customer choice in a category—and identifying emerging business models in the competitive landscape—foretells the challenges players are likely to encounter and offers insights on how to address them. The lesson is that when it comes to customer choice, more is not necessarily better. It's tempting to think that it is, given the ingrained ethos of choice in American culture, and the ease with which customers exercise free choice in the market. But close examination of customer choice, in any category, reveals that it's always constrained; there is no such thing as completely free choice. Of course, production technology will continue to evolve, and car manufacturers might someday offer complete choice of color or even an easy change of color. But that will mean production technology and customer choice have reached a different equilibrium in one corner of one category; it won't signal the advent of completely free choice.

Is completely free choice the ideal? The chaotic market of early personal computing is one free-choice scenario. But another scenario is complete commoditization. For example, if customers want to select not only the capacity of their PC's hard drive, but also the brand, all brands will need to be virtually interchangeable. And to a large degree, they are. But would that be desirable in all categories? The point is, the freer the choice, the more commoditized the elements must be; the production process isn't going to bend. Heavy-truck manufacturers could continue giving customers component brand choice if component suppliers agreed to build their products to the same specifications, eliminating the need for costly engineering by truck builders. But that's unlikely to happen, because component builders would lose their ability to differentiate, which is exactly what has happened with PC components: Although performance specifications might vary, all components essentially are plug-ins.

And what about pickles and lettuce? Today, it's hard to find a mom-and-pop joint that will serve a burger with a big, juicy slice of Jersey tomato. In fast-food establishments, customers can articulate only whether they want a topping—and tomato isn't always a choice. So is it really possible to have something our way? Who knows. Perhaps the demands of the growing "think globally, act locally" customer segment, along with evolving supply-chain technology, someday will enable us to get a Jersey tomato on our burgers. And maybe that's when the Carmelite sisters will open their fast-food restaurant.

GEORGE H. LEON is vice president of the technology practice at National Analysts, a market research and consulting firm in Philadelphia. He may be reached at gleon@nationalanalysts.com.

From *Marketing Management,* January/February 2006, pp. 40, 42–45. Copyright © 2006 by American Marketing Association. Reprinted by permission.

UNIT 3

Developing and Implementing Marketing Strategies

Unit Selections

Key Points to Consider

- Most ethical questions seem to arise in regard to the promotional component of the marketing mix. How fair is the general public's criticism of some forms of personal selling and advertising? Give some examples.

- What role, if any, do you think the quality of a product plays in making a business competitive in consumer markets? What role does price play? Would you rather market a higher-priced, better-quality product or one that was the lowest priced? Why?

- What do you envision will be the major problems or challenges retailers will face in the next decade? Explain.

- Given the rapidly increasing costs of personal selling, what role do you think it will play as a strategy in the marketing mix in the future? What other promotion strategies will play increased or decreased roles in the next decade?

Student Web Site
www.mhcls.com

Internet References

American Marketing Association Homepage
http://www.marketingpower.com
Consumer Buying Behavior
http://www.courses.psu.edu/mktg/mktg220_rso3/sls_cons.htm

"**M**arketing management objectives," the late Wroe Alderson once wrote, "are very simple in essence. The firm wants to expand its volume of sales, or it wants to handle the volume it has more efficiently." Although the essential objectives of marketing might be stated this simply, the development and implementation of strategies to accomplish them is considerably more complex. Many of these complexities are due to changes in the environment within which managers must operate. Strategies that fail to heed the social, political, and economic forces of society have little chance of success over the long run. The lead article in this section provides helpful insight suggesting a framework for developing a comprehensive marketing plan.

The selections in this unit provide a wide-ranging discussion of how marketing professionals and U.S. companies interpret and employ various marketing strategies today. The readings also include specific examples from industry to illustrate their points. The articles are grouped in four sections, each dealing with one of the main strategy areas: product, price, distribution (place), and promotion. Since each selection discusses more than one of these areas, it is important that you read them broadly. For example, many of the articles covered in the distribution section discuss important aspects of personal selling and advertising.

Product Strategy. The essence of the marketing concept is to begin with what consumers want and need. After determining a need, an enterprise must respond by providing the product or service demanded. Successful marketing managers recognize the need for continuous product improvement and/or new product introduction.

The articles in this subsection focus on various facets of product strategy. The first article describes a methodology pinpointing how to conduct the right product market investigations in the right way. The second article provides some thoughtful ideas about premium products. The last article in this subsection analyzes how Howard Schultz is trying to revitalize Starbucks.

Pricing Strategy. Few elements of the total strategy of the "marketing mix" demand so much managerial and social attention as pricing. There is a good deal of public misunderstanding about the ability of marketing managers to control prices and even greater misunderstanding about how pricing policies are determined. New products present especially difficult problems in terms of both costs and pricing. The costs for developing a new product are usually very high, and if a product is truly new, it cannot be priced competitively, for it has no competitors.

"Rocket Plan" relates how companies can fuel success with a rigorous pricing approach. In the second article, the authors delineate how segmentation based on buying behavior can uncover a dynamic force. The last article in this subsection, "Boost Your Bottom Line By Taking the Guesswork Out of Pricing," examines the importance of starting your pricing analysis by asking potential customers what they believe your product is worth.

© 2007 Keith Eng

Distribution Strategy. For many enterprises, the largest marketing costs result from closing the gap in space and time between producer and consumer. In no other area of marketing is efficiency so eagerly sought after. Physical distribution seems to be the one area where significant cost savings can be achieved. The costs of physical distribution are tied closely with decisions made about the number, the size, and the diversity of marketing intermediaries between producer and consumer. The articles in this subsection scrutinize the ways retailers Costco, QVC, and Wal-Mart can create value for their customers and be very competitive in the marketplace.

Promotion Strategy. The basic objectives of promotion are to inform, persuade, or remind the consumer to buy a firm's product or pay for the firm's service. Advertising is the most obvious promotional activity. However, in total dollars spent and in cost per person reached, advertising takes second place to personal selling. Sales promotion supports either personal selling and advertising, or both. Such media as point-of-purchase displays, catalogs, and direct mail place the sales promotion specialist closer to the advertising agency than to the salesperson.

The articles in this final unit subsection cover such topics as the significance of successful sales approaches, the necessity of effective advertising, and the importance of product placement.

The Very Model of a Modern Marketing Plan

Successful companies are rewriting their strategies to reflect customer input and internal coordination.

SHELLY REESE

It's 1996. Do you know where your marketing plan is? In a world where competitors can observe and rapidly imitate each other's advancements in product development, pricing, packaging, and distribution, communication is more important than ever as a way of differentiating your business from those of your competitors.

The most successful companies are the ones that understand that, and are revamping their marketing plans to emphasize two points:

1. Marketing is a dialog between customer and supplier.
2. Companies have to prove they're listening to their customers by acting on their input.

What Is a Marketing Plan?

At its most basic level, a marketing plan defines a business's niche, summarizes its objectives, and presents its strategies for attaining and monitoring those goals. It's a road map for getting from point A to point B.

But road maps need constant updating to reflect the addition of new routes. Likewise, in a decade in which technology, international relations, and the competitive landscape are constantly changing, the concept of a static marketing plan has to be reassessed.

Two of the hottest buzz words for the 1990s are "interactive" and "integrated." A successful marketing plan has to be both.

"Interactive" means your marketing plan should be a conversation between your business and your customers by acting on their input. It's your chance to tell customers about your business and to listen and act on their responses.

"Integrated" means the message in your marketing is consistently reinforced by every department within your company. Marketing is as much a function of the finance and manufacturing divisions as it is the advertising and public relations departments.

Integrated also means each time a company reaches out to its customers through an advertisement, direct mailing, or promotion, it is sending the same message and encouraging customers to learn more about the product.

Why Is It Important?

The interaction between a company and its customers is a relationship. Relationships can't be reproduced. They can, however, be replaced. That's where a good marketing plan comes into play.

Think of your business as a suitor, your customers as the object of your affection, and your competitors as rivals. A marketing plan is your strategy for wooing customers. It's based on listening and reacting to what they say.

Because customers' priorities are constantly changing, a marketing plan should change with them. For years, conventional wisdom was 'prepare a five year marketing plan and review it every year.' But change happens a lot faster than it did 20 or even 10 years ago.

For that reason, Bob Dawson of The Business Group, a consulting firm in Freemont, California, recommends that his clients prepare a three year plan and review it every quarter. Frequent reviews enable companies to identify potential problems and opportunities before their competition, he explains.

"Preventative maintenance for your company is as important as putting oil in your car," Dawson says. "You don't wait a whole year to do it. You can't change history but you can anticipate what's going to happen."

Essential Components

Most marketing plans consist of three sections. The first section should identify the organization's goals. The second section should establish a method for attaining them. The third section focuses on creating a system for implementing the strategy.

Although some plans identify as many as six or eight goals, many experts suggest a company whittle its list to one or two key objectives and focus on them.

"One of the toughest things is sticking to one message," observes Mark Bilfield, account director for integrated marketing of Nissan and Infiniti cars at TBWA Chiat/Day in Los Angeles, which handles national advertising, direct marketing, public relations, and promotions for the automaker. Bilfield argues that a

Illustration by Kelly Kennedy

focused, consistent message is easier to communicate to the market place and to different disciplines within the corporation than a broad, encompassing one. Therefore, he advises, "unless there is something drastically wrong with the idea, stick with it."

Section I: Goals

The goals component of your plan is the most fundamental. Consider it a kind of thinking out loud: Why are you writing this plan? What do you want to accomplish? What do you want to achieve in the next quarter? The next year? The next three years?

Like taping your New Year's resolution to the refrigerator, the goals section is a constant reminder of what you want to achieve. The key difference between a New Year's resolution and your marketing goals, however, is you can't achieve the latter alone.

To achieve your marketing goals you've got to convince your customers to behave in a certain way. If you're a soft drink manufacturer you may want them to try your company's latest wild berry flavor. If you're a new bank in town, you need to familiarize people with your name and convince them to give your institution a try. Or perhaps you're a family-owned retailer who needs to remind customers of the importance of reliability and a proven track record in the face of new competition.

The goals in each of these cases differ with the audiences. The soft drink manufacturer is asking an existing customer to try something new; the bank is trying to attract new customers; the retailer wants to retain existing customers.

Each company wants to influence its customers' behavior. The company that is most likely to succeed is the one that understands its customers the best.

There's no substitute for knowledge. You need to understand the demographic and psychographic makeup of the customers you are trying to reach, as well as the best methods for getting their attention.

Do your research. Learn as much as possible about your audience. Trade associations, trade journals and government statistics and surveys are excellent resources, but chances are you have a lot of data within your own business that you haven't tapped. Look at what you know about your customer already and find ways to bolster that information. Companies should constantly be asking clients what they want and how they would use a new product.

"If you're not asking people that use your end product, then everything you're doing is an assumption," argues Dawson.

In addition, firms should ask customers how they perceive the products and services they receive. Too often, companies have an image of themselves that they broadcast but fail to live up to. That frustrates consumers and makes them feel deceived.

Companies that claim to offer superior service often appear to renege on their promises because their definition of 'service' doesn't mesh with their customers', says Bilfield.

"Airlines and banks are prime offenders," says Bilfield. "They tout service, and when the customers go into the airport or the bank, they have to wait in long lines."

The problem often lies in the company's assumptions about what customers really want. While an airline may feel it is living up to its claim of superior service because it distributes warm towels and mints after a meal, a business traveler will probably place a higher value on its competitor's on-time record and policy for returning lost luggage.

Section II: The Strategy

Unfortunately, after taking the time and conducting the research to determine who their audience is and what their message should be, companies often fail by zooming ahead with a plan. An attitude of, "OK, we know who we're after and we know what we want to say, so let's go!" seems to take over.

More often than not, that gung-ho way of thinking leads to disaster because companies have skipped a critical step: they haven't established and communicated an internal strategy for attaining their goals. They want to take their message to the public without pausing to get feedback from inside the company.

For a marketing plan to work, everyone within the company must understand the company's message and work cooperatively to establish a method for taking that message to the public.

For example, if you decide the goal of your plan is to promote the superior service your company offers, you'd better make sure all aspects of your business are on board. Your manufacturing process should meet the highest standards. Your financial department should develop credit and leasing programs that make it easier for customers to use your product. Finally, your customer relations personnel should be trained to respond to problems quickly and efficiently, and to use the contact as an opportunity to find out more about what customers want.

"I'm always amazed when I go into the shipping department of some company and say, 'What is your mission? What's the message you want to give to your end user?' and they say, 'I don't know. I just know I've got to get these shipments out on time,'" says Dawson.

Because the success of integrated marketing depends on a consistent, cohesive message, employees throughout the company need to understand the firm's marketing goals and their role in helping to fulfill them.

"It's very important to bring employees in on the process," says James Lowry, chairman of the marketing department at Ball State University. "Employees today are better than any we've had before. They want to know what's going on in the organization. They don't want to be left out."

Employees are ambassadors for your company. Every time they interact with a customer or vendor, they're marketing your company. The more knowledgeable and helpful they are, the better they reflect on your firm.

At Nordstrom, a Seattle-based retailer, sales associates are empowered to use their best judgment in all situations to make a customer happy.

"We think our sales associates are the best marketing department," said spokeswoman Amy Jones. "We think word of mouth is the best advertising you can have." As a result, although Nordstrom has stores in only 15 states, it has forged a national reputation.

If companies regard marketing as the exclusive province of the marketing department, they're destined to fail.

"Accounting and sales and other departments have to work together hand in hand," says Dawson. "If they don't, you're going to have a problem in the end."

For example, in devising an integrated marketing campaign for the Nissan 200SX, Chiat/Day marketers worked in strategic business units that included a variety of disciplines such as engineers, representatives from the parts and service department, and creative people. By taking a broad view of the business and building inter-related activities to support its goals, Chiat/Day was able to

Getting Started

A Nine-step Plan That Will Make the Difference Between Writing a Useful Plan and a Document That Gathers Dust On a Shelf

by Carole R. Hedden and the *Marketing Tools* editorial staff

In his 1986 book, *The Goal,* Eliyahu M. Goldratt writes that most of us forget the one true goal of our business. It's not to deliver products on time. It isn't even to manufacture the best widget in the world. The goal is to make money.

In the past, making money depended on selling a product or service. Today, that's changed as customers are, at times, willing to pay for what we stand for: better service, better support, more innovation, more partnership in developing new products.

This section of this article assumes that you believe a plan is needed, and that this plan should weave together your desires with those of your customers. We've reviewed a number of marketing plans and come up with a nine-step model. It is perhaps more than what your organization needs today, but none of the steps are unimportant.

Our model combines some of the basics of a conventional plan with some new threads that we believe will push your plan over the edge, from being satisfactory to being necessary. These include:

- Using and improving the former domain of public relations, image, as a marketing tool.
- Integrating all the business functions that touch your customers into a single, customer-focused strategic marketing plan.
- Borrowing from Total Quality theories to establish performance measures beyond the financial report to help you note customer trends.
- Making sure that the people needed to deliver your marketing objectives are part of your plan.
- "Selling" your plan to the people whose support is essential to its success.

Taking the Plan Off the Shelf

First, let's look at the model itself. Remember that one of the primary criticisms of any plan is that it becomes a binder on a shelf, never to be seen again until budget time next year. Planning should be an iterative process, feeding off itself and used to guide and measure.

Whether you're asked to create a marketing plan or write the marketing section of the strategic plan for your business, your document is going to include what the business is trying to achieve, a careful analysis of your market, the products and services you offer to that market, and how you will market and sell products or services to your customer.

1. Describe the Business

You are probably in one of two situations: either you need to write a description of your business or you can rely on an existing document found in your annual report, the strategic plan, or a capabilities brochure. The description should include, at minimum:

- Your company's purpose;
- Who you deliver products or services to; and
- What you deliver to those customers.

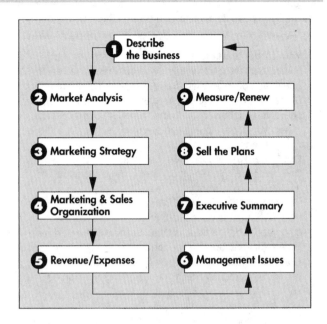

Too often, such descriptions omit a discussion about what you want your business to stand for—your image.

This is increasingly important as customers report they are looking for more than the product or service; they're in search of a partner. The only way to address image is to know who you want to be, who your customers think you are, and how you can bridge the gap between the two.

Part of defining your image is knowing where you are strong and where you are weak. For instance, if your current yield rate is 99.997 percent and customers rate you as the preferred supplier, then you might identify operations as a key to your company's image. Most companies tend to be their own worst critic, so start by listing all your strengths. Then identify weaknesses or the threats you face, either due to your own limitations or from the increased competency of a competitor.

The description also includes what your business delivers to its owners, be they shareholders, private owners, or employees. Usually this is stated in financial terms: revenue, return on investment or equity, economic value added, cash generated, operating margin or earnings per share. The other measures your organization uses to monitor its performance may be of interest to outsiders, but save them for the measurement section of your plan.

The result of all this describing and listing is that you should have a fairly good idea of where you are and where you want to be, which naturally leads to objectives for the coming 6, 12, or 18 months, if not longer.

2. Analyze the Market

This is the section you probably believe you own. *Marketing Tools* challenges you to look at this as a section jointly owned by most everyone working with you. In a smaller company, the lead managers may own various pieces of this section. In a larger organization, you may need to pull in the ideas and data available from

(continued)

other departments, such as logistics, competitor intelligence, research and development, and the function responsible for quality control or quality assurance. All have two things in common: delivering value to customers, and beating the competition.

Together, you can thoroughly cover the following areas:

- **Your target markets.** What markets do you currently compete in? What do you know about them in terms of potential, dollars available, and your share of the market? Something frequently prepared for products is a life cycle chart; you might want to do the same for your market. Is it embryonic, developing, mature or in decline? Are there new markets to exploit?
- **Customer Knowledge.** Your colleagues in Quality, Distribution, Engineering, or other organizations can be helpful in finding what you need.
  The customer's objectives. What threats do your customers face? What goals does the customer have? Work with your customer to define these so you can become a partner instead of a variable component.
  How is the customer addressing her or his markets? Do you know as much about your customer's position as you know about your own? If not, find out.
  How big is each customer, really? You may find you're spending more time on a less important customer than on the customers who can break you. Is your customer growing or in decline? What plans does the customer have to expand or acquire growth? What innovations are in development?
  What does your customer value? Price, product quality, service, innovation, delivery? The better you know what's driving your customer's purchasing decision, the better you'll be able to respond.
- **Clearly identify the alternatives your customer** has. As one customer told employees at a major supplier, "While you've been figuring out how to get by, we've been figuring out how to get by without you." Is backward integration—a situation in which the customer develops the capability in-house—possible? Is there an abundance of other suppliers? What is your business doing to avoid having your customers looking for alternatives?
- **Know your competition.** Your competitors are the obvious alternative for your customer, and thus represent your biggest threat. You can find what you need to know about your competitors through newspaper reports, public records, at trade shows, and from your customers: the size of expansions, the strengths that competitor has, its latest innovations. Do you know how your competition approaches your customers?
- **Describe the Environment.** What changes have occurred in the last 18 months? In the past year? What could change in the near future and over a longer period of time? This should include any kinds of laws or regulations that might affect you, the entry or deletion of competitors, and shifts in technology. Also, keep in mind that internal change does affect your customers. For instance, is a key leader in your business planning to retire? If so, decision making, operations or management style may change—and your customer may have obvious concerns. You can add some depth to this section, too, by portraying several different scenarios:

- What happens if we do nothing beyond last year?
- What happens if we capitalize on our strengths?
- What might happen if our image slips?
- What happens if we do less this year than last?

3. The Marketing Strategy

The marketing strategy consists of what you offer customers and the price you charge. Start by providing a complete description of each product or service and what it provides to your customers. Life cycle, again, is an important part of this. Is your technology or product developing, mature or in decline? Depending on how your company is organized, a variety of people are responsible for this information, right down to whoever is figuring out how to package the product and how it will be delivered. Find out who needs to be included and make sure their knowledge is used.

The marketing strategy is driven by everything you've done up to this point. Strategies define the approaches you will use to market the company. For instance, if you are competing on the basis of service and support rather than price, your strategy may consist of emphasizing relationships. You will then develop tactics that support that strategy: market the company vs. the product; increase sales per client; assure customer responsiveness. Now, what action or programs will you use to make sure that happens?

Note: strategy leads. No program, regardless of how good it is, should make the cut if it doesn't link to your business strategies and your customer.

The messages you must craft to support the strategies often are overlooked. Messages are the consistent themes you want your customer to know, to remember, to feel when he or she hears, reads, or views anything about your company or products. The method by which you deliver your messages comes under the heading of actions or programs.

Finally, you need to determine how you'll measure your own success, beyond meeting the sales forecast. How will you know if your image takes a beating? How will you know whether the customer is satisfied, or has just given up complaining? If you don't know, you'll be caught reacting to events, instead of planning for them.

Remember, your customer's measure of your success may be quite different from what you may think. Your proposed measures must be defined by what your customer values, and they have to be quantifiable. You may be surprised at how willing the customer is to cooperate with you in completing surveys, participating in third-party interviews, or taking part in a full-scale analysis of your company as a supplier. Use caution in assuming that winning awards means you have a measurable indicator. Your measures should be stated in terms of strategies, not plaques or trophies.

(continued)

4. The Marketing and Sales Organization

The most frequently overlooked element in business is something we usually relegate to the Personnel or Human Resources Office—people. They're what makes everything possible. Include them. Begin with a chart that shows the organization for both Marketing and Sales. You may wish to indicate any interdependent relationships that exist (for instance, with Quality).

Note which of the roles are critical, particularly in terms of customer contact. Just as important, include positions, capabilities, and numbers of people needed in the future. How will you gain these skills without impacting your cost per sale? Again, it's time to be creative and provide options.

5. Revenue and Expense

In this section, you're going to project the revenue your plan will produce. This is usually calculated by evaluating the value of your market(s) and determining the dollar value of your share of that market. You need to factor in any changes you believe will occur, and you'll need to identify the sources of revenue, by product or service. Use text to tell the story; use graphs to show the story.

After you've noted where the money is coming from, explain what money you need to deliver the projected return. This will include staff wages and benefits for your organization, as well as the cost for specific programs you plan to implement.

During this era of budget cuts, do yourself a favor by prioritizing these programs. For instance, if one of your key strategies is to expand to a new market via new technologies, products, or services, you will need to allocate appropriate dollars. What is the payback on the investment in marketing, and when will revenues fully pay back the investment? Also, provide an explanation of programs that will be deleted should a cut in funding be required. Again, combine text and spreadsheets to tell and to show.

6. Management Issues

This section represents your chance to let management know what keeps you awake at night. What might or could go wrong? What are the problems your company faces in customer relations? Are there technology needs that are going unattended? Again, this can be a collaborative effort that identifies your concerns. In addition, you may want to identify long-term issues, as well as those that are of immediate significance.

To keep this section as objective as possible, list the concerns and the business strategy or strategies they affect. What are the short-term and long-term risks? For instance, it is here that you might want to go into further detail about a customer's actions that look like the beginnings of backward integration.

7. Executive Summary

Since most senior leaders want a quick-look reference, it's best to include a one-page Executive Summary that covers these points:

- Your organization's objectives
- Budget requirements
- Revenue projections
- Critical management issues

When you're publishing the final plan document, you'll want the executive summary to be Page One.

8. Sell the Plan

This is one of the steps that often is overlooked. Selling your plan is as important as writing it. Otherwise, no one owns it, except you. The idea is to turn it into a rallying point that helps your company move forward. And to do that, you need to turn as many people as possible into ambassadors for your marketing efforts.

First, set up a time to present the plan to everyone who helped you with information and data. Make sure that they feel some sense of ownership, but that they also see how their piece ties into the whole. This is one of those instances where you need to say your plan, show your plan, discuss your plan. Only after all three steps are completed will they *hear* the plan.

After you've shared the information across the organization, reserve some time on the executive calendar. Have a couple of leaders review the plan first, giving you feedback on the parts where they have particular expertise. Then, present the plan at a staff meeting.

Is It Working?

You may think your job is finished. It's not. You need to convey the key parts of this plan to coworkers throughout the business. They need to know what the business is trying to achieve. Their livelihood, not just that of the owners, is at stake. From their phone-answering technique to the way they process an order, every step has meaning to the customer.

9. Measure/Renew

Once you've presented your plan and people understand it, you have to continuously work the plan and share information about it. The best way to help people see trends and respond appropriately is to have meaningful measures. In the language of Total Quality, these are the Key Result Indicators—the things that have importance to your customers and that are signals to your performance.

For instance, measure your ability to deliver on a customer request; the amount of time it takes to respond to a customer inquiry; your productivity per employee; cash flow; cycle time; yield rates. The idea is to identify a way to measure those things that are critical to you and to your customer.

Review those measurements. Share the information with the entire business and begin the process all over again. Seek new ideas and input to improve your performance. Go after more data and facts. And then renew your plan and share it with everyone—all over again.

It's an extensive process, but it's one that spreads the word—and spreads the ownership. It's the step that ensures that your plan will be constantly in use, and constantly at work for your business.

Carole Hedden is a writer and communication/planning consultant living in Elmira, New York.

create a seamless campaign for the 200SX that weaves advertising, in-store displays, and direct marketing together seamlessly.

"When everybody understands what the mission is, it's easier," asserts Bilfield. "It's easier to go upstream in the same direction than to go in different directions."

After bringing the different disciplines within your company on board, you're ready to design the external marketing program needed to support your goals. Again, the principle of integrated marketing comes into play: The message should be focused and consistent, and each step of the process should bring the consumer one step closer to buying your product.

In the case of Chiat/Day's campaign for the Nissan 200SX, the company used the same theme, graphics, type faces, and message to broadcast a consistent statement.

Introduced about the same time as the latest Batman movie, the campaign incorporates music and graphics from the television series. Magazine ads include an 800 number potential customers can call if they want to receive an information kit. Kits are personalized and include the name of a local Nissan dealer, a certificate for a test drive, and a voucher entitling test drivers to a free gift.

By linking each step of the process, Chiat/Day can chart the number of calls, test drives, and sales a particular ad elicits. Like a good one-two punch, the direct marketing picks up where the national advertising leaves off, leveraging the broad exposure and targeting it at the most likely buyers.

While the elaborate 200SX campaign may seem foolproof, a failure to integrate the process at any step along the way could result in a lost sale.

For example, if a potential client were to test drive the car and encounter a dealer who knew nothing about the free gift accompanying the test drive, the customer would feel justifiably annoyed. Conversely, a well-informed sales associate who can explain the gift will be mailed to the test driver in a few weeks will engender a positive response.

Help Is on the Way

Three Software Packages That Will Help You Get Started

Writing a marketing plan may be daunting, but there is a variety of software tools out there to help you get started. Found in electronics and book stores, the tools are in many ways like a Marketing 101 textbook. The difference lies in how they help.

Software tools have a distinct advantage: They actually force you to write, and that's the toughest part of any marketing plan. Sometimes called "MBA In a Box," these systems guide you through a planning process. Some even provide wording that you can copy into your own document and edit to fit your own business. Presto! A boiler plate plan! Others provide a system of interviewing and questioning that creates a custom plan for your operation. The more complex tools demand an integrated approach to planning, one that brings together the full force of your organization, not just Sales or Advertising.

1. Crush

Crush, a modestly named new product from a modestly named new company, HOT, takes a multimedia approach. (HOT stands for Hands-On Technology; *Crush* apparently stands for *Crushing the Competition*)

Just introduced a few months ago, *Crush* is a multimedia application for Macintosh or Windows PCs. It features the competitive analysis methods of Flegis McKenna, marketing guru to Apple, Intel and Genentech; and it features Mr. McKenna himself as your mentor, offering guidance via on-screen video. As you work through each section of a complete market analysis, McKenna provides germane comments; in addition, you can see video case studies of marketing success stories like Intuit software.

Crush provides worksheets and guidance for analyzing your products, customers, market trends and competitors, and helps you generate an action plan. The "mentor" approach makes it a

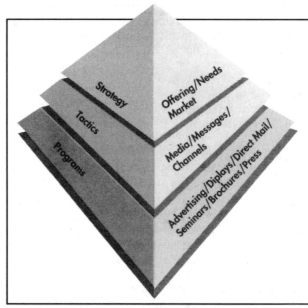

Pyramid Power: Plan Write's pyramid approach asks the user to define the messages for a business as part of the tactics.

useful tool for self-education; as you work through the examples and develop your company's marketing plan, you build your own expertise.

2. Marketing Plan Pro

Palo Alto's *Marketing Plan Pro* is a basic guide, useful for smaller businesses or ones in which the company leader wears

(continued)

a number of different hats, including marketing. It includes the standard spreadsheet capability, as well as the ability to chart numerical data. *Marketing Plan Pro* uses a pyramid process.

I liked the pyramid for a simple reason: It asks you to define messages for your business as part of your tactics. Without a message, it's easy to jump around, reacting to the marketplace instead of anticipating, leaving customers wondering what really is significant about your company or your product.

The step-by-step process is simple, and a sample plan shows how all the information works together. The customer-focus aspect of the plan seemed a little weak, demanding only sales potential and buying capacity of the customers. Targeted marketing is increasingly important, and the user may want to really expand how this section is used beyond what the software requires.

The package displays, at a glance, your strategy, the tactics you develop for each strategy, and the action plan or programs you choose to support the strategy. That could help when you're trying to prioritize creative ideas, eliminating those that really don't deliver what the strategy demands. Within each of three columns, you can click on a word and get help. Click on the heading program: a list of sample actions is displayed. They may not be what you're looking for, but if this is your first plan, they're lifesavers.

I also really liked *Marketing Plan Pro's* user's manual. It not only explains how the software works with your computer, it helps with business terms and provides a guide to planning, walking you through step-by-step.

3. Plan Write

Plan Write, created by Business Resource Software, Inc., is exponentially more powerful than *Marketing Plan Pro. Plan Write* brings together the breadth of the business, integrating information as far flung as distribution systems and image. And this software places your marketing strategy within the broader context of a business plan, the approach that tends to prove most effective.

As with *Marketing Plan Pro, Plan Write* provides a sample plan. The approach is traditional, incorporating a look at the business environment, the competition, the product or service mix you are offering, the way you will tell customers about that mix, pricing, delivery, and support.

Among the sections that were particularly strong was one on customer alternatives and people planning. Under the heading of customer alternatives, you're required to incorporate competitive information with customer information. If you don't meet the customer's needs, where could he or she go? Most often we look only at the competition, without trying to imagine how the customer is thinking. This exercise is particularly valuable to the company who leads the market.

The people part of planning too often is dumped on the personnel guy instead of being seen as a critical component of your organization's capabilities. *Plan Write* requires that you include how marketing is being handled, and how sales will be accomplished. In addition, it pushes you to define what skills will be needed in the future and where the gaps are between today and the future. People, in this plan, are viewed as a strategic component.

Plan Write offers a fully integrated spreadsheet that can import from or export to most of the popular spreadsheet programs you may already be using. Another neat feature allows you to enter numerical data and select from among 14 different graphing styles to display your information. You just click on the style you want to view, and the data is reconfigured.

Probably the biggest danger in dealing with software packages such as *Marketing Plan Pro* and *Plan Write* is to think the software is the answer. It's merely a guide.

—*Carole Hedden*

Section III: Execution

The final component of an integrated marketing plan is the implementation phase. This is where the budget comes in.

How much you'll need to spend depends on your goals. If a company wants to expand its market share or promote its products in a new region, it will probably have to spend more than it would to maintain its position in an existing market.

Again, you'll need to create a system for keeping your employees informed. You might consider adding an element to your company newsletter that features people from different departments talking about the marketing problems they encounter and how they overcome them. Or you might schedule a regular meeting for department heads to discuss marketing ideas so they can report back to their employees with news from around the company.

Finally, you'll need to devise a system for monitoring your marketing program. A database, similar to the one created from calls to the 200SX's 800 number, can be an invaluable tool for determining if your message is being well received.

It's important to establish time frames for achieving your goals early in the process. If you want to increase your market share, for instance, you should determine the rate at which you intend to add new customers. Failing to achieve that rate could signal a flaw in your plan or its execution, or an unrealistic goal.

"Remember, integrated marketing is a long-range way of thinking," warns Dawson. "Results are not going to be immediate."

Like any investment, marketing requires patience, perseverance, and commitment if it is to bear fruit. While not all companies are forward thinking enough to understand the manifold gains of integrated marketing, the ones that don't embrace it will ultimately pay a tremendous price.

SHELLY REESE is a freelance writer based in Cincinnati.

Making Inspiration Routine

It's not about brilliance. Valuable new ideas are the product of hard work and smart, disciplined processes.

A. G. LAFLEY AND RAM CHARAN

First, an observation about the Disney World analogy. P&G relies on innovation to drive growth; and, yes, it has developed a very effective arsenal of programs, processes, and techniques to generate ideas and convert them into revenue. It has no choice. P&G operates in more than 150 countries with 85 on-the-ground operations, and it has 138,000 employees in 21 business divisions. This diversification, complexity, and bureaucracy can become innovation's enemies. Small companies may seem like backyard swing sets by comparison, but backyard swing sets are where children's imaginations roam free. In fundamental ways, small companies have significant advantages over large corporations when it comes to innovation. Where small companies generally fall down, however, is in building disciplines around the creation, capture, and execution of new ideas. Most small companies develop from a single great notion, usually the brainchild of a brilliant founder. But entrepreneurs can't afford to remain the sole font of innovation at their businesses any more than they can remain the sole salesperson. Nor can they rely on the passions of their staff and the mental sparks created when 30 people interact each day in close quarters. Innovation requires work. Work requires structure. For companies, invention is 1 percent inspiration, 49 percent perspiration, and 50 percent smart routine.

Inc. asked us to choose an industry for our imagined company, and the swing-set reference put us in mind of toys. For this exercise, toys also have the advantage of being, a consumer product that P&G is not involved in. We narrowed our focus to nonelectronic playthings, a category in which we must innovate to appeal to generations weaned on computers. Our goal is to design processes that will ensure that our growing company innovates repeatedly and reliably.

1. Select the Strategy Looking for an Underserved Market

Our first step is to ask ourselves: Where do we play? Invading adjacent markets and inventing whole new business categories is tempting, especially for entrepreneurs with low boredom thresholds. But this is a small company, and we don't have the resources to create a new customer base or extend the brand. So we will look for ways to understand our existing customers better and segment them. Interestingly, segmentation itself can be an innovative act, if we identify a corner of our market that is rarely treated as a segment. Can we look at toy buyers through some other lens than such tired demographics as gender, age, and income? For a small company, identifying an overlooked segment is less expensive than inventing a new technology and may sprout even more opportunities.

2. Connect to Customers the Social Network as Idea Collector

The best pointers to that elusive new market are parents and children themselves. But how will we reach them? At P&G, many of the best ideas are born of customer-immersion experiences. About 70 percent of P&G executives have spent several days either in a customer's house—eating, playing, and shopping with the family—or in a small shop, working behind the counter. But with a staff of 30, our toy company can't spare employees to spend days or weeks observing 6-year-olds at home and school to understand what incites their imaginations. Instead, most ideas will have to come from employees. So we will hire creative people and make them conduits to consumers. And we will teach them to sharpen their observational powers during the course of their everyday lives.

The concept of social networks has become commonplace; generally, companies use them to push out marketing messages. In our company, we will use such networks to pull in ideas. We will require every employee to conduct ongoing conversations with his or her own social network—at least five friends or relatives who have children—about what they and their kids look for in toys. To get them started, we will create a discussion guide or list of questions. "What parts of the toy store does your child gravitate toward? Does he prefer toys that allow him to create things or that challenge him to solve a problem?" We will ask employees to occasionally film their children and their friends' children at play. Then we review those videos and look for patterns or anomalies. And we Hill keep asking questions. "Why did the child prefer this toy over another? What does her body language tell us? What might she have been thinking or feeling?"

We will give our social networks a good shake, and now we imagine an idea tumbles out. Among those subjects we observe are children with learning disabilities, who engage differently with some ordinary toys. Their parents work hard to find games at which they can succeed, and in conversations with our employees the parents emphasize their children's strengths. We see an opportunity: toys that allow children with special needs to make the most of their individual talents. This meets our requirement for creating a new market segment.

3. Generate Ideas
Brain-Storming Done Right

Our focus narrowed, we begin the process of identifying potential new products. At this point we will bring members of employees' networks into the office to brainstorm. Fortunately, P&G's brainstorming practices are perfectly scalable. For example, session leaders ask participants to write down their ideas on a big sheet of paper rather than leave that chore to the facilitator. That forces participants to refine their thinking. Session leaders use props: P&G's or a competitor's products, or bits and pieces of relevant materials. They discourage negative comments and tolerate—even encourage—digressions. As we continue to pursue new ideas in this category, we will hold employee-consumer brainstorming sessions every quarter.

And we will invite child psychologists, teachers, and nurses to join those sessions. While we have these experts in the office, we will also ask them to view the videos made earlier in the process and point out signals we may have missed. Again, our goal is to develop a

staff so interested in and knowledgeable about children that staff members revert to field-research mode whenever they are around children. In small companies, some people invent and many people execute, but everyone must observe.

As a result of brainstorming, talking to their social networks, and constantly observing children, employees will naturally start generating ideas. But many of those ideas will have the brightness and weight of balloons; lacking ballast, they will tend to drift off into the ether. Rather than have employees bombard us with one-sentence, off-the-top-of-their-heads e-mails, we want them to add that ballast on their own. So we will ask them to compose one-page, detailed descriptions of their ideas, accompanied by a sketch rendered digitally or in pencil (or even crayon—this is a toy company, after all). That will help us understand the concept and make it easier to discuss with others. We will also ask that before submitting ideas they pair up with another employee, much like how members of Congress seek co-sponsors on proposed legislation. That partner can help them hash out details and identify potential objections and obstacles. If the project is approved, the two will continue working as a team, which fosters collaboration.

4. Select an Idea Time to Separate the Good from the Great

Now that we have a process for harvesting ideas, we will have to cull them. Although we will have our own pet projects, we won't let emotion override practicality. So we will set criteria based on projected revenue and profit goals, and view proposed projects collectively, as a portfolio.

We also want input from employees and, ideally, potential customers. For this, we will borrow the format of P&G project reviews. Once every quarter, project teams will create displays that lay out their ideas, sketches, market research, and other relevant material—no more than fits on a poster board. We will place the posters on easels where staff members can view them. We will also ask employees to invite one or two kids from their social networks to take a look. As we examine the posters, we will ask their creators questions and make comments and suggestions, and urge employees to do the same.

Good leaders reward behavior they desire, so creating an incentive system for innovation is critical. At this stage in the company's growth, we will keep it simple. We will give small awards—$100, perhaps, or dinner for two—for ideas we like. We will make those awards at the quarterly review, to publicly celebrate the ingenuity of our staff. Later, if we proceed with any of those ideas, their creators might receive $500. For ideas we take to market, we will pay more.

5. Prototype and Test
Bring in the Customers

Say we have chosen one idea to pursue: a puzzle that can be assembled into any kind of picture based on a child's imagination rather than the way pieces fit together. The goal now is to quickly get some version into children's hands. Innovative small companies excel at performing inexpensive, frequent experiments. For that reason, prototypes are our friends. We may be able to create the initial design ourselves, using simple prototype software. But we will also hire an outside company to produce physical prototypes, which can often be done for a few hundred dollars. Prototypes are enormously important. With consumer products especially, the sooner you have a visual, the sooner you can start making adjustments based on specific feedback and suggestions.

Prototypes in hand, we will invite members of employees' social networks—which by this time have become like our own extended family—to the office for a play party. We will include both children with special needs and those without. Why the latter group? From these children we may gain additional insights into our target market and also, potentially, ideas for innovations in new markets down the road. As always, we will observe all the children carefully. And we will bring back those teachers and nurses to tell us what they see.

Much as we value the tangible, we won't want to waste money producing prototypes in every color, shape, and texture imaginable. So we will bring to the party other products, such as clothes or chairs or dishes, that reflect those characteristics and see which the children like best. We won't show them food items or other toys, because with items of that nature, a personal preference for the thing itself might influence their decisions.

6. Go to Market
Cookies versus Cookie Dough

After all that brainstorming and observing and prototyping and testing, we will be lucky to find two products a year worth bringing to market. That's fine: A company of our size will likely stumble if it reaches for more. And we won't necessarily worry about perfecting those products ourselves. As a small company, we may have difficulty manufacturing and distributing our products on a large scale, so we will be open to partnership with a large competitor. (Even P&G has gone this route—for example, collaborating with a competitor like Glad.) Big companies are always scouting for innovative products they can add to their portfolios. Often they prefer not a finished product but one that is half-baked, so that their own designers and engineers can contribute to the recipe. We won't insist on offering cookies if we gain more by offering cookie dough.

7. Adjust for Growth
the Process Evolves

As our company grows, so will the resources we devote to innovation. When we get to 50 or 100 employees, we will hire four or five innovation leaders—executives with curiosity, openness to all ideas regardless of origin, and a high tolerance for risk. We will deploy these leaders in different parts of the company so that creative energies are expended on creating innovative internal processes as well as innovative products. The person who devises a brilliant strategy for recruiting great employees is as valuable as our most talented designer.

With more staff, we will gain the luxury of a little—just a little—more time for all. We will use some of that to further ingrain innovation into our routine. Employees will continue to work their social networks, but we will also initiate weekly internal idea meetings. They may last no more than 30 minutes to an hour, and everyone will be invited. Three times a month, we will spend those meetings brainstorming—spreading a fine-weave net to capture small, inchoate ideas that pop up as employees attend conferences, listen to the news, and otherwise engage in work and life. Once a month, we will discuss ideas we are already pursuing to evaluate which are progressing well and which should be put out of their misery. All ideas, even innovative ideas, are not created equal. We want to kill the weak ones before they sap too many resources from the strong.

More money and more people mean more structure, but we also want to preserve the energy and spirit that, as we said at the beginning, are among small companies' greatest strengths. So while we continue to observe customers and potential customers at play, we will also observe our employees at work. For example, we may no longer preside over all the brainstorming sessions—in fact, we will train employees in brainstorming techniques so they can take the helm—but we will sit in frequently. Are the social dynamics still conducive to creativity? And we will make sure our innovation leaders are developing not just creative products and processes but also creative people. Are they coaching employees on how to flesh out intriguing but amorphous ideas? Are they listening to new employees with the same attention they give to veterans?

Companies love to say innovation is in their DNA. But that means more than having a founder and employees who are naturally creative. We will give our creative employees the tools and systems they need to turn their brilliant ideas into real, profit-generating products. And we will demonstrate through our continued success that *innovation routine* is not an oxymoron. It is a mandate.

In April, **A. G. LAFLEY**, the chairman and CEO of Procter & Gamble, and Ram Charan, adviser to such business leaders as Jack Welch and Robert Nardelli, published an insider's guide to innovation at P&G and other top corporations. *The Game-Changer: How You Can Drive Revenue and Profit Growth With Innovation* argues that innovation—like learning—must be continuous and pursued at all levels of the organization. The book describes dozens of mechanisms for keeping the idea pipeline full, such as P&G's customer-immersion programs, which send employees to live in consumers' homes, and innovation "hot zones," facilities where product teams spend weeks on creative exercises.

It's a great book, but for owners of small companies, it's a little like reading about Disney World when all you have to play with is a backyard swing set. We wondered: Could P&G's approach to innovation be made to scale for businesses with a tiny fraction of P&G's resources?

We asked **LAFLEY** and **CHARAN** to imagine they were the founders of a company in an industry of their choice, with $4 million in revenue and 30 employees. What would they do to make their business as innovative as possible?

Surveyor of the Fittest

With the correct methodology, companies can effectively assess what market is viable and what market is not.

Hongjun (HJ) Li

Industry research shows that 75% of new-product launches fail in the marketplace (visit www.microsoft.com to read its section about new–product development performance). That number does not even include product concepts that never successfully enter the market. There are many reasons for such failures, but lack of market demand for new products introduced is definitely the most important one.

According to an AMR Research Inc. report released in June 2005: Out of 20 large manufacturers polled about poor performance of product launches, 47% cited failing to understand and meet customer needs exactly—compared with 33% citing being late to market and 23% citing poor pricing.

No company will develop and introduce a new product if it knows beforehand that there will be no market demand. Unfortunately, most companies try to justify new-product development (NPD) expenditures by doing some market analysis—only to find out later that projected market demand has failed to materialize. Thus, a critical question to industry players is how they can become more effective in their market assessment efforts. This article offers a practical methodology that answers the question.

Defining "New Product"

For the purpose of this article, "new product" refers to one of the following:

- a product that creates or implements a new technology
- a product that implements an existing technology on a new platform
- a product that integrates multiple technologies or functions into a single product for the first time
- a product that provides significant enhancements to an existing product category

Executive Briefing

You might be surprised at how many new-product introductions fail every year. Unfortunately, such failure is not necessarily due to lack of market investigation. That is not to state, however, that market investigation is not relevant anymore. On the contrary: The industry's poor performance with new-product introductions pinpoints the importance of doing the right market investigation the right way. Here is a systematic, effective, and easy-to-follow methodology that illustrates exactly how to accomplish that.

The focus of our discussion is the overall market, not company-specific issues that can also lead to new-product introduction failures. There are many cases in which market demand for a new-product category exists but a particular company's product—falling into that category—fails in the market because of poor internal execution. Although internal execution is certainly critical, companies must first and foremost understand whether there will be a market for their new products being conceived or developed. Market investigation, in other words, remains highly relevant.

We will also assume that when a new product is introduced, it works—and its functionality conforms to original design requirements or intentions. Product failures attributed to unintended design flaws or quality problems are excluded from the scope of discussion. Again, such issues are internal and not market-related.

Common Pitfalls

Because so many new-product introduction failures can be attributed to lack of market demand, it is necessary to understand why companies fail to foresee them in the first place. Granted that market forecasting is sometimes a very difficult thing to do, companies can significantly reduce risks of new-product introduction failures if they do some basic market assessment homework the right way.

In general, the following are the common market assessment pitfalls into which companies fall:

- blind faith in one's capability to drive or create market demand
- looking at technological merits only
- selective use of incomplete, biased, or deceiving market data and feedback in line with product concepts or initial decisions
- taking input from direct customers only, without looking at demand from customers' customers (when applicable)
- relying on feedback or data of customer/consumer interest only, without looking at many other market factors that drive actual purchase decisions
- depending on third-party market forecasts only, without looking at or fully understanding the methodology used and assumptions made

Some companies might achieve market success even if they fall into one of these pitfalls, but such success requires really good luck and can hardly be duplicated in different settings.

Assessing the Market

Market assessment can be viewed as a science or an art. The challenge to market research professionals: Although some commonly used research techniques and tools exist, they might not be adequate to address the complete scope of market assessment required for sound business decision making. The challenge to senior executives is that they don't have the time to do detailed market investigations themselves. In addition, they might not have an effective framework for judging the quality and reliability of their subordinates' market assessments.

Both dedicated market research professionals and senior executives can use the methodology suggested here. The former can use it to investigate all the key aspects of a new product's market potential; the latter can use it to evaluate their subordinates' work. The methodology, if used the right way, can help companies avoid the aforementioned pitfalls.

The individual elements in the suggested market assessment framework are nothing new (see Figure 1). What might be new, however, are identification of all major market-related factors that affect demand for a

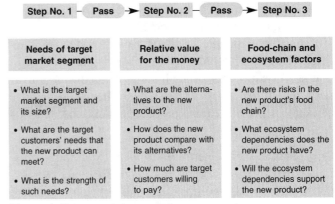

Figure 1 Framework for market assessment.

Note: Customers are those that make purchase decisions (in the case of business-to-business and business-to-consumer). Customers might be different from end users in the case of business-to-business-to-consumer.

new product, categorization of these factors within a systematic framework, and a step-by-step process that is easy to follow: (1) define target segment and needs, (2) analyze relative value, and (3) evaluate food-chain and ecosystem risks.

Defining Target and Needs

With rare exceptions, a particular new product serves only a particular market segment or niche. This is especially true in the consumer-technology market. If a new product to be introduced simply targets "everybody," then it will most likely have a tough road ahead—because different segments and niches have different needs. There is a direct correlation between clarity of market-segment definition and ability to meet target customers' specific needs. Not surprisingly, the phenomenon of "shoot and aim" can explain why so many new products fail.

Defining the target market segment entails a detailed analysis of key segment characteristics such as size, demographics, and purchasing behavior. Without a clear understanding of the target segment, it will be difficult to identify the needs that a new product can meet.

Associating a generic need with a product is easy, and it can mislead companies into believing that their new product meets target customers' needs. To avoid that pitfall, companies can ask a simple question: What, exactly, is the problem that the new product solves?

Take the failed WebTV (a set-top box that consumers connect to their television sets, which allows dial-up Internet connection), for example. Consumers with a personal computer (PC) at home do not need it for Internet access. WebTV does allow non-PC households to access the Internet; unfortunately, the amount of non-PC households with such a need is very small. Moreover, WebTV cannot address that need well because of poor display of Web content on a standard-definition TV.

Even if the specific need for a new product is identified or defined, companies must assess the strength of that need, as different strength levels mean different market sizes. In general, two variables influence the relative strength of the need for a product: cognizance and perceived importance.

Cognizance. This determines to what extent target customers are aware of a particular need. There are two levels: explicit needs and implicit needs. Explicit needs are well-recognized and can be clearly articulated. They normally indicate a high level of need strength. Only new products with meaningful differentiation (to be discussed next) can turn these needs into corresponding market demand. Implicit needs, on the other hand, are not well-recognized or clearly articulated. They typically represent a new market that takes time, resources, and market education to develop.

Perceived importance. Depending on how strong the perceived importance of a particular need is, products meeting a particular need can fit into three categories: must-have, nice-to-have, and can-live-without. Must-have products meet the needs with the highest level of perceived importance and have the broadest market reach. Nice-to-have products address less-important needs and therefore have lower market demand. Can-live-without products generally have the lowest market-penetration rate.

Although measuring need strength can be difficult and subjective, it is a critical element of market analysis. A common method of need-strength assessment is conducting a quantitative survey to ask consumers their interest level in a particular new product or service. The challenge, however, is that different survey designs can yield significantly different results even if the same topic is addressed. Thus, as mentioned, understanding methodologies used and assumptions made is vital to appropriate interpretation of survey results.

One example of different survey results on the same topic is a study on consumers' interest in watching video on mobile devices. A survey by RBC Capital Markets shows that only 24% are interested, whereas a study by The Diffusion Group shows that 32% are interested. The delta can be attributed to differences in measurement scales (true/false versus a 7-point scale) and age groups of survey respondents (ages 21–65 versus ages 15–50). (Read "The Appeal of Mobile Video: Reading Between the Lines" under the TDG Opinions section at www.tdgresearch.com.)

Regardless of which is right (or closer to being correct), consumer interest is only one variable; other factors also drive market demand for a new product. This is why completing the following second step is essential, too.

Analyzing Relative Value

In today's environment, in which new technologies are rapidly emerging, consumers are having more and more choices that meet the same needs. For a new product to succeed in the marketplace, it will need to deliver a more compelling value proposition than alternative solutions by accomplishing at least one of the following: being a better product for a similar price and/or having a better price for a similar product. It is noteworthy that the higher market penetration alternatives have already achieved, the more important it is for new products to have strong differentiation in features/performance or cost.

The main reason voice over Internet protocol (VoIP) has been able to gain traction in both business and consumer markets is that it can deliver the same service as traditional wireline voice but at a lower cost. VoIP also enables certain features not available from "plain old telephone service" (POTS), but lower cost is the main driver of market adoption.

On the other hand, independent VoIP-over-broadband operators (at least those in the United States) have had difficulties quickly penetrating the consumer market without spending tons of marketing dollars. That is because of the availability of four primary alternatives: existing POTS, mobile phone service, Skype-type (a peer-to-peer Internet telephony network) services, and inexpensive VoIP phone cards. Those services either make voice communications an already fulfilled need or deliver cost savings similar to VoIP-over-broadband.

The same thing can be said of telcos' Internet protocol television (IPTV) service. In many markets, especially the United States, cable and satellite television have already made home-video entertainment a fulfilled need. If telcos' IPTV offers only me-too video services, then the most effective way for it to gain market share from cable and satellite television companies is to offer a lower price—as part of a discounted service bundle or a lower cost, stand-alone service. Alternatively, telcos can develop new applications: true video on demand and other innovative, compelling services that leverage the Internet protocol network.

Alternative solutions are not limited to similar products from direct competitors. They also include various other substitutes that address the same need. For example, the use of hands to turn lights on or off is an alternative to a lighting-control home-automation solution that requires a purchase—even though the former is less convenient. As taught in any Economics 101 course, substitutes create a negative impact on demand for a particular product.

Even if a cool new product has no or few existing alternatives and addresses a specific need, affordability or customers' price elasticity will determine its market penetration. A good example is high-end home-control (also called home-automation) systems. Of course they are not truly new products today, as a category, but they were when introduced about three decades ago. Those systems address consumers' need for comfort, convenience, safety, and prestige. However, because of high price tags (typically tens of thousands of dollars), high-end home-control systems have found success only in the custom-installed electronics market. And today's household penetration rate in the United States is still less than 2%, according to Parks Associates (an industry analyst firm).

Evaluating Risks

Suppose a new-product concept passes the test of the previous two steps; there is still no guarantee of market success. This third step prompts companies to identify market risks from a new product's food chain and its ecosystem. In this article, "ecosystem" refers to the interdependency of a certain set of infrastructure elements, platforms, devices, and other components that function as a whole to meet a particular need of customers.

From a market perspective, food-chain risks arise from direct customers' business model issues or uncertainty of demand from customers' customers. Although food-chain risks do not apply to everybody, they can be significant in certain sectors. For example, food-chain issues can explain the failure of some telecommunications equipment companies—and their products—that specifically targeted competitive local exchange carriers (CLECs) in the 1990s in the United States. Various newly developed products for CLECs, at that time, could certainly pass the test of the previous two steps. But they failed eventually because their CLEC customers did not have a sustainable business model after capital market bubbles burst.

Food-chain risks can also apply to a company in the business-to-business-to-consumer market. Assume that a service provider has just approached a vendor of video-phones for the deployment of a new service. To assess how many units the vendor can actually sell, it will need to

carefully assess consumers' potential take rate, partially based on the service provider's marketing and pricing plans. If the service provider cannot sign up many subscribers to the service that involves the use of a video-phone, then the vendor will not be able to sell many units either—no matter how rosy the service provider's deployment plan appears to be.

A new product might also face significant market risks if it has too much dependency on certain ecosystem elements beyond the product developer's control. Products that enable delivery of online video to the television represent a good example. The main device that has such capability is the digital media adapter (DMA), a special set-top box that connects to both the television and a home network. For DMA to succeed as a product category, it will need support from at least the following ecosystem elements:

- wide availability of high-quality online video content, which is subject to Hollywood's receptivity to digital-content distribution and compatible digital-rights management solutions
- attractive pricing from content owners
- high penetration of robust, no-new-wire home networking solutions for multimedia distribution (beyond Ethernet and 802.11b/g, a wireless LAN standard)
- wide deployment of higher-bandwidth broadband access networks beyond ADSL1 or DOCSIS1.0 (Asymmetric Digital Subscriber Line, Data Over Cable Service Interface Specification)

DMA devices first appeared on the consumer market around 2003. Over the past few years, however, very few units have been sold (according to research from Parks Associates and NPD). The poor showing of DMA as a product category can be attributed to not only factors illustrated in the previous two steps but also poor ecosystem support (e.g., very limited availability of quality online video content, various home networking issues). Going forward, though, the DMA market is expected to gain stronger momentum—this time driven by positive developments of the ecosystem.

Implementing the Process

The person or team responsible for market intelligence should (1) develop detailed output based on the key questions in the three aforementioned steps and then (2) provide an overall assessment (see Figure 2). The market intelligence function should present to executives

Steps	Detailed output
Step No. 1: Needs of target market segment	• definition of the target market segment and estimate of the total size of the target segment • definition of the specific needs that the new product can address • categorization of the strength of the identified needs: level of cognizance and importance
Step No. 2: Relative value for the money	• list of alternatives to the new product and their market penetration rate • feature and price comparison between alternatives and the new product • target customers' price elasticity and estimated market adoption rate at specific price points
Step No. 3: Food-chain and ecosystem factors	• analysis of viability of target customers' business model specific to the new product • list of ecosystem elements that the new product depends on • the current status and projected future developments of the identified ecosystem elements
Overall assessment	• qualitative assessment of the viability of the new product's market • quantitative projections of the total available market in terms of units and revenues (if feasible and needed)

Figure 2   The market intelligence function's implementation.

Note: Certain items of the output list can be omitted only if relevant facts (1) are already common knowledge to everybody or (2) do not apply to a particular new product.

Market assessment results		Yellow light	Red light
Needs of target market segment	Difficult-to-define target market segment		X
	Difficult-to-define specific needs of target customers		X
	Implicit needs	X	
	Nice-to-have product	X	
	Can-live-without product		X
Relative value for the money	Presence of alternatives with a high market penetration rate	X	
	High price elasticity of target customers	X	
Food-chain and ecosystem factors	Questionable business model of target customers		X
	Too much ecosystem dependency	X	
	Lack of ecosystem support		X

Figure 3   New-product development risk assessment.

Yellow light: Market demand is limited or has substantial uncertainties.
Red light: Market demand is very limited or has very high uncertainties.

not only the overall assessment but also a summary of the detailed output—so they can see how conclusions are reached.

To judge the quality and reliability of the market intelligence function's work, executives can ask themselves three simple questions:

- Is there clear definition of the target market segment, the specific needs of target customers, and the strength of their needs?
- Is there adequate assessment of the impact from alternatives and customers' price elasticity?
- Are food-chain and ecosystem risks clearly identified and evaluated?

A tool for executive decision making. How should the three-step market assessment process be used for NPD decision-making purposes? As different companies have different business models, financial objectives, market power, and so forth, perhaps there is no clear-cut answer that applies to everybody. However, executives might find Figure 3's risk-assessment framework (based on the

three-step process) a useful tool for distilling output from the market intelligence function and making decisions on NPD projects.

If yellow lights are associated with a new-product concept, then executives will need careful assessment of the new product's value proposition and market positioning before making a "go" decision on product development. If a new-product concept faces one or more red lights, then there will be high risks of market failure—and executives might be better off allocating development resources to an alternative new product that addresses a more viable market.

How often should the process be used? In fast-changing industries or markets, it is probably necessary for that market assessment framework to be used more than once for the entire NPD process. That will allow companies to not only reduce new-product introduction failure risks but also identify new market opportunities in a timely fashion.

Other participants in the market assessment process. Although the market intelligence function and executives are the most direct users of the recommended market assessment framework, a few other functions should be included: product management, sales, marketing, strategic planning, and engineering managers. Their inclusion can take the form of providing input, reviewing output, and communicating relevant findings to individual team members. The more synchronized the internal communication, the more capabilities companies will have for developing and selling new products that meet market needs.

Avoiding the Trap

There have been too many cases in which companies developed new technologies or products looking for problems to solve. To avoid falling into such a trap, companies can complete the aforementioned three simple steps. Afterward, they will be in a much better position to assess the market viability of a new-product concept and whether product development resources should be committed to it.

Hongjun (HJ) Li is director of product marketing at the Plano, Texas, office of Kodiak Networks, a startup specializing in advanced mobile-communication applications headquartered in San Ramon, Calif. He may be reached at hli@kodiaknetworks.com or hongjunli888@yahoo.com. To join the discussion about this article, please visit www.marketingpower.com/marketingmanagementblog.

The Inevitability of $300 Socks

How Ideas Pave the Way for Products

When does an outrageous price for a product become acceptable and even desirable? When the item transforms us from consumers to connoisseurs.

DAN HEATH AND CHIP HEATH

You wouldn't pay $30 for a can of soup. Or $80 for an undershirt. Yet many of you reading this have paid upward of $300 for jeans. What happened to the Lee Jeans era? In a flash, our price threshold for jeans has increased from $50 to $300. And it's not just jeans that have gone ultra-premium, it's markets as varied as bourbon, workout clothes, and even peanut butter. Could we live in a world seven years from now where "normal" people (including you) would pay $300 for, say, a pair of socks? If so, how would it happen?

Products make the leap from pedestrian to premium when their creators think of them as ideas. Some products are heavy on ideas: perfume, spa treatments, life coaching, alcohol. Others are practically idea-free: mailboxes, fax machines, oil changes. Notice anything about those two sets of goods? You make mega-margins on the first and mini-margins on the second. Margins feed on ideas.

Jeans used to be idea-light. They were workmanlike, durable, casual. But workmanlike doesn't become a $700 million-plus-a-year category within a decade. What ideas does a pair of $300 jeans hold that Lee jeans do not? Let's start with expertise. Paige Adams-Geller founded Paige Premium Denim in 2004. Prior to that, she helped shape the fit for many of the top denim brands, including 7 for All Mankind, which deserves much of the credit for the modern jeans boom. The idea presented to the Paige Premium buyer in a pamphlet on each pair is clear: This person has committed her professional life to finding you the perfect pair of jeans.

As if that weren't enough, meet Jose Auguilar, who works for Paige in Los Angeles. His job is to mess with your jeans. He takes each "finished" pair, and, using a piece of sandpaper, starts scraping away at certain spots on the leg, in order to create the color fade the designers desired. Let's admit that paying extra for this service is a bit like paying $50,000 for a Taurus because Jose Auguilar hit it with a hammer a bunch of times. But without Auguilar, without Adams-Geller, those jeans lose their status as a curated item and become more like Lee. Just jeans.

The Premium-Denim Market Proves That Elevating Your Product to an Idea Creates a Sexy Sell

1. The Ideal Rear

Fit model Paige Adams-Geller has the butt that launched a thousand brands—and now her own.

2. The All-American

Earnest Sewn's blue and orange threads are meant to evoke "old Gulf Oil racing cars" and the "fading mystique of American ingenuity and craftsmanship."

3. The Star Maker

Justin Timberlake's brand (named to honor his grandfather) mixes "city slick and Southern sophistication" in the designs.

4. The Mythical Jean

Each basic Odyn style is named for a character from Nordic mythology.

5. The Green Jean

Founded by a Dutch anti-poverty NGO, Kuyichi jeans include an online code that lets you see who picked the cotton and sewed your pair.

Part of the underlying reason for consumers being more receptive to this morphing of products into ideas is that our concept of luxury has evolved. Luxury has become more about personal pleasure and self-expression and less about status. In the 1980s, people generally stuck to their social class, says Zain Raj, executive director of the ad agency Euro RSCG, Chicago: "You wore $200 pants with an $80 shirt and a $65 tie. There was a relative order to the world in terms of value. Today, it's all personal." That's why it's not surprising to see people wear $300 jeans with $8 T-shirts. Or to see folks who can barely make rent pay $15 a pound for Costa Rican organic coffee.

Luxury goods are no longer a sign of status; they're the mark of connoisseurship. Go ahead, ask a rich guy about his $3,900 David Yurman watch. "I love watches," he'll say, and he'll probably tell you about the watch's modern Swiss movement, its antiglare sapphire crystal, and how it's more a work of art than a timepiece. See—he isn't a rich jerk, he's a *watch connoisseur!* Our world is populated by watch people and wine people and coffee people and jeans people. You are, it seems, what you blow a lot of money on.

But we haven't completely left behind the status era, because connoisseurship only works when you are recognized as a connoisseur. What fun would it be to wear the world's nicest watch or jeans, and have no one recognize it? A connoisseur lives to be recognized by fellow aficionados. Kindred spirits can only recognize each other, though, if the product allows some "signal" that insiders can notice, such as the subtle back-pockets of ultra-premium jeans that can only be decoded by other connoisseurs.

Signaling might be the key for socks to launch into the stratosphere. "I could only see it happening if there was a new fashion craze, if people started wearing knickers or long shorts that showed off socks," says Adams-Geller, who knows a bit about phenomena. See, if socks let you signal your community membership, there could be sock people!

But $300 socks might benefit from one or two additional ideas. V.K. Nagrani, a designer of high-end men's socks that retail for about $35, believes socks are a signal of intimacy. Think about it: In a formal situation, you'll rarely see someone's socks. Then, if they take off their shoes—a sign of comfort or familiarity—you'll see their feet. If they recline, and their trousers creep up the leg, you'll see more. The more comfortable they get, the more sock you see. It's a sock tease. Nagrani designs his socks accordingly, so that, as the trousers creep up, you see more and more detail that was once hidden. You're not buying something to keep your feet warm or dry; you're buying seduction. (Though with men, of course, the seductive effect may be extinguished with the first glimpse of hairy calves.)

In this way, slowly but surely, products become ideas. And it dawns on consumers that your product—be it jeans, socks, or a high-end gas range—is a meaningful symbol of their personal aesthetics, their inner selves. Yes, we all know that no one in their right mind would ever pay $300 for socks. But having a right mind is so yesterday.

Rocket Plan

**Companies can fuel success with a rigorous pricing approach—
one that measures customer value, the innovation's nature,
and the product category life cycle stage.**

MARK BURTON AND STEVE HAGGETT

Innovation is the fuel that drives growth. Any good sales executive can tell you that the quickest path to revenue growth is through new product innovation rather than fighting for share in existing markets. Innovation offers immediate differentiation and the chance to command a premium price. Yet the risks of failure are high. Consider this statement from Eric von Hippel, a professor of the Massachusetts Institute of Technology (*Harvard Business Review*, January 2007): "Recent research shows that the 70% to 80% of new product development that fails does so not for lack of advanced technology but because of a failure to understand users' needs."

A new-product launch enjoys many proud parents: the development team that followed a rigorous staged development process, the manufacturing organization that trained Six Sigma black belts, the marketing team that developed creative promotions and toured with industry trade shows, the public relations team that built a compelling publicity campaign, and the sales team that enthusiastically extolled the product's virtues to customers. So why are there high failure rates?

Many companies' innovation efforts are inwardly focused. The results are billions of dollars wasted developing offerings that have little to no appeal to customers. In business-to-business markets there are three principal reasons for that:

Failure to connect customer needs to value: financial, competitive, and strategic benefits to the customer.
PictureTel was an early innovator in the videoconferencing industry 20 years ago, developing a breakthrough technology enabling live videoconferences. Its product launch focused on its leading performance and truly impressive technical capabilities. Yet after PictureTel's great investment and product differentiation, the market did not beat a path to its door. The early value propositions failed to translate the cost of the system into clear value for customers: revenue benefits of reaching more customers or cost savings from travel. In 2000, PictureTel lost $100 million; in 2001, a smaller and more profitable rival purchased it.

Executive Briefing

The majority of new-product launches fail. However, it is seldom the technology itself that's to blame. A rigorous pricing approach can improve customer adoption rates, grow profitability, and increase return on investment. A strategy that quantitatively measures customer value, evaluates the nature of the innovation (whether minor, major, or disruptive), and assesses the stage of the product life cycle can be the difference between success and failure. The authors describe an effective approach.

Use of product-based value propositions centering on technical ability over market needs. Iridium was a triumph of rocket science. In 1987, the wife of a senior Motorola technology leader fumed because she couldn't call home from a boat in the Bahamas. Eleven years and more than $2 billion later, Motorola had successfully launched a necklace of 66 satellites linking $3,000 phone sets for $7-a-minute calls. However, cell phone customers wanted increasingly small units, not 1-pound "shoe phones," and the market for people who needed a dedicated satellite system for $7 a minute was tiny. In 2000, the network was sold for around $25 million—about a penny on the dollar for Motorola's investment.

Overemphasis on the role of pricing in driving customer adoption. Petrocosm launched as an oil industry transaction platform with a $100 million investment from Chevron and top leadership from the oil equipment industry. It offered a cheap source of high-technology drilling equipment. But in an industry requiring billion-dollar offshore platforms poised over explosive hydrocarbon reservoirs, replacing the trust and experience that trained sales and service representatives offer with a low-cost transaction failed to gain a customer base. The customer base didn't want cheap; it wanted cost-effective. Petrocosm faded away.

The good news is that the pricing process is straightforward and will improve the returns on investment in innovations. Most successful innovators follow a few simple rules:

- Define the financial benefits that customers receive from adopting the new solution.
- Align price levels with financial and psychological drivers of customer value.
- Align pricing strategy with the specific nature of the innovation and the product category life cycle status.
- Create outstanding launch programs—taking the emphasis off price by mitigating perceived risks for customers.

Companies that adhere to those principles enjoy significant benefits over their competitors, including (1) a more effective screening process that enables them to focus resources only on those innovations that provide significant value to the customer, (2) compelling launch programs that communicate the business value of innovations, and (3) a coherent pricing strategy that prevents panic discounting to drive sales. Taken together, those benefits translate to greater success rates for new offerings and better pricing for those that make it to market.

The Value-on-Innovation Paradox

In B-to-B markets, technological possibility often drives innovation, not defined customer needs. Living on the uncertain edge of technology, it should be less risky to focus on what's possible rather than invest money in less-certain research based on customer wish lists—trusting in Moore's Law rather than Murphy's Law. (Moore's Law is the observation that the number of transistors on an integrated circuit for minimum component cost doubles every 24 months, described by Intel cofounder Gordon Moore. Murphy's Law states that anything that can go wrong, will.) But the results show the drawbacks of a technology-driven approach.

Often, market research is focused on projections of market size and growth based on customer intent-to-purchase studies. Although this information can be important, it overlooks the most fundamental issue of whether an innovation will be successful: Is there a compelling business reason for customers to go through the upheaval of changing how they do things—to get the potential benefits of adopting your innovation? In short, what value does the customer expect to get, and how does value compare with the costs of switching? That question sets a much higher standard for research. To address it, companies need to focus on the six areas in Figure 1.

Great innovators use the answers to those questions to draw a map of where innovation will have the greatest impact—at both the market and individual customer level. Not until they understand (1) the customer value their innovations create, (2) the barriers, and (3) enablers of adoption do they finalize specifications. These same insights are used to define high-impact value propositions and to establish pricing models and price levels.

Define customer objectives	• How do customers make money? • How do they plan to grow? • How do they differentiate their offerings? • What are their greatest challenges?
Define current solution	• Which business processes support critical customer objectives? • What is the current work flow? • Who are the process owners and what are their priorities?
Define problem solved	• How does our innovation improve performance against key customer objectives and performance of critical business processes? • What is the impact of solving the problem defined? Is it significant enough to go forward?
Define financial impact	• How does our innovation affect revenues and costs relative to current solutions?
Define barriers to adoption	• What and whom in the customer buying group would our innovation affect? • What are the switching costs? • Is our innovation compatible with customer processes and supporting technology? • What is the organizational or political impact of our innovation?
Define likely adopters	• Who will benefit most from a change to our solution? • Who has the power to push for the change?

Figure 1 Customer value.

Defining barriers to adoption and identifying likely adopters are critical. Companies commonly misread how their innovations change the buying center dynamics. Existing customer contacts might not be the right targets for an innovation when relationships with new decision makers and influencers need to be cultivated. Companies often call on the same old contacts and fail to anticipate that those contacts will not have the power to drive change and/or are very much invested in the status quo. When that happens, they find that those relationships actually impede their ability to sell innovations to their current customers.

The smartest road to profitable returns on innovations starts with an understanding of the customer; technology comes second.

Using Value Insights

Translating the results of customer value research into effective pricing for innovations requires answering some challenging questions about value to the customer. Importantly, it is not

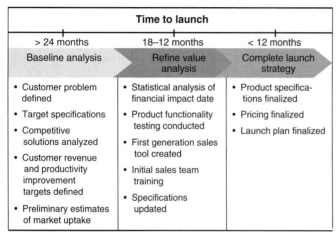

Figure 2 Preparing for effective launch pricing.

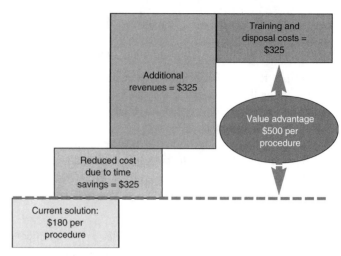

Figure 3 Use customer value data to determine your price.

necessary to exhaustively answer these questions at the start of your customer research and innovation development processes. In fact, one defining characteristic of many leading innovators is that they are comfortable with a certain amount of ambiguity to start. The key is that they continue to (1) ask hard questions about customers and value and (2) refine their views on offering specifications, value positioning, and pricing. They do it early and they do it often.

A leading manufacturer of dental equipment (disguised), which has built its business by entering new markets with innovative offerings, does exactly this. Figure 2 shows a summary of its process.

It is tempting to look at the timeline and say "Our product life cycles are too short for this to be practical." But the fact is that all windows of innovative advantage are shortening. For all companies, it is critical to do value homework and get launch pricing right. Although your business might require far more compressed timelines, the process of establishing and refining your view of value to the customer is the foundational element for successful introduction, pricing, and positioning of innovations.

When the manufacturer was able to employ new technologies, to replace reusable dental instruments with disposable ones, it knew it had a potentially valuable innovation to bring to market. Through direct customer interviews and operational studies, it determined that such a device would improve procedure-room utilization by reducing cleanup time. The device also provided a market opportunity for oral surgeons seeking to differentiate themselves by advertising that they use the safest and most advanced equipment.

Using this information to establish a range for pricing is a three-step process: Determine the total costs to the customer of his current solution options, define the financial benefits that your innovation delivers over and above current alternatives, and identify the switching costs for customers who want to move to your solution.

In the case of our dental equipment manufacturer, that meant determining the following:

- the cost per procedure of current solutions—by amortizing the total lifetime costs of current and reusable equipment over the number of procedures performed
- the cost savings due to greater procedure-room utilization
- the increases in revenues from patients brought in through oral surgeons advertising use of the new equipment
- switching costs (in this instance, disposal and training costs)

Its findings are summarized in Figure 3.

The results of customer value research yield a band of customer value and establish upper and lower boundaries for price range. Using that information about financial value, the manufacturer was then able to set an initial price that captured a fair share of the value created for customers. To do that, it first defined its value advantage over existing solutions: in this case, $500 per procedure. Next, it added the cost of the current solution to define the maximum range of price options available: $180-$680 (the $180 cost of the current solution plus the $500 value advantage).

To narrow down the range, the manufacturer analyzed the psychological elements of value from the customer's perspective. That included negative perceptions (e.g., risk from adopting the new technology, concerns about moving from the comfortable old solution to something new) and psychological benefits (e.g., pride in being on the cutting edge). Finally, the manufacturer needed to set a price that offered some incentive to purchase. At the end of the process, it decided on $400 per instrument. Although that was at the lower end of the possible range, it ensured a significant profit and gave customers a reasonable incentive to switch.

How do companies best select the right price within the range of customer value? Let's turn to that by looking more closely at pricing strategy.

Pricing Strategy Selection

To really refine the pricing decision, evaluate price ranges against a defined pricing strategy for your innovation. This is an iterative process of checking (1) pricing strategy against market research data and (2) possible price points against your pricing strategy. The best way to get your arms around the pricing strategy element is to think about the following two variables.

What is the nature of the innovation? Is it a minor improvement, such as an interim software update? Is it a major one, such as the introduction of flat-panel TV sets? Or is it disruptive, such as the current move to solid-state flash memory for applications previously covered by high-speed disk drives?

Understanding the nature of the innovation defines the degrees of freedom that the innovator has in selecting a pricing strategy. Minor innovations (e.g., line extensions) are often necessary, but they do little to create advantage over the competition. As such, they provide little to increase pricing power. Innovations that are recognized as major breakthroughs present much greater flexibility in choosing a pricing strategy. This is because companies can keep prices high to skim value until the market develops—and then bring prices down to drive growth.

With disruptive innovations, the decision is a bit trickier. In the groundbreaking article "Disruptive Technologies: Catching the Wave" (*Harvard Business Review,* January 2005), Clayton M. Christensen points out that such innovations fall into one of two categories.

Some, such as flash memory, offer significant performance advantages for niche markets (e.g., aerospace applications) but are too expensive for mainstream applications (e.g., laptop computers). The best approach for these products is to go upmarket and use a skim pricing strategy—until costs and complementary technologies make it possible to enter main-stream markets.

Alternately, some offer inferior performance on many key attributes but offer clear benefits in one or two areas for some customers. That was the case with 3.5-inch disk drives when they were introduced. In that instance, the best approach is to go down-market and use a penetration pricing strategy with prices set below established alternatives.

In what stage of the life cycle is the product category?
This element is critical but often overlooked. Failure to consider the life cycle dimension can result in disastrous financial consequences. That happened with flat-panel TVs. Early entrants initially played the game well. Prices for the early sets were high, reflecting both costs and the value that enthusiasts placed on them. As process technologies improved, prices dropped precipitously and customer adoption took off. Unfortunately, as the market started to show signs of maturity, most manufacturers were slow to take their feet off the pricing gas. The result has been terrible margin pressures due to low prices and overcapacity—at exactly the time that consumers are becoming sophisticated enough to value and actively seek out differentiation.

Taken together, those two variables point to default pricing strategies for each combination type and stage of the product category life cycle.

Driving Customer Adoption

In addition to doing their homework on value to frame initial prices as fair and reasonable, great marketers take the focus off price by targeting the right customers, working to mitigate the risks of adopting a new technology, and making it easy

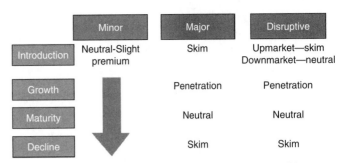

Figure 4 Pricing strategies change with market conditions.

for customers to see the value for themselves (as Figure 4 shows).

When rolling out a true innovation, marketers are often focused on identifying and converting early adopters. Those customers are desirable because they become references for later adopters. The motivations for early adopters run the gamut from (1) exploiting the latest technologies to get ahead of the competition to (2) desiring to satisfy the emotional need to be on the cutting edge. Regardless of the specific motivation, early adopters are traditionally less price-sensitive. However, they are still concerned about the potential challenges in adopting an innovation; even the most motivated aren't completely careless about how much risk they will take on. And if the price is too high for an unknown product and its unproven benefits, then the product might never get off the ground.

To address those concerns, marketers should build their launches on what does drive adoption of new technologies. And they should use that knowledge to support sales. Key drivers of customer adoption include the following:

- compelling advantages over existing technology
- the ability to observe and measure the impact of those advantages
- the complexity of the new solution
- compatibility with existing processes and technologies
- the ability to try out an innovation before making a full commitment

Note that price is not on the list. What the list represents is customer desire to mitigate the risks inherent in adopting an innovative new technology. Too often, companies fail to take into account these drivers of adoption when launching an innovative new offering. Instead, the approach is: "Our specifications are set. Our product is so innovative that it's hard to prove value or understand risk until we get it into customers' hands. Once they have it, they'll see the genius of what we have created."

Consider how Azul Systems addressed adoption drivers in the launch of an entirely new server for handling Java applications. In addition to being a new player in the business, Azul's product did not replace any existing customer equipment—further squeezing already tight information technology budgets. Yet it enjoyed a successful launch. Here's how:

- an economic advantage program: "A free, private consulting engagement helps customers quantify the financial gains their organization will realize through a computer pool deployment." (See www.azulsystems .com for more information.)

- integration of its technology that required changing only one line of code
- a relationship with IBM to provide global support, services, and spare parts to address customer concerns about ongoing support and maintenance
- documented adherence to widely accepted industry standards for interfacing with existing platforms
- a no-cost 45-day evaluation program for qualified accounts

Successful introduction of new products is challenging, but some simple things can be done to greatly improve your chances. More than anything, companies need to understand what ease of adoption will mean to their customers.

An alternative method of enlightening customers is often absurdly low introductory price deals. That compounds the perception of risk by leading customers to think: "If this technology is so good, then why do they seem so desperate for customers?" Price dealing to get those early "reference accounts" can also dramatically affect future revenues. Once low prices are out on the street, it is very difficult to raise them.

Pricing for Success

Price strategy can be the lever that maximizes return on the risky investment or the velvet rope that bars customers from your service. Get it right and your company enjoys a commanding market position, increased profits, and well-earned confidence across the team. Get it wrong and your company limits both sales and profitability and suffers from a weakened market position, financial performance, and team capabilities.

Lessons from successful new-product launches demonstrate an effective process for innovation price strategy.

First, implement a customer-value measurement process as rigorous as the technology development process. Answers to the questions posed in Figure 1's six customer value areas will enable the company to (1) offer a quantified value message as compelling as the technology and (2) estimate a price range corresponding to customer value. Without a solid understanding of quantified customer value, the launch process is unnecessarily risky.

Second, within that range of customer value, set prices based on the interaction of the innovation's nature (minor, major, or disruptive) and the stage of product life cycle (introduction, maturity, growth, or decline). This simple matrix allows companies to plot a price point that maximizes both adoption and profitability.

The rules laid out here offer a guideline of where to set a price for a product or service innovation. That process can help companies overcome the long odds of new-product success—and fuel growth in both revenues and profitability.

MARK BURTON is vice president of Holden Advisors in Concord, Mass., and may be reached at mburton@holdenadvisors.com. **STEVE HAGGETT** is a client manager for Holden Advisors and may be reached at shaggett@holdenadvisors.com. To join the discussion about this article, please visit www.marketingpower.com/marketingmanagementblog.

Authors' note—*Pricing with Confidence: Ten Ways to Stop Leaving Money on the Table* (John Wiley & Sons), Mark Burton's book with co-author Reed Holden, will be published in February 2008.

Customer-Centric Pricing:
The Surprising Secret for Profitability

Companies spend enormous amounts of energy and capital in creating value for customers, but less regard is given to actually capturing the value they have created. Segmentation based on buying behavior uncovers a tremendous differential in willingness to pay for subjective product attributes such as convenience, status, and quality. Purchase decisions are made through an assessment of a myriad of factors balancing perceptions of value components against price in a subtle, complex, and often sub-conscious decision matrix. Customer-centric pricing requires the simultaneous and continuous assessment of product attributes, customer perceptions, and the circumstances of time and place by listening to customers' actions. It is a means of assuring that companies assess the value they create for customers and extract that value from the marketplace.

ROBERT G. CROSS[a,b] AND ASHUTOSH DIXIT[c*]

1. In Search of Opportunity

Despite recent productivity gains, pressures on profitability persist. Due to an uncertain economy and fierce global competition, profits will continue to be inconsistent. Many companies have already cut costs and squeezed productivity to the extent that they are now cutting flesh, not fat. They need to find new ways to consistently grow the bottom line.

Companies spend billions on enhancing brand preference and product differentiation. However, when faced with the prospect of extracting the benefits of these efforts through price differentials, they often fail. Firms tend to respond to lower-priced competition in one of two ways: either by capitulation (cutting prices to meet competition), or by inaction (not responding and ultimately surrendering market share to competitors) (Porter, 1979). They do not often expend the effort to determine the appropriate price differential for their products in the marketplace, an oversight that results in billions of dollars of lost opportunity.

2. Back to the Future

Prior to the industrial revolution, all sales transactions were customer-centric, as each transaction was subject to individual bargaining and negotiation. After the industrial revolution tapped mass markets, however, face-to-face negotiations became impractical. Mass-market expansion led to standardized means of production and standardized sales terms. Accordingly, companies became more product-centric. This product centricity encompassed all aspect of the product, including product features, distribution, service, and price.

Currently, most pricing is still product-centric. Product managers focus on the cost of the product, its physical attributes (size, features, and functions), and the margins they seek from the product. Product positioning vis-à-vis the company's other offerings and competitive offerings may also play a role. This mostly internal focus often creates a disparity between what product managers and customers perceive a product's value to be. This disparity in value perception leads to lost profit opportunities from under-pricing (creating consumer surplus) or over-pricing (lost sales).

However, many businesses are becoming more conscious of the need to look externally, with greater frequency, at the customer perception of value when setting and revising prices. This phenomenon is a function of increased product differentiation and customer segmentation (Porter, 1979), as well as an increase in the knowledge and technology associated with predicting customer response (Cross, 1997).

[a] Revenue Analytics, Inc., USA
[b] Terry College of Business, University of Georgia, Athens, GA 30602, USA
[c] James J. Nance College of Business Administration, Cleveland State University, 2121 Euclid Avenue, BU 458, Cleveland, OH 44115-2214, USA
[*] Corresponding author. E-mail address: a.dixit1@csuohio.edu (A. Dixit).

3. The Customer-Centric Pricing Process

Successful companies go beyond the concept of value creation to the reality of value extraction. While value creation is about getting into the heads of the consumer, value extraction is about getting into their wallets. It is only when the customer agrees with the value proposition and pays for the goods or services that the efforts in value creation pay off. Key to this process is setting customer-centric prices that accurately reflect the perceived value of their products to each customer segment (Anderson & Narus, 2003; Cross, 1997; Dolan, 1995).

Price should be seen as a communicative device between buyer and seller which continually reflects constantly changing market variables such as brand preference, the availability of supply, substitutable alternatives, and a host of other factors (Hayek, 1945). Companies which understand this function and use a customer-centric approach to pricing will be able to extract more from their value-creation strategies.

The customer-centric pricing process is described in Fig. 1. Companies can take advantage of customer heterogeneity by careful attention to:

1. customer segmentation;
2. measuring customer value;
3. capturing the value created by pricing;
4. continual reassessment of the product's perceived value in the relevant market. (Fleischmann, Hall, & Pyke, 2004).

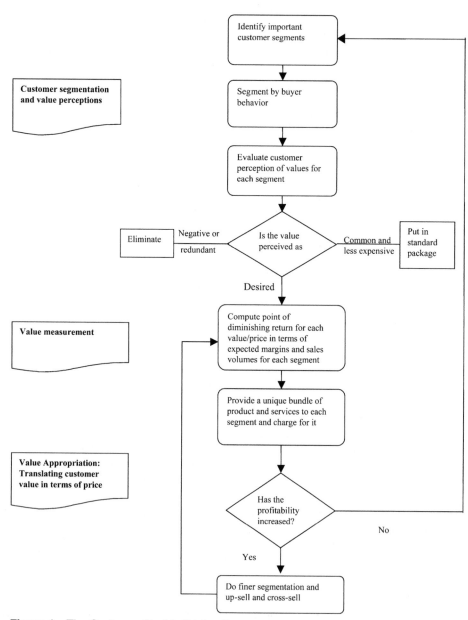

Figure 1 The Customer-Centric Pricing Process.

4. Segmentation Based on Value Perceptions and Buyer Behavior

Significant profit potential comes from understanding the value each customer segment places on individual products, then charging prices that accurately reflect that perceived value (Anderson & Narus, 2003, 2004; Nagle & Holden, 2002). Assessing and capturing the value that a firm creates for a specific market segment requires segmenting the customers into groups with similar perceptions of value and willingness to pay. Since customers define value by a wide variety of metrics, this is not an easy task. Conventional market segmentation techniques include demographic variables such as age, sex, race, income, marital status, education level, and geographical location, as well as psychographic variables such as activities, interests, opinions, and life-style (Assael & Roscoe, 1976; Wells, 1975).

These traditional methodologies have been able to effectively classify relatively homogeneous groups for purposes of product development, promotions, communications, advertising, and other marketing mix variables. (Smith, 1956; Haley, 1968; Frank, Massy, & Wind, 1972; Wansink & Park, 2000). They are not, however, necessarily effective in segmenting customers by willingness to pay, which varies based upon the customer's specific circumstances of time and place (Belk, 1975; Smith & Nagle, 2002). For example, demographic and psychographic segmentations do not adequately account for who will pay for the convenience of an ATM and when and where they will accept an additional fee.

To extract value from the marketplace through customer-centric pricing, we must answer the question: "What is this customer willing to pay at this point in time?" Segmentation by buying behavior is required to determine the answer. Unlike demographics and psychographics that attempt to define who the customers are, segmentation by buying behavior focuses on predicting how they will respond at the time of purchase. The hospitality industry has discovered that such customer-centric segmentation is a much better indicator of price sensitivity than either demographics or psychographics.

Take a sales executive for a pharmaceutical company, for example. She may be very specific about hotel location (proximate to the hospital she is calling on), but relatively indifferent to price if she is on an expense account. However, the same individual, whose demographics and psychographics remain the same, is likely to be more flexible about hotel location and significantly more price conscious if she is traveling with her family on a personal budget.

A customer's perception of the value of any product may change based on subjective factors, some related to the product itself, and others related to the individual's particular circumstances vis-à-vis the product. Factors that may tremendously influence the price a customer is willing to pay for a product include such seemingly difficult to isolate and quantify concepts as status, loyalty, convenience, urgency, and quality. In fact, these subjective, intangible factors may be more meaningful and valuable to the consumer than the product's tangible attributes.

4.1. The Surprising Secret to Profitability

Segmentation based on buying behavior uncovers a tremendous differential in willingness to pay for subjective product attributes such as convenience, status, quality, and need. These price differentials are far greater than most businesses assume, and they can be the basis for substantial profits. It is this price differential that companies could have or should have which is essential to incremental profit. For example, price increases which recognize value creation based on brand preference can reduce consumer surplus. If they do not reduce sales, the additional revenue drops directly to the bottom line. Similarly, discounts offered to micro-market segments of customers which have only a casual need for the product or who are brand indifferent might spark incremental sales. Both present profit-generating opportunities. Unfortunately, these opportunities are sometimes missed.

The desire for an edgy prestige among professionals has helped Harley Davidson leverage a relatively low-tech motorcycle into a premium-priced American icon. Accordingly, the value created by the brand image was captured. Comparable cravings were created when BMW launched its exotic Z8 sports car. However, many of the first buyers sold their cars for more than twice the sticker price to other eager customers who could not get on BMW's waiting list; thus, BMW did not extract all the value it had created. Similarly, extraordinary demand for Microsoft's Xbox game console (launched just prior to Christmas, 2001) caused many of the first units, bought at retail for $199, to be sold for over $1000 on auction sites. In each of these cases, the subjective value in status overwhelms the objective value of the item itself. Moreover, the consumer surplus sometimes shows up as profit to arbitrageurs, not as incremental profit to the entity that created the value in the first place.

Sporting events, concerts, and theaters often do not appreciate the vast differentials in perceived customer value they create. Super Bowl seats are often resold by "brokers" at prices that are generally five times what the NFL charges. When Mel Brooks' musical, "The Producers" first came out, the $35 Balcony seats were sold out for the next five months, and the $99 Orchestra seats were not available for another year, except from "brokers" who charged up to ten times the original price.

Customer-centric pricing aligns the price charged with the value created for the specific customer segment at the relevant time and place. This alignment reduces consumer surplus and significantly enhances profits as the incremental revenue from pricing precision becomes incremental profit. Accordingly, with customer-centric pricing, the company that creates the value captures the benefit of that value, not brokers or other resellers.

Not long ago, the Washington Opera was faced with a revenue shortfall. Rather than attempting to raise across-the-board ticket prices by 5% as they had always done in the past, they evaluated each seat based upon "customer experience" criteria. They found significant differences in the quality of the experience, even within the Orchestra section. The back row at the side of the Orchestra section was extremely different from the tenth row center, yet the price was the same. They also recognized that weekend performances were always sold out, but weekday performances invariably had empty seats. Previously, all seats were sold at one of three price levels: $47, $63, and $85. After customer-centric segmentation, they applied customer-centric prices that were aligned with the perception of value for each seat, for each day of the week. Nine different price levels were

---

Application of Principles

Miss Margaritte's Salon

Margaritte Jackson owns a hair styling salon in a suburban office building. Her clients range from professional women working in the building to retirees living in the neighborhood. She has two stylists dedicated to "cut and style." She currently charges $50 for that service (which takes about one hour), and the two stylists perform, on average, 50 of these services per week, generating $2500 in revenue. This weekly revenue barely covers her costs. Her shop is extremely busy on Fridays and Saturdays, but virtually empty on Tuesdays and Wednesdays. To reduce her costs, she has considered asking each of her stylists to take one of those midweek days off with no pay.

Margaritte was reluctant to ask her employees to take a cut in pay. Fortunately, she understood the concept of value creation. She renovated her shop and switched to an exclusive line of hair care products. She expected these actions to increase the perceived value of her services by 20 percent. Accordingly, she raised her price by 20 percent to $60 and maintained the same number of customers, generating a 20 percent increase in revenue to $3000.

Despite this increase in revenue, she was still not netting much more income because of paying for the renovations and the increased cost of her supplies. Tuesdays and Wednesdays were still slow, and Fridays and Saturdays were still completely booked. She wished that she could spread the customers more evenly throughout the week, but she knew that most of them wanted their hair freshly done for the weekend. She decided to segment her customers by the perceived value they put on different days of the week. For Friday and Saturday cuts, she raised her price to $65. She gave a price incentive to customers who were willing to move to Tuesday and Wednesday, lowering the cost to $45. As it turns out, many of her retired customers were time-flexible and were glad to move to weekdays for a discount. Margaritte was still able to fill her Friday and Saturday schedules with those women who were less price conscious and more style conscious.

To Margaritte's surprise and delight, by increasing her sales midweek and charging more on weekends, she increased her revenue another 20 percent. Only this time, it cost her nothing. The additional $600 per week was pure profit. It came from understanding that customers valued her services differently on different days of the week. This is customer-centric pricing.

---

installed with a broader dispersion of prices. Ticket prices were spread between $29 and $150, with midweek and weekend differentials. Seats in the balcony that would otherwise go unsold on weekdays were filled with people who could now afford the opera. Raising the price of the prime Orchestra seats closer to market value reduced the consumer surplus. As a result, the Washington Opera increased its revenues the next year by 9%, almost double what it could have only hoped for under a 5% across-the-board increase (Cross, 1997). These customer-centric pricing techniques are available to any business, irrespective of the level of sophistication, as illustrated by Miss Margaritte's Salon.

5. Customer Perceptions of Value Components

Customer-centric pricing requires the simultaneous and continuous assessment of product attributes, customer perceptions, and the circumstances of time and place. Customers' purchase decisions are made through an assessment of a myriad of factors balancing perceptions of value components against price using subtle, complex, and often sub-conscious decision variables.

Customer-centric pricing requires understanding and utilizing these decision variables, in order to optimize revenue opportunities. For example, airlines have been adept at exploiting an urgency factor through revenue management to price-ration seats for last-minute, high-fare travelers while offering deeply discounted seats to advance purchase customers who have time to shop for the lowest fare (Cross, 1997).

Brand loyalty is prized for fostering customer retention and raising competitive barriers. However, it also creates a significant opportunity for price premiums. Gillette has continued to invest in product improvement and promotion, and has created and leveraged brand loyalty successfully to raise razor prices, extracting very healthy margins from relatively ordinary shaving items. These profits enable Gillette to invest in R and D for new products, thus assuring market leadership.

Customer-centric segmentation by buying behavior helps distinguish customers' decision patterns that are price-insensitive. Price-insensitive attributes identify where customer value is high and price premiums can be charged. Business managers frequently miss capturing the value they create. The Ritz Carlton hotel chain established an extraordinary reputation for luxury, quality, and customer service; however, it did not fully extract the value it created in the market, and was only marginally profitable for years. When Marriott International acquired the Ritz Carlton chain, it used sophisticated revenue optimization technology to understand when and where it could increase price. In its first five years of ownership of Ritz Carlton, Marriott was able to extract the value Ritz Carlton had created through its reputation for quality, consistency, and customer service. Marriott increased the average daily rate of the Ritz Carlton properties by 26%, compared to only a 6% increase in its other full service hotels.

On the other hand, Marriott stays attuned to the desires of price-sensitive customer segments, as well. They introduced capacity-controlled discount rates with advance purchase restrictions. During the first summer these rates were offered, almost a quarter of a million room-nights were sold at this rate. Two-thirds of these room-nights represented incremental business (Hanks, Cross, & Noland, 1992).

6. Value Measurement: Listening to Customer Actions

Most firms that attempt to align product prices with customer value perceptions do so by gathering information through customer focus groups, surveys, or similar methods. Unfortunately, customers often say one thing, but do another. For example, Philips conducted a focus group of teenagers to assess their color preferences for boom boxes, and a majority of the participants listed "yellow" as their preferred color. However, at the end of the session, when participants were given their choice of picking a yellow or black boom box as they left the room, most took black boom boxes, even though they had marked "yellow" as their preferred color.

That actions speak louder than words should not come as a surprise. How many people would tell Coca-Cola, through a survey or traditional focus group, that they are willing to pay $4 for a 12 oz. can of Coke? Yet millions of $4 cans have been sold through hotel mini-bars. It is not that consumers would necessarily try to bias the results of the market research efforts; it is just that the consumers, themselves, may not be able to predict exactly what they would do, until faced with the decision. At that time, their decision will be influenced by the particulars of time and place. In this example, they may not be able to predict how thirsty they will be and whether there will be suitable alternatives.

At the critical point in the purchase decision, customers scan the immediate offerings in the marketplace and develop a consideration set based upon factors particular to their individual preferences. Within these factors, they develop a hierarchy based on their perceived values for different offerings (Zeithaml, 1988), and their purchase behavior is correlated to these perceptions of value at the instant of the decision.

The difficulties presented for customer-centric pricing are twofold. A consumer considering an automobile purchase will assign a wide range of values to each product attribute. Some will be relatively objective economic values such as fuel efficiency, maintenance, warranty, and resale value. Others will be subjective hedonic values such as design, safety, comfort, and status. Moreover, the consumer may not know in advance of making the purchase decision exactly how much weight he or she may give to each component in the value equation. Accordingly, adept companies must capture and analyze detailed customer transaction data to determine how typical members of the relevant micro-market respond to the offerings in similar circumstances. From this, they can model and predict future customer behavior.

Ford Motor Company has pioneered the application of these techniques in the automobile industry to determine what features the customers in each micro-market segment most desire and what they are willing to pay for them. Understanding the wide range of customer preferences across a broad product line and expansive geographical market requires significant experimentation, data gathering, and analysis. Customers' perception of value will vary based on geography (trucks are more highly valued in the Southwest than the Northeast), vehicle type (truck buyers are more sensitive to cash rebates than car buyers), and product configuration (certain add-ons are much more valuable than their incremental cost).

How much rebates will affect market volume and profitability must be continually tested and analyzed. Through such market testing and analysis, Ford found that a $700 rebate for its Ranger Super Cab could encourage almost half of the customers considering the base model Ranger to upgrade to the more accommodating Super Cab. Despite the cash rebate, Ford still made thousands of dollars more profit on a Super Cab than a base model, since the customers' perception of incremental value is significantly more than the incremental cost to Ford in making the upgraded model. The automaker applied such "smarter pricing" techniques across its product lines, and Lloyd Hansen, Ford's Controller for Marketing and Sales, estimates that about $3 billion in pre-tax profits came from a series of such revenue management initiatives (Leibs, 2000).

7. From Value Creation to Value Appropriation

Customer-centric pricing involves identifying key customer segments, understanding what these customers value, creating customer value by offering unique bundles of products or services, and charging for it appropriately. Value creation is the basis for growth. The better a product is aligned with specific customers' preferences, the more it is valued. The more it is valued, the higher the probability that it will have competitive success. That is the premise behind customer focused value-creation strategies such as One-to-One Marketing and Mass Customization (Peppers & Rogers, 1993; Siminson, 2005; Zipkin, 2001).

These strategies understand the demise of the mass market and the rise of individualistic micro-market segments that demand products that address their specific needs, requirements, and desires. One-to-One Marketing and Mass Customization are successful to the extent they can differentiate both customers and products by recognizing enormous diversity in the global marketplace.

Most of these efforts at value creation focus on gaining market share or customer share in order to increase revenue and profitability. What they miss is the understanding that not only do customers want individualized products, they are often willing to pay a significant premium for them. The more differentiated a product, the less price-sensitive it will be.

Price should be a function of perceived value (Zeithaml, 1988). As companies engage in value-creation strategies and the perceived value increases to the specific customer set, the price should escalate. Often it does not. The result is what economists term a "consumer surplus," that is, a gap between what a customer is willing to pay, and what he or she actually pays.

There have been numerous predictions that the Internet would lower consumer search costs and enable software agents and shop-bots to drive costs down to the lowest common denominator. This phenomenon, however, has not occurred (Baker, Marn, & Zawada, 2001). Purchase decisions are still subjective. For the most part, they are not objectively driven by economically defined measures that can be incorporated into shop-bots. Consumers still place extraordinary value on their individual, subjective perceptions of the supplier related to factors such as reliability, convenience, and trust. These values are typically not predefined, and they vary based on circumstances of time and place. Accordingly, prices in the virtual world of commerce have exhibited the same degree of price dispersion as in the physical world.

One of the keys to customer-centric pricing is having a wide range of prices that address the relative values customers actually place on the products. As firms continue to attempt to differentiate themselves through customer value-add and more fully understand capturing the value they create through customer-centric pricing, the potential for even greater price differentiation exists.

Getting the optimal price has a salubrious effect on the bottom line. For companies with 8% profit margins, a 1% differential in price results in a 12.5% margin difference (Dolan, 1995). Through customer-centric pricing, firms set prices based on the perceived value of a product or service to specific customers or segments of customers. This strategy minimizes consumer surplus and maximizes profitability. Resourceful firms can use customer-centric pricing to leverage the value they have built in the marketplace and appreciably increase profits.

8. Sustaining Value

Building and sustaining customer value that generates a source of continual revenue requires long-term customer relations. Customer relationship management (CRM) processes and techniques have evolved to manage the effective interaction with customers over time (Lemon, White, & Winer, 2002; Sheth & Parvatiyaar, 1995). However, customer-centric prices are essential to complete the customer retention cycle.

Invariably, if the price is not right, the customer relationship is endangered. This is obvious if the price is too high, but it can also be true if the price is too low. Sports fans have always understood the tremendous difference in experience from one event to another. Unfortunately, during the highest demand times such as play-off games, often a majority of fans seeking to attend the games must resort to ticket brokers, thus bypassing the customer relationship process with the team altogether. The inability of the team to accurately assess the true value of the game and to price it accordingly causes awkwardness for the fan, who must seek out third party intermediaries. Not only does this error in pricing disrupt the customer relationship, it allows a third party arbitrageur to steal the financial premium that customers put on the event.

Major league baseball teams are just now discovering that fans are willing to pay significantly more for unique experiences such as big rivalries, or for big names such as Barry Bonds. On the other hand, these teams are also recognizing that ordinary games on weekdays against weak teams require significant discounts to fill the stands. The New York Yankees, despite setting a franchise attendance record in 2002, offered cheap $5 upper deck seats for weekday games in 2003 that would have otherwise gone unsold. A wide dispersion of prices can work to give different segments of fans the seats they desire, at the games they want, at prices they are willing to pay.

Let us revisit how Microsoft could have taken advantage of customer-centric pricing to create greater value for its customers and itself when it launched the Xbox in 2001. Microsoft knew the demand for the game console would far outstrip its ability to produce enough units to satisfy the pre-Christmas demand. Many of the most valuable gaming customers (the ones who wanted the latest product and were willing to pay a premium for it) were required to go to EBay and other auction sites and pay prices that were often five times the retail price. Microsoft could have simply raised the price to ration the early demand. That would have reduced the consumer surplus and kept the customers from going through third parties, but it would also have created the perception that the early purchasers were "ripped off" once productive capacity was brought in line with demand and prices dropped.

Following a customer-centric approach as outlined in Fig. 1, Microsoft could have created a "Collector's Edition" for the first few million units it was able to produce prior to the 2001 Christmas season. It could have included some free games, gold-tipped cables, a Collector's Edition box, and other features that were low in cost, but high in perceived value to the enthusiastic customer segment. Microsoft could have charged $499 (instead of $199) for the first few million units, kept its relationship with the most passionate gamers, and generated far greater profits. In addition to enhancing customer satisfaction for this group, Microsoft could have then created the perception of a bargain for the ordinary game console at a price of $199.

The innovative bundling of various product components with pricing aligned to the price sensitivities of each micro-market segment is the way to create sustainable value in the marketplace. A firm that optimizes revenue through customer-centric pricing not only increases profit, but is in a better position to offer price-sensitive customers lower-priced products with only attributes they value.

9. Economic Benefits

Understanding customer value creation and capturing that value through customer-centric pricing is a step toward a pareto optimal in the economy. A pareto optimal is a relationship in which all parties are better off, and no one is worse off (Pareto, 1906). Accordingly, both producers and consumers benefit.

Producers benefit from understanding customer willingness to pay for tangible product attributes such as product features, functions, warranties, and customer service. More importantly, using the feedback from customer-centric pricing, producers can assess the market value that various customer segments place on more subjective attributes such as brand preference, status, quality, and reliability.

Customer-centric pricing is more than just establishing price; it is a means of constantly communicating with consumers through the price mechanism and using that communication as a means to balance what the firm offers in terms of product attributes. For price-insensitive customers, that might mean a higher degree of reliability, or access to a product at the last minute. On the other hand, price-sensitive customers communicate their willingness to forgo certain product features or attributes for a lower price. Southwest Airlines, for example, has demonstrated that airline passengers do not want to pay a premium for a meal or assigned seating, but they will pay up to three times as much for a last-minute seat on certain flights at certain times. Accordingly, Southwest gives its customers what they want when they want, but not more, thereby increasing Southwest's profitability.

Finding these incremental revenue opportunities requires an accurate assessment of who will pay what amount at what time. These opportunities cannot be accurately predicted by surveys or focus groups. They require monitoring the real-time decision-making of millions of consumers in a dynamic marketplace and responding appropriately with a customer-centric focus. Missing these opportunities could result in missing a chance to extract a brand premium in certain market segments or undermine a competitor's advantage in others with precision discounting. These missed opportunities are a stealthy thief of profits. Money a firm could have had or should have had is hard to find, but extremely profitable if captured, as these revenues from existing assets fall right to the bottom line.

Profit-seeking companies must seize these opportunities. Once missed, they are gone forever. Customer-centric pricing is a means to assure that the value a firm creates is accurately assessed and captured through the price mechanism. This is the secret to profitability.

References

Anderson, J. C., & Narus, J. A. (2003). Selectively pursuing more of your customer's business. *Sloan Management Review, 44*(3), 42–49.

Anderson, J. C., & Narus, J. A. (2004). *Business market management: Understanding, creating, and delivering value.* Upper Saddle River, NJ: Prentice Hall.

Assael, H., & Roscoe Jr., A. M. (1976, October). Approaches to market segmentation analysis. *Journal of Marketing, 40,* 67–76.

Baker, W., Marn, M., & Zawada, C. (2001). Price smarter on the net. *Harvard Business Review, 79*(2), 122–127.

Belk, R. W. (1975). Situational variables and consumer behavior. *Journal of Consumer Research, 2*(3), 157–164.

Cross, R. G. (1997). *Revenue management: Hard-core tactics for market domination.* New York: Broadway Books.

Dolan, R. (1995). How do you know when the price is right? *Harvard Business Review, 73*(5), 174–183.

Fleischmann, M., Hall, J. M., & Pyke, D. F. (2004). Smart pricing. *Sloan Management Review, 45*(2), 9–13.

Frank, R. E., Massy, W. F., & Wind, Y. (1972). *Market segmentation.* Englewood Cliffs, NJ: Prentice Hall.

Haley, R. I. (1968, July). Benefit segmentation: A benefit oriented research tool. *Journal of Marketing, 32,* 30–35.

Hanks, R. D., Cross, R. G., & Noland, R. P. (1992). Discounting in the hotel industry: A new approach. *The Cornell H.R.A. Quarterly, 33*(1), 15–23.

Hayek, F. A. (1945). The use of knowledge in society. *American Economic Review, 35*(4), 519–530.

Leibs, S. (2000). Ford heeds the profits. *CFO Magazine, 16*(9), 33–35.

Lemon, K. N., White, T. B., & Winer, R. S. (2002). Dynamic customer relationship management: Incorporating future considerations into the service retention decision. *Journal of Marketing, 66*(1), 1–14.

Nagle, T. T., & Holden, R. K. (2002). *The strategy and tactics of pricing.* Englewood Cliffs, NJ: Prentice Hall.

Pareto, V. (1906). *Manuale d'economia politica.* Milan: Societ Editrice Libraria.

Peppers, D., & Rogers, M. (1993). *The one to one future.* New York: Currency Doubleday.

Porter, M. E. (1979). How competitive forces shape strategy. *Harvard Business Review, 57*(2), 137–145.

Sheth, J. N., & Parvatiyaar, A. (1995). Relationship marketing in consumer markets: Antecedents and consequences. *Journal of the Academy of Marketing Science, 23*(4), 255–271.

Siminson, I. (2005). Determinants of customers' responses to customized offers: Conceptual framework and research propositions. *Journal of Marketing, 69*(1), 32–45.

Smith, G. E., & Nagle, T. T. (2002). How much are your customers willing to pay? *Marketing Research, 14*(4), 20–25.

Smith, W. R. (1956, July). Product differentiation and market segmentation as alternative product strategies. *Journal of Marketing, 21,* 3–8.

Wansink, B., & Park, S. (2000). Comparison methods for identifying heavy users. *Journal of Advertising Research, 40*(4), 61–72.

Wells, W. D. (1975). Psychographics: A critical review. *Journal of Marketing Research, 12*(2), 196–213.

Zeithaml, V. A. (1988). Consumer perceptions of price, quality and value: A means–end model and synthesis of evidence. *Journal of Marketing, 52*(3), 2–22.

Zipkin, P. (2001). The limits of mass customization. *Sloan Management Review, 42*(3), 81–87.

Boost Your Bottom Line by Taking the Guesswork Out of Pricing

Do you know how much your product is *really* worth?

ALISON STEIN WELLNER

Every time he closed a sale, Kris Simmons kicked himself. That's because Simmons, president of Fire Eye Productions, a video production company based in Chattanooga, Tenn., knew he'd done it again: He'd set his price way too low. A client would ask for a quote, and Simmons would toss out a number based on some combination of his company's cash flow at the moment, his own fear of losing a customer, and what he'd begun charging when he founded Fire Eye four years earlier. "Basically, I'd throw a price out there and see what they'd take," he says.

From the outside, Fire Eye looked like a big success; Simmons was even nominated for the 2004 Young Entrepreneur of the Year Award given by Tennessee's small-business administration. But inside, the company was falling apart. Working 18-hour days to keep up with demand, Simmons had no time to make sales calls, which meant that cash flow was always erratic. He would hire employees, let them go when receivables dipped—and then hastily hire them back when the work flowed in again.

By August 2004, Simmons was fed up and exhausted. He knew what he had to do. He had to raise prices. A price hike would mean he could work fewer hours, earn more money, hire employees, and buy new equipment. On the other hand, if he raised his prices too high—and who knew how high was too high?—he would risk alienating his longtime customers. If he lost them, Simmons knew, Fire Eye would not survive. "These clients are my bread and butter," he thought. "If I make them mad and they leave, then I'm in a whole different kind of bad situation."

There's no more important number than the one on your price tag, and nothing provokes a case of the cold sweats like the thought of raising it. After years of almost no inflation, relentless downward pressure from places like China and India on the price of almost everything, and comparison shopping at the click of a mouse, it's more competitive than ever

out there. It's easy to see why fewer than one-third of business owners surveyed by the National Federation of Independent Business reported in February that they had increased their prices over the previous three months.

But that could be a big mistake—especially today, which might be the best opportunity companies have had to raise prices in some time. In March, the consumer-price index rose 3.1% over the previous year. If you're holding prices steady at a time when they are generally increasing nationwide, you may be surrendering more of your margin than you need to. "This is a very important time for everyone to review their prices," says Brent Lippman, CEO of Khimetrics, a pricing consultancy in Scottsdale, Ariz.

On the other hand, you can't raise prices if you haven't set them appropriately in the first place. Ask entrepreneurs how they arrived at their prices, and once you get past the usual stuff about optimization, segmentation, and market conditions, you'll often hear things like "it was pretty arbitrary" or "we go by our gut." Unfortunately, the gut often gets it wrong. "Entrepreneurs tend to keep prices too low," says Reed K. Holden, founder of Holden Advisors in Concord, Mass., and the co-author of *The Strategy and Tactics of Pricing,* a widely used text on the subject. Robert J. Dolan, dean of the Ross School of Business at the University of Michigan and co-author of *Power Pricing: How Managing Price Transforms the Bottom Line,* agrees. "You're likely leaving money on the table," Dolan says.

How do you make sure that money ends up in your pocket instead? Every industry has a dynamic of its own, and it would be hard to find two businesses that take the same approach to pricing. Still, there has been plenty of recent research into how consumers behave, examining how they assign value to goods and services and how smart managers can alter those perceptions. These insights can be valuable for any entrepreneur, in any industry.

But before we get to that, a quick primer on the wrong way to set prices: Many business owners base their prices on their costs, adding in a certain profit margin on top. "They say, 'Hey, if I could get my costs, plus 20%, that's not a bad business,'" says Dolan. Well, it could be a better business—if you could get a 40% margin. Others look at what their competitors charge and seek to bring their own prices in line or charge less. That may be your only option if your product or service is identical to that of the competition. But how do you know that your rivals know more about pricing than you do? And if you undercut them, you risk sparking a margin-killing price war. Then there are those who consult with customers before arriving at a price. But customers, obviously, have a powerful incentive to get you to keep your prices as low as possible. Setting prices based on what your salespeople report back can lead to similar problems. "Sales-people want to close deals, and they use price as a way of doing that," says Holden. "But that can be inconsistent with the real need of the business—profitability."

Of course, you can't make smart pricing decisions without taking your costs, competitors, customers, and sales-people into account. But nearly all experts agree that making any of those factors the primary basis for your decision is a big mistake. Instead, the right price for a product or service should rest on one thing—the value that a product or service provides.

When determining your prices, says John Gourville, a marketing professor at Harvard University who studies pricing, the first question to ask is this: How much would a rational consumer be willing to pay for your product, assuming the consumer had a perfect understanding of its actual worth? It sounds easy. But while most business owners spend a good chunk of their time touting the benefits of their products and services, "they haven't tried to monetize those benefits," says Brent Lippman. The first step toward creating a pricing strategy, then, is to do just that—think through the benefits of your product and make a rough calculation of what you think they're worth in dollar terms.

Marc Cenedella
The Ladders.com, New York City

Web-based job-search service
Price per month, 2004
$50
Price per month, 2005
$25
"From our point of view, we're charging only a fraction of the value we provide."

Marc Cenedella went through this process in 2003, when he was setting subscription rates for his start-up, TheLadders. com, an electronic job-search service that lists only positions paying more than $100,000. Most career sites allow job seekers to search for free and make money by charging employers. Cenedella's strategy is different: He charges job seekers and lets employers list their six-figure positions for free. After many meetings with "way too much pizza," Cenedella and his team arrived at their value figure: somewhere between $10,000

and $40,000. Their assumption was that a job seeker who used their site would find a position at least one month faster than one who didn't. Since that job would pay $100,000 or more, the value of the company's service translated to roughly one month's take-home pay, or somewhere between $10,000 and $40,000, depending on the job.

Fair enough. Of course, it's hard to imagine anyone coughing up tens of thousands of dollars for a weekly e-mail newsletter. And indeed, you'd be hard-pressed to find a pricing expert who would suggest that as an appropriate price.

That's because there are two kinds of value: objective value and perceived value. The former is what Cenedella came up with: the price of a product or service assuming the customer has a perfect understanding of its value—and understands it in the same way the seller does. Think of objective value as the most that you could rationally charge for a product. At the other end of the spectrum, the least you could rationally charge

---

Do You Offer Discounts? (Maybe You Shouldn't)

Nearly every company offers discounts, promotions, incentives, and giveaways. Such tactics are time-honored ways of keeping clients happy—and luring new ones into the store.

But you might be giving away the store if you're not careful. And you'd be surprised at how many savvy managers are anything but savvy when it comes to discounts, says Robert J. Dolan, dean of the University of Michigan's Ross School of Business and a business consultant. The problem, Dolan says, is that discounts are offered by different departments at different times for different reasons. Sales and marketing execs give breaks to help close deals, for example, while inventory managers cut rates to move excess stock. It adds up fast. The consulting firm McKinsey studied this phenomenon in 2003, dubbing it the "pocket-price waterfall"—that is, the amount of money you actually pocket per transaction drips away bit by bit until the small leak turns into a deluge.

How to avoid a soaking? First, get a handle on all of the discounts you offer. Next, think about the customer behavior you're trying to encourage—or discourage. Do you want people to pay by cash instead of credit? Settle accounts by the end of the month? Don't give away a penny without a clear understanding of what you're trying to accomplish. Another big mistake: grandfathering in discounts forever. Companies often offer discounts to close a particular deal, only to have the client insist on the same low price in the future. What was supposed to be a one-time incentive becomes official company policy. Let customers know when they're getting a special deal. After all, a discount that's expected isn't much of a perk.

—Alison Stein Wellner

for a product would be the incremental cost of producing it—a breakeven price. Somewhere between the two lies what is known as the perceived value of your product—that is, what a person actually is willing to spend. In a perfect world, your customer would see the value of your offering and be willing to fork over the full amount. But in many circumstances, there's a disconnect, and what people are willing to pay is very different from your product's objective value. (In those cases, you'll have to use marketing and other tricks to try to change your customer's perception of value. But more on that later.)

How do you determine what people are willing to pay? Study after study has demonstrated that when it comes to purchasing decisions, people are irrational. In one classic study, researchers asked consumers whether they would be willing to travel an additional 20 minutes to save $5 on a calculator that costs $15. Most said yes. Then they were asked the same question about a $125 jacket. Most answered no. Now, rationally, $5 is $5, whether you're buying a calculator or a jacket. But it's seldom that simple, according to Richard H. Thaler, a professor at the Graduate School of Business at the University of Chicago and author of "Mental Accounting Matters," an article published in 1999 in the *Journal of Behavioral Decision Making*. "People make [purchasing] decisions piecemeal, influenced by the context of the choice," writes Thaler, who won a Nobel Prize for his work in behavioral economics.

As it happens, the greatest influence on the context of a purchasing decision is whether the consumer believes the price is fair. Expectations play a big role in this. In a 1985 study conducted by Thaler, people were asked to consider the following hypothetical situation: You're lying on a beach on a hot day and you crave a cold beer. A friend offers to get one and wants to know what you're willing to spend. When she offers to go to a small grocery store, the median response is $1.50. But if the friend is buying the same beer at the bar of a fancy resort hotel, the price jumps to $2.65. Context and expectation drive the price up nearly 80%. Because we expect to pay more for a beer at a resort, we're willing to pay more.

The real trick in setting prices, then, is to understand—and try to shape—your customers' expectations. One of the key ways people set their expectations is to base them on what they've paid for similar products or services. Academics call this the "reference price," and it's one of the easiest pieces of competitive intelligence to gather. Simply shop your competitors.

Overcoming the power of the reference price is not an easy thing to do. At TheLadders.com, for example, the maximum objective value was $40,000. The product's reference price, however, was quite a bit lower: zero, since most job-listing services are free. There's a lot of room between nothing and $40,000, and free is the most difficult reference price to overcome. But it can be done. Satellite radio companies, for example, have been able to charge annual subscription fees of as much as $142—even though most listeners are accustomed to getting radio for free. How do they do that? Primarily through marketing, which in this context means taking the customers' reference price and making the case that they offer more value.

But starting at zero definitely limits how much you can charge. Cenedella priced a monthly subscription at $50—a

number he admits to pulling out of thin air. Unsatisfied with the number of people signing up, he cut it to $35, and finally settled on $25. TheLadders.com now has nearly 300,000 subscribers, but Cenedella is far from satisfied. "From our point of view, we're charging only a fraction of the value we provide," he says. But he's stumped as to how to fix the situation.

Plenty of entrepreneurs are in the same boat. "The price you get for a product is a function of what it's truly worth—and how good a job you do communicating that value to the end user," says John Gourville. If Cenedella, for example, could guarantee customers that subscribing would shave a month off their job searches, he might be able to charge more. Or he could try to change his customers' reference price. E-mail newsletters may have a going rate of zero, but a good career counselor can cost hundreds, if not thousands, of dollars. If your marketing can convince people to put you into a different price category, it'll be a lot easier to charge more money for it. It's also important to remember that different customers have different expectations and reference prices. Cenedella might, for example, offer a special newsletter for investment bankers at a higher price than he would for, say, marketing executives.

Sam Calagione
Dogfish Head Craft Brewery Milton, Del.

**Premium microbrewed beer
Average price per case in 1999
$18
Average price per case in 2005
$24.60
"When we add new products, we always add them at higher prices. So while our median price level has increased significantly, we can honestly say that we've never raised prices."**

Sam Calagione, president of Dogfish Head Craft Brewery in Milton, Del., is a master at playing with pricing expectations. Dogfish Head's revenue grew 52%, to $8 million, in 2004—in large part because of Calagione's approach to pricing. Some Dogfish Head beers retail at about twice the price of most microbrews and four times that of most mass-market brands. How does Calagione do it? He encourages customers to use fine wine, rather than competing beers, as their reference price. "Wine customers," he says, "understand that an amazing bottle of pinot noir should command four times the price of an average bottle." He conveys this message, in part, with smart packaging. The company, for example, sells its premium Pangaea beer in 750 milliliter cork-finished wine bottles—at a cost of $14 a bottle. That's well above an average beer drinker's price expectation. But it's right in line with that of a wine connoisseur.

Calagione borrows more than the wine industry's packaging. He shuns the consumer advertising used by competing brands,

Get the Price You Want—And Avert the Dreaded Price War

Every salesperson has met one: the customer who cares only about price. High quality? Tell it to the other guy. Superior service? Forget it, the customer says. I won't pay a dime more than I have to.

Reed K. Holden, founder of Holden Advisors, a pricing strategy firm in Concord, Mass., calls them "price buyers," and they're particularly prevalent in the purchasing departments of large corporations—where they'll often release a request for proposal with a set of specs, pick the lowest bid, and call it a day. Such buyers are a huge pain to deal with. For one thing, they're not particularly loyal because they're always ready to drop you for a lower bidder. They're also not afraid to spark price wars. "These companies want their vendors to beat their brains out," says Holden.

If you have too many of these kinds of clients, you'll never have strong margins. But there are ways to cope. The key is to do business with a price buyer only when you can do it profitably—if you have excess inventory, for example, a price buyer might be exactly what you're looking for. (Case in point: Airlines often sell excess capacity to vacation-tour operators but don't create extra capacity to serve that market.) Another option with price buyers is to sell only what they're buying. "If people want a lower price, always be willing to give it to them," says Holden. "But be sure to take away some value."

An electronics company that Holden worked with, for example, gave one customer the price it demanded—but only on older technology. Newer, more innovative products were reserved for those willing to pay for them.

Whatever you do, don't tell yourself that you'll take a hit on one sale and make it up the next time. Price buyers rarely change. If you're in the grip of one, walk away. It may seem scary, but remember: If you must get a price buyer back, you can always do it by lowering your price.

—*Alison Stein Wellner*

instead hosting "beer dinners" attended by beer enthusiasts, early adopters who are likely to spread the word about new products that excite them. Calagione expected to host 18 such dinners in May alone. Taking another page from the wine industry, every time he launches a new product, he makes sure that there's not enough of it to satisfy demand. "We're not a commodity," he says. "By not satisfying demand initially, we create more demand for the future" People understand that a scarce product commands a higher price.

Calagione segmented his market by eschewing the typical American beer drinker and going after customers with high reference prices. Doing so enabled him to do something most businesses only dream about: align prices with objective value. And though he didn't think of it in those terms, that's precisely what Kris Simmons needed to do at his video production company, Fire Eye. His first step was to figure out what his competitors were charging—the reference price. He learned that he

was charging about one-third less than most of his rivals. That was good news. Because his customers' reference prices were a good deal higher than Fire Eye's, a price hike would not seem unreasonable.

Simmons acted immediately. Fire Eye's prices, he decided, would go up 25% across the board. Had he done more research—say, conducting an in-depth value calculation akin to what Cenedella did at TheLadders.com—he might have selected a gutsier number. But 25% was the most his nerves could take. "I didn't want to alienate myself from my customers," Simmons says. "And I thought it was a fair increase." His heart pounding, he began meeting with clients to break the news. He explained his company's situation. He argued that he could be a stronger vendor if he could invest in his infrastructure and hire new, experienced staffers. He also said he'd understand if clients wanted to take their business elsewhere. Simmons had made his play. How would his customers react?

D etermining your new, higher price is one thing. Actually selling it to customers is something else. Simmons's approach—simply explaining the situation—is among the most effective. "People are actually very sensitive to what they think something costs to make," says Gourville. When costs increase, and a company cites that as a reason to justify a price hike, few customers react badly. Indeed, just as people appreciate a fair deal for themselves, they also tend to understand that a company has to stay in business as well.

Some customers may even urge you to raise prices: "We want you to be around."

In some cases, customers may even urge you to raise prices. That's what happened to Henk Keukenkamp, CEO of Scope It, a software company in El Dorado Hills, Calif. In 2003, Keukenkamp pegged the price of his project-costing software to that of a similar product offered by Microsoft: $795 per user, per year. When no one balked at the figure, he boosted it to $995. Even then, he found customers were shocked at the low price—so shocked that Keukenkamp began to feel foolish. "We thought the value we were providing was comparable to Microsoft," he says. "We were wrong. Our customers thought our value was nothing like Microsoft." A pricing theorist would call this a case of misperceived reference price. Finally, Keukenkamp recalls, a customer took him aside and said, "Look, $995 isn't very expensive. How are you going to make any money? We want you to be around to handle updates." Over the next 12 months, Keukenkamp raised the price of a license to $2,295 a year. "I still think we can push it higher," he says.

Keukenkamp's customers had a powerful motivation to keep him in business—they wanted him around to service the software. It's an enviable situation. But even if you're not as fortunate as Keukenkamp, you can still raise prices. You just have to do a better job explaining the reasons for the move. "It makes sense to try to justify why your prices are what they are," says Gourville. "It's better than having consumers feel like they're getting ripped off." And it's not necessary to raise prices across the board, all at once. Sometimes, a wise step is to test out new prices with small samplings of your customers.

If you don't trust your communication skills—or if you're reluctant to confront clients directly—you can slide a price hike in through the back door. One way is to eliminate discounts or change your terms and conditions. "People are more sensitive to list price than to discount terms," says Robert Dolan. Eliminating a discount of, say, 2% to clients who pay within 30 days, for example, is much easier to sell than a 2% increase in prices. (See "Do You Offer Discounts?") Or, conversely, you can raise prices but offer discounts to your most important customers.

You can also stop the gravy train and begin charging for add-on services you currently provide gratis. Another option is to keep prices constant but reduce the amount of product or service you're providing. If you're smart about it, according to Dolan, many customers won't notice the difference. Dogfish Head, for example, sells some of its beer in four-packs, rather than six-packs, which boost the price per bottle. Price hikes also can be masked by bundling an array of products or services together. Studies have shown that people think they're getting a better deal when they cannot determine the costs of the individual items they're purchasing.

Just keep in mind that psychology can also work against you. "People are going to use your past price as a reference point," says Dolan. There are two ways around this. You can convince customers that the new, higher price is accompanied by greater value. Or you can "destroy the reference point," Dolan says—through, say, a redesign or relaunch. If that's not pos-

sible, introducing "premium" versions of your service can help raise reference prices across the board. Every time Calagione releases a new product, for example, he charges more than he has in the past, a move that increases Dogfish Head's average selling price while adding to his customers' reference prices.

Six months after his own price hike, Fire Eye's Simmons couldn't imagine why he didn't do it sooner. Apparently, he did a good job explaining the increase to his customers—not a single one jumped ship. "They were very understanding" Simmons says. He's invested his newfound profits into four new employees, freeing himself to pitch new customers. He's landed some large corporate clients, who, he's since learned, didn't take him seriously at his previous price. That's not the only change. In the past, Simmons routinely failed to charge for overtime. Now, if a project requires 10 more hours, it's added to the bill and those terms are explicitly spelled out in his contracts. He also altered his billing policies, asking for 50% payment up front rather than taking all of it upon a project's completion. This reduced the cost of his receivables, giving him a subtle increase in margin. "It's been rebirth, a new beginning," Simmons says.

Of course, there has been some fallout. Prior to the price hike, Fire Eye closed about 80% of the projects it bid on; today, the number is closer to 40%. On the other hand, today's deals are coming with far better margins, which is steadily improving the overall health of the company. "I'm only spending time with people who want to play my way," Simmons says. "I'll still work with clients on their budgets. But for the most part, I'm in business to make my life better. These prices are making life better for me"

Contributing editor **ALISON STEIN WELLNER** is a New York City-based freelance writer.

Big Retailers Seek Teens (and Parents)

Hip fashions seen as key to fighting off specialty stores.

JAYNE O'DONNELL AND ERIN KUTZ

Having lost shoppers to hip specialty shops, department stores are reinventing themselves to attract both adults and their style-minded children.

J.C. Penney, Macy's, Bloomingdale's, Saks Fifth Avenue and Kohl's are all adopting approaches—from celebrity-designed fashions to mobile marketing to better fitting rooms—to try to lure young shoppers without turning off their parents.

With consumers cutting back on spending, many retailers have decided the best way to recapture them is to deliver a more cutting-edge experience and trendier clothing to attract their kids. The reasoning: Even as parents tighten their belts, they still spend freely on their children. If kids can get their parents to drive them to stores, the parents will end up shopping for themselves, too.

Middle-class teens, it turns out, represent a fairly recession-proof demographic, with outsize influence on household purchases.

That thinking has led J.C. Penney, long known as "my mom's store," to overhaul its teen merchandising, introduce new brands and redesign its teen departments. The retailer, which slashed its first-quarter earnings forecast by a third late last month and last week posted a larger-than-expected 12.3% March sales drop, will announce the changes today. Many of its rivals are taking similar steps, though the 106-year-old Penney chain, with its core clientele of middle-age and older shoppers, faces an especially stiff challenge and is making the biggest push.

While Penney says it commands the biggest share of the market for 13- to 20-year-old girls and women, CEO Mike Ullmann acknowledges his stores are most popular with teens until they get their own driver's license and credit card. At that point, Penney tends to lose them—until they grow up and return with kids of their own.

"With the teens, we have to capture them with a brand and a look," says Mike Boylson, Penney's chief marketing officer.

Today, teens influence up to an estimated 90% of grocery and apparel purchases, according to studies by digital marketing agency Resource Interactive. Even beyond their sway over household budgets, teen buyers, with their willingness, even eagerness, to spend, are highly sought-after consumers in their own right.

That's especially true in a shaky economy that's cut into sales at most retailers. Exhibit A: the success of Aéropostale, Urban Outfitters and some other youth-oriented specialty shops, which have been outperforming stores that cater more to older shoppers.

Penney, like other department stores, faces an uphill battle. By virtue of its size, it commands a huge share of the teen market, ranking first among mall-based stores for teens, according to market research firm TRU. But TRU trends director Rob Callender notes that those studies ask teens where they shop most often—not where they *like* to shop most often. Unless it can forge the kind of loyalty from teens enjoyed by such specialty stores as Abercrombie & Fitch and Forever 21, Penney will remain a destination that teens will follow their parents to, not one they'll seek out.

If drawing teens is crucial to gaining both the youth and adult crowds, some retailers face an institutional problem, too: Department stores can feel too physically unwieldy for teenagers, says Dan Hill of research firm Sensory Logic: "It's very hard to hug a giant."

> ### "It's somewhat of a natural process to reject the kinds of retail environments that your parents are associated with."
> — Leon Schiffman, a marketing professor at St. John's University

Some teens may even eschew department-store shopping as a way to distance themselves from their parents, says Leon Schiffman, a marketing professor at St. John's University in Queens, N.Y.

"It's somewhat of a natural process to reject the kinds of retail environments that your parents are associated with," Schiffman says.

That can frustrate parents. Wendy Queal of Hutchinson, Kan., says her 15-year-old son and 12-year-old daughter are "addicted" to American Eagle Outfitters and also favor Abercrombie & Fitch and Hollister.

"They like the stores with the loud music playing when they go in," Queal says. "They both told me to not buy them things from Dillard's anymore, which is where I have always bought a majority of their clothes. At this point in their lives, their shopping tends to be all about the name."

Well aware of this, Penney executives are stressing its brands' names—not its company name—much as Oldsmobile did years ago, when it began introducing trendier cars. Penney last month announced an exclusive new apparel line, Fabulosity, designed by reality TV star and former model Kimora Lee Simmons. In July, it will launch another brand, Decree, which Boylson says is "more updated than Abercrombie . . . with the same look, same feel, at half the price."

The clothes will be sold in departments with better lighting and more displays showing how to wear different outfits. (Penney's research found teens were seeking more fashion guidance from stores.) Apparel will be divided into different "lifestyles," ranging from wholesome active wear to hip city styles.

The Decree brand will be marketed "as if it's a national brand," Boylson says. "We don't beat them over the head with J.C. Penney."

The Teen Psyche

Youths are among the few categories of shoppers who seem comfortable spending freely these days. Other factors driving the interest in the teen market:

- Teens say they're closer with their families than the previous generation, Gen X, said at the same age, according to TRU. A recent TRU survey found that nine out of 10 teens say they're "close" to their parents; 75% agreed they "like to do things with their family"; and 59% say family dinners are "in."
- Teens are their households' de facto technology officers. They set up iPods and iPhones, troubleshoot PCs and spend hours with cellphones and social-networking sites. These 24/7 modes of rapid-fire communication allow teens—as well as brand marketers—to ignite interest in shopping trends faster than ever.

An informal USA TODAY survey of its panel of shoppers found teens are quick to name small specialty stores, such as American Eagle, as favorites. But they're habitually inconsistent.

John Crouch of Charleston, W.Va., says his 15-year-old daughter, Elizabeth, loves Delia's, American Eagle and Aéropostale. Yet, in the past two years, she's also become a fan of Penney and says it's now stylish. How about Sears? No way. Crouch says Elizabeth calls Sears' apparel "old ladies' clothing."

Schiffman says Bloomingdale's and other upscale department stores appeal to teens because their assortments and atmospheres are superior. "If you offer enough," he says, "you can get teens to go anywhere. J.C. Penney and Sears are just not pulling that."

But Adriene Solomon, like Elizabeth Crouch, disagrees, stressing the other side of the Penney story.

Seeing Penney as Hip

"My children love to shop at the 'trendy' stores: Hollister, Aéropostale, Abercrombie & Fitch, Wet Seal, Journeys, Champs (Sports) and any other tennis shoe store," says Solomon of Missouri City, Texas. "They most definitely don't like to shop at the top department stores like Macy's and Dillard's, but they will shop at J.C. Penney," because its styles seem trendy.

Roland Solomon, 15, says he'd go to Penney even if his mom weren't driving there, because he likes their jeans and shirts.

Yet, even the label "teen" is fraught with contradictions. A 13-year-old shopper bears little resemblance to a teen heading to college—at which point, says retail brand consultant Ken Nisch, high school posturing suddenly seems uncool.

"Things like resale gets to be a big trend in college, because there's more sense that it's not OK to show off what you have too much," Nisch says. "You might have needed an 'outfit' to go to high school, but when you go to college, God forbid if you have an 'outfit.' That means you're trying too hard."

LittleMissMatched, which sells brightly colored and patterned socks, loungewear and other apparel, finds that sales drop once kids head to college. They don't want to draw as much attention to clothes or to be viewed less seriously, says co-founder Arielle Eckstut.

But teen shoppers do want to look as if they know how to dress. Like Penney, the young women's apparel store Dots is redesigning stores to provide more fashion guidance. The retail design and branding firm FRCH, which is handling the redesign, is using splashy graphics and style tips. The goal, says managing creative director Steve McGowan, is to establish an "emotional connection" with shoppers.

"It's retail theater," McGowan says.

But how to reach the elusive teens in the first place?

"Newspaper and direct mail are useless against teens, and TV is not very effective," Boylson says. "Teens are much more in the digital space."

Several retailers are using social-networking sites as marketing tools. They're creating store profile pages, just the way teenagers build personal pages. H&M's boasts 60,000 "fans"—Facebook users who add a link to the H&M page on their own profile pages.

Some of the retail pages include photo albums of the store's seasonal collections and let fans upload photos of themselves wearing the store's clothing. Others provide podcasts of interviews with designers and links to virtual dressing rooms. And they send e-mails alerting fans to sales and discount codes.

American Eagle, which has nearly 30,000 fans, has a Facebook page. So do Hollister, Target, Forever 21 and Abercrombie & Fitch.

Facebook is "such a game-changer," says Dave Hendricks of Datran Media, which helps brands reach online consumers. "Facebook allows retailers to create a more viral experience. The taste-makers among youth spend all of their time in social media."

Penney is targeting teens through ads in theaters, interactive website features and mobile marketing.

"Teens know when they're being marketed to, so you have to be very careful," Boylson says.

Nor can you change their perceptions overnight.

"We understand it's about getting them to love the brands—not just J.C. Penney," says Liz Sweney, Penney's EVP for women's and girl's apparel.

Why Costco Is So Damn Addictive

A day with Jim Sinegal, the MERCHANDISING MAESTRO who gets shoppers to buy 2,250-count packs of Q-Tips and mayo by the drum.

MATTHEW BOYLE

A man who looks like Wilford Brimley moseys into the Costco warehouse store in the Seattle suburb of Issaquah, Wash., on a bright Columbus Day morning, easily blending into the throngs of shoppers picking up Cheerios, toilet paper, and cashmere sweaters.

But as soon as Costco CEO Jim Sinegal crosses the threshold of this vast, 150,000-square-foot theater of retail, it's abundantly clear that he's not just a spectator—he's the executive producer, director, and critic. "Jim's in the building!" crackles over the walkie-talkie of warehouse manager Louie Silveira. In the apparel section, Silveira's infectious grin morphs into a look of slight panic.

A sudden hop in his step, Silveira, who can log 15 miles a day walking the aisles, scurries over to Sinegal. Unsmiling, hands in his pockets, a coffee stain on his $12.99 Costco shirt, Sinegal turns out to be a no-nonsense connoisseur of detail. He greets his manager with a barrage of questions: "What's new today?"

"We just moved this $800 espresso machine to an end-cap," Silveira responds, meaning he moved it out from the middle of the aisle to a more prominent location at the end.

"How are in-stocks?"

"We're good there."

"What did we do in produce last week?"

"$220,000."

Wielding a bar-code scanner like a six-shooter, Silveira answers each query to Sinegal's satisfaction, but evidently that's not often the case. "When he starts looking at an item too long," Silveira confides later, "I say, 'Oh, shit.'"

Sinegal makes a beeline for a table full of $29.99 Italian-made Hathaway men's dress shirts, located just off the "racetrack," which is retail lingo for the U-shaped path along the perimeter—down one side, across, and back up the other side—that most shoppers follow upon entering the warehouse. He takes a shirt out of the box, fingers it, ponders a moment, then puts it back. He walks away, but soon returns to the table. He looks concerned.

In keeping with Costco's low-price, limited-selection philosophy, the Hathaway shirts are all the same size—a 34/35-inch sleeve. Today, at least, if you want a more precise length, you're out of luck. "I'm anxious to see how it does," says Sinegal, bending to pick up a bit of trash off the floor.

Sinegal needn't worry. The shirts, like everything else at Costco, will no doubt sell out within days, to be replaced by another item in the company's carousel of ridiculously priced high-quality inventory. With $59 billion in sales from 488 warehouse locations, Costco, No. 28 in the FORTUNE 500, is the fourth-largest retailer in the country and the seventh-largest in the world. In the 23 years since Sinegal co-founded Costco with Jeff Brotman (now chairman), it has never reported a negative monthly same-store sales result. Yet he's modestly compensated—Sinegal earned $450,000 in salary and bonus last year, chump change by CEO standards. Add in his stockholdings and he's worth $151 million. (One note on that: On Oct. 12, Costco disclosed that an internal review of stock-option granting identified one grant to Sinegal that was "subject to imprecision" and "may have benefited [Sinegal] by up to $200,000." Sinegal says he takes "full responsibility.")

The company counts nearly 48 million people as members, and those customers are not only slavishly devoted (averaging 22 trips per year, according to UBS analyst Neil Currie), but surprisingly affluent as well (more than a third have household incomes over $75,000). While Wal-Mart stands for low prices and Target embodies cheap chic, Costco is a retail treasure hunt, where one's shopping cart could contain a $50,000 diamond ring resting on top of a 64-ounce vat of mayonnaise. Despite having 82 fewer outlets than its nearest rival, Wal-Mart's Sam's Club, Costco generates about $20 billion more in sales.

Clearly, Costco is doing something right—but what? And how? To figure that out, we shadowed Sinegal, who has spent 52 of his 70 years in the retail business. He got his start working for Sol Price, who created the warehouse-club format, and left Price to launch Costco in 1983. Over the years, he's become a merchandising grand master, an exceedingly shrewd practitioner of the unglamorous but elusive art of getting the right product in the right place at the right time for the right price.

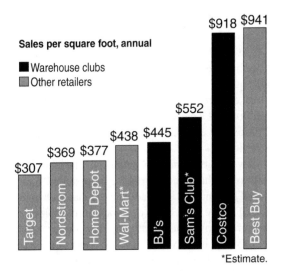

Sales per square foot, annual
■ Warehouse clubs
■ Other retailers

$307 Target
$369 Nordstrom
$377 Home Depot
$438 Wal-Mart*
$445 BJ's
$552 Sam's Club*
$918 Costco
$941 Best Buy

*Estimate.

Big Box, Big Bucks Costco sells more efficiently than its low-margin peers. It even outdoes plusher names like Nordstrom, and holds its own against higher-markup "category killers" like Best Buy.

BERTO'S STORE BY THE NUMBERS

TOTAL MEMBERSHIP 232,000

ANNUAL SALES $285 million

DAILY TRANSACTIONS 7,000

AVERAGE CUSTOMER BILL PER TRIP $150

ROTISSERIE CHICKENS SOLD PER YEAR
283,000

GALLONS OF MILK 375,000

ROLLS OF TOILET PAPER 8.4 million

When Jim Sinegal told Sol Price that he was launching a warehouse club to compete with Price's own Price Club, "Sol was pissed," recalls Sinegal, sipping Starbucks coffee (black) in his modestly appointed office at Costco headquarters in Issaquah. Price had a point: His erstwhile protégé was now his top rival in the fast-growing warehouse-club business. Wal-Mart launched Sam's Club that same year; Price Club and Costco later merged, in 1993.

And what a strange business it is. Costco refuses to mark up any item more than 14%, in contrast to supermarkets and department stores, which often carry markups of 25% and 50%, respectively. "We always look to see how much of a gulf we can create between ourselves and the competition," Sinegal says. "So that the competitors eventually say, 'Fuck 'em, these guys are crazy. We'll compete somewhere else."

To illustrate, Sinegal recounts a story about denim. "Some years ago we were selling a hot brand of jeans for $29.99. They were $50 in a department store. We got a great deal on them and could have sold them for a higher price, but we went down to $29.99. Why? We knew it would create a riot." Low markups may create excitement, but they also mean lower profits: Costco ekes out pretax margins of around 3%. Despite the microscopic margins, Costco earned $1.1 billion last fiscal year through its membership fees—$50 per year of pure profit—and its spartan approach to costs. The company doesn't use pricey ad agencies. Products move right from the delivery truck to the charm-free concrete sales floor. Signage looks like it was made with a cheap laser printer. There are no commissioned salespeople. There aren't even any shopping bags. The only cost that Costco doesn't skimp on is wages and benefits, which are the envy of big-box employees nationwide.

And yet Costco's card-carrying legions come in droves, waiting anxiously in fancy foreign cars on Saturday mornings for the store to open. Carts in hand, they display a fervor not usually seen outside of houses of worship. Why? Because we all love a bargain, and Lord help us if we miss one. "We only carry about 4,000 items," says Sinegal, "compared with 40,000 in a typical supermarket and 150,000 in a Wal-Mart supercenter. Of that 4,000, about 3,000 can be found on the floor all the time. The other 1,000 are the treasure-hunt stuff that's always changing. It's the type of item a customer knows they'd better buy because it will not be there next time, like Waterford crystal. We try to get that sense of urgency in our customers." (It should be mentioned that showing up on the sales floor of a discount emporium doesn't necessarily fit the marketing strategies of your Waterfords and Calvin Kleins and other high-end brands. Whatever those companies think, Costco wants to sell their products and makes a practice of acquiring them—legally—on the gray market.)

The limited-variety approach isn't for everyone, though. Sinegal explains: "We carry a 325-count bottle of Advil for $15.25," he says. "Lots of customers don't want to buy 325. If you had ten customers come in to buy Advil, how many are not going to buy any because you just have one size? Maybe one or two. We refer to that as the intelligent loss of sales: We are prepared to give up that one customer. But if we had four or five sizes of Advil, as grocery stores do, it would make our business more difficult to manage. Our business can only succeed if we are efficient. You can't go on selling at these margins if you are not."

The more efficient the product sourcing, the more latitude Sinegal can give his store managers in how they lay out those big bottles of Advil. "There are certain merchandise displays that all warehouses do," he says. "TVs are always in the front, for example. But the intent is not to tell these guys how to run their places. Our managers are entrepreneurs, not somebody who just comes in and unlocks the doors." Indeed, with some locations doing upwards of $300 million in sales a year, each warehouse is a mini-corporation, and each manager a de facto CEO. (See "Down In the Aisles.")

Costco differs from other retailers in many ways, but it's not as if Sinegal feels he has nothing to learn from them. "Whole Foods has a lot of theater to it," he says. "It's difficult to walk in there and not buy something." He also learned a lot from

Down in the Aisles

How to be great at Costco? Know before they do

If Jim Sinegal is Costco's general, his 488 warehouse managers are field commanders. With the average warehouse generating $128 million in sales a year, they effectively run their own small companies. Humberto "Berto" Yniguez heads the 139,000-square-foot warehouse in Marina Del Rey, Calif., which employs about 500 people and moves $285 million of product a year—the highest-grossing store in the U.S. (Actually it's No. 2; No. 1 is in Honolulu, where everything's so expensive you'd have to pay shoppers to stay away from Costco. So we're sticking with Berto.) "His store hums," says Sinegal.

That hum does not happen by chance. Yniguez is a model student of Sinegal's approach to retailing. Superstars at Costco have the usual skills recruiters look for: people skills, smarts. A yen for crisis management is a plus. Yniguez has that down: A brief stint as a police officer in his early 20s taught him how to settle disputes quickly, which comes in handy when you're dealing with wild-eyed coupon clippers all day.

But Sinegal looks for something else in his employees too: that rare ability to know just what item will sell best in a given spot at a given time. It's more than just pushing candy near Halloween or air conditioners during a heat wave. "Berto's a great merchant," says Sinegal. "When you walk into his warehouse, you feel like you are enveloped in merchandise. It's all around you." And you have to know your customers: "A lot of our members are affluent, and they have higher expectations," Yniguez says. "I could sell a $45,000 diamond in this building, but it would not sell elsewhere."

Yniguez's merchandising ideas often take root elsewhere, like when he started selling large plants to local real estate developers at up to $350 a pop. To keep the plants from cluttering the sales floor, Yniguez leaves them in the parking lot for same-day pickup. Now a handful of other Costcos are doing the same—not surprising, given that seven of his former assistants are running their own warehouses. The student, in turn, becomes the teacher. "Without folks like Berto, we fail," Sinegal says. "It's that simple." —*M.B.*

Being a CEO was the last thing on 18-year-old Jim Sinegal's mind when he took a job unloading mattresses at Fed-Mart, Sol Price's precursor to Price Club. "It wasn't that great a job," Sinegal recalls. "I was getting a buck and a quarter an hour. But it was exciting. Sol was a major part of that excitement. He was not big on compliments, but you never doubted what was on his mind. Ever. He was always able to discover everything we were doing wrong. He just had a knack for it."

Price saw that the young Sinegal had the knack too, and chose him to overhaul Fed-Mart's flagship store. "When I was 26," Sinegal continues, "Sol made me the manager in the original San Diego store, which had become unprofitable. I was supposed to narrow down the selection and get out of troublesome categories like apparel. We had way too much apparel. So here I was, this kid, and I was given a tremendous responsibility. As a result of simplifying the process, we were able to get it back into the black."

If Wal-Mart is low prices and Target is cheap chic, Costco is a treasure hunt.

Sinegal embraced Price's iconoclastic approach. "An awful lot of what we did at Fed-Mart was counterintuitive to people who were in the merchandising business at that time," Sinegal says. "We didn't advertise or accept major credit cards. It was all self-service. Also, you had to be a member of the club. People paid us to shop there."

Most counterintuitive of all was Price's stubborn refusal to wring an extra buck from his customers. "Many retailers look at an item and say, 'I'm selling this for ten bucks. How can I sell it for 11?' We look at it and say, How can we get it to nine bucks? And then, How can we get it to eight? It is contrary to the thinking of a retailer, which is to see how much more profit you can get out of it. But once you start doing that, it's like heroin."

Sinegal works diligently to prevent that addiction from entering Costco's bloodstream. Now that he's in Price's role—retail sage—how does he impart what he's learned, and how does he know who his best students are? Step one is obvious: Hire smart young workers. "One of the first places we recruit is at the local university," Sinegal says. "These people are smarter than the average person, hard-working, and they haven't made a career choice." Those who demonstrate smart and strong people skills move up the ranks. But without merchandising savvy—that ability to know what product would sell best on an end-cap on any given Saturday—an employee has no chance to become warehouse manager. "People who have the feel for it just start to get it," says Sinegal. "Others, you look at them and it's like they are staring at a blank canvas. I'm not trying to be unduly harsh, but that's the way it works. They are not going to become a Louie."

Back in his warehouse, Louie Silveira is perhaps wishing he'd become someone else. He's still facing an Issaquah inquisition from Sinegal, who's convinced he saw a digital piano—$1,999

Stew Leonard's, a supermarket chain in the Northeast: "When we did our fresh foods, we studied them closely." And Target: "They have high standards, but they do that without being boring. That's the trick."

Sinegal has taken Costco where no warehouse club had gone before—pharmacy, fresh bakery and meat, store brands one could be proud to serve in the home, and international expansion. Sinegal's son Michael is currently heading Costco's Japanese operations. Will he run the company someday? Sinegal won't go there.

at the Issaquah warehouse—priced lower in one of his Florida locations the week before. He's not sure which, but tells Silveira to track it down. Silveira checks on a few, but they are all priced the same as his. Sinegal isn't satisfied.

The following day, after hours of boring budget meetings, Sinegal finds, to his delight, that the piano was indeed marked down to $1,499 in the Kendall, Fla., outlet. No victory is too small. "Every time you go someplace, you see something that excites you," Sinegal says. "I was just in the South of France, and there was this gelato stand. I could not believe the excitement it created. I haven't figured out how we will do it at Costco, but it's in my noodle."

Wal-Mart's Midlife Crisis

Declining growth, increasing competition, and not an easy fix in sight.

ANTHONY BIANCO

John E. Fleming, Wal-Mart's newly appointed chief merchandising officer, is staring hard at a display of $14 women's T-shirts in a Supercenter a few miles from the retailer's Bentonville (Ark.) headquarters. The bright-hued stretch T's carry Wal-Mart's own George label and are of a quality and stylishness not commonly associated with America's *über*-discounter. What vexes Fleming is that numerous sizes are out of stock in about half of the 12 colors, including frozen kiwi and black soot.

Fleming may be America's most powerful merchant, but a timely solution is beyond him even so. Wal-Mart failed to order enough of these China-made T-shirts last year, and so they and other George-brand basics will remain in short supply in most of its 3,443 U.S. stores until 2007's second half, depriving the retailer of tens of millions of dollars a week it sorely needs. "The issue with apparel is long lead times," says the quietly intense Fleming, who spent 20 years at Target Corp. before joining Wal-Mart Stores Inc. "We will get it fixed."

For nearly five decades, Wal-Mart's signature "everyday low prices" and their enabler—low costs—defined not only its business model but also the distinctive personality of this proud, insular company that emerged from the Ozarks backwoods to dominate retailing. Over the past year and a half, though, Wal-Mart's growth formula has stopped working. In 2006 its U.S. division eked out a 1.9% gain in same-store sales—its worst performance ever—and this year has begun no better. By this key measure, such competitors as Target, Costco, Kroger, Safeway, Walgreen's, CVS, and Best Buy now are all growing two to five times faster than Wal-Mart (table, page 54).

Wal-Mart's botched entry into cheap-chic apparel is emblematic of the quandary it faces. Is its alarming loss of momentum the temporary result of disruptions caused by transitory errors like the T-shirt screwup and by overdue improvements such as the store remodeling program launched last year? Or is Wal-Mart doing lasting damage to its low-budget franchise by trying to compete with much hipper, nimbler rivals for the middle-income dollar? Should the retailer redouble its efforts to out-Target Target, or would it be better off going back to basics?

If Wal-Mart seems short of answers at the moment, it might well be because there aren't any good ones. Increasingly, it appears that America's largest corporation has steered itself into a slow-growth cul de sac from which there is no escape. "There are a lot of issues here, but what they add up to is the end of the age of Wal-Mart," contends Richard Hastings, a senior analyst for the retail rating agency Bernard Sands. "The glory days are over."

Simple mathematics suggest that a 45-year-old company in an industry growing no faster than the economy as a whole will struggle to sustain the speedy growth rates of its youth. In Wal-Mart's case, this difficulty is exacerbated by its great size and extreme dominance of large swaths of the U.S. retail market. Wal-Mart already controls 20% of dry grocery, 29% of nonfood grocery, 30% of health and beauty aids, and 45% of general merchandise sales, according to ACNielsen.

However, the expansion impulse is as deeply embedded in Wal-Mart's DNA as its allegiance to cut-rate pricing. Wal-Mart was able to boost total U.S. revenues by 7.2% last year by opening new stores at the prodigious rate of nearly one a day. According to Wal-Mart CEO H. Lee Scott Jr., the company plans to sustain this pace for at least the next five years. In fact, he is on record saying that room remains in the U.S. for Wal-Mart to add 4,000 Supercenters—the largest of its store formats by far—to the 2,000 it now operates.

Does Scott, 58, recognize any limits whatsoever to Wal-Mart's growth potential in the U.S., which accounted for 78% of its $345 billion in sales last year? "Actually, and I know it's going to sound naive to you, I don't," he replies. "The real issue is, are [we] going to be good enough to take advantage of the opportunities that exist?"

Too Close for Comfort

Wall Street does not share Scott's bullishness, to put it mildly. Wal-Mart shares are trading well below their 2004 high and have dropped 30% in total since Scott was named CEO in 2000, even as the Morgan Stanley retail index has risen 180%. "The stock has been dead money for a long time," says Charles Grom, a JPMorgan Chase & Co. analyst.

Even money managers who own Wal-Mart's shares tend to see the retailer as a beaten-down value play, not a growth company.

"I'd be surprised if true growth-oriented investors were involved at this point," says Walter T. McCormick, manager of the $1.2 billion Evergreen Fundamental Large Cap Fund, which began buying the stock a year ago. "The issue the Street has is market saturation: We may be in the seventh inning of a nine-inning game."

One can argue that the deceleration of Wal-Mart's organic growth is a function of the aging of its outlets, given that same-store sales rates slow as stores mature. Outlets five years or older accounted for 17% of all U.S. Supercenters in 2000 and 44% in 2006, and will top 60% in 2010, according to HSBC analyst Mark Husson. "There's an inevitability of bad middle age," he says.

Meanwhile, the underlying economics of expansion have turned against Wal-Mart, even as it relies increasingly on store-building to compensate for sagging same-store sales. On balance, the new Supercenters are just not pulling in enough sales to offset fully the sharply escalating costs of building them. Part of the problem is that many new stores are located so close to existing ones that Wal-Mart ends up competing with itself. All in all, the retailer's pretax return on fixed assets, which includes things such as computers and trucks as well as stores, has plunged 40% since 2000.

Even many analysts with a buy on Wal-Mart want it to follow the lead of McDonald's Corp. and cut way back on new-store building to concentrate instead on extracting more value from existing stores, which vary wildly in their performance. Wal-Mart disclosed a year and a half ago that same-store sales were rising 10 times, or 1,000%, faster at the 800 best-managed outlets than at the 800 worst-run ones. Equally shocking was its admission that 25% of its stores failed to meet minimum expectations of cleanliness, product availability, checkout times, and so on.

Scott is acutely aware of the Street's discontent. "We have to find a way to give our shareholders back the returns that they need through some mechanism," he acknowledges. In March, Wal-Mart boosted its dividend 31%. Apparently, the board also is considering spinning off Sam's Club, the warehouse club division that is a perennial also-ran to Costco.

Wal-Mart announced late last year that it would trim its customary 8% annual addition to U.S. square footage to 7% in 2007. At the moment, though, slamming on the brakes is out of the question. Says Scott: "If you stop the growth at Wal-Mart, you'd be silly to think that [alone] means you're going to have better stores."

Wal-Mart's "home office" has taken a series of steps to improve the performance of its far-flung store network. Last year it implemented a whole new supervisory structure that required many of its 27 regional administrators to move out of Bentonville and live in the districts they manage. In April, Scott removed the executive in charge of U.S. store operations and put her in charge of corporate personnel instead.

The number of stores falling below the threshold of minimum customer expectations has declined but remains "more than would be acceptable," says Scott, who is surprisingly philosophical about the persistence of mediocrity. Asked why it has been so difficult to fix bad stores, HE replies: "That's a very good question. It's a question I ask all the time."

The polite, self-deprecating Scott is no Robert L. Nardelli, whose ouster as Home Depot Inc.'s (HD) chief had as much to do with his abrasive personality as the chain's business problems. That said, Wal-Mart's stock has performed worse under Scott than Home Depot's did under Nardelli. "The Street is going to look to the back half of 2007 for evidence of improvement," says an adviser to a large, longtime Wal-Mart shareholder. "If that doesn't happen, you're going to see a tremendous amount of pressure."

Scott & Co. already are struggling to cope with mounting sociopolitical backlash to Wal-Mart's size and aggressive business practices. Over the past decade, dozens of lawsuits were brought by employees claiming to be overworked and underpaid, including the mother of all sex discrimination class actions. Organized labor set up two Washington-based organizations to oppose the antiunion employer at every turn. And hundreds of municipalities across the country erected legal obstacles of one kind or another.

Wal-Mart's initial reaction to the gathering storm of opposition was to ignore it and maintain the defiant insularity that is a legacy of its Ozarks origins. "The best thing we ever did was hide back there in the hills," Sam Walton, the company's legendary founder, declared shortly before his death in 1992.

In the past few years, Scott has reluctantly brought Wal-Mart out from behind its Bentonville barricades. Virtually from scratch, this famously conservative company has built a large public and government relations apparatus headed by Leslie A. Dach, a veteran Washington political operative of pronounced liberal bent. Few CEOs have embraced environmental sustainability as avidly as has Scott, who also broke with the Republican orthodoxy of his predecessors by advocating a hike in the federal minimum wage.

It's not just rhetoric: Wal-Mart has indeed made substantive reforms in some areas. It has struck up effective working relationships with many of the very environmental groups it once disdained. No less dramatically, the company has added three women (one is Hispanic) and two African American directors to its board and also tied all executive bonuses to diversity goals.

It turns out, though, that there is a dark, paranoid underside to Wal-Mart's visible campaign of outreach. What began as an attempt by Wal-Mart's Threat Research and Assessment Group to detect theft and pro-union sympathies among store workers grew into surveillance of certain outside critics, consultants, stockholders, and even Wal-Mart's board. Bruce Gabbard, a security technician fired for allegedly unauthorized wiretapping of a *New York Times* reporter, has described himself as "the guy listening to the board of directors when Lee Scott is excused from the room."

Wal-Mart's spreading Spygate scandal is perhaps the most damaging in a long sequence of PR disasters, including last year's conviction of former No. 2 executive, Thomas M. Coughlin on fraud and tax evasion charges stemming from embezzlement of company funds. Coughlin, a Walton protégé who had been Scott's leading rival for the CEO post, is serving a sentence of 27 months of house arrest.

There is no way of measuring how much business Wal-Mart is losing to competitors with more benign reputations. According to a recent survey conducted by Wal-Mart itself, though, 14% of Americans living within range of one of its stores—which takes in 90% of the population—are so skeptical of the company as to qualify as "conscientious objectors."

But the Arkansas giant's fundamental business problem is that selling for less no longer confers the overwhelming business advantage it once did. Low prices still define the chain's appeal to its best customers, the 45 million mostly low-income Americans who shop its stores frequently and broadly. But the collective purchasing power of these "loyalists," as Wal-Mart calls them, has shriveled in recent years as hourly wages have stagnated and the cost of housing and energy have soared.

More affluent shoppers also walk Wal-Mart's aisles in great numbers, but they tend to buy sparingly, loading up on toothpaste, detergent, and other "consumables" priced barely above cost while shunning higher-margin items such as clothes and furniture. To the selective middle-income shopper, quality, style, service, and even store aesthetics increasingly matter as much as price alone. "Here's the big thought Wal-Mart missed: Price is not enough anymore," says Todd S. Slater, an analyst at Lazard Capital Markets.

Backwoods Knowhow

At first, Wal-Mart management blamed its loss of momentum mostly on rising gasoline prices—a theory undercut when same-store sales kept falling even as the cost of gas receded during the latter half of 2006. Today, Wal-Mart executives are more willing to acknowledge the X factor of intensified competition. Says Fleming: "We're now up against world-class competitors that are each taking a slice of our business."

Wal-Mart not only was slow to recognize this threat but also responded haphazardly once it did. The nub of the problem was that the discounter had relied for so long on selling for less that it did not know any other way to sell. Wal-Mart did not begin to build a marketing department worthy of the name until Fleming was named to the new position of chief marketing officer in spring, 2005, an appointment Scott hailed as "an extraordinary move for us."

Founded in 1962, Wal-Mart rose to dominance on the strength of its mastery of retailing's "back-end" mechanics. Forced by the isolation of the Ozarks to do for itself what most retailers relied on others to do for them, Wal-Mart built a cutting-edge distribution system capable of moving goods from factory loading dock to store cash register faster and cheaper by far than any competitor. It added to its cost advantage by refusing to acquiesce to routine increases in wholesale prices, continually pressing suppliers to charge less.

Walton, who was both a gifted merchant and a born tightwad, also pinched pennies in every other facet of business, from wages and perks (there were none) to fixtures and furnishings. Aesthetics counted for so little that when the retailer finally put down carpet in its stores it took care to choose a color that matched the sludgy gray-brown produced by mixing dirt, motor oil, and the other contaminants most commonly tracked across its floors. To Wal-Mart, the beauty of its hideous carpet was that it rarely needed cleaning.

Low costs begat low prices. Instead of relying on promotional gimmickry, Wal-Mart sold at a perpetual discount calculated to make up for in volume what it lost in margin. Walton's philosophy was price it low, pile it high, and watch it fly. His belief in everyday low prices made him a populist hero even as he built America's largest fortune. (His descendants still own 40% of Wal-Mart's shares, a stake worth $80 billion.) Regulators forced "Mr. Sam" to modify his slogan of "Always the lowest price" to the hedged "Always low prices!" But hundreds of retailers went broke trying to compete with Wal-Mart on price just the same.

In many ways, Wal-Mart has remained reflexively tight-fisted under Scott, a 28-year company veteran who trained at Walton's knee and rose to the top through trucking and logistics. Last year, Wal-Mart began remodeling the apparel, home, and electronics sections in 1,800 stores, replacing miles of that stain-colored carpeting with vinyl that looks like wood. To Fleming, the new "simulated wood" floor is all about aesthetic improvement. His boss takes the classical Wal-Mart view. "The truth is that vinyl costs less," Scott says. "And the maintenance on the vinyl costs less than the maintenance on the carpet."

Yet Wal-Mart is neither as low-cost nor as low-price a retailer as it was in Walton's day, or even when Scott moved up to CEO. Most dramatically, overhead costs jumped 14.8% in 2006 alone and now amount to 18.6% of sales, compared with 16.4% in Scott's first year—a momentous rise in a business that counts profit in pennies on the dollar.

The imperatives of reputational damage control have prompted Bentonville to add hundreds of staff jobs in public relations, corporate affairs, and other areas that the company happily ignored when it was shielded by the force field of Walton's folksy charisma. And as the nation's largest electricity consumer and owner of its second-largest private truck fleet, Wal-Mart was hit doubly hard by the explosion of energy costs.

Wal-Mart also has purposefully, if not entirely voluntarily, inflated its cost base in expanding far beyond its original rural Southern stronghold. It is far more expensive to buy land and to build, staff, and operate stores in the large cities that are the final frontier of Wal-Mart's expansion than in the farm towns where it began. Then, too, the company is encountering mounting resistance as it pushes deeper into the Northeast, Upper Midwest, and West Coast, requiring it to retain legions of lawyers and lobbyists to fight its way into town.

Narrowing the Gap

Under Scott, Wal-Mart even blunted its seminal edge in distribution by letting billions of dollars in excess inventories accumulate at mismanaged stores. A dubious milestone was reached in 2005 as inventories rose even faster than sales. "You'd see these big storage containers behind stores, but what was more amazing was that [local] managers were going outside Wal-Mart's distribution network to subcontract their own warehouse space," says Bill Dreher, a U.S. retailing analyst for Deutsche Bank.

Over the past decade, top competitors in most every retailing specialty have succeeded in narrowing their cost gap with Wal-Mart by restructuring their operations. They eliminated jobs, remodeled stores, and replaced warehouses, investing heavily in new technology to tie it all together. Unionized supermarkets even managed to chip away at Wal-Mart's nonunion-labor cost advantage, signaling their resolve by taking a long strike in Southern California in 2003–04. The end result: Rival chains gradually were able to bring their prices down closer to Wal-Mart's and again make good money.

Consider the return to form of Kroger Co., the largest and oldest U.S. supermarket chain. Cincinnati-based Kroger competes against more Wal-Mart Supercenters—1,000 at last count—than any other grocer. Which is why until recently the only real interest Wall Street took in the old-line giant was measuring it for a coffin. Today, though, a rejuvenated Kroger is gaining share faster in the 32 markets where it competes with Wal-Mart than in the 12 where it does not.

A recent Bank of America survey of three such markets—Atlanta, Houston, and Nashville—found that Kroger's prices were 7.5% higher on average than Wal-Mart's, compared with 20% to 25% five years ago. This margin is thin enough to allow Kroger to again bring to bear such "core competencies" as service, quality, and convenience, says BofA's Scott A. Mushkin, who recently switched his Kroger rating to buy from sell. "We're saying the game has changed, and it looks like it has changed substantially in Kroger's favor," he says.

While Wal-Mart vies with a plethora of born-again rivals for the trade of middle-income Americans, it also must contend on the low end of the income spectrum with convenience and dollar-store chains and with such "hard discounters" as Germany's Aldi Group. These no-frills rivals are challenging Wal-Mart's hold over budget-minded shoppers by underpricing it on many staples.

To right Wal-Mart's listing U.S. flagship division, Scott installed Eduardo Castro-Wright as its president and CEO in fall, 2005. The Ecuador-born, U.S.-educated Castro-Wright, now 51, worked for RJR Nabisco and Honeywell International Inc. before joining Wal-Mart in 2001. In Castro-Wright's three years as CEO of Wal-Mart Mexico, revenues soared 50%, powered by sparkling same-store sales growth of 10% a year.

To date, Castro-Wright has fallen so far short of replicating the miracle of Mexico that in January he had to publicly deny rumors that he was about to be transferred back to international. Instead, Scott shifted the vice-chairman over Castro-Wright to new duties. That the U.S. chief now reports directly to Scott both solidifies Castro-Wright's status and ups the pressure on him to show results.

Castro-Wright can point to progress on the cost side of the ledger. By tightening controls over the stores, headquarters has halved the growth rate of inventories to 5.6% from 11.5% two years ago. Wal-Mart also has squeezed more productivity out of its 1.3 million store employees for eight consecutive quarters. This was done by capping wages for most hourly positions, converting full-time jobs to part-time ones, and installing a sophisticated scheduling system to adjust staffing levels to fluctuations in customer traffic.

Wal-Mart has found other new ways to economize, notably by cutting out middlemen to do more contract manufacturing overseas. The company's much publicized green initiatives have tempered criticism from some left-leaning opponents but are perhaps best understood as a politically fashionable manifestation of its traditional cost-control imperative.

By any conventional measure, Wal-Mart remains a solidly profitable company. Rising overhead costs have cut into net income, which in 2006 rose a middling 6.7%, a far cry from the double-digit increases of the 1990s. Return on equity continues to top 20%, however, and U.S. operating margins actually have widened a bit under Castro-Wright, as costs have risen a bit slower than Wal-Mart's average selling price.

Evidently, though, it is going to take a lot more than Castro-Wright's workmanlike adjustments to revive Wal-Mart's moribund stock. In the end, Scott's aversion to a McDonald's-style strategic about-face leaves Wal-Mart no alternative but to try to grow its way back into Wall Street's good graces. But if opening a new Wal-Mart or Sam's Club almost every day can't move the dial, what will?

Foreign markets present an intriguing mix of potential and peril for Wal-Mart, which first ventured abroad in 1992. Although the company now owns stores in 13 countries, the lion's share of those revenues comes from Mexico, Canada, and Britain. In 2006 international revenues rose 30%, to $77 billion. At the same time, though, Wal-Mart's long-standing struggles to adapt its quintessentially American low-cost, low-price business model to foreign cultures was underscored by the $863 million loss it took in exiting Germany.

Wal-Mart is the rare U.S. company that is more politically constrained at home than abroad in angling for outsize growth opportunities. In March it withdrew its application for a Utah bank charter just before a congressional committee was set to convene hearings. The retreat marks an apparent end to its decade-long campaign to diversify into consumer banking.

Although Wal-Mart regularly makes sizable acquisitions abroad, it is in no position to respond in kind to such domestic dagger thrusts as CVS's $26.5 billion acquisition of pharmacy benefits manager Caremark Rx. "That deal is a real threat, but Wal-Mart would have huge antitrust problems if it made an acquisition of any size," says a top mergers-and-acquisitions banker. "They are kind of stuck."

In the end, Wal-Mart seems unlikely to regain its stride unless it can solve what might be the diciest conundrum in retailing today. That is, can it seduce tens of millions of middle-income shoppers into stepping up their purchases in a major way without alienating its low-income legions in the process?

Largely because of the pressing need to differentiate itself from Wal-Mart, Target began grappling with this very puzzle more than a decade ago and gradually solved it with the cheap-chic panache that transformed it into "Tar-zhay." Says the president of a leading apparel maker: "Target has an awareness of what's happening in fashion equal to a luxury player, maybe greater. They have set the bar very high."

Scott acknowledged as much in making former Target exec Fleming chief marketing officer, reporting to Castro-Wright. Fleming, who had been CEO of Wal-Mart.com, went outside to fill every key slot in building a 40-person marketing group from scratch. He supported Wal-Mart's move into higher-priced, more fashionable apparel and home furnishings with the splashiest marketing the retailer had ever done, buying ad spreads in *Vogue* and sponsoring an open-air fashion show in Times Square.

Wal-Mart's top management all the way up to and including Scott presumed that Wal-Mart could run like Tar-zhay before it had learned to walk. "What Wal-Mart tried to do smacks of a kind of arrogant attitude toward fashion—that you can just order it, put it down, and people will buy it," says Eric Beder, a specialty retailing analyst at Brean Murray, Carret & Co.

Crash Course

Wal-Mart did everything at once and precipitously, introducing ads even as it was flooding stores with new merchandise and before it could complete its store remodeling program. Bentonville was learning marketing on the fly and did not even attempt to adopt the sort of formal, centralized merchandise planning at which Target and many big department-store chains excel. Instead, Wal-Mart relied on dozens of individual buyers to make critical decisions as it pushed hard into unfamiliar product areas.

How else to explain why a retailer whose typical female customer is thought to be a size 14 loaded up on skinny-leg jeans? Or why Wal-Mart's cheap-chic Metro7 line got off to a flying start in 350 stores only to crash and burn as it was rolled out to 1,150 more? Or why Wal-Mart not only severely misread demand for George-brand basics but also is unable to replenish its stocks for months on end while "fast-fashion" chains such as H&M easily turn over entire collections every six weeks?

Scott loved Wal-Mart's bold new direction until he hated it, his enthusiasm diminishing in sync with same-store sales throughout much of 2006. "We are going to sell for less," Scott says now, emphasizing a return to Wal-Mart's first principles.

"I believe that long after we are gone, the person who sells for less will do more business than the person who doesn't."

Yet Scott also signaled his continuing commitment to the pursuit of the middle-income shopper by promoting Fleming to yet another new post, chief merchandising officer, as part of a January shakeup of the senior ranks. Although Wal-Mart no doubt has sponsored its last glitzy runway show, Fleming insists that the company is sticking with its underlying strategy of "customer relevance"—that is, of moving beyond a monolithic focus on price to try to boost sales by targeting particular customers in new ways. "We're not going to back off," he vows. "We've learned certain lessons. Some things we'll build on, some things we won't."

While the look of its stores is primarily a function of how much Wal-Mart chooses to spend on them, the retailer is unlikely ever to come up with an ambience conducive to separating the affluent from their money without changing its whole approach to labor. The chain's dismal scores on customer satisfaction surveys imply that it is understaffing stores to the point where many of them struggle merely to meet the demands of its self-service format.

It is entirely possible even so that Wal-Mart in time will figure out how to sell vast quantities of dress-for-success blazers, 400-thread-count sheets, laptop computers, and even prepackaged sushi. But as Wal-Mart closes in on $400 billion in annual revenues, it is going to have to overachieve just to get same-store sales rising again at 3% to 5% a year.

The odds are that Scott, or his successor, will have to choose between continuing to disappoint Wall Street or milking the U.S. operation for profits better reinvested overseas. Only by hitting the business development equivalent of the lottery in countries like China, India, or Brazil can the world's largest retailer hope to restore the robust growth that once seemed like a birthright.

With Mara Der Hovanesian, Lauren Young, and Pallavi Gogoi in New York.

Sell It!

The bottom line is that your business comes down to one thing: sales. That's why we went straight to the source—the experts, entrepreneurs and even customers—to find out what really works.

AMANDA C. KOOSER, MINDY CHARSKI, CATHERINE SEDA ET AL.

How to Sell to Your First Department Store

You'd think selling an innovative new beauty line to a department store would be easy, right? Wrong. No one would take my calls! But being a squeaky wheel finally paid off when I got hold of a buyer who gave me 30 seconds to make my pitch. That's when I got crafty: I explained that several (rival) stores were interested, but hers was my top choice. Sold! Flattery works every time.

MAUREEN KELLY, 34, launched Tarte Cosmetics in 2000 and had sales of $15 million last year.

How to Sell to Hispanics

Don't assume your marketing resonates with the country's nearly 42.7 million Hispanics, who are projected to have $863 billion in buying power this year. To reach out successfully, get to know the culture, says Joe Zubizarreta, COO of Zubi Advertising in Coral Gables, Florida. Understand that language isn't the only differentiator, he adds. Be in the local community, have a bilingual website and staff, and prepare operationally to handle your new customers.

MINDY CHARSKI is a Dallas-based freelancer who regularly writes about marketing to Hispanics.

How to Use Tech to Power up Sales

Technology won't make sales happen, but it can definitely make selling easier. Some tools to check out:

- Condense your phone, e-mail, web access and documents into one small device. The Hewlett-Packard iPAQ 510 Voice Messenger smartphone features Windows Mobile 6 Standard and advanced voice controls.
- Online tools are hot commodities right now. Jigsaw (www.jigsaw.com) is like a massive, multiuser Rolodex where sales professionals can share contacts.

- Need a lightweight, portable projector? Check out the 2.8-pound Planar PR6020 for $1,399.
- Store your presentations and sales materials on the ultracompact, $15 1GB Kingston DataTraveler Mini Fun USB 2.0 Flash drive.

AMANDA C. KOOSER is *Entrepreneur*'s assistant technology editor.

How to Sell on eBay

Through my astounding journey growing my $1 million eBay business, Koss DVD, I discovered two things: 1) Many eBay business owners don't understand how their eBay/PayPal fees and costs of running their business impact their profits, and 2) I do. I learned to track every detail of listing and selling items, and I trained myself to shy away from risky behavior—such as choosing the wrong listing format—that could lead to profit loss. Watching these details saved me a ton of money!

COREY KOSSACK (pictured at right), 23, is founder of ProfitBuilder-Software.com and author of *eBay Millionaire or Bust* (eBay User ID: kossdvd).

How to Sell Overseas

Choose exporting, a relatively easy and fast way to enter foreign markets. It involves comparatively low levels of commitment and risk, yet allows you to go global quickly. Pick a market where consumers speak your language and want your product. Check out BuyUSA.gov to learn as much as you can about the culture and market. The site can also help you find customers through customized research, an international partner search or a single company promotion program.

LAUREL DELANEY is *Entrepreneur*'s "Global Village" columnist.

How to SEO Like a Pro

Spiders love links—search engine spiders, that is. So don't just optimize your website for keywords and rest on your laurels. To climb to the top of search results—for free—get links. Not all links are created equal, though. To engage in ethical search engine optimization, think quality before quantity. Find quality blogs, magazines and sites where your content will be relevant. Next, submit a helpful comment or article. If it's accepted, you'll get a link. Here's the essential step: Link your most important keyword phrase to your site. You'll improve your rankings because spiders will follow the links from authority sites to yours—and so will customers.

Internet marketing strategist **CATHERINE SEDA** is author of the new book *How to Win Sales & Influence Spiders*.

How to Sell an Expensive Product

Presentation is everything, so make your products look as attractive as possible. Whether you're promoting the item via the web, a catalog or a brochure, invest in good photography. It encourages an emotional response. Also pay close attention to the copy. If something about a product is unique, make sure you describe how. And if you want repeat business, differentiate yourself from the competition by offering something your competitors don't, be it personalized service or exclusive products.

KASSIE REMPEL (pictured at right), 34, is founder of Simply-Soles (*www.simplysoles.com*), a million-dollar online boutique and print catalog featuring women's designer shoes.

How to Create Buzz

Our efforts at creating buzz have had to do with simply empowering our users—giving them a suite of creative tools and encouraging them to innovate. By listening and adapting to our community and creating a scenario in which our users had a vested interest in the product, we were nine-tenths of the way to creating the early buzz we experienced. In today's computing and business environments, interactivity and participation are paramount.

PHILIP ROSEDALE (pictured above), 38, founded San Francisco-based Linden Lab, creator of virtual world Second Life, in 1999.

How to Get Out of a Sales Slump

Selling yourself out of a slump starts with a proactive attitude. Get out there and meet with as many customers and prospects as you can—whether it's face-to-face meetings, networking events or follow-up appointments. Then it's just a matter of moving contacts to the next step in the sales cycle. Sell them on a presentation, demonstration, product test or anything else that will bring them closer to buying. Progress builds confidence. Lastly, compile ideas on how you can help your prospects and customers grow their businesses. Remove what you're selling from your mind. Think instead about what your customers are buying. What motivates them? If you focus on building your customers' businesses, you'll end up building your own.

BARRY FARBER is *Entrepreneur*'s "Sales Success" columnist.

How to Make Cold Calls

Having a positive and resilient attitude is critical to success. Relationships are everything today, so when you call someone you don't already know, you're going to hit a great deal of resistance from the start. But don't let a few bad calls affect your attitude during the next call. Another key is to listen. Your prospect will warm up once you're able to get them talking about what they do, their goals or their challenges. Lastly, don't forget to follow up. I've secured more meetings and business simply by making those extra calls and catching the prospect at a better time.

BARRY FARBER (www.barryfarber.com) is *Entrepreneur*'s "Sales Success" columnist.

How to Sell to the Government

The government market is vast, but don't let that intimidate you. Here are some quick tips to help you get started: First, start local and find nearby government agencies. Check out the Federal Executive Board website (www.governmentexpress.com), for details on the 28 U.S. cities that have federal executive boards. The contact information will lead you to a list of all federal offices in your area. Then visit the Government Express website, click on "Resources," then click the "DoD Procurement Tech Assistance Centers" link. PTACs offer low- and no-cost courses on doing business with the government. The rest of the site is full of useful information, too. Once you've found the local agencies, go in and meet people. Call and set appointments with the small-business office. Relationships help you sell in government, just like in business.

MARK AMTOWER (www.governmentexpress.com) has been helping companies win government business since 1985.

How to Hire an Ad Agency

Ask other business owners about good agencies in your area. Focus on firms that do more than just advertising. Usually, a mix of services—ads, PR, direct mail, online tactics—will deliver a bigger bang for your buck. Find an agency that asks good questions. Chemistry is critical to a lasting relationship, so make sure you meet—and like—the staffers who would be working on your business's account. And be sure to call current and past clients for references.

GARY SLACK is chairman and CEO of Slack Barshinger, an award-winning Chicago marketing communications agency.

How to Put Your Customers to Work for You

Your customers want to see you succeed and to make you a part of their identity. If you've majored in relationships and follow-up, more than a few runners might show up at your 5K run, some even wearing your T-shirt. Let them tell the world about you. How? One restaurateur, for example, asked some customers to picket his place, carrying placards that read, "The food here can't be beat!" and "Best restaurant value in town!" The "picketers" drew in other customers.

Another restaurateur who was opening a new location invited 12 people to enjoy a free dinner with all the trimmings. The only thing he asked in return was that they agree to spend half an hour waiting in line outside his restaurant the next evening. They did. Others noticed the line, the restaurant filled, and it has remained popular ever since. This restaurateur's customers were the makings of his business—in just half an hour.

JAY CONRAD LEVINSON (www.guerrillamarketingassociation.com) the father of guerrilla marketing, has sold more than 15 million books in 43 languages.

How to Sell to Teens

Teens care about the hottest brands and latest fashions. Most of us buy stuff more often than our parents, and we're more concerned with quality and the prestige that comes from wearing certain brands. But style is always evolving and there are so many brands, stores and options that we get bored quickly. Before I go shopping, I look to magazines and celebrities for the current trends, then I go to the mall to see what's available at what price.

CASSIE KREITNER (pictured at right, center) is a freshman at Syracuse University. She is majoring in magazine journalism and marketing.

Selling to teens means selling to their peers. Teens trust their friends, so if you reach their peers, you eventually reach them—in large numbers. You need to brand—teens bond to brands, so do whatever it takes to get your logo and brand message in front of them—repeatedly. Also, be interactive—be high-tech and high-touch. Entice teens with contests or send postcards inviting them to your website to give their opinions.

ANN A. FISHMAN (ann@annfishman.com) is a leading expert in generational marketing.

How to Keep Your Brand Fresh

Conduct a "brand audit" once a year. Look at how your product or service is marketed and branded (your marketing messages), analyze your brand positioning (i.e., ask customers what they think of your brand), then compare the two to see how well they connect. A coffee-house owner, for example, might think she serves great coffee, while convenience or ambience may be a bigger selling point from the customer's perspective. An annual brand audit keeps you on track.

Adapted from *Start Your Own Business: The Only Startup Book You'll Ever Need* (4th Edition) by Rieva Lesonsky and the staff of *Entrepreneur* magazine.

How to Motivate Your Sales Team

1. Communicate both sales goals and reasons why.
2. Offer not only sales strategies, but also specific tactics.
3. Use short-, mid- and long-term incentives.
4. Set sales goals collaboratively with the team.
5. Reward both team performance and individual effort.
6. Don't dictate activity—only results.
7. Use praise and recognition, never humiliation or punishment.
8. Share sales success stories, not just numbers.
9. Reward peer coaching and mentoring.
10. Create a databank of sales tools and documents.

DAVID NEWMAN produces sales, finance and HR audio conferences for Business 21 Publishing (www.b21pubs.com/audio).

How to Sell by Social Networking

Want to get people talking? Newsflash: They already are! They're online—chatting, collaborating, blogging, podcasting—so join their conversations. Social networking enables you to find and target niche markets easily, quickly and absolutely free. So jump in! Start an active dialog. Get to know your audience. Show them how much you care—just never lie about who you are. Your honesty and integrity add real value to your business. Get typing!

JENNIFER KUSHELL (pictured below, l) co-founded YSN.com (Your Success Network), an online universe for ambitious movers and shakers.

Attention-Deficit Advertising

Madison Avenue is betting distracted consumers will respond to pitches that deliver helpful services.

Burt Helm

It's the catch-22 of today's advertising world. Marketers, only too aware that consumers are ignoring traditional ads, have adopted the "more is more" approach and have begun advertising everywhere—in taxis, fitness clubs, hospital waiting rooms. But the clutter is numbing consumers to all the messages. When they're not fast-forwarding through TV commercials or clicking away from ads online, people are getting pretty good at tuning them out.

That fact is challenging admakers worldwide, forcing them to look for new ways to capture consumers' attention. One trick you will start seeing a lot more of: messages that, in and of themselves, provide a service. Nick Law, chief creative officer of the agency R/GA, has been doing this kind of thing for years, most notably with Nike+, a site that helps runners track their performance. "You have to ask, why would anyone care about this [ad]?" says Law. "In the traditional advertising world, that was never a question asked with much rigor."

Taking a cue from the social-networking and texting crazes, marketers are rolling out services that help people connect with one another. A pioneer in this area is the Chicago-based mobile ad firm Vibes Media. At a series of outdoor concerts during the Final Four weekend of the NCAA Basketball Tournament, Vibes displayed viewers' text messages on screens above and next to the stage. Messages rooting for teams, shouting out to friends, and sending birthday wishes appeared below prominent AT&T or Coca-Cola logos. Some 5,000 people sent in 11,000 messages, according to Vibes. The firm also has been offering bar patrons in Chicago, Los Angeles, New York, and Atlanta the chance to send text messages to the television screens at their local watering holes. Alex Campbell, Vibes' CEO, says pick-up lines typically abound, from "The blonde at the bar is smoking hot!" to "Turn around, I'm right behind you." As patrons stare at the screen waiting for their messages to pop up, they can't miss the Bud Light ads placed between them.

Passing It On

Some of these newfangled ads don't just cut through the clutter, they inspire consumers to spread the message themselves. At the Hong Kong International Airport last year, travelers saw

a familiar, if unexpected, sight when they checked into the gate area: photos of the friends and family who had just dropped them off. Through a special promotion, Motorola enabled loved ones to "Say Goodbye" via photos and messages sent from their phones to digital billboards in the departure area. The photos appeared there inside the image of a giant Motorola mobile phone. Motorola got thousands of Hong Kong's ad-inundated consumers to stare at a billboard longer than usual. It also invited departing travelers, via special instructions displayed on the billboard, to use their phones to send a Motorola-branded goodbye video featuring soccer star David Beckham and Asian pop star Jay Chou to their friends and families. As travelers sent the videos out, Motorola ads proliferated throughout the world.

In an age when widgets—small, Web-based programs—are all the rage, companies are increasingly creating online tools that offer to help their customers. Clorox, for instance, wanted homemakers to know that it sells a range of cleaning products beyond bleach. It introduced TimeWise, a Web program where consumers could schedule reminders for cleaning tasks and kids' chores. The brand name was prominent on the site, naturally, as were offers for complementary products. Clorox won't discuss the promotion's efficacy, but it has been discontinued.

Appearing useful is of particular interest to marketers keen to place ads on mobile phones, a tricky prospect since the potential annoyance factor is so high. Hoping to sell more of its

Johnnie Walker whisky in Singapore, liquor giant Diageo, with the help of OgilvyOne Worldwide, created a "digital personal assistant" for drinkers' mobile phones. An avatar named "Jennie" sends out VIP invitations, information about hot night spots, and Johnnie Walker promotions. For the inebriated, the service includes a "take me home" button that, when pressed, uses GPS to call a cab.

Companies are even wrapping ads around community outreach. Eager to reinvigorate its image as a basketball brand, Converse this fall began organizing games for Miami's inner-city youth. Kids got to try out new shoes and meet Miami Heat guard Dwyane Wade, who signed autographs and refereed. The program is moving to more cities and, to get kids interested, Converse created an application on Facebook that allows people to sign up friends to play an online basketball game. Converse says it now has more than 40,000 people to add to its database of potential customers, as well as information on where they live. Now *that's* useful.

Product Placement—You Can't Escape It

Frustrated by Fragmented Audiences, Marketers Seek More Places to Pitch

LAURA PETRECCA

To hype the fall TV season, CBS plastered pictures of its shows' stars on postage stamps and across the insides of elevator doors. It laser-coated its eye logo on more than 35 million eggs, and carved the name of a new program, Jericho, into a 40-acre Kansas cornfield.

CBS added those blips to the marketing storm sweeping the nation. Advertising is intruding on more previously untouched corners of life, including novels, hotel shower curtains, school buses and the bellies of pregnant women. Golfer Fred Couples is often followed around the course by a gaggle of woman paid to wear the name Bridgestone Golf, his sponsor.

It's advertising ad nauseam. And it's getting worse.

"I've never seen things changing as much as they are now," says Rance Crain, editor-in-chief of trade magazine Advertising Age and a 40-plus-year observer of marketing. "Advertisers will not be satisfied until they put their mark on every blade of grass."

Ad-zapping devices—and a decrease in consumer attention spans—have created doubts about the effectiveness of traditional TV, radio and print ads. In response, marketers have become increasingly invasive.

"It's out of control," says Jenny Beaton, a mother of three in Westlake, Ohio. "I don't know how advertisers can think they're selling more products. It's just annoying everybody."

Many, such as Beaton, are tuning out.

"Advertising is so ubiquitous that it's turning people off," Crain says. "It's desensitizing people to the message."

The more consumers ignore ads, the more ads marketers spew back at them, says Max Kalehoff of marketing research firm Nielsen BuzzMetrics. "It's like a drug addiction. Advertisers just keep buying more and more just to try to achieve prior levels of impact. In other words, they're hooked."

This year, marketers will spend a record $175 billion on ads in major media, such as TV, radio, print, outdoor, movie theaters and the Internet, says ad-buying firm ZenithOptimedia. That's up 5% over 2005. Add direct mail and other direct-response ads, and the total will hit $269 billion.

The increase comes from advertisers trying to out-yell each other, says J. Walker Smith, president of the consulting firm Yankelovich. If a marketer feels drowned out, "They just turn up the volume."

Here's how loud it's getting:

- The average 1970s city dweller was exposed to 500 to 2,000 ad messages a day, Smith says. Now, it's 3,000 to 5,000.
- In 2005, MTV viewers had to put up with 21% more prime-time commercials per hour than in 2004, says TNS Media Intelligence and media firm MindShare.
- Marketers shelled out 71% more—$941 million—to integrate brands into TV shows in 2005 vs. 2004, PQ Media says.
- There are now ad-supported TV screens at airports, gas stations, health clubs and on buses and subways. Wal-Mart has its own network. ABC signed with the In-Store Broadcasting Network to promote TV shows in Kroger supermarkets.
- Spending for on-screen movie theater ads swelled 21% to $453 million in 2005 vs. 2004. Off-screen ads, such as lobby promotions, rose 18% to $75 million, according to the Cinema Advertising Council.
- Marketers raised "out-of-home" spending, from billboards to elevator ads, by 9% last year to $6.3 billion, the Outdoor Advertising Association of America says.

There's more to come. Marketers see small-screen devices—iPods, cellphones, laptops and video games—as the growth frontier:

- Spending for ads on Web-enabled mobile phones is expected to be $150 million this year, up threefold vs. 2005, according to consulting firm Ovum. By 2009, that will swell 766% to $1.3 billion.
- In 2005, $21 million was spent to place products in video games, a 38% rise over 2004, PQ Media says.
- Last year, companies shelled out $13 billion on Internet classified, search and display ads, JupiterResearch says. That's expected to double to $26 billion by 2011.

Brain Freeze

"The human brain doesn't process things any better than it did 30 years ago. But there are more people competing for that processing time," Yankelovich's Smith says. "It's no surprise that consumers are pushing back."

They've put more than 130 million phone numbers on the federal government's telemarketer-thwarting national Do Not Call Registry as of Sept. 5.

Use of pop-up ad blockers on computers nearly tripled from June 2003 to January 2006, to 71%, according to Arbitron/Edison Media Research provided by eMarketer. Users with spam blockers more than doubled to 73%.

Web Gives Consumers Voice

The Internet has emerged as a soapbox for irate consumers.

After Columbia Pictures said it would cover Major League Baseball bases with Spider-Man 2 logos in 2004, tens of thousands voted against it in ESPN.com and AOL.com polls. Within 48 hours, the studio called it off, citing the polls.

On a more micro level, football fans watching the Auburn vs. Louisiana State game on Sept. 16 saw CBS serve up Ruby Tuesday eatery ads with the computer-generated first down line. Among the post-game comments on an LSU online forum: "It was very distracting. . . . Please join me in voicing your displeasure." The posting included Web links to Ruby Tuesday and CBS corporate sites.

"Never before in history have consumers been able to spit back at marketers they way they have now," says BuzzMetric's Kalehoff.

But the onslaught goes on. Driving it, Crain says: "Desperation."

Marketing Under Pressure

Companies are under more pressure than ever to deliver rosy quarterly results, and top marketing executives have less time than ever to prove their mettle. The average tenure of a chief marketing officer at a major U.S. company has declined to 23.2 months, according to search firm Spencer Stuart.

It's no wonder they'll sign off on increasingly bizarre ideas.

For instance, a recent promotion for the Paramount Pictures film Jackass: Number Two appears on urinal mats when the mat is hit with a stream of "number one."

Even conservative Procter & Gamble has loosened up. It put print ads for Crest Night Effects whitening gel inside women's restroom stalls—at eye level when the user sits down.

"Marketers are saying, 'We must be more innovative—to zig when others zag,'" says Richard Notarianni, executive creative director of media at ad firm Euro RSCG.

"The industry is desperate to find clever ways to reach people, whether or not it has any legitimate value. . . . When someone says, 'Let's put advertising in bathroom stalls,' another says 'That's great. It's a captive audience.'"

'Your Brand Here'

The desperate ad buyers are finding willing co-conspirators.

As more companies, cities, school districts—even individuals—hawk ad space, others feel as if they are leaving money on the table if they don't join in.

"This is about economics," says James Twitchell, consumer culture expert and author of Branded Nation and Adcult USA.

Elementary and high schools now pipe commercial radio onto buses and TV into classrooms. The Scottsdale Unified School District in Arizona is one of several districts across the USA that has sold ads on the outside of school buses.

Taking a page from the pro-sports arena, schools also hawk naming right deals for facilities. In Sheboygan, Wis., two high schools just sold sponsorship rights to their cafes to Associated Bank.

In May, Robert Reames III, 27, a father of three girls who was looking for money to replace the family car, sold rights to a permanent tattoo on his neck to Web-hosting company Globat.

The company also bought a temporary tattoo ad on the pregnant belly of Asia Francis, 21, of St. Louis. Globat would not disclose what it has paid for "body art."

No space is too odd. US Airways is in talks to sell ads on airsickness bags, spokeswoman Valerie Wunder says. It already makes about $10 million a year from ads on tray tables and napkins, she says.

"The game has become one of finding the next blank space that hasn't been covered," says Yankelovich's Smith.

Most marketing executives know they have a problem. Many of the firms that buy ads are the same ones that put out research reports on the dangers of deluging and angering consumers.

"Advertisers love to talk about advertising clutter," Twitchell says. "That's like the doctor shooting a patient up with amphetamines and then saying that the patient is acting really frenetic."

Hoping to Get 'Engaged'

In its search for salvation, the marketing industry has glommed onto the concept of "engagement"—a quality-over-quantity idea.

The basic theory: Instead of, for example, running dozens of radio ads, create messages that the consumer seeks out, such as an entertaining Web video, and perhaps even passes on to friends.

"Message clutter is not going to go away. If anything, it's going to proliferate," says Mike Donahue, executive vice president, American Association of Advertising Agencies. "If you're looking at 10 messages and two of them really involve you, engage you and connect with you, those ads will be less annoying and a lot more effective."

Andrew Hertz, 39, general manager of Miami Seaquarium, thinks they might be on to something.

"When advertisers make the ads fun and interactive, they're not so bad," he says, citing a Mini Cooper magazine ad that included stickers of fancy wheels and other accessories that consumers could peel off to customize the car on the page.

What Hertz can't stand: ads in his face, including Internet pop-up ads, and paper subscription cards that fall out of magazines. "The thing that annoys me is when advertising is intrusive," he says.

BuzzMetric's Kalehoff says marketers have to stop pitching so hard, fast, loudly and frequently.

Kalehoff says they need to understand—and respond to—gripes from frustrated consumers such as Hertz. Only then will they be able to produce marketing that sells, he says.

"If you want to make friends with your customers, you have to stop hitting them over the head."

UNIT 4

Global Marketing

Unit Selections

Key Points to Consider

- What economic, cultural, and political obstacles must an organization consider that seeks to become global in its markets?

- Do you believe that an adherence to the "marketing concept" is the right way to approach international markets? Why, or why not?

- What trends are taking place today that would suggest whether particular global markets would grow or decline? Which countries do you believe will see the most growth in the next decade? Why?

- In what ways can the Internet be used to extend a market outside the United States?

Student Web Site
www.mhcls.com

Internet References

International Trade Administration
   http://www.ita.doc.gov
World Chambers Network
   http://www.worldchambers.net
World Trade Center Association OnLine
   http://iserve.wtca.org

It is certain that marketing with a global perspective will continue to be a strategic element of U.S. business well into the next decade. The United States is both the world's largest exporter and largest importer. In 1987, U.S. exports totaled just over $250 billion—about 10 percent of total world exports. During the same period, U.S. imports were nearly $450 billion—just under 10 percent of total world imports. By 1995 exports had risen to $513 billion and imports to $664 billion—roughly the same percentage of total world trade.

Whether or not they wish to be, all marketers are now part of the international marketing system. For some, the end of the era of domestic markets may have come too soon, but that era is over. Today it is necessary to recognize the strengths and weaknesses of our own marketing practices as compared to those abroad. The multinational corporations have long recognized this need, but now all marketers must acknowledge it.

International marketing differs from domestic marketing in that the parties to its transactions live in different political units. It is the "international" element of international marketing that distinguishes it from domestic marketing—not differences in managerial techniques. The growth of global business among multinational corporations has raised new questions about the role of their headquarters. It has even caused some to speculate whether marketing operations should be performed abroad rather than in the United States.

The key to applying the marketing concept lies in understanding the consumer. Increasing levels of consumer sophistication is evident in all of the world's most profitable markets. Managers are required to adopt new points of view in order to accommodate increasingly complex consumer wants and needs. The markets in the new millennium will show further integration on a worldwide scale. In these emerging markets, conventional textbook approaches can cause numerous problems. The new marketing perspective called for by the circumstances of the years ahead will require a long-range view that looks from the basics of exchange and their applications in new settings.

The selections presented here were chosen to provide an overview of world economic factors, competitive positioning, and increasing globalization of markets—issues to which each and every marketer must become sensitive. "How China Will Change Your Business" investigates the ever-increasing presence and influence China has in our lives. The second article describes how multinationals and local firms are squaring off on China's rapidly growing middle market. "Three Dimensional" shows how the markets of Japan, Korea, and China are far from homogeneous. The fourth article reveals the significant impact that technology will have globally. "Brand Loyalty Goes Global" shows how brand loyalty programs can create stronger relationships with customers in competitive new ways. The last article examines the challenges that Fisher-Price has faced in developing toys for the global marketplace.

How China Will Change Your Business

Ted C. Fishman

C hina's miracle economy can come at you in a lot of ways, from all directions.

- Mention an interest in China to your old friend who owns an industrial toolmaking shop and he confides that his factory, which was started by his father and has bought a comfortable suburban life for three generations of his family as well as good wages to hundreds of workers, "is getting killed by the people over there."
- Stop at the auto supply store for windshield-wiper fluid. Half the store is now a showroom for small Chinese motor scooters, some of which look like half-Harleys, others like Ducatis. Most cost less than $300.
- Decide at last to plunge into digital photography. Photo magazines all rave about a small new camera from Nikon, an engineering wonder that can shoot fast, captures dimly lit scenes, and costs half the price of similar machines a year ago. Nikon is one of Japan's marquee brands, but when you bring the camera home from the store you spot the words in small print on the product itself: "Made in China."
- Wake up in Santa Barbara, Calif., one morning to a sky that looks as though it is painted a shiny white. The morning's newspaper reports that the sunlight is playing tricks on something known as the Asian Brown Cloud, a mass of dust that has drifted over the Pacific from China. The cloud contains particles of loose earth from deforested land mixed with arsenic and other industrial pollutants from the country's factories.

Powered by the world's most rapidly changing large economy, China is an ever increasing presence and influence in our lives, connected to us by the world's shipping lanes, financial markets, telecommunications, and above all, by the globalization of appetites. China sews more clothes and stitches more shoes and assembles more toys than any other nation. It has become the world's largest maker of consumer electronics, pumping out more TVs, DVD players, and cell phones than any other country. And more recently, it has ascended the economic development ladder higher still, moving quickly and expertly into biotech and computer manufacturing. It is building cars (there are more than 120 automakers in China), making parts for Boeing 757s, and exploring space with its own domestically built rockets.

Americans tend to focus on the huge inequality in trade between the two countries. It is a worry Americans help to create by buying ever more from China's humming factories. In 2004, the Chinese sold the United States $160 billion more in goods than they bought. Contrary to common wisdom, however, the trade deficit with China does not mean that Americans are spending down the national wealth at a faster pace than ever before. So far, most of China's gains with American buyers have come at the expense of the other countries that once lured American dollars, especially other Asian economies. Americans—and the world—get more stuff in the bargain.

Ever since China started on the capitalist road, opinions about its prospects have figuratively, and literally, been all over the map. The present mood is a combustible mix of euphoria, fear, admiration, and cynicism. On those emotions ride great tides of capital, the strategic plans of businesses great and small, and the gravest political calculations in the world's capitals and city halls.

Yet few working Americans have a full awareness of China's rise. How could they? Nothing like this has ever happened before, and it's occurring on the other side of the globe. Yet Americans—particularly anyone involved in running a business—need to know what is happening today in China and to understand how China's fate has become inextricably bound with our own. Conceding China's rise does not mean conceding to China. But it does require acknowledging some important truths:

1. China's economy is much larger than the official numbers show. In 2003, China's official GDP was $1.4 trillion. By that measure, it was the seventh-largest economy in the world. As with nearly all economic statistics from China, however, that measure is suspect. One reason the real number may be much higher is that, in competition for development funds, local Chinese authorities have considerable incentive to underreport their growth rates to the nation's central planners. Another reason is that the government measures only China's legal economy. Its underground economy, made up of both unsavory businesses and more mundane ones that lack a government stamp (and tax bill), is enormous but uncountable.

Economists also note that China's official GDP underplays the true size of its economy because China uses the massive power of its foreign currency reserves to keep the world price of the yuan marching in lockstep with the dollar. If the dollar had not dropped against the euro and other world currencies over the past few years, China's ranking would be a notch or two bigger. Critics of China's currency policies, including American domestic manufacturers such as steel mills, casters, plastics molders, and machine-tool makers, argue that China artificially depresses the value of its currency against the dollar by as much as 40%.

A dollar spent in China buys almost five times more goods and services than a dollar spent in a typical American city like Indianapolis. Taking purchasing-power parity into account, the U.S. Central Intelligence Agency estimates that China's economy looks more like one with a GDP of $6.6 trillion. Put another way, it makes more sense to think of China's economy as closer to two-thirds the size of the U.S. economy than to one-seventh.

2. The growth of China's economy has no equal in modern history.

China's economy has grown so fast that it has taken on the mythic qualities of one of Mao's showcase farms. Since China set about reforming its economy a generation ago, its GDP has expanded at an annual rate of 9.5%. Countries in the early stages of economic reform often come up fast, but not like China. The country is closing in on a 30-year run during which its economy has doubled nearly three times. Neither Japan's nor South Korea's postwar boom comes anywhere close. Nicholas Lardy, an economist at the Institute for International Economics, notes that China grew mightily even during the worldwide economic doldrums of 2001–02.

China is so committed to economic growth that the Chinese often talk as though they can will it to happen. It is a necessary optimism that pervades official Chinese communication. Orville Schell, the author of *Virtual Tibet* and the dean of the school of journalism at the University of California, Berkeley, draws a parallel between the unity of focus the Chinese demonstrated for anti-capitalism and their focus now on capitalism. Schell argues that in both instances there is a willingness to suspend logic and see only bright tomorrows. Both lead to excess. In its capitalist present, China has been willing to overlook the dark side of modernization, seeing economic progress as the solution to all the country's challenges. Even so, every time the worst is predicted for China's economy, it seems to grow faster, create stronger industries, import more, and export more.

3. China is winning the global competition for investment capital.

One reason China's economy is growing so fast is that the world keeps feeding it capital. According to Japan's Research Institute of Economy, Trade and Industry, one-third of China's industrial production was put in place by the half-trillion dollars of foreign money that has flowed into the country since 1978. In 2003, foreigners invested more in building businesses in China than they spent anywhere else in the world. The U.S. used to attract the most foreign money, but in 2003 China took a strong lead, pulling in $53 billion to the U.S.'s $40 billion.

With money comes knowledge. The catalytic role of foreigners in the country is still growing quickly; every day China receives a river of European, Asian, and American experts in manufacturing, banking, computing, advertising, and engineering. In 2003, exports and imports by foreign companies operating in China rose by over 40%. More than half of China's trade is now controlled by foreign firms. Many of these import goods into the country that they then manufacture into exports. Foreign companies have pumped up China's trade volume enough to make it the third-largest trading country in the world, behind the U.S. and Germany and now ahead of Japan.

4. China can be a bully.

China can spend, it can hire and dictate wages, it can throw old-line competitors out of work. In just a three-year period from 2000 to late 2003, for example, China's exports to the U.S. of wooden bedroom furniture climbed from $360 million to nearly $1.2 billion. During that time, the work force at America's wooden-furniture factories dropped by 35,000, or one of every three workers in the trade. China now makes 40% of all furniture sold in the U.S., and that number is sure to climb.

5. China's economy is an entrepreneurial economy.

China's industrial competitors, including the U.S., often misapprehend the source of China's productive strength. They fear that another centrally governed, well-planned assault on strategic industries is being plotted in Beijing. The world has already seen how effective the Japanese, Koreans, and Taiwanese can be when they focus on sectors they mean to conquer. Even Chinese government planners like to talk as though they are aping the centrally coordinated, government-financed assaults on strategic global industries that their Asian neighbors have pulled off over the past 40 years. However, in looking at how Chinese businesses really take shape—locally and opportunistically—Kellee Tsai, a political scientist at Johns Hopkins University and a former analyst at Morgan Stanley, argues that nothing could be further from the truth. For a world fretting over Chinese economic competition, the entities to fear are not government planners but enterprises that spring on the scene lean and mean, planned and financed by investors who want to make money quickly.

An emblem of the Zbejiang province in China is Hong Dongyang, an entrepreneur whose story is now well-known throughout the country. Hong was once a schoolteacher. She began making socks in the 1970s on a home sewing machine. At first Hong sold them along the roads near her home. She opened a stand and christened her embryonic enterprise Zhejiang Stocking Company. Hong's sock company was predictably copied en masse by others. Today, the province is the Chinese sock capital, with more than 8,000 companies spinning out eight billion pairs a year, one-third of the world's supply. In 2001, the Chinese makers produced 1% of the socks on U.S. feet. In just two years, sock imports from China to the U.S. jumped two-hundred-fold and now make up 7% of the U.S. market, James J. Jochum, assistant secretary for export administration at the U.S. Department of Commerce, has noted that the Chinese manufacturers cut their prices by more than half in 2003 and helped drive one in four U.S. sock makers out of business.

6. The most daunting thing about China is not its ability to make cheap consumer goods.

The American economy won't crater just because the Chinese can produce sofas and socks for less than we can. The Japanese, for their part, have lost the television business. The Italians are losing the fine-silk business. Consumer goods trade on the surface of the world's economy and their movement is easy for the public to watch. The far bigger shift, just now picking up steam, is occurring among the products that manufacturers and marketers trade with each other: the infinite number and variety of components that make up everything else that is made, whether it is the hundreds of parts in a washing machine or computer or the hundreds of thousands of parts in an airplane.

THE CYCLE OF CODEPENDENCY
China is at one moment our greatest threat, the next our friend. It is siphoning off American jobs; it is essential to our competitive edge. China exports deflation; it stokes soaring prices.

Given how quickly China is climbing the industrial ladder, perhaps the next question is whether any commercial technology is beyond an imminent challenge from China. Gal Dymant, an American Israeli venture capitalist in Beijing, believes the answer is that few will be. One of the companies Dymant works with, a database publisher named Asia Direct, produces an annual China Hi-Tech Directory. Tracking the directory's updates year to year gives Dymant an informal measure of the shifts in Chinese industry.

The first thing one notices about the directories, he says, is how much thicker they grow every year, particularly in industries where there have been large foreign investments. In 2003, Asia Direct's volume grew considerably fatter in the sections devoted to China's domestic mobile-phone manufacturers and suppliers, broadband communications, and in companies establishing themselves in cities outside of China's eastern powerhouses. The manufacture and sale of integrated chips is also soaring, along with healthy gains in China's software and information-services markets. Then again, every section in the directory has grown, including biotechnology, semiconductors, and Internet development, areas in which Chinese firms have newly established themselves, many now in partnership with the world's leading technology-driven companies.

For his part, Dymant is putting together an investor group to Build a Chinese version of one of the world's most advanced and costly medical devices, the magnetic resonance imaging (MRI) machine. "The talent is here to build anything," Dymant says. "We think we can develop MRIs for about 60% of the price they are built for in the U.S."

7. China is closing the research and development gap—fast.
The ability of American industry to stay ahead of its international competition rests on the national gifts and resources that the U.S. devotes to innovation. The research gap between the U.S. and China remains vast. In December, Washington authorized $3.7 billion to finance nanotechnology research, a sum the Chinese government cannot easily match within a scientific infrastructure that would itself take many more billions (and years) to build.

Yet when it comes to more mainstream applied industrial development and innovation, the separation among Chinese, American, and other multinational firms is beginning to narrow. Last year, China spent $60 billion on research and development. The only countries that spent more were the U.S. and Japan, which spent $282 billion and $104 billion, respectively. But again, China forces you to do the math: China's engineers and scientists usually make between one-sixth and one-tenth what Americans do, which means that the wide gaps in financing do not necessarily result in equally wide gaps in manpower or results. The U.S. spent nearly five times what China did but had less than two times as many researchers (1.3 million to 743,000). China's universities and vocational schools will produce 325,000 engineers this year—five times as many as the U.S.

For now, the emphasis in Chinese labs is weighted overwhelmingly toward the "D" side—meaning training for technical employees and managers. Nevertheless, foreign companies are moving quickly to integrate their China-based labs into their global research operations. Motorola alone has 19 research labs in China that develop technology for both the local and global markets. Several of the company's most innovative recent phones were developed there for the Chinese market.

8. China now sets the global benchmark for prices.
Big news can be found in little places. In its November 2003 circular, a dryly written four-page publication, the Chicago Federal Reserve Bank noted complaints from American makers of automotive parts that "automakers had been asking suppliers for the 'China price' on their purchases." The bank's analysts observed that U.S. suppliers had also been asked by their big customers to move their factories to China or to find subcontractors there.

Over much of the business world, the term China price has since become interchangeable with lowest price possible. The China price is part of the new conventional wisdom that companies can move nearly any kind of work to China and find huge savings. It holds that any job transferred there will be done cheaper, and possibly better.

It is plainly understood that asking suppliers to lower prices is merely another way of telling them they ought to be prepared to meet the best price out of China, even if they are making their products in Japan or Germany. General Motors, which buys more than $80 billion worth of parts a year, now has a clause in its supply contracts that gives its supplier 30 days to meet the best price the company can find worldwide or risk immediate termination.

In fact, in the U.S. between 1998 and 2004, prices fell in nearly every product category in which China was the top exporter. "The manufactured goods that have dropped in price the most are those made by China," says W. Michael Cox, chief economist for the Federal Reserve Bank of Dallas, citing figures assembled by the bank for its 2003 annual report, published in 2004. Personal computers, the most outstanding example, fell by 28%, televisions by nearly 12%, cameras and toys by around 8%, while other electronics, clothing of all sorts, shoes, and tableware also dropped in price.

9. China's growth is making raw materials more expensive.
Even as China puts pressure on U.S. manufacturers to lower prices, it's squeezing them from a different direction. Its voracious demand for raw materials has caused prices to spike. Copper prices jumped 37% last year, aluminum and zinc both rose about 25%, and oil was up 33%. In 2003, according to the calculations of Stephen Roach, chief economist at Morgan Stanley, the Chinese bought 7% of the world's oil, a quarter of all aluminum and steel, nearly a third of the world's iron ore and coal, and 40% of the world's cement. The trend is for bigger amounts yet to come.

The squeeze is leaving U.S. manufacturers with no alternative but to become more productive. Better machines, software, and advanced management techniques, for instance, now mean that U.S. companies on average produce far more per worker than they did a quarter of a century ago when manufacturing employment was high. From 1977 to 2002, productivity throughout the U.S. economy grew by half, but in manufacturing it more than doubled. Surprisingly, despite losing huge numbers of workers, U.S. manufacturers actually finished 2003 making more stuff than they did in 2001. Output was up, if only by half a percent.

10. No company has embraced China's potential more vigorously than Wal-Mart. And no company has been a bigger catalyst in pushing manufacturers to China. Estimates of how much of Wal-Mart's merchandise comes from abroad today range from 50% to 85%. Chinese factories are, by far, the most important and fastest-growing sources for the company. In 2003, Wal-Mart purchased $15 billion worth of goods from Chinese suppliers. A whopping portion of between 10% and 13% of everything China has sent to the U.S. winds up on Wal-Mart's shelves. Writing in *The Washington Post,* Peter Goodman and Phillip Pan reported in February 2004 that "more than 80% of the 6,000 factories in Wal-Mart's worldwide database of suppliers are in China." The company has 560 people on the ground in the country to negotiate and make purchases.

Wal-Mart is often demonized for its part in shipping U.S. manufacturing jobs overseas. It is difficult, however, to separate the role of Wal-Mart's thousands of suppliers in the migration of manufacturing out of the U.S. from the larger global trends realigning how and where the world makes things. If Wal-Mart has a unique part in the trend, it is in how expertly the company has managed that trend and, in so doing, accelerated it. China's low-cost manufacturing machine feeds Wal-Mart's critical mass by allowing companies to build assembly lines that are so huge that they achieve ever-greater economies of scale and drive prices downward all the more.

The next question is whether any commercial technology is beyond an imminent challenge from China.

Wal-Mart's Chinese suppliers can achieve startling, market-shaking price cuts. By selling portable DVD players with seven-inch LCD screens from China for less than $160, for instance, Wal-Mart recently helped cut the price of these trendy devices in half. Even with superlow prices, Chinese factories can sell in such giant quantities that they willingly oblige. To get ready for its big Thanksgiving sale in 2002, Wal-Mart picked Sichuan Changhong Electric, one of the world's largest makers of televisions, to supply sets under the Apex Digital brand. Changhong makes 15 million TVs a year, most of them for export. Eight of 10 shipped overseas go to the U.S. In 2002, its sets at Wal-Mart sold for far less than comparable models from other makers, sometimes undercutting the competition by $100 or more. The models the company delivered for the sale helped the event net $1.4 billion.

In late December, state-owned Changhong reported nearly half a billion dollars in losses, purportedly linked to unpaid bills owed by Apex. The scandal, though mired in murky details, nevertheless highlights both the ability of China's big firms to sustain losses and keep running and their willingness to satisfy American retailers' demands for ever-lower prices.

11. There are hidden costs associated with doing business in China. Companies that engage with China must expect pressure to transfer their technology and thus create their own competition in the country. The Chinese use the carrot of their vast market to extract concessions from foreign firms that will help build China's industrial might. It is a policy worthy of grudging admiration. When viewed from the Chinese side, it has a long record of success.

Motorola virtually invented China's mobile-phone market. Its corporate archives show that the company knew that eventually the transfer of technology to China would sow formidable rivals. Nevertheless, Motorola decided its best strategy was to get into China early and to bring its best technology. The proof today is in the size and efficacy of the country's mobile communications network: Calls get through to phones in high-rises, subway cars, and distant hamlets—connections that would stymie mobile phones in the U.S.

What no one at Motorola anticipated was how crowded the Chinese market would become. Nokia and Motorola now battle for market share in the Chinese handset business. German, Korean, and Taiwanese makers figure strongly. And all these foreign brands are now facing intense competition from indigenous Chinese phone makers. More than 40% of the Chinese domestic handset market now belongs to local companies such as Ningbo Bird, Nanjing Panda Electronics, Haier, and TCL Mobile. The domestic makers have become so strong that when Siemens found its mobile handset business in China wanting, it joined with Ningbo Bird to gain both low-cost manufacturing and a developed distribution channel. Yet Motorola can't exit the Chinese market. If it did, says Jim Gradoville, Motorola's vice president of Asia Pacific government relations, the Chinese companies that emerged would be the leanest and most aggressive in the world, and a company like his would have no idea what hit it. So Motorola stays. Already the largest foreign investor in China's electronics industry, Motorola plans to triple its stake there to more than $10 billion by 2006.

12. Piracy is a problem. Foreign companies have little defense against even outright theft of their technology in China. China's failure to police intellectual property, in effect, creates a massive global subsidy worth hundreds of billions of dollars to its businesses and people. By investing in the country's manufacturing infrastructure, by providing the expertise, machines, and software China needs to produce world-class products, the world is also helping assemble the biggest, most sophisticated, and most successful "illegal" manufacturing complex in the world.

Seen another way, China's loose intellectual property rules turn the tables on the Western colonial powers and the Japanese who throughout the nineteenth and early twentieth centuries violated China's land and people. As China grows into a great power, the wealth transferred into the country by expropriating intellectual property will propel it forward.

13. China's heavy buying of U.S. debt has lowered the cost of money in the U.S. In the first half of 2004, China's total foreign exchange reserves topped $460 billion. In size, that puts China's cumulative dollar account at roughly equal to a third of its gross domestic product. If China simply spent its dollars, it would flood the world market with American currency and drive the dollar down. But China, no fool, is not interested in pushing the dollar down. So instead of selling its dollars, it lends them back to the U.S.

China keeps tight wraps on the value, composition, and trading of its portfolio, but Wall Street commonly assumes that the country owns a large amount of high-grade U.S. corporate bonds, intertwining its national fortunes with America's blue chips (many of them the same corporations reaping fortunes in China itself).

China also has almost certainly built a large stake in the market for bonds issued by Fannie Mae and Freddie Mac, the companies that buy home mortgages from banks and thrift institutions and resell them as bundled securities. This means that billions of dollars' worth of investments belonging to the Chinese are plowed indirectly into the American real estate market, and that an ever-increasing share of Americans' mortgage payments pour into the coffers of the government of China.

As long as China is an aggressive lender, Americans—whether borrowing for their own private purchases or acting in the roles of taxpayers—can borrow money at lower rates than they would otherwise have to pay. Much of the recent boom in real estate prices in America, especially in the East and West Coast markets, is attributable to these low rates.

14. Americans and Chinese have become reliant on each other's most controversial habits.

The Chinese need a low-priced currency to keep their export machine going and create jobs. But maintaining the yuan's low price also means that Chinese consumers are stuck with a currency that would otherwise buy more for them on the world market. China's diligent savers suffer too since their bank deposits are tied up in accounts that earn low government-mandated rates of return, as the government, in effect, siphons off money from savers to maintain its currency peg.

Relatedly, China's vast export earnings earn less than they ought to when they are invested in U.S. debt securities that offer modest yields, when investments in the Chinese economy can return 10 times as much (albeit on riskier terms). Seen from that view, the people of China, who earn on average just one-fortieth what Americans do, are indirectly subsidizing the insatiable shopping of Americans, who acquire ever more goods at the same time that Chinese consumers are hampered from buying goods from abroad.

The people of China are indirectly subsidizing the insatiable shopping of Americans.

The obverse of this peculiar relationship is that China lends America all the money it needs to spend itself silly. The cycle of codependency, which former U.S Treasury Secretary Lawrence Summers labels a "balance of financial terror," isn't sustainable. The U.S. cannot take on ever-bigger debt and amass huge trade deficits indefinitely. In the worst scenario, the U.S.'s willingness to fritter away its national wealth to finance private consumption and unproductive government spending would extract a permanent price on the economy, sending the U.S. in a downward spiral that would be hard to escape.

Thus do the routes to prosperity chosen by China and the U.S. put both countries at risk. Without the U.S. to buy Chinese goods, China cannot sustain its growth; without China to lend money to the U.S., Americans cannot spend. Without the twin engines of the U.S. and China stoking the fortunes of other nations, the rest of the world might also sputter.

How can the U.S., perhaps with its traditional allies, adjust to a competitive challenger that has strengths unlike any other that America has faced? Are the transfers of talent, technology, and capital part of an inevitable dynamic? Or does the U.S., or any other country, have the power to shape a future in which everyone prospers?

Americans looking for answers and action must also find a way to move America's leadership to see China's rise as every bit as worthy of national attention as the rumblings in more obvious political hot spots. While all eyes turn to the so-called clash of civilizations between Islam and the West, China will have the more profound impact on the world in the long run. And yet, despite occasional misgivings offered in factory towns and tariffs slapped on imports at the height of campaign season, American leaders tend to view China's rise as the fulfillment of a free marketer's dream, where global investors will shepherd the country into wealth, democracy, and peaceful interdependence with the rest of the free world.

It is a lovely theory, and it may ultimately be true. There is, however, no evidence upon which to base such a prediction. Which exactly of the world's large, highly nationalistic, dictatorial, Communist-capitalist countries offers a historical analogue? Answer: There is no such country.

This article was adapted from **TED C. FISHMAN'S** book, *CHINA, INC.*, published by Scribner, an imprint of Simon & Schuster.

The Battle for China's Good-Enough Market

Multinationals and local firms for the first time are squaring off in China's rapidly growing middle market—a critical staging ground for global expansion and the segment from which world-beating companies will emerge.

Orit Gadiesh, Philip Leung, and Till Vestring

Caterpillar, the world leader in construction equipment, is having trouble making deeper tracks in China. The U.S.-based manufacturer of tractors, backhoes, road graders, and other devices began selling equipment in China in 1975, a year before the death of Chairman Mao. As the Chinese government invested massively in infrastructure, Caterpillar helped pave the way, literally, for economic growth and modernization in the world's fastest-growing market for construction equipment.

Like many foreign players in any number of industries, Caterpillar got its start in China by selling goods to the Chinese government—the only possible customer before the era of economic reform—and then began selling high-quality equipment to the private sector as a premium segment of the market emerged. But it never broadened its focus to include other segments, and by the early 2000s, Komatsu, Hitachi, Daewoo, and other competitors from Japan and Korea were in the middle market with tools and equipment that cost less but were still reliable. Meanwhile, a tranche of local manufacturers that had previously been focused only on the low end of the market were burrowing up to battle the established players, designing and releasing their own products targeted squarely at middle-market consumers.

As the experiences of Caterpillar and other multinationals suggest, a critical new battleground is emerging for companies seeking to establish, sustain, or expand their presence in China: It's the "good-enough" market segment, home of reliable-enough products at low-enough prices to attract the cream of China's fast-growing cohort of midlevel consumers.

Harvard professor Clay Christensen, author of *The Innovator's Dilemma,* has used the phrase "good enough" to suggest that start-up companies developing and releasing new products and services don't necessarily need to aim for perfection to make inroads against established players. The phrase can be similarly applied to middle-market players in China that have been able to steal a march on incumbents by developing and releasing good-enough products that are displacing premium ones.

These forward-thinking companies (multinational and domestic firms alike) are doing more than just seizing share of wallet and share of mind in China's rapidly expanding middle market—in and of itself a major achievement. They are conditioning themselves for worldwide competition tomorrow: They're building the scale, expertise, and business capabilities they'll need to export their China offerings to other large emerging markets (India and Brazil, for instance) and, ultimately, to the developed markets. Given China's share of global market growth (Goldman Sachs estimates that China will account for 36% of the world's incremental GDP between 2000 and 2030) and the country's role in preparing companies to pursue opportunities in other developing regions, it's becoming clear that businesses wanting to succeed globally will need to win in China first.

In the following pages, we'll explore the importance of China as a lead market. We'll describe the surge of activity in China's middle market; when (and whether) multinationals and Chinese companies should enter this vibrant arena for growth; and, most important, how they can compete effectively in the good-enough segment. As Caterpillar and other foreign players have learned, achieving leadership in China's middle market isn't easy.

An Evolving Opportunity

Historically, there has been a simple structure to China's markets: at the top, a small premium segment served by foreign companies realizing solid margins and rapid growth; at the bottom, a large low-end segment served by local companies offering low-quality, undifferentiated products (typically 40% to 90% cheaper than premium ones) that often lose money—when producers do their accounting right. Between the two is the rapidly expanding good-enough segment. (For an example of how one market sector breaks out, see Figure 1)

Premium (Narrow)	Good-Enough (Rapidly Expanding)	Low-End (Evolving Base)
Definition: High-end products purchased by discerning customers with significant purchasing power.	**Definition:** Products of good quality, produced by local companies for a rapidly expanding group of value-seeking consumers with midlevel incomes.	**Definition:** Products of lower quality, meeting basic needs, produced by local firms for a large group of consumers with low incomes.
Leading Vendors: Panasonic, Philips, Sony	**Leading Vendors:** Hisense, Skyworth, TCL	**Leading Vendor:** Konka
Product Features: LCD and plasma screens, many state-of-the art user features, priced according to their status as international brands.	**Product Features:** LCD, plasma, and large cathode-ray tube screens, with limited user features, priced to undercut foreign brands.	**Product Features:** Cathode-ray tube screens with basic standard user features and low-cost components, priced to sell.
Share of Market in 2005: 13%	**Share of Market in 2005:** 62%	**Share of Market in 2005:** 25%

Figure 1   The Structure of China's Market for Televisions.

The good-enough space in China is growing for many reasons, not the least of which are recent shifts in consumer buying patterns and preferences. These shifts are coming from two directions: Consumers with rising incomes are trading up from the low-end products they previously purchased. At the same time, higher-income consumers are moving away from pricey foreign brands and accepting less expensive, locally produced alternatives of reasonable quality. The same holds true on the B2B front.

Consequently, China's middle market is growing faster than both the premium and low-end segments. In some categories, the good-enough space already accounts for nearly half of all revenues. Eight out of every ten washing machines and televisions now sold in China are good-enough brands. It should come as no surprise, then, that China—and, in particular, its opportunity-rich middle market—is increasingly capturing multinational executives' resources and attention. As Mark Bernhard, chief financial officer of General Motors' Shanghai-based GM China Group, recently told the *Detroit News:* "For GM to remain a global industry leader, we must also be a leader in China."

The automaker's strategy in China embodies that belief. GM had traditionally been an underperformer in the market for small cars. However, its acquisition of Korea's ailing Daewoo Motor in 2002 enabled it to compete and ultimately take a leadership position in China. The deal allowed GM to develop new models for half what it would cost the company to develop them in the West. Daewoo-designed cars now make up more than 50% of GM's sales in China, currently its second biggest market. What's more, GM is using these vehicles to compete against Asian automakers and sell small cars in more than 150 markets around the world, from India to the United States.

Colgate-Palmolive made similar moves in China. It entered into a joint venture in the early 1990s with one of China's largest toothpaste producers, and it acquired China's market leader for toothbrushes a decade later, allowing it to scale up and then leverage its production processes to compete in other parts of the

world. As a result, Colgate more than doubled its oral hygiene revenues in China between 1998 and 2005, and it now exports its China products to 70 countries.

Local Chinese competitors pose the biggest challenge to multinationals seeking to capitalize on their business ventures in China and beyond. In the auto industry, for instance, domestic carmakers like Geely and Chery have eaten away at Western companies' market share in China by introducing good-enough cars for local consumption. Several of these automakers have started exhibiting vehicles at car shows in the United States and Europe, buying available Western brands, and exporting vehicles to other emerging markets. True, these players face enormous challenges in meeting safety and emissions standards and in building up the required distribution networks to compete in Europe and North America. But no Western company should underestimate the determination of Chinese firms to figure out how to meet international quality standards and make their global mark.

European and North American companies producing major appliances, microwaves, and televisions know this all too well. They abdicated China to low-cost local competitors in the 1990s and now find themselves struggling to compete globally against those same Chinese companies. Haier, which started making refrigerators in 1984, went on to become one of China's best-known brands and then used its hard-won scale advantages and manufacturing skills to crack, and then dominate, foreign markets. Today, it is one of the largest refrigerator companies in the world, controlling 8.3% of the highly fragmented global market. The company sells products in more than 100 markets, including the United States, Africa, and Pakistan.

Obviously, the stakes in China have changed. Local companies are using booming domestic markets to hone their strategies at home before taking on the world. Multinationals, therefore, need to defend their positions in China not only to profit from the economic growth in that country but also to prevent local competitors from becoming global threats. The good-enough space is where multinationals and Chinese firms are going head-to-head—and it's the market segment from which the world's leading companies will emerge.

Making an Entrance

It's one thing to recognize the importance of China's middle market; it's another thing entirely to turn that awareness into action. The first step in winning the battle for China's good-enough market is determining when—or when not—to enter the fray. That will depend on the attractiveness of the premium segment: Is it still growing? Are companies still achieving high returns or are returns eroding? Another consideration is your company's market position: Are you a leader or a niche player? (See Figure 2)

Foreign companies grappling with the good-enough decision in China will need to consider these factors and perform thorough market and competitor analyses, along with careful customer segmentation and needs analyses—classic strategy tools, of course, but applied in the context of a rapidly changing economy that may lack historical data on market share, prices, and the like. Senior managers will need to establish the factors that are key to success in everything from branding to pricing to distribution. This knowledge will inform important decisions

about whether companies should expand organically into the middle market, acquire an existing player in that space, or find a good-enough partner.

Generally speaking, competing in the good-enough space is neither necessary nor wise for multinationals operating in stable premium segments. These companies should instead focus on lowering their costs and innovating to maintain their premium or niche positions and to sustain their margins. We studied one large manufacturer of automation equipment, for example, that wisely decided to stand pat in the premium segment. Market research suggested that its customers were still willing to pay more for reliability, even with a variety of lower-cost choices out there. The company continued to invest in R&D, hoping to further differentiate its products from those of local players; it expanded its distribution and service networks to improve its responsiveness to customers; and it cut costs by taking advantage of local production resources.

Multinationals will need to tear apart the cost structure of their good-enough competitors to understand how they make money while charging such low prices.

STATE OF THE PREMIUM MARKET SEGMENT

		STRONG	WEAK OR ERODING
COMPANIES' COMPETITIVE POSITION	**STRONG**	**Maintain strong premium status** Hold off on entering the good-enough segment of the market — for now. Drop prices as required to remain competitive; lower costs and innovate to defend premium status and sustain margin. Regularly reevaluate the decision not to enter.	**Attack from above or buy your way in** Premium players employ an offensive-defense approach to enter the middle market. That is, they enter the good-enough segment in order to defend against the rise of local competitors and the erosion of the premium segment.
	WEAK OR ERODING	**Innovate to maintain current premium status** Hold off on entering the good-enough segment of the market — for now. Increase innovation efforts to capture a niche position in the premium segment. Regularly reevaluate the decision not to enter.	**Burrow up from below or buy your way in** Value players enter the good-enough segment using a breakthrough approach — with a merger, for instance, or by developing China-specific products or business models — to steal share from incumbents and attain market leadership.

Figure 2 Should You Enter the Middle Market? Multinationals deciding whether to move into China's middle market need to first consider the attractiveness of the premium segment and their current market position. If conditions warrant, they can attack aggressively from above. Chinese firms can burrow up from below. Both can acquire their way into the good-enough space.

Few multinationals find themselves in such a fortunate position, however. If growth in the premium segment is slowing and returns are eroding, multinational corporations will need to enter the good-enough space. Even those companies that because of their strong competitive position initially abstain from entering the middle market should revisit their decision frequently to guard against emerging competitive threats. For their part, Chinese companies will need to move upmarket as the lower-end segment becomes increasingly competitive.

Our research and experience indicate that companies contemplating a move into the good-enough space go about it in one of three basic ways: Leading multinationals in the premium segment *attack from above*. The goal for these organizations is to lower their manufacturing costs, introduce simplified products or services, and broaden their distribution networks while maintaining reasonable quality. Meanwhile, Chinese challengers in the low-end segment tend to *burrow up from below*. These companies aim to take the legs out from under established players by providing new offerings that ratchet up quality but cost consumers much less than the premium products do. And, finally, multinationals that can't reduce their costs fast enough, and domestic players looking for more skills, technology, and talent, *buy their way in*.

Each of these moves comes with its own set of traps. The challenge, then, for companies eyeing the middle market is to understand why those that went before them failed in this space—and how to sidestep the pitfalls they encountered. Let's take a closer look at these three approaches.

Attacking from Above

Whether they're selling toothpaste or power transmission equipment, multinational companies dominate China's small but high-margin premium segment—the only one in which foreign players have traditionally been able to compete successfully. So a move toward the middle certainly holds a fair amount of risk for those already thriving in the premium space. A chief concern is cannibalization. After all, selling to consumers in less-than-premium segments could negatively affect sales of high-end products. These companies also run the risk of fueling gray markets for their wares. If, say, a business sells a T-shirt for $10 in China but $20 in the United States, there's a good chance an enterprising distributor will find a way to buy that T-shirt in China and export it to the United States for sale there.

Multinational managers, therefore, need to conduct careful market analyses to understand the differences between China's premium and good-enough segments. There may be, for instance, strong geographic distinctions a company can capitalize on. Consider the strategy GE Healthcare employed to expand sales of its MRI equipment in China. The company created a line of simplified machines targeted at hospitals in China's remote and financially constrained second- and third-tier cities—places like Hefei and Lanzhou, where other multinationals rarely ventured. That good-enough territory had all the right conditions: It was a fast-growing market whose customers' purchasing criteria weren't likely to change soon. GE's cost structure allowed it to compete with other middle-market players in the industry. And there was little risk that the company would cannibalize its premium line of diagnostic machines; large city hospitals were not keen on downgrading their MRI equipment.

Markets are dynamic, and there's no place on the planet where they are shifting as quickly or as dramatically as in China. So multinational executives also need to think about the degree to which the premium and good-enough segments will converge over time. Managers can use traditional forecasting methods (scenario planning, war gaming, consultations with leading-edge customers, and so on) to pick up on emerging threats and impending opportunities. Which brings us back to GE Healthcare's MRI expansion plans: The company's long-held commitment to health care development in China meshed perfectly with Chinese leaders' publicly stated desire to improve health services in less-privileged areas of the country. Given the government's aims, GE Healthcare understood there would eventually be some overlap of the premium, middle, and low-end markets—and profitable opportunities in the good-enough space.

After weighing the risks that cannibalization and dynamic markets pose to their company's premium positioning, managers in multinationals need to consider their possible opportunities in the good-enough space: Can they take advantage of their lower purchasing costs, greater manufacturing scale, and distribution synergies? Then they have to determine which capabilities they may need to develop: How adept is their organization at designing products, services, brands, and sales approaches that will attract customers in the middle market without diminishing their company's position in the premium space? They may need to convene teams dedicated solely to studying the opportunities and resources required in the good-enough segment, as GE Healthcare did. (See the sidebar, "Penetrating the Good-Enough Market, One County Hospital at a Time.") They may also want to recruit local management talent—individuals with experience competing in the middle space—or purchase local companies to gain new technologies or expertise.

Those multinationals that decide to enter the middle market tend to employ an "offensive-defense" strategy—aggressively staking claims in the good-enough space to box out emerging local players and established global competitors seeking to gain their own scale advantages. By entering the good-enough space ahead of the pack, for instance, GE Healthcare was able to defend its position against local upstarts, including Mindray, Wandong, and Anke. The company is still trying to develop the optimal product portfolio and is addressing such issues as how best to service the equipment. Even so, GE captured 52% of the $238 million market in 2004, generating roughly $120 million in sales. Having honed its approach to the good-enough space, GE is replicating the strategy in new markets in several developing countries, including India.

Multinationals are bound to find it tough to jump in from above. Apart from the risks of cannibalization and all the challenges always associated with going down-market, companies will need to adapt fast, as customers' preferences change and competitors react. And they will probably need to tear apart the cost structure of their good-enough competitors to understand how those firms make money while charging such low prices. Just switching to local sourcing, for instance, may not be sufficient for large multinationals to match the lower production costs of their domestic competitors.

Burrowing Up from Below

Multinationals for years underestimated the ability and desire of local players in the low end of the market to move up and compete—a miscalculation that may now be coming home to roost. Recent developments have strengthened local competition in China and facilitated Chinese companies' moves upmarket and beyond.

Let's start with consolidation. For years, there were often hundreds of companies in a single industry catering primarily to customers in the low end of the market and typically focusing on regional needs. Many of those companies operated unprofitably—think of Red Star Appliances or Wuhan Xi Dao Industrial Stock. Because of China's free-market reforms, however, the weakest of those competitors are folding, and industries are experiencing waves of consolidation. Red Star, Wuhan Xi Dao, and 16 other money-losing concerns shifted and reshifted throughout the 1990s to form appliance maker Haier. A competent player or two, like Haier, have risen in each industry, often benefiting from national support. China's booming economy has enabled these survivors to build scale and develop market capabilities such as R&D and branding. As we have seen, over time, several of these emerging domestic champions have become direct challengers to global companies in a variety of industries.

Next, look at the rapidly expanding customer base in the middle space. Chinese customers—whether individual consumers, businesses, or government agencies—are becoming less willing to shell out 70% to 100% premiums for international products. At most, they may pay 20% to 30% more for world-class brands. The Italian dairy giant Parmalat discovered exactly that when it tried selling fruit-flavored yogurt for the equivalent of 24 cents a cup. Instead, consumers went with local brands at half the price. It seemed that brand, innovation, and quality—the hallmarks of multinationals in China—were no longer critical points of differentiation in customers' minds. This price sensitivity is opening up new ground for ambitious Chinese companies traditionally focused on the low end. These firms are designing and releasing good-enough products that overcome buyers' skepticism about quality at much lower prices, which generate higher margins than their low-end products. The often brutal competitive dynamics in the low-end segment also serve as a huge incentive for the better-managed local companies to move up. Until consumer demand began to explode in China, however, there really wasn't anywhere for these firms to go. Now there is.

The journey from low end to good-enough to global usually takes a decade and then some—but more and more Chinese companies are embarking on it. For instance, Lenovo, founded in 1984, entered the good-enough segment via a joint venture, flourished in the middle market, and then went on to establish its international brand with the purchase of IBM's PC division in 2005 for $1.75 billion. It is currently the world's third-largest PC maker. Similarly, Huawei Technologies has grown since 1988 to the point where 31 of the first 50 firms on Standard & Poor's ranking of the world's top telecom companies are clients of the Chinese maker of mobile and fixed telecommunications networks.

Penetrating the Good-Enough Market, One County Hospital at a Time

Ge healthcare already had a successful business selling high-end medical equipment in China when the Chinese government set a goal for the next decade of improving the health care available in less-privileged locales. To support the government's efforts and also to break out of the high end of the market, GE developed a business case for manufacturing and selling medical devices for China's good-enough market. CEO Jeff Immelt's visits and conversations with Chinese leaders motivated the company to pursue the opportunity. In the end, GE's research and analysis identified a substantial demand from thousands of mid-tier and low-end Chinese hospitals in less affluent provinces that were not served by multinationals. GE knew that it could design new products and business models to serve this market. GE also knew that by using techniques like Six Sigma to eliminate manufacturing waste, it could make its costs competitive.

A team was charged with observing operations in the target hospitals and meeting with the hospital administrators and physicians to help determine what sort of medical equipment customers wanted, the specific features they needed, possible price points, and the kinds of distribution and services that would be required. Armed with this information, the fact-finding team considered stripping out some of the expensive equipment features and adding others that these target customers valued more. For instance, doctors in China's high-end hospitals preferred to program the medical equipment themselves, whereas physicians in the midlevel and low-end hospitals, who considered themselves less computer savvy, preferred preprogrammed machines.

The team worked with staffers in GE's R&D and manufacturing groups to build the right products at the right price points for the good-enough market. Because GE's existing sales, distribution, and service systems were not geared to the target customers, the company also had to reconfigure its networks of existing representatives and recruit new ones. This middle-market initiative is still a work in progress, but GE Healthcare has taken an enormous first step in establishing itself—and defending itself against rivals—in the good-enough segment.

Chinese customers are becoming less willing to shell out 70% to 100% premiums for international products. At most they may pay 20% to 30% more for world-class brands.

Just as foreign players approaching the market from above come face-to-face with their shortcomings—high costs, limited distribution capabilities, and the possibility of cannibalizing their own products—local companies moving up encounter their own limitations. Foremost is the shortage of managerial talent, especially for international businesses. Growing numbers of Chinese students are pursuing MBAs and studying abroad. They are slowly distinguishing themselves from the large cohort of current Chinese managers, whose command-and-control leadership style dominates local manufacturing houses. But catching up remains difficult, as China's surging economic growth outpaces the country's ability to educate and apprentice twenty-first-century managers.

Another obstacle for Chinese companies is their inability to compete with global players through innovation or by establishing a strong brand because of their limited size and their lack of management tools and experience. A question like "How much should we spend on advertising?" can stymie local managers looking at expansion. Long used to competing solely on price, they have little experience in understanding and addressing segment-specific needs, linking those needs to R&D and brand-building efforts, and creating the required infrastructure in sales and distribution.

Consider the early successes enjoyed by Chinese handset manufacturer Ningbo Bird. It was among a group of small, local companies that took 20% to 30% of the telecom market between 2000 and 2002 from the likes of Nokia and Motorola. Ningbo Bird prevailed by competing on price. But its success was short-lived, its march toward global expansion thwarted. The company just didn't have the expertise and resources the foreign corporations had in customer segmentation, R&D, innovation, and distribution.

By contrast, Huawei has been able to successfully navigate such roadblocks. Initially established as a network equipment distributor, Huawei has built and acquired the technical and managerial capabilities it needed to rise up from the low end of the market. From its inception, Huawei invested 10% of its sales in R&D. It developed its own products to penetrate new segments in China and forged technical alliances to further broaden its product mix. With government support, Huawei prompted consolidation in the domestic market, gaining massive scale in the process. The company now controls 14% of the local market for telecom networks. Firmly established in the good-enough space at home, Huawei built brands to meet the requirements of global customers. It established 12 R&D centers around the world, pioneering next-generation technologies (customized communication networks and voice access systems) and partnering with global brands such as 3Com to build customer awareness of its own brands.

Huawei has broadened its reach in stages over 14 years. The company first focused on establishing itself in developing regions of China, where multinationals had less incentive to compete. It then penetrated countries with emerging economies, such as Russia and Brazil. Finally, it attacked the developed countries. It has expanded internationally through aggressive sales and marketing, by taking advantage of low-cost China-based R&D, and by leveraging its ability to outsource some of its manufacturing processes to other players in China. A little more than a decade ago, Huawei was a regional company in a local market that few multinationals considered important. With 2005 revenues of $8.2 billion, it is now second only to Cisco, according to InfoTech Trends' ranking of the networking hardware industry. It could never have ascended the way it has without using China's good-enough segment as a springboard for growth.

Buying Your Way In

For multinational companies that can't alter their costs or processes quickly enough to compete with local players, and for Chinese firms that lack the production scale, R&D mechanisms, and customer-facing capabilities to compete with foreign players, there is still a breakthrough option for entering the middle market—mergers and acquisitions.

China's entry into the World Trade Organization in 2001 fueled a surge in M&A activity. Now, however, foreign acquirers are facing tougher approval processes. China's public commitment to open markets remains strong, but several high-profile deals have gotten stuck at the provincial or ministerial level, owing to increasing public concerns about selling out to foreign firms. For instance, in its bid to buy Xugong Group Construction Machinery, China's largest construction machinery manufacturer and distributor, the U.S. private equity firm Carlyle Group met with unexpected resistance from the government and ended up twice reducing its stake, ultimately to 45%. In rejecting successive Carlyle bids, officials in Beijing insisted the nation's construction equipment industry should be controlled by "domestic hands."

As the Carlyle Group learned, gaining regulatory and political approval for M&As in China is a major undertaking. Foreign companies seeking such approval may need to draft (and redraft) a compelling business case for the acquisition, one that cites up front the benefits for local companies and authorities. Like Carlyle, they must be willing to adjust (and readjust) the structure, terms, and conditions of a deal to gain government support. They may also need to engage in heavy-duty relationship building, investing the time and resources required to woo critical players in the deal.

As is always the case with M&As the world over, it's all about fit: There should be cost and distribution synergies between the multinational and its target and little chance that the local company's products will cannibalize the multinational's premium brands. Successful acquirers in China—multinationals and Chinese firms alike—use a clear strategic rationale to select the right target. They over invest in the due diligence process. They take a systematic approach to post-merger integration.

Many Chinese companies believe they must forge ahead and buy established Western brands and distribution systems whether or not they have the experience and management tools to handle them.

That was the game plan behind Gillette's 2003 acquisition of Nanfu, then China's leading battery manufacturer. Gillette's Duracell division throughout the 1990s was losing market share in China to lower-priced competitors. By 2002, Duracell's share of the Chinese domestic battery market was 6.5%. By contrast, Nanfu controlled more than half the market. After careful analysis, Gillette's management team recognized that its Duracell unit was at a cost disadvantage compared with its rivals and concluded it would be difficult to broaden the brand's market penetration. Facing such odds, Gillette decided to buy into the good-enough market, acquiring a majority stake in Nanfu. But Gillette was extremely careful to protect both Duracell's and Nanfu's brands in their respective segments. Gillette continues to sell premium batteries in China under the Duracell brand and has maintained Nanfu as the leading national brand for the mass market. The dual branding, cost synergies, sales growth, broadened product portfolio, economies of scale, and distribution to more than 3 million retail outlets in China have paid off for Gillette, which has seen significant increases in its operating margins in China.

Buying into the good-enough segment also worked for consumer-goods giants Danone, L'Oréal, and Anheuser-Busch—companies that saw the vast potential in China but couldn't get their costs low enough to compete. For instance, in 2004, Anheuser-Busch outbid its competitor SABMiller to acquire Harbin, the fourth-largest brewer in China. That acquisition allowed Anheuser-Busch to reach the masses while preventing Harbin from swimming upstream. The next year, it increased its stake in Tsingtao Brewery, from 9.9% to 27%. Both moves enabled the global brewer to rapidly increase its share among China's drinkers of less-than-premium beer.

Chinese companies are also wrapping their arms around acquisition strategies, attempting to establish their presence in the middle market by purchasing brands, talent, and other resources from target companies in Europe and North America. To date, they've met with mixed results. On the one hand, Lenovo's acquisition of IBM's PC division turned the Chinese computer maker into the world's third-largest PC company. On the other hand, the acquisition experiences of TCL, a major Chinese consumer electronics manufacturer, have been less successful.

TCL built a strong position in the Chinese market by producing and distributing basic cathode-ray tube TVs at astonishingly low prices. It also engaged in contract and private-label manufacturing for the U.S. and European markets. But TCL realized it would need a strong brand to rise up from the low end of the China market and that growing organically in a mature industry like TV manufacturing would be prohibitively expensive. So TCL acquired French firm Thomson, which owned a number of well-known brands, including RCA. Unfortunately, Thomson also owned some high-cost and unproductive manufacturing facilities in France. TCL has struggled since acquiring Thomson,

as the market for TVs has shifted from cathode-ray to plasma and LCD technologies. In 2006, the company lost $351 million from operations. Many Chinese companies believe that in order to play in the global arena, they must simply forge ahead, buying established Western brands and distribution systems—whether or not they have the experience and management tools to handle such acquisitions. But, as TCL's story suggests, executing such a plan is hardly cut-and-dried.

In the 1960s and 1970s, the mantra for many organizations was "Capture U.S. market share, capture the world." Today, China—and its middle market in particular—has become the object of multinationals' ardent pursuit. The enormous market potential of the country's population, the formidable growth of the economy, and China's established position in low-cost sourcing and manufacturing are providing competitive advantages for many companies—benefits these organizations are then leveraging both inside and outside the nation.

Local Chinese companies know their futures depend on entering the good-enough space and attacking global leaders (and their premium positioning) by offering low-cost products of reasonable quality that they can eventually take to the world. Multinationals are beginning to recognize that ceding the middle space to Chinese firms may breed competitors that will ultimately challenge them on a global scale. Ironically, Chinese companies that have already gone global are on the defensive as well. A recent *Forbes Asia* article reported that as Haier has attacked international markets and won share abroad, both local companies and multinationals have been nibbling away at its share of China's middle market—which fell from 29% in 2004 to 25% last year.

The stakes are high. All the more reason, then, for companies that have stumbled in China in the past to redouble their efforts. Danone's high product costs thwarted its early attempts to sell dairy products in China's middle market. But that obstacle was removed when the firm reengaged in the fight, lowering its costs by buying a local dairy.

Likewise, Caterpillar hasn't diverted its focus away from China and the importance of the good-enough space. The company plans to triple its sales by 2010, opening more manufacturing plants and dealerships and forming more joint ventures with local companies. "Operational and sales success in China is critical for the company's long-term growth and profitability," said Rich Lavin, vice president of Caterpillar's Asia Pacific Operations Division, in November 2006. Shortly thereafter, the company moved its divisional headquarters—from Tokyo to Beijing.

ORIT GADIESH (orit.gadiesh@bain.com) is the chairman of Bain & Company in Boston. **PHILIP LEUNG** (philip.leung@bain.com), a Bain partner in Shanghai, leads the firm's Greater China health care practice. **TILL VESTRING** (till.vestring@bain.com), a Bain partner based in Singapore, leads the firm's Asia-Pacific industrial practice.

Three Dimensional

The markets of Japan, Korea, and China are far from homogeneous.

Masaaki Kotabe and Crystal Jiang

Asia is one of the world's most dynamic regions, and offers multiple opportunities for businesses and investors. In terms of its nominal gross domestic product (GDP) in 2005, Japan has the largest economy ($4.80 trillion), followed by China ($1.84 trillion) and Korea ($.72 trillion). China's real purchasing power exceeds $7 trillion, Japan's is estimated at $4 trillion, and Korea's is estimated at $1 trillion. These giants' combined purchasing power is comparable to the $12 trillion U.S. economy.

One of the challenges faced by American and other Western multinational companies is a tendency to lump together these markets and assume that Asian consumers have similar tastes and preferences, moderated by different income levels. This is not only a very shortsighted view, but also a risky assumption when entering these markets.

Asian countries have distinct cultural, social, and economic characteristics that affect consumer behavior, with consumers in Japan, Korea, and China differing in brand orientations, attitudes toward domestic and foreign products, quality and price perceptions, and technology feature preferences. A comparative analysis of consumer behaviors can help companies identify effective marketing strategies, and enable them to successfully tackle these Asian markets (see Table 1).

Brand Orientation

Japan. Of all the developed countries, this is the most brand-conscious and status-conscious. It is also intensely style-conscious: Consumers love high-end luxury goods (especially from France and Italy), purchasing items such as designer handbags, shoes, and jewelry. Since 2001, Hermes, Louis Vuitton (commonly referred to as LVMH), and Coach have opened glitzy flagship stores in Tokyo and enjoyed double-digit sales growth. And the country represents 20% of Gucci's worldwide revenue, 15% of LVMH's, and 12% of Chanel's. It seems that a slumping economy has not inhibited its consumers.

Eager to "know who they are," they prefer brands that contribute to their senses of identity and self-expression. These highly group-oriented consumers are apt to select prestigious merchandise based on social class standards, and prefer products that enhance their status. Accordingly, they attach more

Executive Briefing

Globalizing markets might not mean that markets have become similar. Although multinational companies tend to believe that all Asian markets are the same, a comparative analysis proves that consumers in Japan, Korea, and China differ in their brand orientations, attitudes toward domestic and foreign products, quality and price perceptions, and product feature preferences. To ensure success, companies must set aside narrow and risky assumptions, and tailor country-specific strategies to target these consumers.

importance to the reputation of the merchandise than to their personal social classes.

Noticeably, the country's consumer markets have expanded to China and Korea. In Shanghai or Seoul, you can see the influence of Japan's fashion trends and products. There's even a Chinese word for this phenomenon: ha-ri, which means the adoration of Japanese style.

Korea. Consumers have very sophisticated tastes, show immense passion for new experiences, and favor premium and expensive imported products. In 2004, the Korean Retail Index showed continuous growth of premium brands in certain product categories, such as whiskey, shampoo, and cosmetics. Consumers also demonstrate great interest in generational fads (expressions of their generations and cultures, not just of their economics or regions), thereby selecting products that follow their generations' judgments and preferences.

China. Roughly 10 million–13 million Chinese consumers prefer luxury goods. The majority of them are entrepreneurs or young professionals working for foreign multinational firms. Recent studies found that 24% of the population, mostly in their 20s and 30s, prefers new products and considers technology an important part of life. (Those in their 40s and 50s are price-conscious, brand loyal, and less sensitive to technology.) With higher education and purchasing power, this generation is brand- and status-conscious. It considers luxury goods to be personal achievements, bringing higher social status.

Table 1   Market Characteristics of the Three Largest Asian Economies

	Japan	Korea	China
Population (2005)	127 million	48 million	1,306 million
Nominal GDP (2005)	$4.80 trillion	$ .72 trillion	$1.84 trillion
GDP purchasing power parity (2004)	$3.7 trillion	$ .92 trillion	$7.3 trillion
GDP per capita purchasing power parity (2004)	$29,400	$19,200	$5,600
GDP real growth rate of country (2004)	2.9%	4.6%	9.1%
Degree of luxury brand consciousness	Very strong	Strong	Varied
Preference for foreign products	Strong (particularly for European products)	Weak	Very strong
Price/quality perception	Extremely quality demanding	Polarization of consumption	Very price conscious
Importance of high-tech features on new products	Very high	Very high	Varied

Sources: Central Intelligence Agency, World Factbook, and Index Mundi

Purchasing behavior tends to vary regionally. Consumers in metropolitan areas follow fashions/trends/styles, prefer novelty items, and are aware of brand image and product quality. These consumers live on the eastern coast—in major cities such as Shanghai, Beijing, Shenzhen, and Dalian. There, luxury brands such as Armani, Prada, and LVMH are considered prominent logos for high-income clientele.

According to LVMH, this country is its fourth-largest market in terms of worldwide sales. It's no wonder that many high-end firms label these consumers "the new Japanese": a group of increasingly wealthy people hungry for brands and fanatical about spending.

Domestic vs. Foreign

Japan. Although consumers are extremely demanding and have different perceptions of products made in other countries, they are generally accepting of quality foreign products. However, Japan is mostly dominated by well-established companies such as Canon, Sony, and Toyota. Many globally successful firms experience great difficulty gaining footholds.

In this market, Häagen-Dazs Japan Inc. succeeded the exit of competitor Ben & Jerry's, dominating the premium ice cream market with a 90% market share. It successfully delivered the message of a "lifestyle-enhancement product" with word-of-mouth advertising, garnering a flood of free publicity. The company flourished by promoting high quality with local appeal.

Korea. These consumers hold negative attitudes toward foreign businesses; the majority believes that these businesses transfer local wealth to other countries, and crowd out small establishments. Consumers are very proud, and demonstrate a complicated love-hate relationship with foreign brands.

Very few consumers understand or speak English, let alone the languages of their closest trading partners: Japan and China. Often, Korean campaigns require significant rebranding—use of localized brands—to influence local perceptions. According to an official at Carrefour (the world's second-largest retailer), the company has difficulty expanding its investments into other provinces because of excessive regulations, and hasn't done enough research to keep up with Korean consumers' needs.

Nevertheless, the country is increasingly comfortable with the presence of foreign companies in previously closed industries. (In fact, the society is much too uncritical and passive in the acceptance of foreign—especially American—products.) And consumers are far less brand-conscious than before, and will embrace new products from unknown companies.

China. Attitudes toward foreign products differ, depending on consumers' age groups. Companies can no longer view this country's youth through the lens of traditional cultural values; this generation considers international taste a key factor in making decisions. Conversely, the mature generation (55 years and older) expresses a definite preference for locally made products. In general, consumers believe imported products under foreign brand names are more dependable.

Many foreign companies (e.g., Nike, Nokia, Sony, McDonald's) have replaced unknown local brands. The country retains more than 300 licensed Starbucks outlets, and chairman Howard Schultz says of this market: "In addition to the 200 million middle-to-upper-class segments of the population that are typically customers for upscale brands, there is a growing affinity from the younger, affluent consumer for Western brands."

However, some foreign companies—with an increased focus on local appeal—have lost their prominent brands' images to domestic rivals, ultimately forfeiting their market share. After all, when this country's consumers are inspired by design and function, they prefer domestic brands because of their good value for the money.

Quality and Price

Japan. These consumers are the world's strictest when it comes to demand for product quality, and they clearly articulate their needs/desires about a product or packaging operation. They view information other than price (e.g., brand, packaging, advertising) as important variables in assessing quality and making decisions. Compared with Chinese and Korean consumers, they have much higher expectations for products—and are willing to pay premium prices for them. In agricultural produce, for example, they are less tolerant of skin blemishes, small size, and uniformity.

Foreign companies that don't fully understand and meet consumers' needs/expectations struggle with their investments. Although Wal-Mart dwarfs the competition (with $285 billion in 2004 global sales) and owns 42% of all Japanese supermarket chains, it faces losses there. Its "everyday low prices" philosophy doesn't seem to attract Japanese consumers, because they often associate low price with low quality: yasu-karou, warukarou—cheap price, cheap product.

To cater to these consumers, manufacturers have adopted a total quality approach. To survive fierce local competition, Procter & Gamble sought the best available materials for product formulations and packaging. In the process, it learned some invaluable lessons on how to improve operations, and obtained new product ideas from consumers. (Interestingly, the company took this education on the Japanese way of interacting with consumers and applied it globally.) Today, the country serves as Procter & Gamble's major technical center in Asia, where it develops certain global technologies.

And McDonald's opened its first store in Tokyo's Ginza district, which is identified with luxury brand-name goods. It purchased expensive land—not justified by the limited profits of a hamburger establishment—to boost the quality image of its product. Today, McDonald's Japan has grown to become the country's largest fast-food chain.

In terms of cost, the younger generation prefers low-priced products—everything priced at 100 yen (similar to U.S. dollar stores). The "two extreme price markets" segmentation model explains how consumers value lower prices for their practical use while paying premium prices for self-satisfaction, social status, and the quality of products—especially those from Europe. As a result, anything that falls in the middle of the price range—such as the country's designer brands—generates petty profits.

Korea. Consumption has been sluggish since the Asian financial crisis of 1997–1999. However, the younger generation is at the forefront of a new and emerging pattern; it holds opposing expectations of/preferences for low-priced and high-priced goods. When purchasing high-tech or fashion-related items, these consumers prefer well-known brands, and tend to purchase expensive goods to attain psychological satisfaction. Yet they are willing to purchase unbranded goods with low prices, as long as the basic features are guaranteed. It has taken several decades for discount stores to surpass the retail market.

China. Most consumers are price sensitive, and try to safeguard part of their income for investment. In 2005, many global automakers readjusted their strategies in this country, based on demand predictions that most consumers would purchase cars priced less than $12,000. One popular Chinese automaker, Chery, priced its QQ model between $5,500 and $7,500; another aggressive domestic automaker, Xiali, priced its cars at similarly affordable prices.

Although this market is lucrative with growing demand, foreign brands (e.g., Honda, General Motors, Volkswagen Group) cannot compete with Chinese automakers' competitive prices. And when the younger generation worships Western and luxury brands—in eagerness to establish its social identity—it might prefer pirated versions to domestic ones, making anticounterfeiting control a major issue for companies.

Technology Features

Japan. Because of the country's harmonic convergence of the domestic market and the industrial sector, consumers have always preferred high-tech gadgets. According to an estimate by The World Bank Group, the country possesses 410,000 of the world's 720,000 working robots (which perform useful chores and provide companionship). Its electronics companies create gizmos by borrowing new concepts from the computer industry, such as personal video recorders, interactive pagers, and Internet radios.

Instead of looking for cost or value, consumers are willing to pay for better and cooler features and technological sophistication. Largely because of Japan's small living quarters, manufacturers have become experts at miniaturizing and creating multifunction devices. For instance, Sony's PlayStation Portable compacts the power of the original PlayStation into a palm-sized package. According to the company, it can deliver music and MPEG-4 video, can display photos, and even offers a Wi-Fi connection for wireless gaming and messaging. It's also no wonder that the country welcomed Baroke, the first company to successfully produce quality sparkling and still wine in a can.

Korea. The most wired country in the world is a leader in Internet usage and high-tech industries such as mobile phones, liquid crystal displays, and semiconductors. It also has widespread broadband, and high volumes of personal computer ownership. While mobile phone sales have cooled in Japan, these consumers continue to trade in phones for newer models about every six months.

Largely because of Japan's small living quarters, manufacturers have become experts at miniaturizing and creating multifunction devices.

According to a Samsung Research Institute survey, consumers prefer to express themselves without following social conventions. The Cyworld virtual community Web site, for instance, provides a subscriber with a private room, a circle of friends, and an endless range of "home" decoration possibilities and cool music. Ever-widening cyberspace reaches more than one-fourth of the population. The younger generation in particular enjoys virtual shopping malls and e-commerce.

China. It is imperative for companies to understand the major differences in consumer behavior between generations. Young Chinese consumers (typically affluent segments in the prosperous cities) are passionate about the latest developments. Recent studies found that 24% of the population—most with ages in the early 20s or 30s—prefer new products and consider technology an important part of life. Those in their 40s–50s, on the other hand, are price conscious, brand loyal, and less sensitive to technology.

Advice and Recommendations

Marketers need to tailor country-specific strategies to target consumers in Japan, Korea, and China. The existence of strategically equivalent segments (e.g., the younger generation, with its propensity to purchase high-quality, innovative, and foreign products) suggests a geocentric approach to global markets. These similarities allow for standardized strategies across national boundaries. By aggregating such segments, companies not only preserve consumer orientation, but also reduce the number of marketing mixes they have to offer—without losing market share, marketing, advertising, research and development, and production throughout Asia.

Moreover, because product design, function, and quality determine consumers' experiences, companies must simultaneously incorporate all areas—such as product development and marketing—to establish commanding positions in mature markets. Once they create positive images in these countries, success will be forthcoming.

Japan:

- This is the most profitable market for luxury goods companies. The key to success is promotion of high quality, local appeal, and a sense of extravagance.
- As one of the most volatile markets, it requires a steady flow of new stimuli with an improved rhythm of innovations. To survive, companies must continuously develop new products and establish prestigious brand value. If they can succeed there, then they can do so anywhere.
- Picky Japanese consumers clearly articulate their requirements about products or packaging operations. As a result, companies can use the country as their technical center—to gain firsthand experience in satisfying consumers in the region.
- These consumers are willing to pay for better and cooler features and technological sophistication. Companies can win their hearts by introducing gizmos.
- Because significant differences exist among generations, and those differences will translate into diverse consumer behaviors, segmentation marketing (identifying variations based on age, region, and gender) is best. Companies must be aware of these differences, and understand what kinds of products/services can meet the market segment's needs. For example: Coca-Cola has introduced more products here than anywhere else, including coffee and green tea beverages that appeal to Japanese tastes. As a result, its net operating revenue represents more than 60% of the total Asian segment (20% of its worldwide revenue).

Korea:

- A consumer-oriented approach is crucial for identifying tastes and blending in, rather than being viewed as foreign. Careful market, brand, and advertising testing is imperative.
- It can be difficult to enter this market alone; strategic alliances with domestic companies are a practical way to understand local preferences when introducing a global brand.
- If foreign companies make greater efforts to intensify their involvements with—and long-term commitments

to—the country's economic development, then consumers' perceptions of an "invasion" will dissipate over time.

- Product design directly affects a company's competitiveness. This and brand power can overcome product quality, and even product functions. To present the best product design to its consumers, Samsung Electronics hired an influential British industrial designer. According to the company's Economic Research Institute, a good design "provides a good experience for consumers"; it looks different, feels good, is easy to use, and has an identity.

China:

- Foreign companies can no longer wait; the market for consumer goods is growing rapidly, stimulated by a strong economy.
- Its diversity and the vastness of its consumer base make it critical for companies to segment consumers based on demographic, geographic, and psychographic/lifestyle variations.
- Because of the younger generation's brand orientation, promoting symbolic value is imperative for conspicuous and inconspicuous foreign products.
- Multinational companies can't assume that their first-mover advantages will be rewarded for brand recognition and established distribution channels.
- Cost-conscious consumers are quite unpredictable, so companies should avoid a too-high premium price strategy. Instead, they should research quantitatively acceptable price/value trade-offs by category.
- Because local brands are on the rise, foreign companies must work harder to localize research and development and the contents of their products. They must also better evaluate the market and the potential for long-term growth. Without competitive pricing and world-class product design/quality, companies will have a tough time surviving.

Company executives must remember that not all countries are created equally. By understanding and learning to appreciate the differences and similarities between these three Asian purchasing giants, companies from other countries can immerse their organizations seamlessly.

MASAAKI KOTABE is the Washburn Chair of International Business and Marketing and director of research at the Institute of Global Management Studies at Temple University's Fox School of Business and Management in Philadelphia. He may be reached at mkotabe@temple.edu. **CRYSTAL JIANG** is a PhD candidate in strategy and international business at the Fox School of Business and Management. She may be reached at crystalj@temple.edu. To join the discussion on this article, please visit www.marketingpower.com/marketingmanagementblog.

From *Marketing Management*, Vol. 15, no. 2, March/April 2006, pp. 39–43. Copyright © 2006 by American Marketing Association. Reprinted by permission.

Tech's Future

With affluent markets maturing, tech's next 1 billion customers will be Chinese, Indian, Brazilian, Thai . . . In reaching them, the industry will be deeply transformed.

Steve Hamm

In recent months, the Andhra Pradesh province in southern India has been the site of a rash of farmer suicides. Drought and low-quality seeds have left poor farmers with failed crops and no way to pay their debts. Many have swallowed lethal doses of pesticides as their only escape. Government officials estimate the toll since May at more than 60.

Against this bleak backdrop, a ray of hope: Neelamma, a 26-year-old woman, has found opportunity as a new type of entrepreneur. She's one of a dozen itinerant photographers who walk the streets of their farming communities carrying small backpacks stuffed with a digital camera, printer, and solar battery charger. As part of an experiment organized by Hewlett-Packard Co., Neelamma and the others are able to double their family incomes by charging the equivalent of 70¢ apiece for photos of newborns, weddings, and other proud moments of village life.

To make this happen, HP had to throw out its notions of how the tech business works. Anand Tawker, the company's director of emerging-market solutions in India, and his colleagues wrestled with fundamental questions: Does computing technology have a place in villages where electricity is fitful? Could it improve people's lives? How could villagers living in poverty pay for the latest digital wonders? And they came up with answers. In place of standard electricity, HP designers created the portable solar charger. Instead of selling the gear outright, HP rents the equipment to the photographers for $9 a month. "We asked people what they needed. One thing kept coming up: 'We want more money in our pockets,'" says Tawker. "So we do experiments. We launch and learn."

Why go to all that trouble? The answer is fast becoming obvious. During the first 50 years of the info-tech era, about 1 billion people have come to use computers, the vast majority of them in North America, Western Europe, and Japan. But those markets are maturing. Computer industry sales in the U.S. are expected to increase just 6% per year from now to 2008, according to market researcher IDC. To thrive, the industry must reach out to the next 1 billion customers. And many of those people will come not from the same old places but from far-flung frontiers like Shanghai, Cape Town, and Andhra Pradesh. "The robust growth opportunities are clearly shifting to the developing world," says Paul A. Laudicina, managing director at management consultant A.T. Kearney Inc.

Tech companies are scrambling to cash in on what they hope will be the next great growth wave. Led by China, India, Russia, and Brazil, emerging markets are expected to see tech sales surge 11% per year over the next half decade, to $230 billion, according to IDC. What makes these markets so appealing is not just the poor, but also the growing ranks of the middle-class consumers. Already, there are 60 million in China and 200 million in India, and their numbers are growing fast. These newly wealthy consumers are showing a taste for fashionable brands and for products every bit as capable as those available to Americans, Japanese, and Germans.

That tantalizing opportunity is drawing all of tech's big players. Microsoft is hawking software in Malaysia, Intel is pushing its chips in India, Cisco Systems is in Sri Lanka, and on and on. IBM says emerging markets are now a top priority. "We'll be even more aggressive," says IBM Chief Executive Samuel J. Palmisano. In Brazil, where IBM's revenues just zoomed past $1 billion, Big Blue plans on hiring 2,000 people and spending an additional $100 million on market development.

A Rival in Every Port

For tech's giants, this is the equivalent of America's basketball stars playing Argentina in the Olympics under international rules. The leaders are just as vulnerable to upset because they're facing companies that grew up in these markets and know them intimately. Just look to China, where homegrown Lenovo Group Ltd. has fought off Dell and other invaders to remain the top PC player. The Western powers may be accustomed to dominating in the developed world, but as the competition shifts to new terrain, their lock on the future is far from secure. They face stiff challenges from service companies in India, online gaming pioneers in Korea, security outfits in Eastern Europe, and network gearmakers in China. Even mighty Microsoft is vulnerable. Open-source software, with growing support in developing countries, could stunt its growth.

How the Tech Industry Is Changing

The rapid growth of sales in developing countries is having a profound impact on the tech industry. Companies must reimagine how they design products and do business.

Design

Products have to be simpler and more durable. TVS Electronics, an Indian printer maker, is producing devices for India's 1.2 million small shops. They're an all-in-one computer, cash register, and inventory-management system. They can be operated with icons, because many clerks are illiterate. And they tolerate dust and heat.

Innovation

Companies have to innovate for the peculiarities of emerging markets. Electricity often is unavailable or unreliable. That prompted Hewlett-Packard to design a small solar panel to charge digital printers for itinerant photographers in India. In South Africa, HP is working with a solar fabric that's cheaper and less fragile.

Pricing

There's pressure on prices, so some companies are using pay-as-you-go schemes. Poland needed to modernize its drivers' licensing system but couldn't afford it. So Hewlett-Packard agreed to install Poland's new computer system in exchange for a cut of the fees drivers pay each time they get a new license or renew an old one.

Business Development

The old strategies may not work anymore, so companies are trying new ones. IBM figures it can do well in China by supplying technology to local companies. Example: It developed a low-cost, $12 microprocessor and a simple network computer for China's Culturecom, which is selling computers and Net-access services in the country's rural backwaters.

Competition

Companies like Cisco, Dell, and Microsoft dominate in the developed world. But now a host of new challengers are using their low costs and intimate knowledge of local markets to give the giants trouble. Chinese networking upstart Huawei can charge 50% less for gear than Cisco, and is starting to make inroads worldwide.

The closest historical precedent for what's happening now is the PC revolution of the late 1970s and early 1980s. Before the PC, computers were the province of technical druids in giant corporations and government offices. Then with Apple Computer Inc.'s Macintosh and IBM's PC, the tech industry underwent a huge market-expanding shift. Computers began to show up on the desktops of everyone from schoolchildren to small-business owners. The result was seismic change. Microsoft, Intel, and Dell became the new champions, while dinosaurs like Digital Equipment lumbered off to the tar pits. Now, with rapid diffusion of technology into emerging economies, the industry is again reaching a gigantic new audience. And a new generation of companies will try to kick their elders in the teeth.

Expect a power shift from West to East. That's because the PC-centric era, dominated by U.S. companies, is fast giving way to the wireless age. The trend is most apparent in Asia, where cell phones with Net access are the computing gizmo of choice. While 30 million PCs are expected to be sold there this year, that pales in comparison to the 200 million cell phones capable of handling e-mail and Web surfing that researcher Yankee Group projects. That gives an advantage to Korea's Samsung Group and LG, which make cell phones as well as PCs. In the past four years they've come from nowhere to become the No. 3 and No. 6 mobile-phone makers in the world. "In the 20th century the torch came across the Atlantic from Europe to America. Now the torch is crossing the Pacific," says Geoffrey A. Moore, managing director at tech consultancy TCG Advisors LLC.

The challenges of succeeding in emerging markets are forcing the Western powers to come up with bold new strategies.

They're under pressure to innovate like crazy, pioneer new ways of doing business, and outmaneuver their feisty new competitors. "The pattern in the past was to sell the same stuff to the same kind of customers. But that won't work, and it has to change," says C.K. Prahalad, business professor at the University of Michigan Business School and author of *The Fortune at the Bottom of the Pyramid*, a book about commerce in the developing world. "What's required is a fundamental rethinking of how to design products and make money."

The result is an outpouring of innovation, from both the old guard and the up-and-comers, that could rival that of the PC era. The Indian photographer's setup is just the start. New innovations designed for the developing world range from the Simputer, a durable handheld being sold in India, to e-Town, a package of all of the products and services rural Chinese towns need to provide Net access for their residents. And who would have thought up a cell phone designed for the world's 1.4 billion Muslims? Nobody—until now. Tiny Dubai-based Ilkone Mobile Telecommunication has just started selling a phone that not only comes loaded with the Koran but also alerts people at prayer times and, with the help of a compass, points them toward Mecca.

BRAZIL

IBM's revenues here recently sailed past $1 billion. No wonder it has plans to hire 2,000 people and spend big bucks here.

Developing countries require new business strategies as well as new products. Most families in rural China or India can't afford a PC. In many instances, a handful of computers have to be shared by a whole village to be economically feasible. A new class of businesses—tech kiosk operators—is emerging to provide computing as a service. With cash often in short supply, pay-as-you-go programs are not only boosting cell-phone usage but are catching on with computers and Web access as well.

When these technologies cycle back into the mature markets, it could change everything from pricing to product design. To succeed in the developing world, devices and software have to be better in many ways: cheaper, easier to use, extra-durable, more compact—and still packed with powerful features. The resulting improvements will ultimately benefit everybody from New Delhi to New York. One possibility: HP is testing a solar fabric with itinerant photographers in South Africa that costs 80% less than the traditional solar panels that they use in India and won't crack. If this works out, people around the world could recharge their portable electronics by dropping them into carrying cases made of the material.

Creating Consumers

For tech's powerhouses, this shift to emerging markets cuts both ways. They have a chance to round up many new customers, but only if they're smarter than their new competitors. They'll have to invest substantial sums of money up front. Yet, for many products, prices will of necessity be very low. While the first billion customers produced an industry with more than $1 trillion in annual revenues, sales for the second billion won't be anything close to that. And ultimately, lower prices in the emerging markets will put pressure on prices everywhere. You could end up with an industry that, while it delivers a lot of value to a lot of people, it won't be able sustain the revenue growth rates or the profit margins of its glorious past.

On the brighter side, tech's spread into emerging markets could have a snowball effect on the world economy and the tech industry's fortunes. Investments in technology stoke national economies—boosting productivity, gross domestic product, and consumption of all sorts of products, including more technology. And as computer-factory workers in China and software programmers in India increase their incomes, they become consumers. A.T. Kearney figures that the number of people with the equivalent of $10,000 in annual income will double, to 2 billion, by 2015—and 900 million of those newcomers to the consumer class will be in emerging markets. "If you have a middle class that provides a sufficient market for consumer goods, you have the basis for rapid industrial expansion and jobs for poor people," says Sarbuland Khan, head of the information-technology task force at the U.N. "It becomes a virtuous cycle rather than a vicious cycle."

Strategic Rethinking

Cintia Arantes and Eduardo Severino de Santana are the embodiment of that hope. The Brazilians, both 22, grew up poor in Recife, on the country's northeastern coast. But both are climbing the social ladder thanks to a local program that trains disadvantaged Brazilian youths in computer skills. De Santana, who had been unemployed last year, quickly turned one computer course into a job helping to manage the tech facilities at a national law firm.

RUSSIA
The nation's large companies are beginning to see the point of investing in information technology.

Arantes' trajectory could take her even higher. Her laborer father doesn't have steady work, so she helps support the family of six by working nights at a phone company call center. Thanks to a tip from a teacher at a school where she was an administrative assistant, she started taking computer courses last year. Now she's an intern at a local software company in the mornings, takes courses in the afternoon, and hopes to enter a university computer engineering program next year. Her goal: to become a programmer. "I'll keep on battling until I get there," she vows. In the meantime, she's trying to save up the $700 or so it would cost to buy a PC.

In many cases, tech companies will only succeed in emerging markets if they're willing to ditch the strategies that made them successful in the developed world. Take Dell. In 2000 it introduced a consumer PC in China, called SmartPC, that was different from any it had sold before. It came preconfigured rather than built to order, and it was manufactured not by Dell but by Taiwanese companies. At less than $600, the SmartPC has helped Dell become the top foreign supplier in China. Its share of the PC market there rose from less than 1% in 1998 to 7.4% today.

Still, Dell is anything but the dominant force in China that it is in the U.S. A key reason is that Dell's practice of selling direct to customers, over the Net or the phone, doesn't work very well in the Middle Kingdom. Chinese typically want to lay their hands on computers before they buy them. That means the best way to reach them is via vast retailing operations—the strength of local players Lenovo and Founder Electronics, which both rank ahead of Dell with market shares of 25.7% and 11.3%, respectively, according to IDC. Dell set up kiosks to demonstrate its SmartPC and other products. But in August, the company withdrew from the consumer market in the face of competitors selling stripped-down PCs for as little as $362. "In the fastest-growing large market in the world, the local PC makers are winning," says Philippe de Marcillac, a senior vice-president at IDC.

Cultural Customization

There's no easy formula for selling in emerging markets. Some corporate or government customers in Russia and Brazil are as big as any in the U.S., and their needs are just as sophisticated. Russian Railways, with 1.2 million employees, spent $2 billion over the last three years building a modern data communications system. "We're very proud," says Anna Belova, deputy minister of the railway. "We have a huge scale of tasks, and we find creative solutions." Now other giant Russian enterprises see it as a role model and are boosting their tech purchases, too.

To target innovations that will resonate in these markets, companies are conducting in-depth studies of peoples' needs. Intel, for instance, has a team of 10 ethnographers traveling the world to find out how to redesign existing products or come up with new ones that fit different cultures or demographic groups. One of its ethnographers, Genevieve Bell, visited 100 homes in Asia over the past three years and noticed that many Chinese families were reluctant to buy PCs, even if they could afford them. Parents were concerned that their children would listen to pop music or surf the Web, distracting them from school work.

Intel turned that insight into a product. At its User-Centered Design Group in Hillsboro, Ore., industrial designers and other specialists created "personas" of typical Chinese families and pasted pictures that Bell had taken of Chinese households on their walls. They even built sample Chinese kitchens—the room where a computer is most often used. The result: Late this year, Intel expects a leading Chinese PC maker to start selling the China Home Learning PC. It comes with four education applications and a physical lock and key that allows parents to prevent their kids from goofing off when they should be studying.

Many products designed for consumers and small businesses in emerging markets will have to fit some demanding specifications: They need to be simple to use and capable of operating in harsh environments. A handful of products have already come out with these factors in mind—and many more are on the way. India's TVS Electronics Ltd., for instance, is selling a new kind of all-in-one business machine called Sprint designed especially for that country's 1.2 million small shopkeepers. It's part cash register and part computer, designed to tolerate heat, dust, and power outages. The cost: just $180 for the smallest of three models.

Pricing is often the make-or-break factor. In rural South Africa, where HP has set up a pilot program similar to the one in India for developing technologies for poor people, the average person makes less than $1 a day. Clearly, not too many can afford to buy their own personal computers. HP's solution? The 441 PC (as in four users for one computer). It's a machine set up in a school or library that connects to four keyboards and four screens, so multiple people can get on the Net or send e-mail at the same time.

Some of the best ideas for the developing world have the potential for catching on everywhere—including the U.S. It's already starting to happen. Kishore Kumar first developed a simple PC-based remote health-monitoring system for distant villages in his native India. Now his company, TeleVital Inc. of Milpitas, Calif., is marketing the technology in the States. The first U.S. customer, Battle Mountain General Hospital in Battle Mountain, Nev., couldn't afford patient-monitoring equipment—or people to operate it. Now it's hooking up with a hospital 100 miles away to track its patients. Says Battle Mountain administrator Peggy Lindsey: "We in rural America can really use equipment like this."

When tech companies modify their existing products for emerging markets, they can end up with improvements that have a broader impact. That's what happened at Nokia Corp. when it set out to reduce the costs of setting up and operating wireless telephone networks. One improvement, called Smart Radio technology, can cut in half the number of signal-transmission sites operators need. Wrap that and other new technologies together, and operators can build networks for up to 50% less than before. Nokia has been rolling out these innovations from Thailand to Peru. DTAC, the No. 2 Thai cellular operator, is installing the new gear around Bangkok. "If this works, we can use this concept to penetrate into much more remote areas up-country," says Sigve Brekke, the company's CO-CEO.

Dell already has translated emerging-market innovations into successes in its traditional markets. After SmartPC took off in China, Dell in 2001 introduced a version for the U.S., for the first time going after bargain hunters. A year later, Dell absorbed the SmartPC into its mainstream consumer product line as sales took off. "We try to take some of the best ideas we have seen that are happening in local environments and make it a global product," says Dell Senior Vice-President William J. Amelio.

Dell, Nokia, and other Western giants need all of the innovations they can muster, especially as the field of competition shifts to emerging markets, and they're confronted by a stampede of aggressive challengers. Chinese communications-equipment maker Huawei is giving Westerners fits in its home market, where it has captured a 16% share in the crucial router business, second only to mighty Cisco, according to IDC. And thanks to prices up to 50% lower than rivals', Huawei is expanding everywhere from Russia to Brazil. It already ranks No. 2 worldwide in broadband networking gear, says market researcher RHK. "Huawei is being very aggressive," says Cicero Olivieri, director of engineering and planning for GVT, a large telecom company in Brazil.

Momentum Shift

The most serious challenge lies ahead. Huawei is pouring money into Internet Protocol version 6, or IPv6, the standard for the next-generation of the Internet that will have more security, speed, and capacity. China is planning to adopt IPv6 more rapidly than any other country in the world. And if Huawei's close ties to the Chinese government help it become the early leader in the technology, it could get the jump on rivals such as Cisco, Alcatel, and Lucent. "The Ciscos of the world will have to change their business models to compete—and try to out-innovate these small, nimble companies," says William Nuti, a former Cisco senior vice-president and now CEO of Symbol Technologies.

Throughout the developing world, new players are popping up like obstacles in a *Super Mario Brothers* game. Take the online game business itself. Upstart NCsoft has taken advantage of Korea's lead in broadband penetration to build the world's largest online game business, with more than 5 million monthly subscriptions. NCsoft CEO Kim Tack Jin is now expanding in Taiwan, China, Japan, and the U.S.—where 228,000 copies of its *City of Heroes* game were sold in the first three months after

Up-and-Comers

With the tech action in emerging markets, local players have a chance to become players on the world stage. Here are some bright prospects:

	Business	Global Expansion
NCSOFT	The world's No. 1 seller of online PC games, with more than 5 million monthly subscribers. The South Korean company is predicting revenue growth of 55% this year, to $221 million, and 70% growth outside its home market.	After taking off in Korea, NCsoft is expanding in Taiwan, China, Japan, and the U.S. China and Japan present the most growth opportunity. In the U.S., its *City of Heroes* was an instant hit when it launched in April.
I-FLEX SOLUTIONS	The Indian company, which offers banking software and services, claims the world's top software suite for managing consumer, corporate, Internet, and investment banking. In a slow-growth worldwide enterprise software industry, revenues grew 26% last quarter.	I-flex sells in 108 countries and just inked a $10 million deal with Banco Du Chile, the largest commercial bank in the country. Prospects are bright: i-flex's Internet-based systems and low-cost Indian programming give it a huge advantage.
TCL MOBILE	A subsidiary of electronics conglomerate TCL Corp., it's one of the top two Chinese handset makers, specializing in moderately priced phones. It recently formed a joint venture with Alcatel to expand into higher-end products.	It's starting to expand into developing markets in Asia, Africa, and the former Soviet Union. Though TCL faces tough competition, its solid position in the No. 1 cellular market gives it a decent chance at emerging as a strong global player.
KASPERSKY LABS	Anti-virus software. Founded by Eugene Kaspersky, one of the world's leading experts on computer security, the Russian company's products protect computers against viruses, hackers, and spam. Sales are forecast to grow 50% this year.	Kaspersky is expanding in Europe, the U.S., China, and Japan, targeting consumers and small businesses. With viruses rampant, Kaspersky is well placed to tap growing demand for security products by capitalizing on Russia's renowned programming skills.

its April release, according to market researcher NPD Group. The key to NCsoft's success: It has come up with a combo of fantasy and action gaming that's a hit with players.

Even mighty Microsoft is vulnerable to the competitive threats. Linux is emerging as a viable alternative to its Windows in developing markets and could cut into its market share. China, Japan, and Korea are collaborating on a version of the free open-source software package. A number of governments are considering policies that favor open-source software packages, and one, Israel, has already decided to stop using Microsoft's products. While that affects only tens of thousands of government workers, if other countries take the same path, millions of their employees could end up using open-source software, rather than Windows and Office.

Microsoft doesn't have an answer—at least not yet. In October the company, which declined to comment for this story, will begin to sell a cheaper Windows in Thailand, Indonesia, and Malaysia in an effort to beat back the open-source threat. But it so far refuses to follow suit in China—where it has had four general managers in six years. "Business as usual won't

work there. They have to find new ways to do things," warns Jack Gao, who ran Microsoft China from 1999 to 2003 and now heads up software maker Autodesk's China operations.

It may turn out that patience is the most important attribute for tech companies trying to get things going in emerging markets. IBM, after all, has been in Brazil for 87 years. Hewlett-Packard has spent three years establishing pilot programs in India and South Africa, and, finally, they're starting to yield products and to improve the lives of the locals. Take Neelamma, the itinerant photographer. She has become a star in the two-room house with a dirt floor that she and her stonecutter husband, Krishnamurthy, share with his parents and brother. What are Neelamma's dreams? "I want to buy a television and a ceiling fan. And I want to build a small photo studio in my home," she says. One young woman's life and aspirations have been changed by the arrival of technology. Another 1 billion new consumers may not be too far behind.

With Manjeet Kripalani, in Bombay; Bruce Einhorn, in Hong Kong and Andy Reinhardt in Paris, and bureau reports.

Brand Loyalty Goes Global

Keeping Customers From Every Corner Of The World Happy Is a Daunting (But Crucial) Task.

MIKE KUST

The business world truly has become a global marketplace over the past 10 years. Brands in all verticals have opportunities to expand their customer base just by tapping into new geographic markets. But today's hotly debated item is not brand opportunity but brand loyalty.

Can a brand inspire loyalty from customers in China, India, France and the United States with a single program? The answer comes in many languages, all translating into a declarative "yes." Brand loyalty programs can create stronger relationships with a company's most valuable customers in competitive new markets. One of the best examples of executing this kind of program can be found in an industry near and dear to the hearts of nearly every sales and marketing executive—the travel industry.

Many hotel chains operate several brands under a global umbrella. No surprise there to anyone who has stayed at a Regent and a Radisson on the same trip (Carlson Hotels) or a W and a Sheraton (Starwood). But if not managed properly, the result can be an inconsistent pattern of traditional marketing metrics and an inconsistent customer experience.

Even with the variety inherent to different brands, hotel chains can address the inconsistencies that many travelers face. For example, how does an executive who travels internationally earn points that accrue to a meaningful level if he has to stay in different hotel chains in different countries? And can that executive count on a positive experience when he has to stay in different hotel franchises, owned by the same company, that will accrue those points in a coherent program?

Brands must create the ability to connect customers of different properties with a common loyalty program—one that rewards recency, frequency and incremental revenue with exclusive experiences or financial incentives. The infrastructure needed to meet a multi-continent, multi-currency, multi-language customer base is demanding. It means that the executive who starts out at a company's luxury property in Beijing, then stays at the mid-level hotel in Oslo and winds up the trip at a family-style suite hotel near Chicago, can accrue points in the same loyalty program and reach the reward thresholds available in that program more quickly.

It also means that all the advantages of being an exclusive member need to be tied into one program. The exec who starts in Beijing should belong to the same frequent guest program as the suite hotel in Chicago. His currency changes should be recorded automatically. The preferences for bed, room service and other amenities also should be communicated automatically.

Also, the program should allow for converting points to airline miles with the participation of global airline partners. Improved benefits for elite members could include best available room, 25% to 50% point bonuses, last room availability, early check-in and late check-out, and elite-only points and cash offers.

One example of a successful program is the Carlson hotels goldpoints plus program. Randy Petersen, editor of *Inside Flyer* and *FlyerTalk,* in addition to a noted frequent travel loyalty expert, had this to say in a October 29, 2007 article that appeared on btbtravel.com: "In an age of member disappointment because of devaluation of their points, it's refreshing to know that there is a hotel company out there doing what's best for its customers. Carlson Hotels has raised the bar for earning more points for their members, 100% for most hotel stays, and yet for the large majority of their rewards they have not raised the requirements for redemption."

This brand connection program model works in many other businesses. In fact, executives in any business can learn from the following best practices for developing brand loyalty:

- **Work across Brands.** Different brands need not compete for the attention and experiences available through separate loyalty programs. The business travel hotel brand is different from the luxury brand, and very different from the atmosphere of the family brand.
- **Build Brand Loyalty Programs** around customers, rather than products or services. Customers are the source of all value. If they see an opportunity to earn more discounts or access to information by buying more of your product, they will buy more. If participating in a loyalty program enhances their overall experience, they will buy more often.

- **Work across Countries.** Customers have common needs even if they have their differences. This model proves that the common need for convenience and familiarity will drive guest loyalty, regardless of what country in which it operates. In Asia, for example, customers expect higher reward levels than they do in North America, so extend that expectation to all countries.
- **Find a Partner** with broad enough capabilities to meet your needs. The infrastructure required to design and deliver such a program must be reliable. The program provider should have a wide array of capabilities to meet your needs, including experts in operations, creative, interactive, IT, decision sciences, fulfillment services and prepaid cards.

Whether or not a company operates in China, Czechoslovakia or Chicago, all brand loyalty is driven by relationship strength. A good loyalty program builds trust. It acts in the best interests of the customer (mutuality) and it aligns the goals of all the brands involved. It encourages customers to stay longer, create more value and refer the program to colleagues, friends and family.

MIKE KUST is the chief marketing officer for the Norwalk, Conn.-based Peppers & Rogers Group.

From *Sales & Marketing Management*, January/February 2008, pp. 24–25. Copyright © by VNU Business Media, Inc. Used with permission from Sales & Marketing Management.

Fisher-Price Game Plan: Pursue Toy Sales in Developing Markets

Nicholas Casey

In developing a line of talking toys aimed at children in China, engineers at Fisher-Price had to struggle to perfect the Mandarin "Sh" sound, which involves a soft hiss that was difficult to encode on sound-data chips embedded in the toys.

Developers finally solved the problem of recording the phrase "It's learning time!" in Mandarin, but new challenges are ahead. The company will soon be examining the LCD screens on learning toys to determine whether Chinese characters can be displayed clearly.

Getting such details right is increasingly important as Fisher-Price and its parent company, Mattel Inc., try to attract more customers overseas.

In the past five years, Fisher-Price's sales in developing markets have more than doubled, and its sales of baby swings and infant rockers in those markets have soared tenfold. Meanwhile, Mattel reported its first quarterly loss in more than three years, in part because Fisher-Price sales fell 13% in the U.S., where electronics have increasingly cut into the market for toys. Though Fisher-Price's international sales were down 7% in the quarter ended March 31, its overseas results have grown rapidly in many previous quarters.

Aiming Fisher-Price toys at preschoolers overseas is also important to Mattel because it helps lay the groundwork for the company's other brands as toddlers graduate from stacking plastic rings to collecting toys like Barbie and Hot Wheels. "Fisher-Price is the tip of the spear for Mattel into these developing markets," says Kevin Curran, Fisher-Price's senior vice president and general manager.

Fisher-Price is in particularly hot pursuit of markets—Brazil, Russia and Poland, for example—where brand-name American toys for toddlers are just beginning to appear and are thus perceived as novelties. Another draw: The countries have fast-growing middle classes with new disposable cash and children they want to pamper, the company says.

To capture consumers, however, the company must distinguish itself from entrenched local toy makers. At the same time, it must keep costs down, to make the products affordable enough to sell in developing countries.

Hitting the mark on products for these markets has presented some unexpected hurdles, like the problem recording Mandarin. Earlier, Fisher-Price ran into trouble with a reading toy called "Storybook Rhymes" that featured a traditional Turkish poem paired with an illustration of a pig. "We realized this wasn't appropriate for a Muslim country," says Kelly Chapman, who heads product design, referring to cultural restrictions on pork. In development, the company replaced the pig with pictures of cats.

Taking an international tack has been quite a stretch for Fisher-Price, which was founded in 1930 and family-run until the retirement of founder Irving Fisher in the late 1960s. Mattel acquired the company in 1993, but Fisher-Price still has its headquarters in the upstate hamlet of East Aurora, N.Y., and still uses photos of local toddlers on its packaging, including on toys sold overseas. Neighborhood children also test products in Fisher-Price's only research lab, which is on the company's small campus.

But the game is changing. "In many discussions [at headquarters], the U.S. is getting treated just as any other country," says Mr. Curran, because "international has been and is the fastest part of what's growing."

Market researchers like Shelly Glick Gryfe have been trotting the globe, scouting out the next big market for preschoolers. Ms. Glick Gryfe, who holds a degree in child psychology, says she began studying families in India more than a decade ago, but for most of that time the lack of a large middle class made a big retail presence difficult for Fisher-Price, whose toy prices range from $3 to $30—far above those of local competitors. Many Indian mothers weren't willing to make the investment in the company's educational toys because, research showed, they didn't perceive the playthings as potential learning tools.

But when new data came in about two years ago, Ms. Glick Gryfe found more Indian parents had begun taking American toys home. "We were seeing a shift in attitude," she says. And Fisher-Price reacted fast. This year the company is offering more than a dozen lines in India.

Fisher-Price is also pursuing the Chinese market, which offers sheer size and big seasonal gift-giving events like Chinese New Year. While the "one child" policy has slowed the country's birth rate, Ms. Glick Gryfe says Fisher-Price can target the large number of adults—including both parents and grandparents—doting on each child.

But expanding a company's international business isn't without risk. John Taylor, a toy analyst at Arcadia Investment Corp. in Portland, Ore., says the presence of cheaper locally made toys means that Fisher-Price's success will depend on the growth of brand consciousness among consumers in new markets. "Chinese kids have been growing for 5,000 years without the benefit of Fisher-Price," he notes.

Glossary

This glossary of marketing terms is included to provide you with a convenient and ready reference as you encounter general terms in your study of marketing that are unfamiliar or require a review. It is not intended to be comprehensive, but taken together with the many definitions included in the articles themselves, it should prove to be quite useful.

A

acceptable price range The range of prices that buyers are willing to pay for a product; prices that are above the range may be judged unfair, while prices below the range may generate concerns about quality.

adaptive selling A salesperson's adjustment of his or her behavior between and during sales calls, to respond appropriately to issues that are important to the customer.

advertising Marketing communication elements designed to stimulate sales through the use of mass media displays, direct individual appeals, public displays, give-aways, and the like.

advertorial A special advertising section in magazines that includes some editorial (nonadvertising) content.

Americans with Disabilities Act (ADA) Passed in 1990, this U.S. law prohibits discrimination against consumers with disabilities.

automatic number identification A telephone system that identifies incoming phone numbers at the beginning of the call, without the caller's knowledge.

B

bait and switch Advertising a product at an attractively low price to get customers into the store, but making the product unavailable so that the customers must trade up to a more expensive version.

bar coding A computer-coded bar pattern that identifies a product. See also universal product code.

barter The practice of exchanging goods and services without the use of money.

benefit segmentation Organizing the market according to the attributes or benefits consumers need or desire, such as quality, service, or unique features.

brand A name, term, sign, design, symbol, or combination used to differentiate the products of one company from those of its competition.

brand image The quality and reliability of a product as perceived by consumers on the basis of its brand reputation or familiarity.

brand name The element of a brand that can be vocalized.

break-even analysis The calculation of the number of units that must be sold at a certain price to cover costs (break even); revenues earned past the break-even point contribute to profits.

bundling Marketing two or more products in a single package at one price.

business analysis The stage of new product development where initial marketing plans are prepared (including tentative marketing strategy and estimates of sales, costs, and profitability).

business strategic plan A plan for how each business unit in a corporation intends to compete in the marketplace, based upon the vision, objectives, and growth strategies of the corporate strategic plan.

C

capital products Expensive items that are used in business operations but do not become part of any finished product (such as office buildings, copy machines).

cash-and-carry wholesaler A limited-function wholesaler that does not extend credit for or deliver the products it sells.

caveat emptor A Latin term that means "let the buyer beware." A principle of law meaning that the purchase of a product is at the buyer's risk with regard to its quality, usefulness, and the like. The laws do, however, provide certain minimum protection against fraud and other schemes.

channel of distribution See marketing channel.

Child Protection Act U.S. law passed in 1990 to regulate advertising on children's TV programs.

Child Safety Act Passed in 1966, this U.S. law prohibits the marketing of dangerous products to children.

Clayton Act Anticompetitive activities are prohibited by this 1914 U.S. law.

co-branding When two brand names appear on the same product (such as a credit card with a school's name).

comparative advertising Advertising that compares one brand against a competitive brand on at least one product attribute.

competitive pricing strategies Pricing strategies that are based on a organization's position in relation to its competition.

consignment An arrangement in which a seller of goods does not take title to the goods until they are sold. The seller thus has the option of returning them to the supplier or principal if unable to execute the sale.

consolidated metropolitan statistical area (CMSA) Based on census data, the largest designation of geographic areas. See also primary metropolitan statistical area.

consumer behavior The way in which buyers, individually or collectively, react to marketplace stimuli.

Consumer Credit Protection Act A 1968 U.S. law that requires full disclosure of the financial charges of loans.

consumer decision process This four-step process includes recognizing a need or problem, searching for information, evaluating alternative products or brands, and purchasing a product.

Consumer Product Safety Commission (CPSC) A U.S. government agency that protects consumers from unsafe products.

consumerism A social movement in which consumers demand better information about the service, prices, dependability, and quality of the products they buy.

convenience products Consumer goods that are purchased at frequent intervals with little regard for price. Such goods are relatively standard in nature and consumers tend to select the most convenient source when shopping for them.

cooperative advertising Advertising of a product by a retailer, dealer, distributor, or the like, with part of the advertising cost paid by the product's manufacturer.

corporate strategic plan A plan that addresses what a company is and wants to become, and then guides strategic planning at all organizational levels.

Glossary

countersegmentation A concept that combines market segments to appeal to a broad range of consumers, assuming that there will be an increasing consumer willingness to accept fewer product and service choices for lower prices.

customer loyalty concept To focus beyond customer satisfaction toward customer retention as a way to generate sales and profit growth.

D

demand curve A relationship that shows how many units a market will purchase at a given price in a given period of time.

demographic environment The study of human population densities, distributions, and movements that relate to buying behavior.

derived demand The demand for business-to-business products that is dependent upon a demand for other products in the market.

differentiated strategy Using innovation and points of difference in product offerings, advanced technology, superior service, or higher quality in wide areas of market segments.

direct mail promotion Marketing goods to consumers by mailing unsolicited promotional material to them.

direct marketing The sale of products to carefully targeted consumers who interact with various advertising media without salesperson contact.

discount A reduction from list price that is given to a buyer as a reward for a favorable activity to the seller.

discretionary income The money that remains after taxes and necessities have been paid for.

disposable income That portion of income that remains after payment of taxes to use for food, clothing, and shelter.

dual distribution The selling of products to two or more competing distribution networks, or the selling of two brands of nearly identical products through competing distribution networks.

dumping The act of selling a product in a foreign country at a price lower than its domestic price.

durable goods Products that continue in service for an appreciable length of time.

E

economy The income, expenditures, and resources that affect business and household costs.

electronic data interchange (EDI) A computerized system that links two different firms to allow transmittal of documents; a quick-response inventory control system.

entry strategy An approach used to begin marketing products internationally.

environmental scanning Obtaining information on relevant factors and trends outside a company and interpreting their potential impact on the company's markets and marketing activities.

European Union (EU) The world's largest consumer market, consisting of 16 European nations: Austria, Belgium, Britain, Denmark, Finland, France, Germany, Greece, Italy, Ireland, Luxembourg, the Netherlands, Norway, Portugal, Spain, and Sweden.

exclusive distribution Marketing a product or service in only one retail outlet in a specific geographic marketplace.

exporting Selling goods to international markets.

F

Fair Packaging and Labeling Act of 1966 This law requires manufacturers to state ingredients, volume, and manufacturer's name on a package.

family life cycle The progress of a family through a number of distinct phases, each of which is associated with identifiable purchasing behaviors.

Federal Trade Commission (FTC) The U.S. government agency that regulates business practices; established in 1914.

five C's of pricing Five influences on pricing decisions: customers, costs, channels of distribution, competition, and compatibility.

FOB (free on board) The point at which the seller stops paying transportation costs.

four I's of service Four elements to services: intangibility, inconsistency, inseparability, and inventory.

four P's See marketing mix.

franchise The right to distribute a company's products or render services under its name, and to retain the resulting profit in exchange for a fee or percentage of sales.

freight absorption Payment of transportation costs by the manufacturer or seller, often resulting in a uniform pricing structure.

functional groupings Groupings in an organization in which a unit is subdivided according to different business activities, such as manufacturing, finance, and marketing.

G

General Agreement on Tariffs and Trade (GATT) An international agreement that is intended to limit trade barriers and to promote world trade through reduced tariffs; represents over 80 percent of global trade.

geodemographics A combination of geographic data and demographic characteristics; used to segment and target specific markets.

green marketing The implementation of an ecological perspective in marketing; the promotion of a product as environmentally safe.

gross domestic product (GDP) The total monetary value of all goods and services produced within a country during one year.

growth stage The second stage of a product life cycle that is characterized by a rapid increase in sales and profits.

H

hierarchy of effects The stages a prospective buyer goes through when purchasing a product, including awareness, interest, evaluation, trial, and adoption.

I

idea generation An initial stage of the new product development process; requires creativity and innovation to generate ideas for potential new products.

implied warranties Warranties that assign responsibility for a product's deficiencies to a manufacturer, even though the product was sold by a retailer.

imports Purchased goods or services that are manufactured or produced in some other country.

integrated marketing communications A strategic integration of marketing communications programs that coordinate all promotional activities—advertising, personal selling, sales promotion, and public relations.

internal reference prices The comparison price standards that consumers remember and use to judge the fairness of prices.

introduction stage The first product life cycle stage; when a new product is launched into the marketplace.

ISO 9000 International Standards Organization's standards for registration and certification of manufacturer's quality management and quality assurance systems.

J

joint venture An arrangement in which two or more organizations market products internationally.

just-in-time (JIT) inventory control system An inventory supply system that operates with very low inventories and fast, on-time delivery.

L

Lanham Trademark Act A 1946 U.S. law that was passed to protect trademarks and brand names.

late majority The fourth group to adopt a new product; representing about 34 percent of a market.

lifestyle research Research on a person's pattern of living, as displayed in activities, interests, and opinions.

limit pricing This competitive pricing strategy involves setting prices low to discourage new competition.

limited-coverage warranty The manufacturer's statement regarding the limits of coverage and noncoverage for any product deficiencies.

logistics management The planning, implementing, and moving of raw materials and products from the point of origin to the point of consumption.

loss-leader pricing The pricing of a product below its customary price in order to attract attention to it.

M

Magnuson-Moss Act Passed in 1975, this U.S. law regulates warranties.

management by exception Used by a marketing manager to identify results that deviate from plans, diagnose their cause, make appropriate new plans, and implement new actions.

manufacturers' agent A merchant wholesaler that sells related but noncompeting product lines for a number of manufacturers; also called manufacturers' representatives.

market The potential buyers for a company's product or service; or to sell a product or service to actual buyers. The place where goods and services are exchanged.

market penetration strategy The goal of achieving corporate growth objectives with existing products within existing markets by persuading current customers to purchase more of the product or by capturing new customers.

marketing channel Organizations and people that are involved in the process of making a product or service available for use by consumers or industrial users.

marketing communications planning A seven-step process that includes marketing plan review; situation analysis; communications process analysis; budget development; program development integration and implementation of a plan; and monitoring, evaluating, and controlling the marketing communications program.

marketing concept The idea that a company should seek to satisfy the needs of consumers while also trying to achieve the organization's goals.

marketing mix The elements of marketing: product, brand, package, price, channels of distribution, advertising and promotion, personal selling, and the like.

marketing research The process of identifying a marketing problem and opportunity, collecting and analyzing information systematically, and recommending actions to improve an organization's marketing activities.

marketing research process A six-step sequence that includes problem definition, determination of research design, determination of data collection methods, development of data collection forms, sample design, and analysis and interpretation.

mission statement A part of the strategic planning process that expresses the company's basic values and specifies the operation boundaries within marketing, business units, and other areas.

motivation research A group of techniques developed by behavioral scientists that are used by marketing researchers to discover factors influencing marketing behavior.

N

nonprice competition Competition between brands based on factors other than price, such as quality, service, or product features.

nondurable goods Products that do not last or continue in service for any appreciable length of time.

North American Free Trade Agreement (NAFTA) A trade agreement among the United States, Canada, and Mexico that essentially removes the vast majority of trade barriers between the countries.

North American Industry Classification System (NAICS) A system used to classify organizations on the basis of major activity or the major good or service provided by the three NAFTA countries—Canada, Mexico, and the United States; replaced the Standard Industrial Classification (SIC) system in 1997.

O

observational data Market research data obtained by watching, either mechanically or in person, how people actually behave.

odd-even pricing Setting prices at just below an even number, such as $1.99 instead of $2.

opinion leaders Individuals who influence consumer behavior based on their interest in or expertise with particular products.

organizational goals The specific objectives used by a business or nonprofit unit to achieve and measure its performance.

outbound telemarketing Using the telephone rather than personal visits to contact customers.

outsourcing A company's decision to purchase products and services from other firms rather than using in-house employees.

P

parallel development In new product development, an approach that involves the development of the product and production process simultaneously.

penetration pricing Pricing a product low to discourage competition.

personal selling process The six stages of sales activities that occur before and after the sale itself: prospecting, preapproach, approach, presentation, close, and follow-up.

point-of-purchase display A sales promotion display located in high-traffic areas in retail stores.

posttesting Tests that are conducted to determine if an advertisement has accomplished its intended purpose.

predatory pricing The practice of selling products at low prices to drive competition from the market and then raising prices once a monopoly has been established.

prestige pricing Maintaining high prices to create an image of product quality and appeal to buyers who associate premium prices with high quality.

pretesting Evaluating consumer reactions to proposed advertisements through the use of focus groups and direct questions.

Glossary

price elasticity of demand An economic concept that attempts to measure the sensitivity of demand for any product to changes in its price.

price fixing The illegal attempt by one or several companies to maintain the prices of their products above those that would result from open competition.

price promotion mix The basic product price plus additional components such as sales prices, temporary discounts, coupons, favorable payment and credit terms.

price skimming Setting prices high initially to appeal to consumers who are not price-sensitive and then lowering prices to appeal to the next market segments.

primary metropolitan statistical area (PMSA) Major urban area, often located within a CMSA, that has at least one million inhabitants.

PRIZM A potential rating index by ZIP code markets that divides every U.S. neighborhood into one of 40 distinct cluster types that reveal consumer data.

product An idea, good, service, or any combination that is an element of exchange to satisfy a consumer.

product differentiation The ability or tendency of manufacturers, marketers, or consumers to distinguish between seemingly similar products.

product expansion strategy A plan to market new products to the same customer base.

product life cycle (PLC) A product's advancement through the introduction, growth, maturity, and decline stages.

product line pricing Setting the prices for all product line items.

product marketing plans Business units' plans to focus on specific target markets and marketing mixes for each product, which include both strategic and execution decisions.

product mix The composite of products offered for sale by a firm or a business unit.

promotional mix Combining one or more of the promotional elements that a firm uses to communicate with consumers.

proprietary secondary data The data that is provided by commercial marketing research firms to other firms.

psychographic research Measurable characteristics of given market segments in respect to lifestyles, interests, opinions, needs, values, attitudes, personality traits, and the like.

publicity Nonpersonal presentation of a product, service, or business unit.

pull strategy A marketing strategy whose main thrust is to strongly influence the final consumer, so that the demand for a product "pulls" it through the various channels of distribution.

push strategy A marketing strategy whose main thrust is to provide sufficient economic incentives to members of the channels of distribution, so as to "push" the product through to the consumer.

Q

qualitative data The responses obtained from in-depth interviews, focus groups, and observation studies.

quality function deployment (QFD) The data collected from structured response formats that can be easily analyzed and projected to larger populations.

quotas In international marketing, they are restrictions placed on the amount of a product that is allowed to leave or enter a country; the total outcomes used to assess sales representatives' performance and effectiveness.

R

regional marketing A form of geographical division that develops marketing plans that reflect differences in taste preferences, perceived needs, or interests in other areas.

relationship marketing The development, maintenance, and enhancement of long-term, profitable customer relationships.

repositioning The development of new marketing programs that will shift consumer beliefs and opinions about an existing brand.

resale price maintenance Control by a supplier of the selling prices of his branded goods at subsequent stages of distribution, by means of contractual agreement under fair trade laws or other devices.

reservation price The highest price a consumer will pay for a product; a form of internal reference price.

restraint of trade In general, activities that interfere with competitive marketing. Restraint of trade usually refers to illegal activities.

retail strategy mix Controllable variables that include location, products and services, pricing, and marketing communications.

return on investment (ROI) A ratio of income before taxes to total operating assets associated with a product, such as inventory, plant, and equipment.

S

sales effectiveness evaluations A test of advertising efficiency to determine if it resulted in increased sales.

sales forecast An estimate of sales under controllable and uncontrollable conditions.

sales management The planning, direction, and control of the personal selling activities of a business unit.

sales promotion An element of the marketing communications mix that provides incentives or extra value to stimulate product interest.

samples A small size of a product given to prospective purchasers to demonstrate a product's value or use and to encourage future purchase; some elements that are taken from the population or universe.

scanner data Proprietary data that is derived from UPC bar codes.

scrambled merchandising Offering several unrelated product lines within a single retail store.

selected controlled markets Sites where market tests for a new product are conducted by an outside agency and retailers are paid to display that product; also referred to as forced distribution markets.

selective distribution This involves selling a product in only some of the available outlets; commonly used when after-the-sale service is necessary, such as in the case of home appliances.

seller's market A condition within any market in which the demand for an item is greater than its supply.

selling philosophy An emphasis on an organization's selling function to the exclusion of other marketing activities.

selling strategy A salesperson's overall plan of action, which is developed at three levels: sales territory, customer, and individual sales calls.

services Nonphysical products that a company provides to consumers in exchange for money or something else of value.

share points Percentage points of market share; often used as the common comparison basis to allocate marketing resources effectively.

Sherman Anti-Trust Act Passed in 1890, this U.S. law prohibits contracts, combinations, or conspiracies in restraint of trade and actual monopolies or attempts to monopolize any part of trade or commerce.

shopping products Consumer goods that are purchased only after comparisons are made concerning price, quality, style, suitability, and the like.

single-channel strategy Marketing strategy using only one means to reach customers; providing one sales source for a product.

single-zone pricing A pricing policy in which all buyers pay the same delivered product price, regardless of location; also known as uniform delivered pricing or postage stamp pricing.

slotting fees High fees manufacturers pay to place a new product on a retailer's or wholesaler's shelf.

social responsibility Reducing social costs, such as environmental damage, and increasing the positive impact of a marketing decision on society.

societal marketing concept The use of marketing strategies to increase the acceptability of an idea (smoking causes cancer); cause (environmental protection); or practice (birth control) within a target market.

specialty products Consumer goods, usually appealing only to a limited market, for which consumers will make a special purchasing effort. Such items include, for example, stereo components, fancy foods, and prestige brand clothes.

Standard Industrial Classification (SIC) system Replaced by NAICS, this federal government numerical scheme categorized businesses.

standardized marketing Enforcing similar product, price, distribution, and communications programs in all international markets.

stimulus-response presentation A selling format that assumes that a customer will buy if given the appropriate stimulus by a salesperson.

strategic business unit (SBU) A decentralized profit center of a company that operates as a separate, independent business.

strategic marketing process Marketing activities in which a firm allocates its marketing mix resources to reach a target market.

strategy mix A way for retailers to differentiate themselves from others through location, product, services, pricing, and marketing mixes.

subliminal perception When a person hears or sees messages without being aware of them.

SWOT analysis An acronym that describes a firm's appraisal of its internal strengths and weaknesses and its external opportunities and threats.

synergy An increased customer value that is achieved through more efficient organizational function performances.

systems-designer strategy A selling strategy that allows knowledgeable sales reps to determine solutions to a customer's problems or to anticipate opportunities to enhance a customer's business through new or modified business systems.

T

target market A defined group of consumers or organizations toward which a firm directs its marketing program.

team selling A sales strategy that assigns accounts to specialized sales teams according to a customers' purchase-information needs.

telemarketing An interactive direct marketing approach that uses the telephone to develop relationships with customers.

test marketing The process of testing a prototype of a new product to gain consumer reaction and to examine its commercial viability and marketing strategy.

TIGER (Topologically Integrated Geographic Encoding and Reference) A minutely detailed United States Census Bureau computerized map of the U.S. that can be combined with a company's own database to analyze customer sales.

total quality management (TQM) Programs that emphasize long-term relationships with selected suppliers instead of short-term transactions with many suppliers.

total revenue The total of sales, or unit price, multiplied by the quantity of the product sold.

trade allowance An amount a manufacturer contributes to a local dealer's or retailer's advertising expenses.

trade (functional) discounts Price reductions that are granted to wholesalers or retailers that are based on future marketing functions that they will perform for a manufacturer.

trademark The legal identification of a company's exclusive rights to use a brand name or trade name.

truck jobber A small merchant wholesaler who delivers limited assortments of fast-moving or perishable items within a small geographic area.

two-way stretch strategy Adding products at both the low and high end of a product line.

U

undifferentiated strategy Using a single promotional mix to market a single product for the entire market; frequently used early in the life of a product.

uniform delivered price The same average freight amount that is charged to all customers, no matter where they are located.

universal product code (UPC) An assigned number to identify a product, which is represented by a series of bars of varying widths for optical scanning.

usage rate The quantity consumed or patronage during a specific period, which can vary significantly among different customer groups.

utilitarian influence To comply with the expectations of others to achieve rewards or avoid punishments.

V

value added In retail strategy decisions, a dimension of the retail positioning matrix that refers to the service level and method of operation of the retailer.

vertical marketing systems Centrally coordinated and professionally managed marketing channels that are designed to achieve channel economies and maximum marketing impact.

vertical price fixing Requiring that sellers not sell products below a minimum retail price; sometimes called resale price maintenance.

W

weighted-point system The method of establishing screening criteria, assigning them weights, and using them to evaluate new product lines.

wholesaler One who makes quantity purchases from manufacturers (or other wholesalers) and sells in smaller quantities to retailers (or other wholesalers).

Z

zone pricing A form of geographical pricing whereby a seller divides its market into broad geographic zones and then sets a uniform delivered price for each zone.

Test-Your-Knowledge Form

We encourage you to photocopy and use this page as a tool to assess how the articles in *Annual Editions* expand on the information in your textbook. By reflecting on the articles you will gain enhanced text information. You can also access this useful form on a product's book support Web site at *http://www.mhcls.com*.

NAME: DATE:

_____

TITLE AND NUMBER OF ARTICLE:

_____

BRIEFLY STATE THE MAIN IDEA OF THIS ARTICLE:

_____

LIST THREE IMPORTANT FACTS THAT THE AUTHOR USES TO SUPPORT THE MAIN IDEA:

_____

WHAT INFORMATION OR IDEAS DISCUSSED IN THIS ARTICLE ARE ALSO DISCUSSED IN YOUR TEXTBOOK OR OTHER READINGS THAT YOU HAVE DONE? LIST THE TEXTBOOK CHAPTERS AND PAGE NUMBERS:

_____

LIST ANY EXAMPLES OF BIAS OR FAULTY REASONING THAT YOU FOUND IN THE ARTICLE:

_____

LIST ANY NEW TERMS/CONCEPTS THAT WERE DISCUSSED IN THE ARTICLE, AND WRITE A SHORT DEFINITION:

We Want Your Advice

ANNUAL EDITIONS revisions depend on two major opinion sources: one is our Advisory Board, listed in the front of this volume, which works with us in scanning the thousands of articles published in the public press each year; the other is you—the person actually using the book. Please help us and the users of the next edition by completing the prepaid article rating form on this page and returning it to us. Thank you for your help!

ANNUAL EDITIONS: Marketing 09/10

ARTICLE RATING FORM

Here is an opportunity for you to have direct input into the next revision of this volume.
We would like you to rate each of the articles listed below, using the following scale:

1. **Excellent: should definitely be retained**
2. **Above average: should probably be retained**
3. **Below average: should probably be deleted**
4. **Poor: should definitely be deleted**

Your ratings will play a vital part in the next revision.
Please mail this prepaid form to us as soon as possible.
Thanks for your help!

RATING	ARTICLE	RATING	ARTICLE
	1. Hot Stuff		25. You Choose, You Lose
	2. The World's Most Innovative Companies		26. The Very Model of a Modern Marketing Plan
	3. How the Creative Stay Creative		27. Making Inspiration Routine
	4. Avoiding Green Marketing Myopia		28. Surveyor of the Fittest
	5. Doing Whatever Gets Them in the Door		29. The Inevitability of $300 Socks
	6. Marketing Myopia		30. Rocket Plan
	7. Putting Customers First		31. Customer-Centric Pricing: The Surprising Secret for Profitability
	8. Customer Connection		32. Boost Your Bottom Line by Taking the Guesswork Out of Pricing
	9. Add Service Element Back in to Get Satisfaction		
	10. School Your Customers		33. Big Retailers Seek Teens (and Parents)
	11. Surviving in the Age of Rage		34. Why Costco Is So Damn Addictive
	12. Attracting Loyalty		35. Wal-Mart's Midlife Crises
	13. Nonprofits Can Take Cues from Biz World		36. Sell It!
	14. Fidelity Factor		37. Attention-Deficit Advertising
	15. Trust in the Marketplace		38. Product Placement—You Can't Escape It
	16. Wrestling with Ethics		39. How China Will Change Your Business
	17. The Science of Desire		40. The Battle for China's Good-Enough Market
	18. Eight Tips Offer Best Practices for Online MR		41. Three Dimensional
	19. Consumers on the Move		42. Tech's Future
	20. A Clean Slate		43. Brand Loyalty Goes Global
	21. Wooing Luxury Customers		44. Fisher-Price Game Plan: Pursue Toy Sales in Developing Markets
	22. The Halo Effect		
	23. Youth Marketing, Galvanized		
	24. Sowing the Seeds		

BUSINESS REPLY MAIL
FIRST CLASS MAIL PERMIT NO. 551 DUBUQUE IA

POSTAGE WILL BE PAID BY ADDRESSEE

McGraw-Hill Contemporary Learning Series
501 BELL STREET
DUBUQUE, IA 52001

NO POSTAGE
NECESSARY
IF MAILED
IN THE
UNITED STATES

ABOUT YOU

Name

Date

Are you a teacher? ❏ A student? ❏
Your school's name

Department

Address   City   State   Zip

School telephone #

YOUR COMMENTS ARE IMPORTANT TO US!

Please fill in the following information:
For which course did you use this book?

Did you use a text with this ANNUAL EDITION? ❏ yes ❏ no
What was the title of the text?

What are your general reactions to the Annual Editions concept?

Have you read any pertinent articles recently that you think should be included in the next edition? Explain.

Are there any articles that you feel should be replaced in the next edition? Why?

Are there any World Wide Web sites that you feel should be included in the next edition? Please annotate.

May we contact you for editorial input? ❏ yes ❏ no
May we quote your comments? ❏ yes ❏ no